AFRIQUE

Other Tactics/Intell. Supplements from Posterity Press:

Strategic Rifleman: Key to More Moral Warfare
Gung Ho: The Corps' Most Progressive Tradition
Global Warrior: Averting WWIII
Expeditionary Eagles: Outmaneuvering the Taliban
Homeland Siege: Tactics for Police and Military
Tequila Junction: 4th-Generation Counterinsurgency
Dragon Days: Time for "Unconventional" Tactics
Terrorist Trail: Backtracking the Foreign Fighter
Militant Tricks: Battlefield Ruses of the Islamic Militant
Tactics of the Crescent Moon: Militant Muslim Combat Methods
The Tiger's Way: A U.S. Private's Best Chance for Survival
Phantom Soldier: The Enemy's Answer to U.S. Firepower
One More Bridge to Cross: Lowering the Cost of War
The Last Hundred Yards: The NCO's Contribution to Warfare

AFRIQUE

A WARNING FOR AMERICA

ILLUSTRATED

H. JOHN POOLE

FOREWORD BY

GEN. ANTHONY C. ZINNI USMC (RET.)

POSTERITY

PRESS

Published by Posterity Press
P.O. Box 5360, Emerald Isle, NC 28594
(www.posteritypress.org)

Cataloging-in-Publication Data

Poole, H. John, 1943-
Afrique
Includes bibliography and index.
1. Infantry drill and tactics.
2. Military art and science.
3. Military history.
I. Title. ISBN: 978-0-981865904 2015 355'.42
Library of Congress Control Number: 2015940355

Coverart composition © 2015 by Posterity Press
Edited by Dr. Mary Beth Poole
Proofread by William E. Harris

First printing, United States of America, September 2015

To all U.S. security personnel presently serving in Africa.

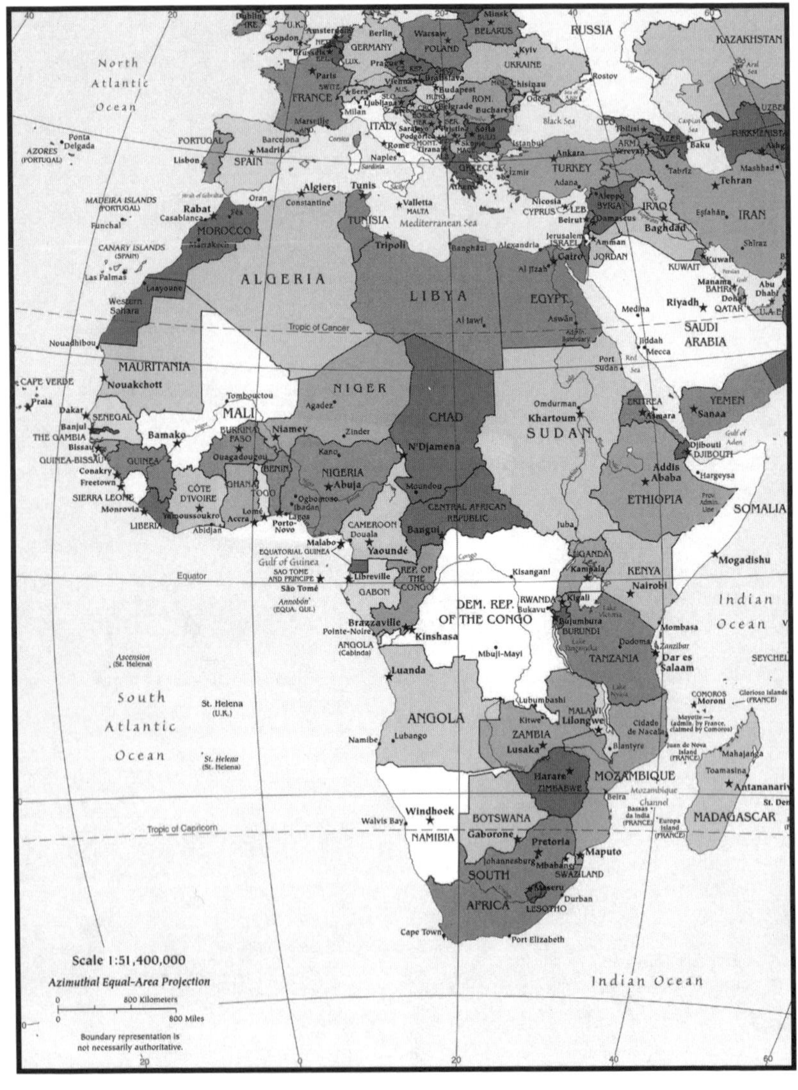

[T]HE TERM "DARK CONTINENT" CAME INTO USE IN THE 19TH CENTURY TO DESCRIBE A ... [LAND MASS] LARGELY UNKNOWN AND MYSTERIOUS TO EUROPEANS—NATIONAL PUBLIC RADIO

(Source: Courtesy of Univ. of Texas at Austin, Castanada Map designator "txu-oclc-238859671-africa_pol_2008.jpg," quote from William Jennings Bryan)

Contents

Part Five: Cooperation between Expansionist Entities

Part Six: How the Trade and Strife Are Connected

Part Seven: Combatting the Main Attack

Illustrations

Maps:

Figures:

Tables

Foreword

Africa has been the exploited, neglected, and forgotten continent for centuries. The legacy of colonialism, tribal conflict, corruption, and poverty have resulted in the developed world ignoring its potential. Only China has begun to invest in Africa in any meaningful way and that creates additional problems for the democratic nations of the world fearing Chinese hegemony and the spread of communist ideology. Failed or incapable states in this region have opened the door to violent extremists to grow in power and influence. Lawlessness in the form of piracy, criminal activity, and genocide is chronic. Our attention has been drawn to Africa only in respect to a metastasized threat from extremists tied to groups from the Middle East and Central Asia with whom we are engaged in a global conflict. Despite all this, Africa promises to be a significant future player on the world stage if it can realize its economic and geographic potential. It could also become significant in a negative sense if the ills that plague it grow and spread. We have growing security interests in Africa. We are, however, dealing with the threats to those interests in a meager, ineffective way. How long can an economy of force approach with minimal resources and lack of focus on understanding the environment stave off those threats? John Poole offers a well thought out course of action that focuses on everything from a strategic understanding of what we face, and what the culture is composed of, to the tactical requirements for small units to succeed on the ground. We should heed his sage advice and look to adopting his recommendation.

Gen. Anthony C. Zinni USMC (Ret.)
former head of U.S. Central Command

Preface

Why the Title?

"Afrique" is a word most often associated with French West Africa—a colonial federation of territories from 1895 to 1960. This federation included the following regions: Mauritania, Senegal, French Sudan (now Mali), French Guinea, Côte d'Ivoire, Upper Volta (now Burkina Faso), Dahomey (now Benin), and Niger. *"Afrique"* was chosen as the title for this U.S.-security-oriented work, not because of any French connection, but because of where many of its most astounding revelations occur.

By-Product of a Military Study

After many years of investigating foreign infantry tactics to assist the American war effort in Southwest Asia, this researcher realized that U.S. ground units were still not getting the right kind of combat intelligence. On almost every actionable aspect of their immediate enemy, all headquarters (or spy agency) insights were either too general, or misinterpreted. That's when the researcher decided to dedicate the first half of every new tactical-technique-manual supplement to the Eastern combatant's quite different way of conducting warfare.

As a Vietnam-era company commander, this same individual had received very little of any value from his battalion S-2.[1] While fighting the world's best light infantry, U.S. line company personnel couldn't care less about the foe's weaponry, general whereabouts, or order of battle. Of more help would be the exact locations of his hidden infiltration routes, way-stations, and protective strongpoints. But, only someone who had closely followed the evolution of small-unit tactics would know that, or how—through patrol debriefings—to determine it.

Of course, that Vietnam-era S-2 had not been alone in his tactical ignorance. The infantry commander, himself, had been no better informed.[2] He mostly knew how to fight someone with indirect fire and air strikes. Then, he (and the rest of the U.S. phalanx) had gotten repeatedly outmaneuvered *on the ground* by tiny increments of skinny little guys with very little resupply, and almost no tank, artillery, or aerial support.

In effect, U.S. intelligence gathering has traditionally focused on the foe's overall capabilities, instead of his local refuges and tactical expertise.[3] Against an opponent who routinely seeks victory through a deluge of small-unit engagements, such a "big-picture" orientation would automatically cause gaps in crucial information.

Pentagon Still Obsessed with Firepower

The "military/industrial complex"—of which President Eisenhower so unexpectedly warned—has been trying hard to ignore/conceal this "tactical chink" in America's armor. Seemingly unaffected by the lack of clear-cut victory in all recent conflicts, it must have complete control and economic stimulation as its principal objectives.

Through a little field experimentation, the average American rifle company could easily refine its own tactical techniques—the maneuvers with which its tiny subordinate elements might outsmart an enemy. Instead, all U.S. infantry commanders must now be satisfied with what inexperienced contractors and non-realistic facilities mostly provide—how those elements could better utilize their weaponry. As long as both providers stick with the officially sanctioned (standardized) squad movements, they are allowed by headquarters to do most of the troop preparation. But, across the board, there is a major conflict of interests with such an approach to national defense. The first "field experimentation" option would allow the U.S. military to keep pace with tactical-evolution worldwide, whereas the second "civilian-interface" option only perpetuates the *status quo*. The more logical first could be done for free, whereas the already existent second costs taxpayers a great deal of money. If Gen. Smedley D. Butler USMC were still around, his next book would be *How We Prepare for War Is a Racket*. Not only is it a racket, but it is almost certainly making a chronic tactical deficiency even worse. For America to win any more wars, its infantry squads must be shown how consistently to gain the tactical advantage over an adversary of any size. That's because, most future wars will be fought by tiny semi-autonomous ground elements. Anything larger runs the risk of instant annihilation by "smart" standoff firepower.

For a while, there was a new prime-time television (TV) program in Eastern North Carolina that repeatedly associated U.S. military service with the latest equipment. Without a doubt taxpayer-funded, it went far beyond the hype of recruiting. Most new Government Issues (GIs) to view this program would have quickly concluded that all that fancy gear makes them world-class warriors. Unfortunately, this so-called "edge" in technology has yet to compensate for their Eastern counterparts' greater mastery of stealth and deception. That may be why America hasn't decisively won a war since World War II (WWII). At least, that's what Sun Tzu would say.

For all those government workers who perceive any move beyond the *status quo* as disloyal, a "more pointed" discussion of how urgently this nation now needs a change to its threat assessment procedures is also offered.

Proof Positive of an Information Processing Problem

As any undercover U.S. cop can confirm, hints of something as monumental as 9/11 would have been "on Muslim streets" for weeks before it actually happened. While all U.S. intelligence and law enforcement agencies have since tried to improve, most still suffer from the same underlying difficulty. They and the American military still rely too heavily on electronic over human intelligence—namely, satellite imagery and radio intercepts instead of spies and frontline observers. That's how "top-down" organizations prefer to operate. Their highest-level leaders must honestly believe that too much troop input poses a threat to good order and discipline.

Tall "top-down" organizations (those with long chains of command) have the hardest time being efficient "where the rubber meets the road." Not only are their top leaders effectively insulated from bottom-echelon insights, but their own instructions often get garbled during their dissemination. Some intermediate-level "boss" either shortstops or modifies them. On the way down the chain, this happens to the "commander's intent." On the way up, it happens to inadequacies as well as opportunities. As each echelon tries to handle its own problems "in house," the next higher never hears of them. Or, if the troops are capable of a small-unit "breakout," their immediate superior thinks it too risky. That's when the overall commander ends up choosing some strategies that his troops can't execute, and avoiding others they could. Over the long term, too many lives get lost, and then too many wars.

This Problem Is Multifaceted and Cultural

There are a number of reasons why present-day U.S. intelligence gathering may be less than ideal. Western bureaucracies suffer from a number of hierarchical pressures. Anything that makes the organization or its parent administration look bad is at risk of being ignored. All too often, the result is incomplete or skewed governmental information.

Then, there are all the "reference traditions" of American university research. Highly deceptive foes seldom leave enough evidence to be implicated in any main-stream media release. With too strict a "source requirement," U.S. intelligence gatherers would come up with very few suspects anywhere in the Eastern World. In effect, any not reported in the *New York Times* would never have happened. Recently, a Chinese takeover in part of Pakistan-occupied Kashmir only qualified for an "opinion editiorial."[4] Police forces must be more realistic than that. Many now rely on a local version of *Wikipedia* to more effectively fight crime. When properly edited, such a network provides eyewitness accounts as well as details nowhere else available. While such details may seldom qualify as unadulterated fact, they still offer a useful framework for future research.

Lastly is the "political-correctness card" with which Washington's ruling party so easily labels constructive criticism as "unsubstantiated garbage." That's why a conservative TV network is now necessary to cover what the mostly liberal news media won't. Many Americans see "political correctness" as a way to demonstrate their national loyalty. Most have yet to realize that procedural *status quos* seldom compensate for a changing world. This nation has civilian experts in almost every field of endeavor. Yet, only rarely is one called to Washington to advise Congress or any government agency. That's why so many citizens now feel that the "cold hard facts" play too small a role in most Beltway decisions.

How to Solve the Intelligence Shortfall

While this book provides a "none too tactful" exposé of America's foreign-policy failures in Africa, it will also serve as a model for future intelligence gathering around the world. Current collection methods need not be scrapped, just supplemented to facilitate a more insightful interpretation.

Through more "open-source" details than are normally allowed in governmental or university studies, *Afrique* uncovers the "bottom-echelon" activity of all foreign entities currently exploiting the world's most resource-abundant continent. By focusing on trends within these tiny details, it then more easily identifies decentralized perpetrators. For the "bottom-up" activity of a Communist, Islamist, or criminal faction, on-site journalism can provide more insight than all the electronic surveillance, top-secret assessments, and U.S.-policy determinations put together. That's because electronic surveillance amasses more data than is easily processed, top secrets often have to do with embarrassment avoidance, and foreign-policy is usually a manifestation of current-administration opinion.

Determining the progress of a "bottom-up-operating" adversary—whether he be Communist, Islamist, or criminal—takes focusing on his actual ground activity (vice his easy-to-falsify communications). Most such clues will be small and "non-confirmable." Yet, once the adversary's historical *"modus operandi"* has been established, those clues that hold promise will be readily distinguishable from the others. Enough such traces (despite the erroneous few) will then collectively paint a picture of not only what has happened, but what is about to happen. That is the future of U.S. military intelligence gathering in any Eastern, insurgent, or criminal environment. It's not new. Many police departments already use such methods. Just as organized-crime factions operate from the bottom up, so do Communist and Islamist forces. That's why this new way of determining their intentions will work so much better than the old.

Armed with such information, small teams of U.S. infantrymen and special operators could better win all the tiny engagements that go into preventing their parent command's "death by a thousand razor cuts."

Those who still doubt the power of this alternative way of collecting intelligence should check the accuracy of Posterity Press' various "predictions" over the years. Almost all have turned out to be correct. To study an Eastern opponent, the Western researcher can't doggedly stick with the traditional ways of assessing things. Once the focus has shifted from "big picture" to small, he (or she) will be more likely to determine that opponent's hidden agenda.

Figure P.1: More "Human-Intelligence" Required
(Source: "The Somalian Update," by SGT.J.T.Manuszak©, U.S.Army Ctr.of Mil.Hist., from url: http://www.history.army.mil/art/Somalia/Manuszak_Somalia_files/image015.jpg)

For the Inveterate "Nay-Sayers"

"Attention to poorly supported detail" may be difficult for non-law-enforcement types to accept. For them, any improvement to America's intelligence apparatus will take much more justification. In effect, the standard U.S. way of studying something works just fine for inanimate and unchanging objects. But, for a highly decentralized and thoroughly deceptive human adversary, it has proven less than adequate over the years. That's why it must now be supplanted on the fields and streets of what has become a worldwide low-intensity combat zone. All human knowledge is nothing more than a glorified hypothesis anyway. That's why one so often hears "Only God knows for sure" or "Things are more complicated than they appear." If any "fact-related" variable has been even slightly misinterpreted, then that fact—in all of its traditional grandeur—may be no fact at all.

While pandering to "conventional wisdom," many recognition-hungry researchers don't even bother to list their sources. So what's wrong with using the *modus operandi* of chronic perpetrators to further interpret a security-related hypothesis? Wouldn't that help to arrive at more realistic projections and strategies? This book provides a good example of how this perfectly logical supplement to the U.S. intelligence effort can produce a more revealing look at recent events in Africa.

Most high-level bureaucrats within the U.S. intelligence community will quickly dismiss any suggestion that they have been considering too little detail. It's true that they've collected massive amounts of electronic minutia. But, communications are far too easy to contaminate with disinformation, and satellite imagery still can't detect most surface anomalies. That's why police departments pay more attention to physical evidence than phone taps and stand-off photography. Only through a myriad of tiny surface clues (fingerprints, DNA, etc.) can they often zero in on the most likely offender. (See Figure P.1.) While the suspect only becomes "guilty" after a formal trial, their initial investigation—by itself—can still deter any further crime while that trial is pending.

One's Ultimate Loyalty is to the Truth

After each international incident, U.S. intelligence agencies tend to gravitate toward evidence that meshes well with America's current foreign policy. A non-affiliated (or independent) criminal investigator would instead pursue clues that fit the historical *modus operandi* of his most promising suspects. While the first "agency" effort invariably comes up with *al-Qaeda* (or the administration's current "bad boy"), the second "more objective" endeavor arrives at an assortment of possible culprits. Within the mutual agenda of more than one culprit may lie evidence of a hidden instigator. When trying to solve a complicated crime, U.S. law enforcement agencies can often shorten their list of suspects by assessing how closely each has been linked to the occurrence. They still look for co-conspirators.

To follow this "pseudo-police model," federal intelligence personnel must first become more familiar with the Eastern thought process and ways of operating "from the bottom up." Most modern-day expansionists, insurgents, terrorists, and criminals follow this alternate paradigm. That means every one of America's intelligence, police, and ground combat units should be interested. By studying this and other Posterity Press titles, their fledgling intelligence gatherers could quickly "come up to speed" on this other way of fighting.

What Have the Communists and Islamists Been Secretly Up To?

If there really does exist a way to improve America's intelligence collection system, then how much harm have her adversaries already done inside U.S. borders without anyone noticing it? Will an in-depth study of every African nation also reveal what has been happening throughout the U.S.? To answer these questions, read this book. It should prove far more exciting than any detective story.

Still intact are America's noble intentions and potential for saving the world. What might usefully change is how her defense agencies go about meeting those aspirations.

LT.COL. H. JOHN POOLE USMC (RET.)
FORMER GY.SGT. (FMCR) AND FORMER
ILLINOIS BUREAU OF INVESTIGATION AGENT

ACKNOWLEDGMENTS

Thanks be to God for all useful insights into the convoluted ways of the world. Any government that makes the mistake of ignoring His presence in its quest for religious tolerance will become increasingly more atheistic in its outlook and efforts. That, in turn, will make it (and its population) more susceptible to the unhealthy influences of the still Communist (and highly expansionist) Peoples Republic of China (PRC). Communism is based on a philosophy of materialism. It denies the existence of God, the spirituality of the human soul, and the existence of heaven.[1]

PART ONE

THE DUAL FACE OF FOREIGN EXPANSION

"IF MY FORCE IS FIVE TIMES THAT OF THE ENEMY, I ALARM HIM TO THE FRONT, SURPRISE HIM TO THE REAR, CREATE AN UPROAR IN THE EAST AND STRIKE IN THE WEST." — CHANG YU, SUN TZU SCHOLAR

(Source: Chang Yu, as quoted in "The Art of War" by Sun Tzu, trans. Samuel B. Griffith [New York: Oxford Univ. Press, 1963], pp. 79, 80)

1 Most African Turmoil Still over Commerce

- Why is Africa so vital to the world's trade in commodities?
- How might Dark Continent instability facilitate that trade?

More than ivory comes out of Africa.

(Source: Courtesy of Classroom Clipart, ©, free download from the following url: http://classroomclipart.com/clipart-view/Clipart/Africa/09-06-08_02R_jpg.htm)

The Growing Sense of Foreboding at Home

U.S. citizens have become quite worried of late, about not only the future of the planet, but of America herself. For years, there has been talk of a "New World Order." If that Order is one and the same with what the Communist (and avowedly atheistic) Chinese have been calling "Globalization," then all material goods are about to be traded freely. Little attention will be paid to the ill effects of any such goods on recipient or provider. All will be "fair" in love and commerce. Within such a freewheeling Order, the country doing most of the world's business might come to control its politics.

Isn't enough money the prerequisite of most elections? To better appreciate the danger, America's "more-ethics-oriented" business community should first consider a circumstantial anomaly from Oceania.

Only *al-Qaeda* has been openly contesting the Indonesian island of Sulawesi that sits squarely atop the second largest petroleum deposit in the Western Pacific. Yet, there is now little doubt of the PRC's interest in the biggest deposit beneath the Paracel and Spratly islands. Thus, one suspects some hidden link between China and *al-Qaeda* with regard to Sulawesi.

Might similar Sino-Arabic connections exist in Africa—wherein lies not only vast reserves of petroleum, but also the world's only supply of rare defense metals? As the earliest writings on strategic deception come from China, such a possibility would best be pursued by a Western veteran of a Far Eastern war without the usual number of cultural biases. But, such a person is hard to find. Most Americans are as adverse to conspiracy theories as they are used to "big-picture thinking." The full extent of a "bottom-up" expansionist's plan for Africa would only be apparent from a proliferation of tiny clues—most of which could never be confirmed. Any U.S. researcher would have to make some sense out of a partially erroneous cloud of hints. But, as every pointillist painter knows, enough "approximate dots" will eventually reveal a recognizable image. Within Africa, this image may be twofold—not only of the repeat offender, but also of his hidden instigator. The image components that can then be substantiated would be the only way to convict either miscreant in a court of law.

Why the Additional Insight Is Now Necessary

Other researchers have already established that the PRC has been swapping regional infrastructure for mineral rights at the governmental level in Africa. But, what of China's more obscure grass-roots strategies? They can only be studied through a detailed look at all Chinese inroads, whether host-country approved or through private interests. *Afrique* makes a concerted effort to uncover such "encroachments" on each nation's well-being by either the Chinese or recently active Islamists. While their respective homelands may be far apart, their ways of operating are much the same. Among the world's very few "revolutionary" regimes are those from China, North Korea, Cuba, Venezuela, Iran, and Sudan.[1] All have tiny—Communist or Islamic revolution-promoting, perpetuating, and monitoring—elements that have been intentionally spread throughout their populations and defense agencies. It is through the collective input of miniscule defense elements that much of their internal discipline and external expansion is accomplished. That's why such governments are said to be operating from the bottom-up, despite what is often autocratic leadership at the top.

For the Chinese, "bottom-up" problem solving has been an integral part of a cultural heritage that predates Communism by thousands of years. Among its best examples is the "covered" supply road that the Chinese built into North Vietnam at the start of the 1950's.[2] Its rapid extension permitted the Viet Minh to unexpectedly overwhelm the well-supported French garrison at Dien Bien Phu. (See Figure 1.1.) Both conduits had been made by thousands of shovel-and-axe-wielding coolies instead of bulldozers. The same decentralized "low-tech" approach would later be used to secretly move the supplies.

Figure 1.1: "Low-Tech" Asian Reds Win First of Many Wars
(Source: Courtesy of Cassell PLC, from "Uniforms of the Indo-China and Vietnam Wars," © 1984 by Blandford Press Ltd.)

> The Red Highway [from China into North Vietnam] was a masterpiece of camouflage. It had been cut through the jungle without allowing as much as ten yards to be exposed to the skies. At a few less densely wooded sections, hundreds of trees had been roped together and drawn closer to one another with the aid of pulley-like contraptions. They had been fastened in such a way that their crown intertwined over the road. In the open ravines, networks of strong wire had been stretched between the slopes to support creepers, which had soon blotted out the road beneath.
>
> The jungle road included permanent bridges, twelve to fifteen feet wide, most of them constructed a few inches underwater to fool aerial observation. Difficult or swampy sections of the road had been "paved" either with stones or with logs leveled with gravel. Along the Red Highway were checkpoints where guerrilla MP's [military police] controlled transport or troop movements. Rest-houses and service stations where carts and bicycles could be repaired were also located on that incredible network of trails. Its very existence was ridiculed by some French statesmen. It was simply too incredible to believe. Yet it was there![3]
>
> — *Devil's Guard,* by George Robert Elford

For the final battle of the war, the Viet Minh simply followed the Chinese model. In just three months, they built a 600-mile road from the Chinese resupply point to Dien Bien Phu.[4] Over that road, they would secretly move 100,000 fighters, 200 heavy guns, and 8000 tons of supplies.[5] While they had some Russian trucks, they relied mostly on 500-pound-carrying bicycles. Because the trail had been so well camouflaged, it was invisible to French observation planes. The Viet Minh had roped the treetops together to create a tunnel of vegetation.[6] Later, they would hide their heavy guns in bunkers overlooking the French-occupied valley.

While this famous example of bottom-up progress is now a bit dated, subsequent advances in technology have made the West no less vulnerable to what large numbers of civilian "volunteers" can accomplish against it. Such volunteers no longer need to militarily invade as at Korea's Chosin Reservoir in late 1950. Now, in large enough numbers, they can actually alter the business and political climate of their new place of residence.

Assembling the Pieces to a Complicated African Puzzle

After identifying trends in the evidential detail, *Afrique* will draw all appropriate conclusions without any attempt at "political correctness." The reader should thereby get a troubling glimpse of what may eventually befall the U.S..

Afrique is not for the faint of heart. It must be read like a detective story, with the ultimate objective of somehow helping America and the world. The personal satisfaction of later being able to connect its tiny clues will be considerable. Many are of a non-martial nature, but their collective influence could prove disastrous to not only the 54 countries of Africa, but also to America herself. At book's end, the reader will be shown the only military way to meet this seemingly impossible challenge.

Best Place to Start

There can be no comprehensive assessment of a Chinese attempt at world domination without the diversion that most Sun Tzu students have come to expect. Within Africa, this diversion need not be of Chinese origin, or even Chinese encouraged. It must only happen at about the same time as some Chinese initiative. Most likely, of course, would be another brutal example of Islamist expansion.

Much of North Africa was formerly part of the ancient Muslim Empire. Many of these same areas are now secular Islamic countries with active *"Salafist"* rebellions. Still sporting the same "revolutionary" government as during the Korean War, the PRC is in no way deterred by such chronic unrest. As most Western businesses tend to shy away from risky places, all the latent violence simply gives China's state-owned corporations more access to Africa's natural resources. It also provides an excuse for more of a military presence from the PRC—in the form of trainers, advisers, and peacekeepers. Either way, China gains sway over local diplomacy and politics.

Absolute Requirement for Any Meaningful Investigation

To try to identify a conspiracy involving 54 separate nations without any attention to their individual histories (or world context) would be futile. Facts that have not been politically edited can be more exciting than fiction. To create the proper framework for further research, this introductory chapter will necessarily make repeated reference to the post-1960 African experience. Most will be action-packed.

Previous Foreign Interest in the Dark Continent

Many years ago, the Colonial Powers were mostly interested in Africa's natural resources. Only within northern Africa's former Muslim Empire did the religious affiliations of its people even come into play. Then, from 1965 to 1980, the Soviet Union and PRC tried—through armed revolt—to shift the politics of the whole southern end of Africa to Communism. What remains of that effort is mostly non-martial. Through immigration and construction, the PRC still discreetly pursues that same objective. All the while, it has been solving two problems at home—too many people and not enough energy.

> On the African continent, the effects of this [PRC] transformation are evident in two key areas: an ever-increasing presence of Chinese expatriated civilians and military forces, and increased economic and political investment.[7]
> — *Joint Forces Quarterly,* March 2009

Any more recent pro-Communist revolt on the Dark Continent would have to serve a specific purpose—like scaring away Western business interests. A good current example may be the Movement for the Emancipation of the Niger Delta (MEND) in Nigeria. MEND has been primarily attacking Western oil companies, kidnapping U.S. workers, and destroying U.S. facilities. In a 2007 *National Geographic* photograph, its fighters were wearing red scarves, carrying shiny Eastern-bloc weapons, and operating brand new Yamaha outboard motors.[8] One could reasonably conclude that someone rich from Asia—who also likes the color red—had been supporting (and possibly directing) them. That someone did not have to be an Islamist.

MEND emerged independent[ly] of either the Wahhabi

> Shari'ah movement in northern Nigeria or the Nigerian Taliban that first appeared in [northeastern Nigeria's] Yobe state in December 2003. . . . Its members are mainly Catholics, though Asari [its jailed leader] is an exception.[9]
>
> — Project for the Research of Islamist Movements

Should the big U.S. oil companies find operating in Nigeria too dangerous, their Chinese counterparts are all set to move in, according to *ABC News*.[10] A Sun-Tzu-like ploy is therefore possible. Against a backdrop of Islamic unrest, the oil-hungry PRC might try to discourage Western competition through a pseudo-Islamic guerrilla proxy.

The Current Threat Is from Two External Sources

Western travelers still marvel at the depth of character of the African people. But, the vast majority of those people continue to suffer from Communist and Islamist duress. By fully researching the activities of these modern-day robber barons, one might arrive at some interesting links between them. Both seem to want oil, but the Islamists will often just sell their petroleum to the Chinese. The Chinese are non-Christian and would rather do business with a non-Western entity. When in pursuit of their global ambitions, they will quickly swap monetary aid for diplomatic favoritism (particularly at the U.N.).

As of 2006, America was buying most of its oil from Nigeria, Angola, Algeria, and Chad, whereas Communist China was getting its supply from Sudan, Angola (People's Republic of Angola until 1992), Chad, and the Congo Republic (People's Republic of the Congo until 1991.)[11] To make any sense out of Africa's mishmash of convoluted intrigue, one has only to identify what foreign nations want from her. At the top of the list is oil, with only a passing regard for its owner's religious or political preferences. (See Map 1.1 and Table 1.1.)

Africa's Islamic North

Most of North Africa is Muslim. While there may seem to be more turmoil along this vast area's boundary (particularly in Ni-

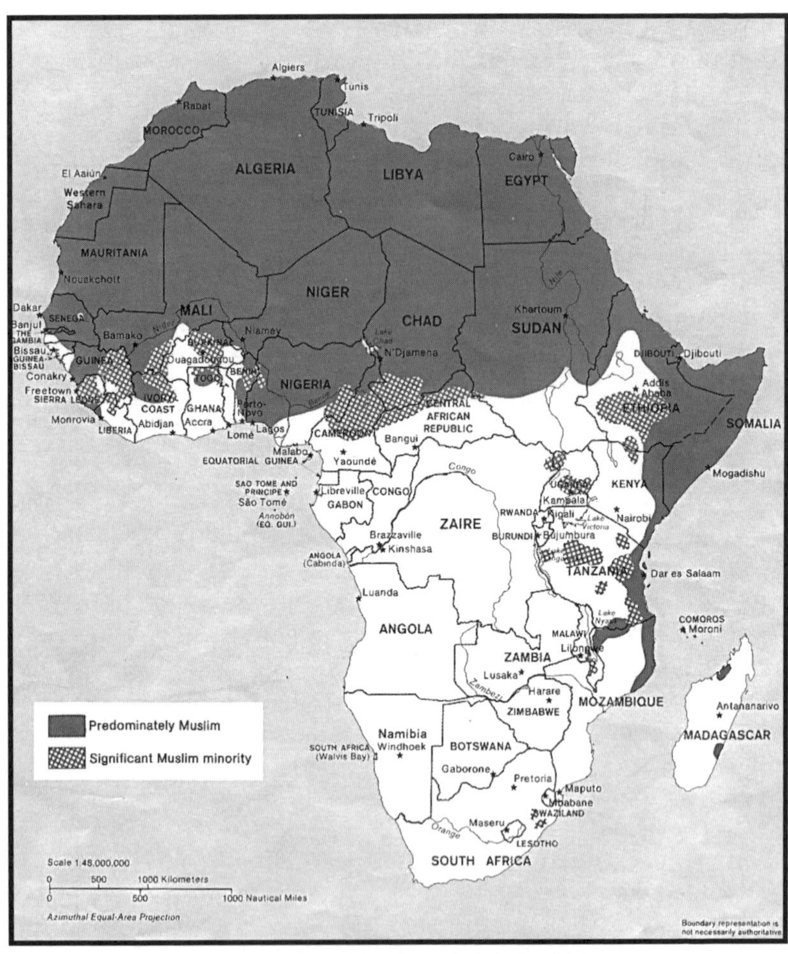

Map 1.1: Modern-Day Islamic Africa

(Source: Courtesy of General Libraries, University of Texas at Austin, from their website for map designator "africa_islam_1987.pdf")

geria), that turmoil cannot be automatically attributed to religious differences. Also at play are tribal animosities and economic competition. For example, most of the current difficulties in South Sudan have nothing to do with who the opposing sides worship.

2014 Oil Stats for Africa's Most Contested Nations

	Oil production (barrels/day)	Gas Production (cubic meters)	Oil Reserves (barrels)	Gas Reserves (cubic meters)
Countries with Islamist Rebellions				
Algeria	1.762 million	78.6 billion	12.2 billion	4.505 trillion
Egypt	700,000	56.63 billion	4.4 billion	2.18 trillion
Libya	310,000	12.19 billion	48.47 billion	1.549 trillion
Tunisia	64,150	1.863 billion	425 million	65.13 billion
South Sudan	220,000	none	3.75 billion	63.71 billion
Niger	20,000	none	150 million	none
Mali	none	none	none	none
Kenya	none	none	none	none
Chad	97,910	none	1.5 billion	none
Countries with both Islamist and Non-Specified Rebellions				
Nigeria	2.367 million	33.71 billion	37.14 billion	5.118 trillion
DRC	20,000	9 million	180 million	991.1 million
CAR	none	none	none	none
Countries with Communist Backgrounds				
Mozambique	20	4.355 billion	none	2.832 trillion
Angola	1.89 million	760 million	9.06 billion	275 billion
Congo Republic	279,000	1.166 billion	1.6 billion	90.61 billion
Namibia	none	none	none	62.29 billion
Ethiopia	100	none	430,000	24.92 billion
South Africa	168,700	1.187 billion	15 million	15.01 billion
Somalia	none	none	none	5.663 billion
Zambia	none	none	none	none
Zimbabwe	120	none	none	none
Guinea-Bissau	none	none	none	none
Other Countries with Strong Economic Ties to Communist China				
Cameroon	62,760	165 million	200 million	135.1 billion
Equatorial Guinea	290,800	6.88 billion	1.1 billion	36.81 billion
Gabon	239,300	90 billion	2 billion	28.32 billion
Sudan (Islamist)	28,830	none	1.25 billion	21.24 billion
Tanzania	10	928.8 million	none	6.513 billion

Table 1.1: Where the Petroleum Is Located in Africa
(Source: CIA World Factbook.)

Figure 1.2: Chinese PT Boat at Tanzania's Only Seaport
(Source: Courtesy of Warboats.com, fig. 190, from the following url: http://www.warboats.org/soviet.htm)

The Previously Communist South

As a result of Apartheid, only local history buffs may realize the extent of Communist subversion within Southern Africa from 1965 to the early 1980's. The Chinese Communist effort was most obvious on Africa's east coast at Tanzania. The People's Liberation Army (PLA) had taken over the training and equipping of that nation's military.[12] The PRC-built "TANZAM Railway" would soon be carrying Chinese-trained rebels to Zambia for further transit to neighboring countries.[13] And Chinese Patrol Torpedo (PT) boats would soon be traversing Dar es Salaam harbor. From 1967 to 1969, six Soviet P-6 Class "Bolshevik" boats were given to Tanzania as part of a military assistance package. The PRC had 80 of the same model at home. As such, it could have easily provided the crews.[14] (See Figure 1.2.)

Meanwhile, the Soviet Communists were busy on Africa's west coast. When a Cuban contingent finally came to the aid of Soviet proxies in Angola in 1975 and a Soviet landing force was allowed to sit just off the West African shore in 1976,[15] the die was cast. Before long, the South Africans had pulled their army out of the fray. There was to be a new era of "peaceful coexistence" throughout southern Africa. Despite so-called "free" elections, only Communist rebel candidates seemed to win. In the early 1990's, the constitutions of four countries were amended to allow multi-party voting: (1) Mozambique;[16] (2) Angola;[17] (3) Tanzania;[18] and (4) Zambia.[19] Still, their ruling parties remained in power.

The problem was simple—the two Communist powers had been competing for the same prizes. This was most obvious through the pincers movement on Rhodesia—Chinese backed ZANLA (Zimbabwe African National Liberation Army) from Mozambique and Soviet-backed ZIPRA (Zimbabwe's People's Revolutionary Army) from Botswana and Zambia. Generally speaking, the rebels from East Africa had Maoist intentions and method, whereas those from West Africa had Soviet ways. But, there were exceptions on both coasts. (See Table 1.2.) Meanwhile, U.S. and South African proxies attempted mostly to stem the Communist takeover of Angola and Namibia. They did far less about the Communist Chinese presence in Tanzania and Mozambique.

> In black Africa, rivalry is keen in Uganda, Kenya, Zambia and the two Congos, and among liberation movements; only in Tanzania do the Chinese appear to be ahead. There have been reports of Chinese naval activities in the Indian Ocean: ships were sighted in May near the Andamans, and China is helping Tanzania build a small naval base near Dar-es-Salaam. However, China's navy is not large enough to provide a significant presence in the Indian Ocean, and its [the navy's] impact there for some years can at best be psychological.[20]
>
> — *Foreign Affairs,* October 1970

China's TANZAM, TAZARA, or "Freedom" Railway

The PRC's grand strategy for Africa became first apparent in Tanzania in the mid-1960's after a visit from Zhou Enlai. A combined labor force was to build a 1160 mile-long railway from Dar es Salaam to Kapiri Mposhi—a town just north of Lusaka where the Copper Belt from the Democratic Republic of the Congo [DRC] ends in Zambia. At the peak of construction in 1972, there were 13,500 Chinese and 38,000 Africans working on this train line.[21] While the following is supposedly a joint statement from the leaders of Zambia and Tanzania, it sounds more of Chinese origin. The three countries signed a formal agreement in 1967.

Political Affiliations of Past and Present Revolts

Nations with Former Communist Rebels or Socialist Ruling Parties

Angola	MPLA (had Soviet support)
	UNITA (policies initially Maoist after Savimbi trained in China)
	FNLA (had Chinese instructors)
Namibia	SWAPO (backed by Soviets)
Mozambique	FRELIMO (got its men from Tanzania, PRC instructors)
South Africa	ANC (initially backed by PRC the switched to Soviets)
	MK (ANC's armed wing, some trained at PRC camps in Angola)
	PAC (ANC offshoot that stayed Chinese)
Zimbabwe	ZANU (PRC backed, ZANLA was its military wing)
	ZANLA (PRC supported, sent men to China for training)
	ZAPU (Soviet backed, ZIPRA was its military wing)
	ZIPRA (Soviet supported, sent men to China for training)
Tanzania	(formerly PRC-backed Socialist regime since 1961)
Zambia	(formerly PRC-backed Socialist regime since 1964)
Malawi	(independent in 1964 but often traversed by guerrilla forces)
Botswana	(independent in 1966 but often traversed by guerrilla forces)
Guinea Bissau	Joao Bernardo "Nino" Viera's guerrillas until 1974 (PRC-backed)
Congo Republic	(formerly Marxist regime since 1960)

Other PRC-Backed Nations with Ongoing Insurrections

DRC	FDLR (same Hutu Interahamwe that did Rwandan genocide)
Ethiopia	ONLF (ethnic Somalis)
South Sudan	Riek Machar's forces (mostly Christian)
Sudan	Sudan Revolutionary Front (Islamist coalition)

Nations with Large Muslim Populations and Ongoing Insurrections

Chad	Union of Forces for Democracy and Development (UFDD)
Somalia	Al Shabaab (formerly al-Qaeda, now ISIS affiliate)
Algeria	AQIM (formerly al-Qaeda, now ISIS affiliate)
Libya	"Libya Dawn" (rival Islamist government in Tripoli)
	Ansar al-Sharia Libya (strong relations with ISIS)
Mali	National Movement for the Liberation of Azawad (MNLA)
	Unity Movement for Jihad in West Africa (MUJAO)
Tunisia	Ansar al-Sharia (strong relations with ISIS)
Nigeria	Boko Haram (formerly al-Qaeda, now ISIS affiliate)
Egypt	Al Gamaat al-Islamiyya (al-Qaeda affiliate)
	Ansar Beit al Maqdis (ISIS affiliate)
Eritrea	Eritrean Islamic Jihad (al-Qaeda affiliate)
Western Sahara	The Polisario Front (Socialist faction that with Algerian backing is working to end Moroccan control)

Table 1.2: All Rebels Have Political Affiliations

> In addition to stimulating economic development in Southern Tanzania and Northeast Zambia, the TAZARA railway was expected to be politically liberating for the entire southern African region. By breaking free from the hegemony of South African mining interests, Zambia could provide inspiration for all those fighting against the white settler and Portuguese colonial rule in Rhodesia, Mozambique, Angola, and South Africa. The railway would also assist Zambia and Tanzania in their support for these liberation struggles: with an independent outlet to the sea, Zambia would no longer be as vulnerable to trade sanctions or border closings for supporting the anti-colonial forces. Meanwhile, the railway could provide the means for shipping . . . military supplies, to the liberation forces through a friendly neighboring country.[22]
>
> — Joint decree of Tanzanian and Zambian leaders

Chinese assistance on the project was mostly provided by the PLA's Railway Engineering Corps. This military unit would turn into China Railway Engineering Corporation (CRECG), a close affiliate of the Ministry of Railways' foreign aid department. Then, that foreign-aid department would become China Civil Engineering Construction Corporation (CCECC).[23] How these (and other) "civilianized" government entities would affect Africa will be later detailed.

Like with Angola's Benguela Railway to the DRC, PRC money has since kept both transportation conduits operational.[24] While their principal purpose may now be natural resource extraction, their upkeep still involves Chinese state-owned corporations and their own security personnel. It is through peacekeepers and corporate security guards that the PRC maintains a ground presence in many of the most strategically important corners of the world.

But Not Only Communists Were on the Move in Africa

Northern Africa is now home to some 15 *al-Qaeda* affiliates, according to U.S. government reports. One or more of these affiliates attacked the U.S. consulate in Benghazi, Libya, on 11 September 2012.[25] (Look again at Table 1.2.)

Between 2010 and November 2013, Islamic militants carried out more than 1,000 attacks in Algeria, Libya, Tunisia, and Morocco. Most were linked in some way to *al-Qaeda*. *Ansar Dine,* had conquered some 300,000 miles of northern Mali, prompting a French military intervention. The *Polisario Front,* an Algeria-based separatist group, had assisted *al-Qaeda in the Islamic Maghreb (AQIM)* to move guns and men across the Sahara into Algeria and Libya. *Ansar al-Sharia* had gained control of some 400 mosques in Tunisia and allied itself with one of the major political parties there. Then, *al-Qaeda*-linked militants attacked a shopping mall in Kenya while their Somali brethren continued to attack American and allied shipping near the Red Sea entrance.[26]

Sudan Has Always Been at the Center of Regional *Jihadism*

When Osama bin Laden was expelled from Saudi Arabia in 1991, he and most of *al-Qaeda's* organizational hierarchy took up residence in Sudan.[27] (See Map 1.2.) About this same time, Sudan's rulers (from its own chapter of the Muslim Brotherhood) started hosting Islamist "summits" and guerrilla training camps. To these, fundamentalists and rebels from all over North Africa were invited.[28] Then, in 1993, American troops landed in Somalia's capital of Mogadishu. Before long they were fighting *al-Qaeda*-trained militiamen.[29]

After *al-Qaeda* was finally evicted from Sudan in 1996,[30] Lebanese *Hezbollah* took over many of its guerrilla training facilities.[31] Through those facilities passed African volunteers for the conflicts in Iraq and the Levant. When the National Congress Party (NCP) (also from Muslim Brotherhood roots) took control of the Sudanese government in 1998,[32] trouble throughout the region showed few signs of abating.

What's So Special about Africa's Northern End?

A sizable portion the world's trade flows through the Suez Canal. Without access to this vital waterway, those who would reconstitute the old Muslim Empire or fully tap Africa's supply of petroleum would have great difficulty doing so. Their holdings would be divided, and their trade routes restricted. Thus, all countries along the Mediterranean and Red Sea approaches to the Suez Canal are of tremendous strategic value to any expansionist. That may help to explain the many insurgencies in this region over the years: (1) Islamic Salvation Front, Armed Islamic Group, and Islamic Salvation Front in Algeria;[33] (2) *En-Nahda* in Tunisia;[34] (3) *Ga'mat al-Islamiya* and Egyptian Islamic Jihad in Egypt;[35] (4) Eritrean Islamic Jihad *(Jamal Jihad),* Eritrean Liberation Front, Eritrean Kunama Movement, and Red Sea Democratic Organization in Eritrea;[36] and (5) the Islamic Union of Mujahideen of Ogaden in Ethiopia.[37] All have enjoyed some measure of foreign support.

Much of sub-Saharan Africa is also a good place to recruit *jihadist* fighters for other continents. "About a third of Africa's 700 million inhabitants are Muslim, so Islamists see Black Africa as their newest theater [of operations]."[38] In Egypt, Libya, Tunisia, Algeria, Morocco, Mauritania, and Sudan, followers of the Prophet Muhammad make up most of the population. In Somalia, Chad, Niger, Mali, Senegal, and Guinea, theirs is the majority religion. They also constitute about half of the citizenry in Nigeria, Eritrea, and Ethiopia; with sizable minorities in Ghana, Ivory Coast, Sierra Leone, Kenya, and Tanzania.[39] As such, every expansionist—whether in search of *sharia*-law or not—could easily capitalize on the differences between Muslim and Christian.

The Extent of Subversion from Khartoum

Salafists of both persuasions (Shiite and Sunni) have long considered Sudan their African base camp. Khartoum once used Iranian funds to promote Islamist uprisings throughout resource-rich East Africa—most notably, Kenya, Uganda, Tanzania, Somalia, and Ethiopia.[40]

> U.S. authorities have evidence that Sudan harbors such militant Islamic extremist organizations as *Hamas, Hezbollah,* the *Palestinian Islamic Jihad [PIJ]* and *al Gamaat al-Islamiyya* [from Egypt], and that it supports other terrorist groups in Algeria, Uganda, Tunisia, Ethiopia and Eritrea.[41]
> — Center for Defense Info., 10 December 2001

After all, it was through a 1990's alliance of militant Islamic organizations that Khartoum had helped to destabilize Eritrea,[42]

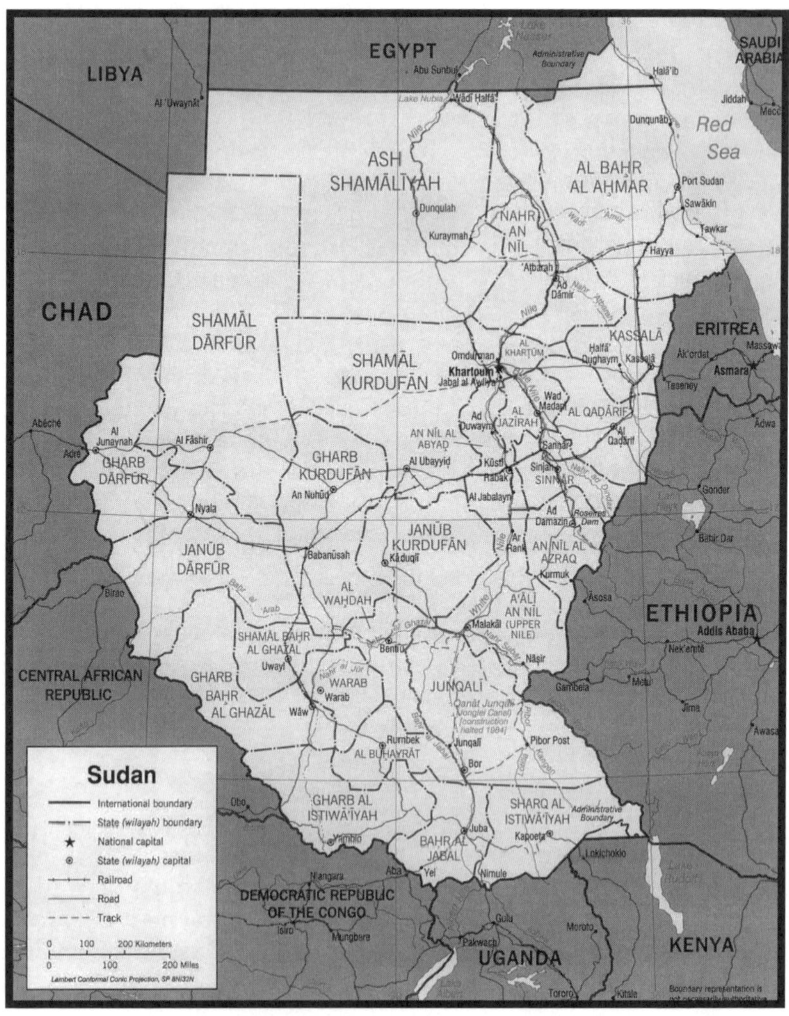

Map 1.2: Sudan's Original Border Areas
(Source: Courtesy of General Libraries, University of Texas at Austin, from their website for map designator "sudan_pol00 copy.tif")

Algeria,[43] Egypt,[44] and Tunisia.[45] Intentionally obscure, that alliance has been variously called the Armed Islamic Movement (AIM);[46] International Legion of Islam;[47] Islamic People's Congress;[48] Islamic People's Conference;[49] and Islamic National Front (INF).[50]

As Africa's Islamist Movement Unfolded

Like Lebanese *Hezbollah* had done in Lebanon, Sudanese AIM functioned as an "umbrella" entity for separate groups across North Africa. By so doing, it could divert unwanted attention from any particular member.

At first, some 40 Islamist parties, movements, and organizations came together under the guise of a Popular Arab and Islamic Conference (PAIC) [51]—the initial title for AIM. Its mission was to counter the Saudi-dominated Organization of Islamic Conference (OIC).[52]

Soon, worldwide *jihad* was being discussed at AIM conferences. To supplement this effort, bin Laden (then living in Khartoum) created the World Islamic Front for the Jihad against Jews and Crusaders (WIFJ). It would serve as an additional umbrella for about 20 other guerrilla and terrorist groups.[53]

Where *Jihadist* Training Occurred in Sudan

Prior to 1991, the Sudanese Army and "Islamic fundamentalist militants from [other countries]" were trained in Sudan by the Iranian Revolutionary Guard Corps (IRGC or *Sepah).*[54] *Egyptian Islamic Jihad, Eritrean Islamic Jihad, Ethiopian Islamic Jihad, Palestinian Islamic Jihad, Hamas,* and *Hezbollah* are just a few of the regional insurgencies to have frequented Sudan in succeeding years.[55] *Sepah* directly supported rebels in Algeria, Tunisia, and Egypt,[56] so Sudan may have at one time been an Iranian satellite of sorts. Both the Iranian air force and navy used Sudanese facilities. After deposing the Shah, the Ayatollah Khomeini had called for a global Islamic revolution by both Shiites and Sunnis.[57] That would have taken the cooperation of *Salafists* (fundamentalists) from both sects, whether they liked each other or not.

One of the Sunni founders of *al-Qaeda*—Abdullah Yusuf Azzam—also had a far-reaching vision. He wanted to recoup all the glories and lands of Islam.[58] Those so-called lands included Palestine, Lebanon, Chad, Eritrea, Somalia, and southern Yemen.[59] So, much of northeastern Africa would have been included. Most of this area did eventually come under insurgent attack.

By 1993, thousands of *jihadists* were being instructed at facilities built by Osama bin Laden in Sudan.[60] "By early 1995, Iranian funding [had] enabled . . . *al-Qaeda* to establish twenty-three training camps throughout Sudan." At some were *Hezbollah* and *Sepah* trainers.[61] Many remained operational after bin Laden's departure in 1996. Among them were the following: "[1] two camps for Arabs at Merkhiyat; [2] one camp for Eritrean, Ethiopian, Ugandan, Somali, and occasionally Palestinian Islamists at al-Qutanynah; [3] one camp for training Palestinian, Libyan, Iranian, Iraqi, [and] Yemeni . . . Islamists in Jabel al-Awliya; [4] one for training Egyptians, Algerians, and Tunisians in Shendi, near Port Sudan; [5] one for treating casualties in Soba; . . . [6] one in Sejara near Omdurman [that] controlled training throughout Sudan."[62] In addition to a protected quay at Port Sudan's mechanized infantry barracks, *al-Qaeda* also enjoyed a base camp at Ras Kamboni—a tiny peninsula on the south coast of Somalia.[63] Graduates of the Ras Kamboni training center have since conducted terrorist attacks in Tanzania, Kenya, Uganda, and elsewhere. While *al-Qaeda* is ultimately responsible for those attacks, Sudan has continued to orchestrate regional trouble. In December 2005, Chad went so far as to declare war on Sudan, accusing various Sudanese militias of making daily cross-border raids.[64]

Did Those *al-Qaeda* Trainers Then Move to Somalia?

When finally asked to leave Sudan in 1996,[65] *al-Qaeda* must have shifted enough of its African contingent to Somalia to run several training camps at Ras Kamboni and Mogadishu.[66] At least part of this same contingent may have stayed on in Somalia. *Al-Qaeda* operatives have since been active in all of its regions—Somalia (including Galmudug), Somaliland,[67] and Puntland.[68] (See Map 1.3.)

> At least 27 people have been killed in heavy fighting near the border of two semi-autonomous regions of Somalia, witnesses said on the eve of a political conference to hammer out a road towards elections in the chaotic country.
>
> Puntland's security ministry said its forces had repelled a two-day attack by *al-Shabaab* militants in the north of Galkayo town, which its troops control, and accused the authorities of the Galmudug region, who control the south of Galkayo, of harbouring the militants.[69]
>
> — *Reuters News,* 3 September 2011

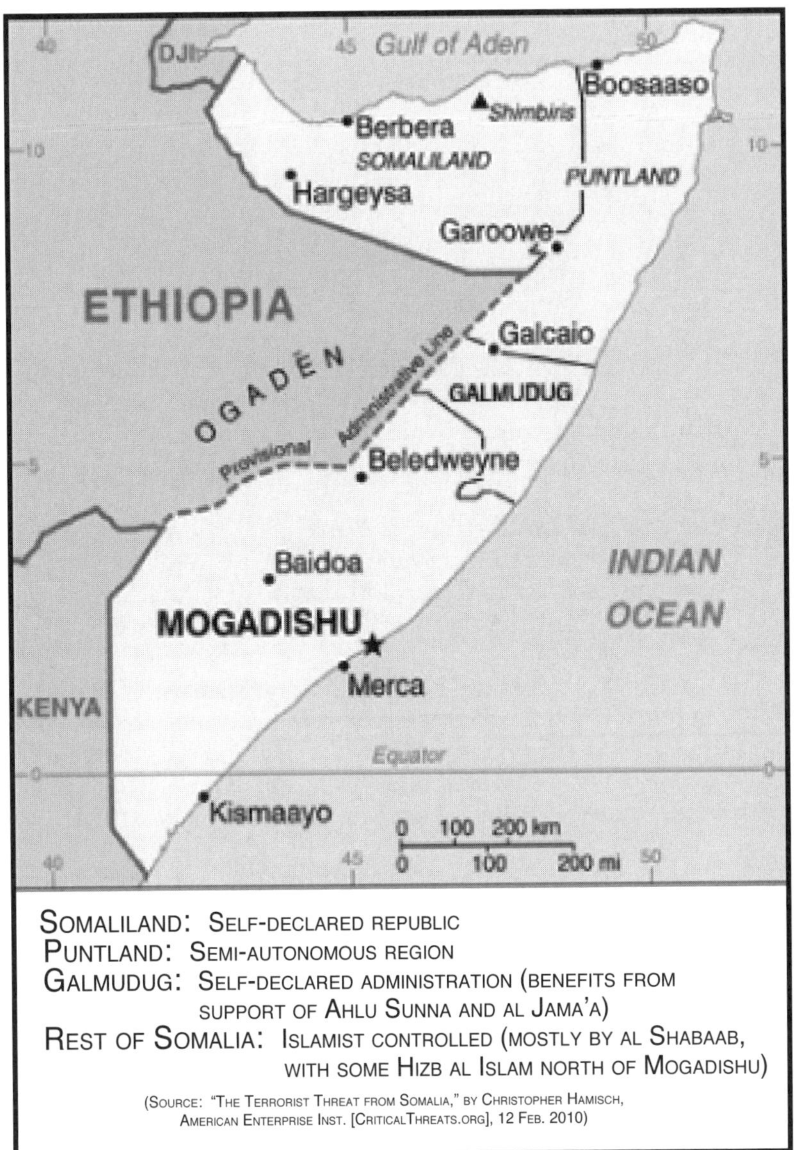

Map 1.3: Somalia Comprised of Semi-Autonomous Regions
(Source: Courtesy of General Libraries, University of Texas at Austin, from their website, for map designator "somalia_sm_2010.gif")

Extent of the Somali Training Camps

How those *al-Qaeda* trainers first came to Somalia may give a clue as to their present role and location.

> Somalia . . . is divided into three parts, each "ruled" by local warlords. . . . *Al-Qaeda* has been transporting men and material through its vast, unguarded coastline for many years. . . .
>
> As the Islamist vanguard, it was incumbent on *al-Qaeda* to manifest Muslim displeasure at the U.S. intervention in the Horn of Africa [in 1993]. Beginning in early 1992, *al-Qaeda* established a network in Somalia. Al-Qaeda's then deputy Emir for military operations, Muhammed Atef, was entrusted with the mission, and frequently visited Somalia in 1992 and 1993. In early 1993, *al-Qaeda's* chief instructor, Ali Muhammad, came to train the attack team drawn from *[al-Itihadd al-Islamiya (AIAI)]*. . . the [Somali chapter of the] Muslim Brotherhood [and forerunner of *al-Shabaab]*. On October 3-4, *al-Qaeda*-trained *[AIAI)]* . . . fighters attacked U.S. forces in Mogadishu, killing eighteen U.S. personnel. The blame focused on General Muhammad Farah Aideed, but Osama [bin Laden] was in fact behind this key operation. . . .
>
> According to Indian intelligence interrogation of Maulana Masood Azhar, the then secretary of *Harkat-ul-Ansar* [an *al-Qaeda* affiliate in Pakistan], . . . a number of Arab *mujahidin* [sic] . . . moved to Somalia. . . . [S]ome 400 went to Sudan and thereafter to Somalia, where they joined *[AIAI]* . . . in 1993. . . .
>
> *Al-Qaeda's* role in expelling U.S. troops from Somalia is acknowledged by local Islamists. . . . On June 8, 1998, the U.S. Attorney General indicted Osama for his role in training the tribesmen who killed eighteen U.S. soldiers in Somalia in 1993.[70]
>
> — *Inside al-Qaeda,* by Rohan Gunaratna

Does *al-Qaeda* Still Run Rebel Schools in Somalia?

In April 2009, the *Christian Science Monitor* reported a recent recruit from the *al-Qaeda* affiliate—*al-Shabaab*— being instructed at the far southern Somali peninsula of Ras Kamboni along with hundreds of other young men.[71] (See Maps 1.4 and 1.5.) After repeated visits by Ethiopian and Kenyan contingents from the African Union (AU) forces designated to help the legitimate Somali regime, Ras Kamboni may no longer be the principal *al-Qaeda* training complex. But, a smaller sequel undoubtedly survives nearby.

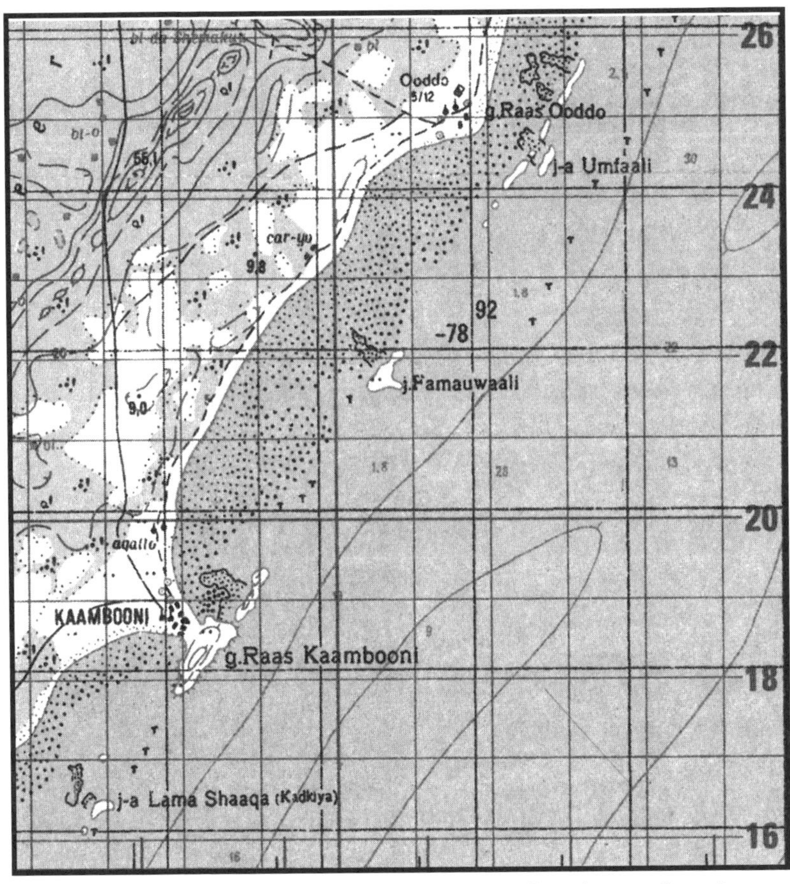

Map 1.4: Ras Kamboni on Somalia's Southeast Coast
(Source: Courtesy of General Libraries, University of Texas at Austin, from their website, for map designator "ras_kaambooni.jpg")

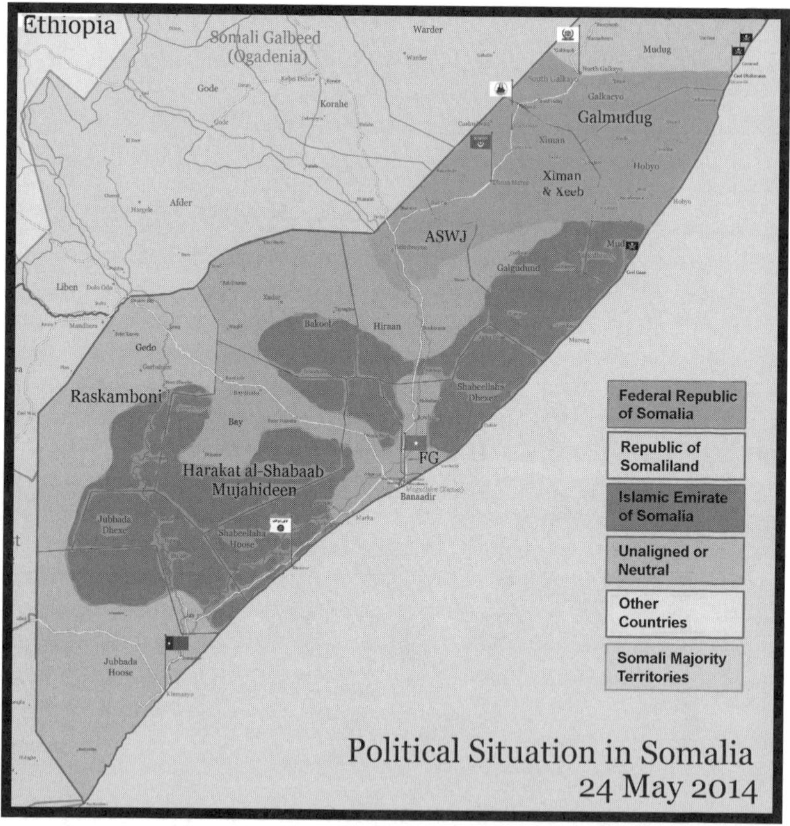

Map 1.5: Al-Qaeda-Controlled Territory as of May 2014
(Source: Wikipedia Encyclopedia, s.v. "Somalia," under provisions of GNU Free Documentation License, map designator "Somalia_map_states_region.png," by Ingoman,©; as retrieved in November 2014 from this url: http://upload.wikimedia.org/wikipedia/commons/archive/9/9f/20140707001427!Somalia_map_states_regions_districts.png)

[A]l-Shabaab was behind the Westgate shopping mall attack in Kenya. Jamal Osman attended one of its training camps in the Somali bush. . . .

Around 300 newly trained fighters, who have completed a six-month course, parade in the training camp. . . .

The men comprise young Muslims from all over the world: Arabs, Kenyans and . . . some from Britain. . . .

The group was one of two fully armed battalions I saw

> during my stay. They are determined men who want to crush the western-backed Somali government in Mogadishu. The weak government is propped up by African Union troops, including Kenyan forces who invaded southern Somalia two years ago. That is why *al-Shabaab* regard the Westgate attack as revenge.[72]
>
> — *Channel 4 News* (U.K.), 16 December 2013

This same nonprofit British news service goes on to describe some of the actual training, names of subordinate *al-Shabaab* elements, and what may even be an approximate location of a new big camp.

> Some of the new soldiers at the graduation ceremony showed off their gymnastic skills to impress Sheik Ali Dhere.
>
> Highly organized, these latest additions will soon decide which unit within *al-Shabaab* to join. They can remain regular fighters, become bomb-makers or work for the Amniyat, *al-Shabaab's* security network.
>
> But the most popular unit is the Istishhadyin unit, the suicide brigade. . . . Believe it or not, there's a long waiting list. . . . With months of training, only the best recruits will be accepted. . . .
>
> I visited Bulo Burte, a key strategic crossing point on the Shabelle river. It's an *al-Shabaab* stronghold. . . .
>
> I followed the Hizbat, the *al-Shabaab* police, on their beat.[73]
>
> — *Channel 4 News* (U.K.), 16 December 2013

Buloburte is in central Somalia near the town of Jalalaqsi on the Shabelle River. It was captured by Somali and AU forces on 13 March 2014. The size of this stronghold alone would indicate a major training facility nearby. In all likelihood, that facility is once again operational.

> Bulobarte was among the remaining few strategically important military bases for *al-Shabaab* militants in central Somalia.[74]
>
> — *Somali News,* 13 March 2014

Somalia's None-Too-Promising Future

As of May 2014, Somalia was still a major refuge for *al-Qaeda* affiliates—most notably, *al Shabaab*. Look back at Map 1.5 for the areas that were—at that time—being called the "Islamic Emirate of Somalia." Its very title infers the nucleus of a new Sunni caliphate. The Muslim Brotherhood in Sudan has continued to do everything in its power to create such an entity at the Horn of Africa. Its Yemeni counterpart may have a complementary vision. Why shouldn't that caliphate span the narrow entrance to Suez?

Oil-Rich Chad May Have Succumbed to Sudanese Pressure

Chad's capital of N'Djamena experienced a good-sized insurrection in early 2008. Since that time, it has faced no major rebel threats. This may be largely due to Chad's 2010 *"rapprochement"* with neighboring Sudan. Khartoum had previously used Chadian rebels as proxies.[75]

Sudan has been confronting two of its own separatist movements—one in the South, and the other in its western region of Darfur. To defeat the latter, Khartoum has largely relied on Arab militiamen called the *Janjaweed*.

Chad's population is predominantly Muslim, and its previously French legal system has been modified to follow Islamic as well as traditional interpretations of the law.[76] So, why would the Sudanese government want to expand its influence in that direction, if not to help some foreign mentor (like the PRC) to further monopolize North Africa's petroleum assets? (Look back at Table 1.1.)

Religious Beliefs Only Partially at Issue

- Where in Africa are differences in belief most pronounced?
- Are they at the root of all strife in these regions?

Africa's spiritual beliefs are still somewhat traditional.

(Source: Correl Gallery Clipart with image designator "31F001.tif")

Africa's Background of Worship

Africa is home to hundreds of ethnic groups. Many still practice some form of traditional veneration. The continent also has nearly equal numbers of Muslims and Christians. While each constitutes around 40-45% of its total population, the traditionalists account for 10-12%.[1] Africa has seen its fair share of colonial proselytizing over the years, and there is some evidence of the Muslim percentage of the whole now growing to as much as 47%. But, religion normally takes a back seat to other reasons for regional strife. Because the northern half of the continent is mostly Muslim and southern half mostly Christian, there are those who would attribute all mid-continent violence to how their Abrahamic ideologies differ. Most African Muslims are Sunni, so one would expect almost as much hatred toward Shiites, tribal animists, and Chinese Communist atheists. Yet, there is little evidence of any portion of the latter. So, one must look beyond religion to find the underlying cause of Africa's chronic turmoil.

Ongoing Trouble in Sudan More about Oil Than Beliefs

The recent breakaway of South Sudan from Sudan offers a microcosm of the religious difference between Africa's opposing ends. As with the continental halves, the preponderant faith of these two nations may differ, but the reasons behind their continued animosity are more complicated. (See Map 2.1.)

Sudan People's Liberation Army (SPLA) was formed in 1983 when Lt.Col. John Garang of the Sudan Police Auxiliary Forces (SPAF) was sent to quell a mutiny in the town of Bor. It involved 500 southern enlistees who were resisting orders to be rotated to the north. Instead of terminating the mutiny, Garang encouraged mutinies in other garrisons and then placed himself at the head of the rebellion against the Khartoum government. Over the years, his SPLA has gotten support from several countries.[2]

More recently, thousands of people are believed to have been killed by fighting that began in mid-December 2013 as a political dispute between South Sudan's President Salva Kiir and his former deputy president, Riek Machar. The conflict, which started as a personal rivalry between Kiir and Machar, has divided South Sudan's army and various communities along ethnic lines, pitting members of Kiir's Dinka tribe against Machar's Nuer.[3] Despite the tribal differences, one suspects the ongoing dispute with Khartoum over shared oil assets to be at the heart of the problem. Marchar is a former assistant to President Bashir of (northern) Sudan. Now that the South is a separate nation, its Abyei Oil Reserve extractions will no longer be moving north to Port Sudan, and in the process earning transit revenues for Khartoum. They will instead be traveling southeastward to Juba and then on to China's new megaport at Lemu, Kenya. (Look again at Map 2.1.)

Below is reliable evidence that Khartoum may still back a Machar who is no longer very popular with his own tribe.

Riek Machar Teny Dhurgon—Rebel leader with SPLA from 1984 until the 1991 split [of Sudan into two parts]. Led breakaway faction from SPLM/A in 1991, forming separate southern rebel movement initially known as SPLA-Nasir (from 1993 the SPLA-United, and from 1994-97 the SSLM/A). Despite espousing independence for the south, *his faction received covert support from the [Khartoum] government* as it fought for years (91-99) against the SPLA.

Map 2.1: Present-Day (Northern) Sudan

(Source: Courtesy of General Libraries, University of Texas at Austin, from their website for map designator "sudan_sm_2013.tif")

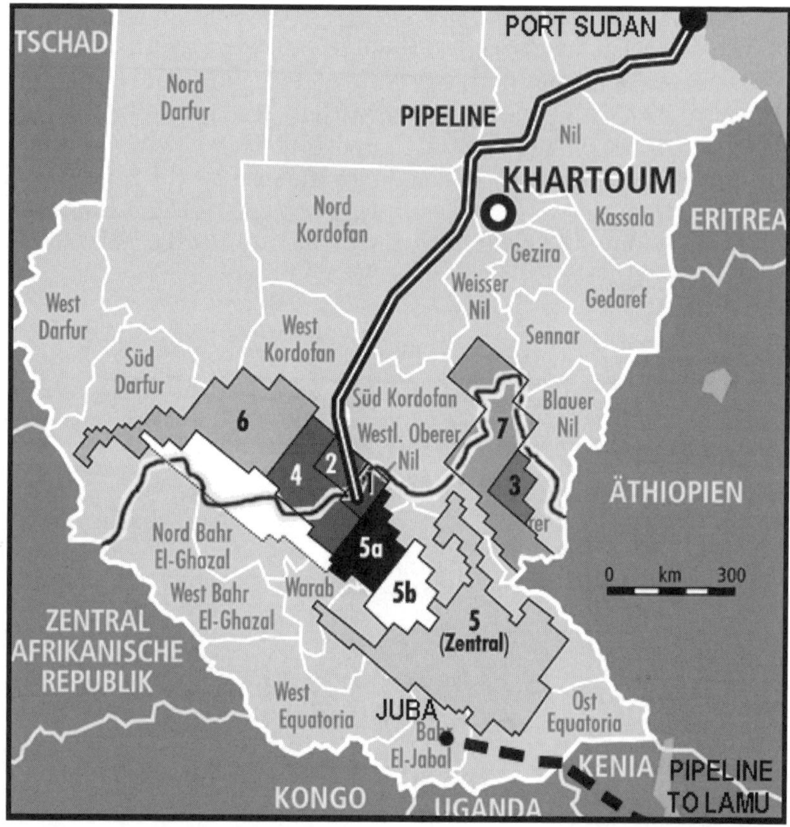

Map 2.2: Petroleum Concessions Stretch across New Border
(Source: Wikipedia Encyclopedia, s.v. "South Sudan," public-domain image from Sven-steffen arndt [2005] with designator "Sudan_Map_Oelgas.png")

> . . . His SSLA rebel forces claimed all the rural land of Western Upper Nile/Unity State except garrison towns. . . . Signed . . . [the] 1997 Khartoum Peace Agreement with the [northern Sudanese] government which . . . appointed

> him president of the Southern States Coordinating Council . . . and assistant to President of Sudan, Omar al-Bashir. Also formed . . . [from Machar's] United Democratic Salvation Front and its military arm under the . . . Agreement, [was the] South Sudan Defense Force. His failure to stem government-forced displacement of civilians from [the] Western Upper Nile/Unity State ended up turning Nuer people against his leadership and . . . led to his . . . resignation from the government and attempt to recreate his army in the south in 2000 as Sudan Peoples Democratic Forces (2000-02). In January 2002 signed agreement with Garang to merge SPDF with SPLA.[4]
>
> – *Human Rights Watch,* 2003

Northern Sudan is predominantly Muslim, whereas South Sudan contains many Christians. In fact, Kiir and Machar are both Christian. From what *Human Rights Watch* has said, one can thus conclude that the continuing turmoil in South Sudan has more to do with money and power than any religious or tribal differences.

> The new nation stands to benefit from inheriting the bulk of Sudan's oil wealth, but . . . rivalries within the governing party, . . . cloud its immediate future.[5]
>
> – *BBC Country Profile* for South Sudan

That South Sudan has three times the oil-producing potential of its longtime-PRC-supported northern sister means much of this influence may ultimately be coming from China. The legitimacy of such a claim will be pursued later. Because most of the Communist influence on Africa has occurred far to the south historically, current Chinese interest in the predominantly Muslim north is often discounted. (Look back at Table 1.1.)

First Must Come Africa's Complete Communist History

Marxist and Maoist Communism are both avowedly atheistic. That fact should put them into direct opposition with southern Africa's predominantly Christian ideology, but it never really has. This would imply consider danger in not fully following one's Trinitarian beliefs.

Part Two

Communist Initiatives

"Communism is not love. Communism is a hammer which we use to crush the enemy." — Mao Tse Tung

(Source: http://www.brainyquote.com/quotes/keywords/communism.html.)

The Formerly Socialist Bloc of Nations

- Which nations were "freed" by Communist rebels?
- How democratic are their current governments?

China mostly went after the East African colonialists.

(Source: Courtesy of Orion Books, from *World Army Uniforms since 1939*, © 1975, 1980, 1981, 1983 by Blandford Press, Part II, Plate 63; FM 5-103 [June 1985], p. 4-19)

African Nations with Communist Backgrounds

From the early-1960's to mid-1990's, most of the countries at Africa's southern end came under prolonged Communist pressure. The Soviet-backed MPLA (People's Movement for the Liberation of Angola) first started fighting the Portuguese in Angola in 1961. (See Figure 3.1.) In 1962, Chinese backed FRELIMO (Mozambique Liberation Front) was founded in Tanzania to expel the Portuguese from Mozambique. That same year, SWAPO (Southwest Africa's People's Organization) emerged to free Namibia from South African (SA) occupation; and Nelson Mandela moved the headquarters of

Figure 3.1: Portugal's Colonial Empire
(Source: DA Pamphlet 550-36 [1991], p. 127)

his now banned ANC (African National Congress of South Africa) from to Dar es Salaam. That east coast port city had now become the PRC's training and resupply center for many of the freedom movements within southern Africa. A Chinese railroad would soon be built to carry reinforcements and resupplies from there to rebel base camps in Zambia. (See Map 3.1.) Thus, the much revered Mandela was no stranger to the Chinese way of doing things.

> Mandela himself arrived [in Tanzania] in 1962 seeking financial and military support [from the PRC], and the ANC set up their office in Dar es Salaam—just across the street from the FRELIMO building. Military training camps were set up in the towns of Morogoro, Mbeya and Bagamoyo.[1]
>
> — *Sunday World* (Zambia), April 2014

Before long, not only *MK* (*Umkhonto we Sizwe,* the ANC's military wing), but also ZANLA and SWAPO fighters were being trained in Tanzania. A few *MK* personnel went as far as Beijing for instruction.[2]

After an ideological split in the mid-1960's, the Chinese and Soviets began to vie for the same areas within Africa, though their respective proxies still occasionally cooperated in a mutual fight for independence. ZANLA and FRELIMO had Chinese advisers,[3] whereas ZIPRA had Soviet.[4] Then, both foreign powers went after Rhodesia (the future Zimbabwe) at the same time. (See Map 3.2.) While Chinese-backed ZANLA invaded the eastern part of that country from Mozambique, Soviet-backed ZIPRA attacked its western side from Botswana.[5] Waiting to confront them were the world-famous Selous Scouts. (See Figure 3.2.)

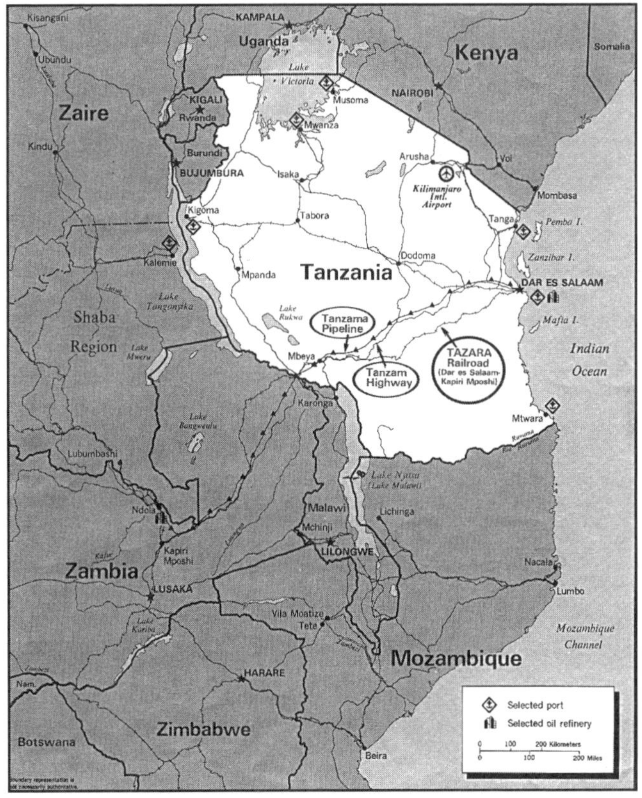

Map 3.1: China's TANZAM Railway, Highway, and Pipeline
(Source: Courtesy of General Libraries, University of Texas at Austin, from their website for map designator "dar_corridor_88.jpg")

By the early 1970's, both Communist camps were trying to gain favor with the other's proxies. Some rebels had been courting both sides at once, so original affiliations began to shift. Most notably, some of the Chinese surrogates became more Marxist as the Soviet Union took a more direct hand in the struggle.

On the eastern side of the continent, FRELIMO had been conducting Maoist guerrilla warfare but then switched—for self-defense reasons—to more conventional Soviet tactics (and advisers). When the Portuguese were finally driven from Mozambique in 1975, FRELIMO's politics (as the new country's ruling party) became decidedly Stalinist.[6] (See Map 3.3.)

In the middle of southern Africa, formerly PRC-backed *MK* was now helping to raid into Rhodesia from Soviet-affiliated ZIPRA's Zambian base camps.[7] (See Map 3.4.) Still facing the region's most

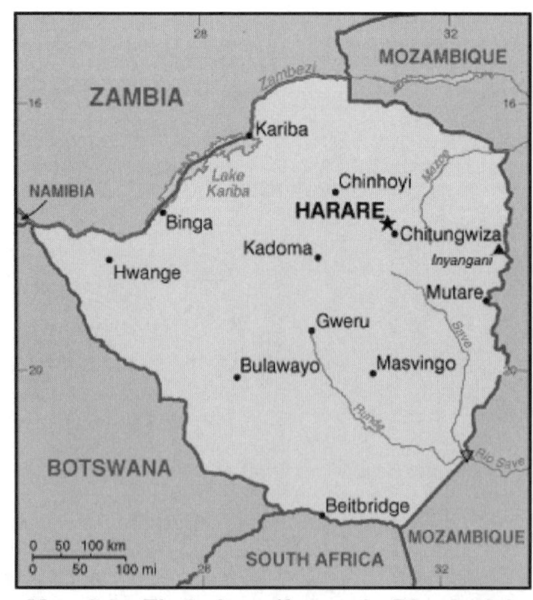

Map 3.2: Zimbabwe (formerly Rhodesia)
(Source: Courtesy of General Libraries, University of Texas at Austin, from their website for map designator "zimbabwe_sm_2014.gif")

Figure 3.2: Selous Scout
(Source: Courtesy of Orion Books, from *Uniforms of Elite Forces,* ©1982)

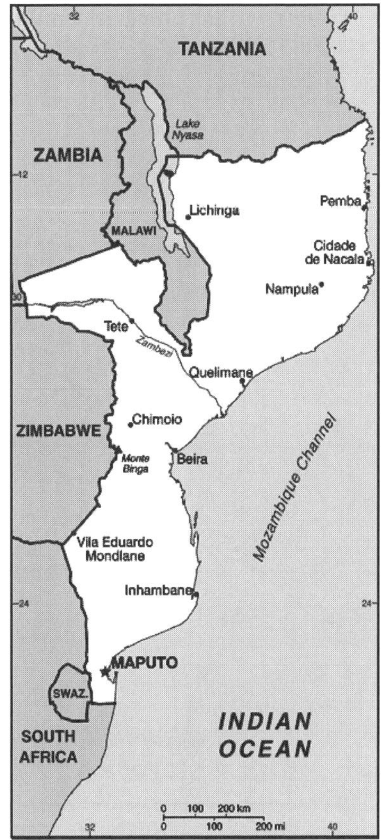

Map 3.3: Mozambique
(Source: Univ. of Texas at Austin website from "mozambique_sm_2014.gif")

powerful national army at home, the ANC may have wanted to keep both avenues of support open. By some accounts, the ANC and its military wing had been partially allied with ZIPRA since the late 1960's.

On the southwestern side of Africa, only the MPLA had been "Marxist-Leninist" with Soviet backing from its very inception in Angola.[8] (See Map 3.5.) However, not all of its rebel counterparts had shared this allegiance. Formed in March 1962, the FNLA (National Front for the Liberation of Angola) at first had Chinese instructors. So did its offshoot—UNITA (National Union for the Total Liberation

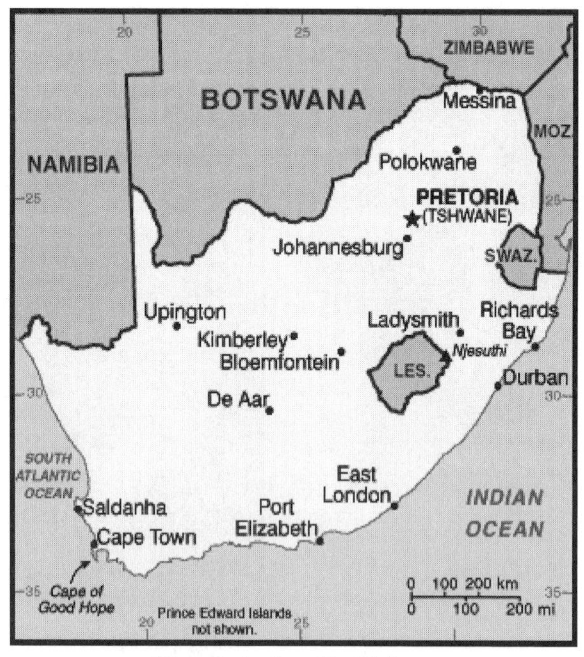

Map 3.4: South Africa

(Source: Courtesy of General Libraries, University of Texas at Austin, from their website for map designator "south_africa_sm_2014.gif")

of Angola)—in 1964. (Only much later would Zaire and the U.S. assume this role with FNLA and UNITA during Angola's ensuing civil war.[8])

Then, from bases in Zambia, SWAPO and *MK* fighters began to assist the MPLA's military wing in Angola. As Soviet successes mounted, the ANC also increased its Soviet affiliation. At some point, it totally withdrew its cadres from the Chinese training camps

Map 3.5: Angola

(Source: Courtesy of General Libraries, University of Texas at Austin, from their website for map designator "angola_sm_2014.gif")

to fully follow the Soviet model.[9] Some of those camps were in Ghana. Others may have been in Angola itself, as many *MK* fighters had been instructed there.[10] Freedom fighters will often accept help from competing sources. Then, as one mentor gains influence, they can more easily join him. While now Soviet backed, Mandela never forgot the help that China had initially provided.[11]

This Fight Was against More Than Just Apartheid

Soon to emerge across the full expanse of southern Africa was an all-out war between the Soviet Union and Western alliance over the political future of every country in the region. Widely portrayed as a struggle against Apartheid, it was also for a Marxist style of government. The size to which this conflagration would eventually grow will surprise most modern-day Americans, as will the fact that the U.N. had forced the West to back down in the face of blatant Communist aggression. Perhaps Communism never did pose much of a threat, or have an insidious domino effect. That particular "ism" has been scarcely mentioned by the U.S. news media for over 20 years. Many younger Americans have come to believe that the breakup of the Soviet Union signalled its demise. East Asians know better, and Eastern Europeans still visibly cringe at the mention of "social democrats."

Then Things Really Started to Heat Up

In November 1975, Fidel Castro began to reinforce the MPLA's military wing with between 15,000 and 20,000 Cuban regulars.[12] The only regional entity strong enough to contest a Cuban expeditionary force was South Africa. It sent in motorized "battlegroups." By December 1975, those SA battle groups—with Western-backed UNITA and some FNLA ground attachments—proliferated in the central part of Angola.[13]

Meanwhile at the northern end of Angola, America's Central Intelligence Agency (CIA) had been preparing FNLA and Mobutu's Zaireans (through wherewithal and training) to open up another front.[14] (See Figure 3.3, then Map 3.6.) The first FNLA drive was in November of 1975 on Quifangondo, a fishing village north of Luanda. Though supported by SA artillery fire, it failed miserably. Before long, most of the FNLA units and their Zairean attachments were chased back into Zaire.[15] At that point, the SA Recce (reconnaissance) teams had little choice but to form small guerrilla bands to work behind MPLA lines.[16] All the while, the South Africans had been trying to keep the extent of their role in the Angolan War secret.[17] Soon the secret was out, and political pressure from the West forced the SA battle groups to withdraw in early 1976. As they departed, the Soviet-backed MPLA and Cubans moved back in. In the aftermath of the SA withdrawal, MPLA and SWAPO declared themselves allies.[18]

To prevent any further interference from the West, the Soviets positioned a small amphibious landing force just off the west African coast in January 1976. Among the ships in that tiny flotilla was a gigantic armor carrier.[19]

In early 1985, the MPLA/Soviet/Cuban alliance reoccupied the strongholds in south central Angola that the South Africans had been forced to vacate by the Lusaka Accord of 1984. To consolidate the gain, the Soviets then sent in large quantities of military hardware. This billion-dollar aid package included MIG-23 fighters

Figure 3.3: South Africans and Zaireans Both Fought the MPLA
(Source: Courtesy Orion Books, from *Uniforms of Elite Forces*, ©1982, Plate 23 [No. 68] and Plate 32 [No. 94])

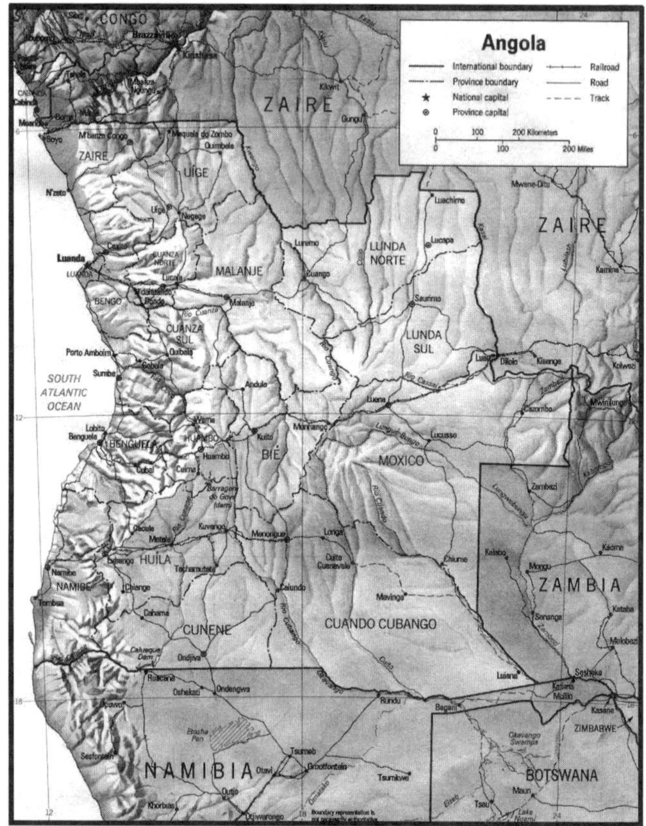

Map 3.6: Zaire Objected to the Soviet Takeover of Angola
(Source: Courtesy of General Libraries, University of Texas at Austin, from their website for map designator "angola_rel90.pdf")

and HIND helicopter gunships. It also brought the total of tanks for FAPLA's (People's Armed Forces for Liberation of Angola—the MPLA's military wing) to 550.[20]

In August of that same year, FAPLA assembled a large force of 20 brigades for a renewed push against UNITA in southeastern Angola. That force included a SWAPO semi-conventional brigade and five *MK* (ANC) battalions.[21] Before long, they were being cut to ribbons by 32 Battalion's air-bursting multi-rocket barrages and SA night-strike aircraft. Among their casualties (according to UNITA intelligence) were 19 Soviets and 116 Cubans.[22] Then, a Soviet general took over all MPLA forces. Backing him up were 3,000 Soviet and East German advisers and 45,000 Cuban ground troops.[23] FAPLA's new mission was conventionally to overwhelm all UNITA bases in southeastern Angola. General Shaganovitch commenced this new offensive in June 1986. Through a series of spoiling attacks, Battalion 32, SA Recce, and UNITA were able to slow the advance. Finally, SA air, artillery, and motorized infantry joined in the struggle. On 29 September 1987, President Botha directed his armed forces to help with a UNITA counteroffensive.[24] The fighting raged until peace talks were re-initiated in the summer of 1988. Then, public sentiment against Apartheid resulted in the West effectively caving in to Communist expansion across the entire region.

> 1993—U.N. imposes sanctions against UNITA. The U.S. acknowledges the MPLA.[25]
>
> — *BBC Country Profile* for Angola (2005)

Erstwhile Cooperation between Soviet and Chinese Reds

While Soviet-backed ZIPRA had most of its base camps in Botswana, it also had a few in Zambia. The Zambian contingent was contesting northern Rhodesia with guerrilla tactics, whereas the Botswana contingent preferred armored columns. A Chinese railroad from Dar es Salaam into Zambia may have resupplied freedom fighters of any description.[26] After all, better armed Soviet surrogates would provide a diversion for Chinese initiatives. Early in the overall freedom movement, a few pro-Soviet fighters may have even been trained in Tanzania. In the early 1960's, there were Cuban (as well as Chinese) instructors in Dar es Salaam.[27] The Chinese were, after all, the experts on rural guerrilla warfare. Any liberation movements (of whichever allegiance) would have welcomed their proximity.

Even late in the struggle, there was occasional cooperation between Communist powers. In 1979, Soviet advisers were spotted helping artillerymen to defend a ZANLA base.[28] The same year, Chinese instructors were seen at a now pro-Soviet FRELIMO collective farm.[29] At various times, both ZANLA and ZIPRA had sent commanders to China for training.[30] When the Soviet Union finally collapsed in 1990, the PRC almost certainly took over its many interests in southern Africa.

Angola's Civil War Then Spread to the DRC

Through a small expeditionary force and FNLA, Zaire's long-time dictator—Mobutu—had initially fought the Soviet-backed MPLA in Angola.[31] In 1998, Mobutu was toppled by a Laurent Kabila led rebellion. A year later, the new Kabila regime (having renamed its country the DRC) was itself challenged by a Rwanda-and-Uganda-backed insurrection. To preserve this new DRC government, several other countries intervened militarily. Not surprisingly, those countries were Zimbabwe, Angola, Namibia, Chad, and Sudan,[32] with Zimbabwe's troops engaged the longest from 1998 to 2002.[33] Because two of these intervening regimes had been Marxist, one Maoist, and another financially indebted to the PRC, one suspects more than the legitimate bolster of a freedom-loving Kinshasa government. The PRC has had thousands of its own troops in Sudan (as peacekeepers and pipeline security personnel) since 2000. It gave Angola a two-billion-dollar line of credit in 2005.[34] China's increasing degree of influence over Namibia and Chad will be discussed shortly.

Political Aftermath of the Fighting

Within Angola and Mozambique, the MPLA and FRELIMO took over their respective governments when the Portuguese left in 1975. Both adopted the Soviet style of administering a nation. At Namibia, SWAPO formed the new regime. In Rhodesia, Mugabe—the head of ZANLA's political party—won the U.N.-brokered election. Mugabe was no ordinary freedom fighter. He had attended the Nanking Military Academy in China.[35] While Angola would initially become a Soviet satellite, Zimbabwe was from the very start a PRC puppet—much to the dismay of its population.

According to the *CIA World Factbook* in 2006, the following nations had Marxist regimes: (1) Mozambique from 1975 to 1989; (2) Namibia, from 1990 onward; and (3) the Republic of the Congo, 1960-1990.[36] *BBC News* says Angola's new government was also Marxist in 1975.[37] It even had "people's tribunals" and "labor camps."[38] To this day, the upper half of Angola's flag contains a yellow star on a red background, whereas its lower half sports a "hammer and sickle."[39]

The new administrations of Tanzania and Zambia were more Maoist (agrarian) in outlook. "President Nyerere had progressively transformed Tanganyika into a one party . . . Socialist state following . . . independence from Britain in 1961."[40] As Tanzania's new president, he issued an official declaration of "Socialism" in 1967. In 1977, the "Party of the Revolution" became Tanzania's only legal political party.[41] To complete the picture, the Tanzanian "People's Army" was thoroughly equipped with Chinese MIG-19 aircraft and T-62 tanks.[42] Meanwhile, Zambia had been nationalizing private enterprise and seizing land for agricultural reform. In 1972, it too became a one-party state.[43] Soon, it was allowing Chinese trains from Dar es Salaam to cross its border carrying weaponry for MK, SWAPO, and other Communist proxies.[44]

After the U.N. intervened, Western observers were shocked to see Communist factions winning elections in at least four of the affected nations—Zimbabwe, South Africa, Namibia, and Angola. While several constitutions were eventually amended to allow multi-party politics [Mozambique (1990),[45] Angola (1991),[46] Tanzania (1992),[47] and Zambia (1992)[48]], Angola and Zimbabwe would become virtual dictatorships.

Most nations within southern Africa are now officially "republics," each having several political parties that will occasionally capture a few seats in its parliament or national assembly.[49] The only real exceptions are Angola and Zimbabwe. Within Angola, Dos Santos has run things since independence from Portugal. He now has considerable Chinese backing. At Zimbabwe, a very old Mugabe is still the elected leader of a supposedly "parliamentary democracy."[50]

The only southern African states to have initially avoided Communist-mentor entanglements after peace was declared are Botswana, Namibia, South Africa, and Malawi. While all now closely interact with the PRC, only the first three were listed by *Freedom House* in 2014 as "Free." Malawi was only "Partially Free," along with Tanzania, Zambia, and Mozambique. "Not Free" were Angola and Zimbabwe.[51] Of all the nations with "less-than-free" status, only the regimes of Angola and Malawi had not been Chinese-backed at some point in their history.

Tanzania

For Tanzania, one-party rule ended in 1995 with the first democratic elections since the 1970's. There have been two elections since then that the ruling party has won despite international observers' claims of voting irregularities.[52]

To Western tourists, Tanzania seems like a thriving and contented place. However, *Freedom House* has noticed a disturbing recent trend.

> The year 2013 saw a general increase in acts of extrajudicial violence committed by security forces, mob and vigilante violence, and political violence. . . . Press freedom deteriorated due to the shutdown of key news outlets and an increase in attacks on journalists.[53]
>
> — "Tanzania—Freedom in the World 2014"
> *Freedom House*

One wonders if a continuing friendship with the PRC may have anything to do with this recent downturn in Tanzanian freedoms. Just since 1990, there have been 10 high-level leadership and 11 military visits from the PRC to Tanzania. In return, Tanzania has dispatched 15 top leaders and eight military emissaries to China. While PRC-Tanzania business cooperation began in earnest in the 1960's with the TANZAM Railway, it has been greatly expanded in recent years. At present, there are eight Sino-Tanzanian joint business ventures inside this strategically located East African country.[54]

Mozambique

FRELIMO moved quickly to create a Stalinist, one-party society in Mozambique. It nationalized most, if not all, of the private property without compensation. It relocated whole tribes to communal villages. Additionally, it established a chain of "reeducation centers" for anyone who didn't want to cooperate.[55] As many as 75,000 people may have perished in those centers.[56]

The FRELIMO party officially abandoned Marxism in 1989. A new constitution the next year provided for multi-party elections and a free market economy. The U.N. negotiated a peace agreement between FRELIMO and RENAMO (Mozambique National Resistance) to end the fighting in 1992. In December 2004, Joaquim Chissano stepped down after 18 years in office. His elected successor, Armando Guebuza (also from FRELIMO), promised to continue the sound economic policies that have encouraged foreign investment. He was reelected to a second term in October 2009. However, the elections were flawed by voter fraud, questionable disqualification of candidates, and FRELIMO use of government resources during the campaign. As a result, *Freedom House* removed Mozambique from its list of electoral democracies.[57]

Since the demise of the Soviet Union, Mozambique has rekindled its affiliation with China. Six Chinese leaders have visited this East African country, and it has reciprocated with 14 high-level emissaries to China. Further, the PRC has forgiven what was left of a Mozambiquan debt that should have been repaid in 1999. Shanghai and Maputo (the capital of Mozambique) have now established a sister-city relationship.[58] Of particular interest are the Maoist themes in Mozambique's current emblem. It's almost identical to that of the PRC. (See Figure 3.4.)

Angola

Angola is still rebuilding after a 27-year civil war that ended in 2002. Peace seemed imminent in 1992 when Angola held national elections, but fighting picked up between the MPLA and UNITA again in 1993. Savimbi's death in 2002 ended UNITA's insurgency and cemented the MPLA's hold on power. The MPLA leader Dos Santos pushed through a new constitution in 2010. Then, 2012 elections saw him installed as president.[59]

Though technically a republic, the *CIA World Factbook* still calls Angola's government a "multi-party presidential regime." According to the 2010 constitution, ballots are cast for parties rather than candidates, and then the majority leader appointed as president. Following the 2012 legislative elections, Dos Santos became president for five years and then eligible for a second term. In actuality, he has been in charge of all Marxist elements in Angola since 1979. Angola still has the same flag it did when called the People's Republic of Angola. While the MPLA may still have Marxist-Leninist leanings, it has accepted considerable monetary assistance from the PRC since the fall of the Soviet Union.[60] Such help always involves

Figure 3.4: Present-Day Emblem of Mozambique
(Source: Courtesy of Wikipedia Encyclopedia, s.v. "Mozambique" [public domain image with designator, '640px-Emblem_of_Mozambique.png']"

political trade-offs. Anyone familiar with how Mao had used teenaged "Red Guards" to better control his population will notice the similarities.

> [The MPLA] dominated August 2012 parliamentary elections, taking more than 70 percent of the vote. While the polls suffered from serious flaws, including outdated and inaccurate voter rolls, the results were endorsed by the African Union. A spate of urban-based anti-government protests that had begun in 2011 continued in 2012, leading to state-backed intimidation of protest leaders, scores of arrests, and the violent dispersal of demonstrations. . . .
>
> . . . The August 2012 legislative elections . . . were not free and fair. . . .
>
> . . . The state owns the only daily newspaper and national

> radio station, as well as the main television stations. And private media are often denied access to official information and events. Libel and defamation are punishable by imprisonment and fines. Journalists, particularly those covering anti-government protests and reporting on corruption, endured harassment, attacks, and detentions by security forces in 2012 According to Human Rights Watch (HRW), state media incited pro-government vigilantes to violence against antigovernment protesters. . . .
>
> . . . In 2012, authorities continued to violently disperse sporadic demonstrations by . . . anti-government protesters, and to arrest and intimidate protest leaders.[61]
>
> — "Angola—Freedom in the World 2013"
> *Freedom House*

Zimbabwe

As of May 2006, the nation of Zimbabwe was reeling from a 1,042% inflation rate and going through an "economic meltdown."[62] To counter the economic crisis, the Zimbabwean army seized many of the private farms, banks, and railways.[63] The underlying problem was simply the shortcomings of a Socialist regime.

In June, 2006 the prestigious *Financial Times* reported that Mugabe's government was being kept afloat by China. That aid included everything from natural-resource harvesting to military technology.[64]

The Maoist land reform of 2005 within Zimbabwe was a disaster. An entire neighborhood had been bulldozed, leaving 700,000 people homeless. As many as one-third of its citizens may have fled the country. The rest face an uncertain future.[65] According to the 2006 World Health Report, Zimbabwean men can now expect to live only to age 37, and Zimbabwean women only to age 34 (the shortest lifespan on earth).[66] Ongoing events provide a glaring example of what help from the Chinese can ultimately entail.

South Africa

After the fighting ended, evidence of Marxist excess followed the ANC party's Nelson Mandela into office.

> Former detainees from ANC prison camps alleged that they had been held in harsh conditions in Angola, Kenya, Tanzania, Uganda, or Zambia. Human rights monitors confirmed that prisoners in these camps had sometimes been tortured and, in a few cases . . . executed. Moreover, they alleged that some of the camps continued to be in operation, even after the ANC had announced the suspension of its armed struggle against Apartheid. Mandela promised to investigate and to end these practices, but would not agree to air the allegations in public.[67]
>
> — *U.S. Library of Congress Country Study*

Before winning the 1994 election, the ANC formed an alliance with the Congress of South African Trade Unions (COSATU) and Communist Party of South Africa (SACP).[68] As late as 2002, South Africa's ruling party was still defining itself as "a disciplined force of the left."[69]

Though South Africa now sports a multi-party system, the ANC has been continually in charge of things since the actual combat stopped. In May 2014, President Jacob Zuma from the ANC party was reelected by the National Assembly for a second five-year term in office. Only overly optimistic Westerners failed to notice the subsequent downward trend.

> Under Jacob Zuma, its new leader, it [the ANC] has quietly adopted a radical platform of social policies. . . .
>
> The ANC . . . has introduced the largest welfare state ever seen in a developing country. . . .
>
> Under the influence of its . . . new secretary-general, Gwede Mantashe, . . . a former . . . chairman of the South African Communist party, it is adopting policies . . . based on left-wing states such as Cuba and Venezuela.[70]
>
> — *The Sunday Times* (U.K.), 25 January 2009

To outsiders, South Africa may still seem relatively stable, but it has been far more supportive of Mugabe's oppressive Chinese-backed regime in Zimbabwe than one might expect.

> A growing number of Zimbabwean asylum seekers in South Africa are reporting being refused refugee protection,

> amid fears that the decision to endorse the Zim elections has resulted in a change of immigration policy across the border.
>
> South Africa's President Jacob Zuma was one of the first regional leaders to openly congratulate Robert Mugabe's highly contested electoral 'victory' last month. . . .
>
> In the weeks since the elections, an influx of Zimbabweans have been crossing the border into South Africa, with many said to be fleeing retribution for voting against Mugabe's ZANU PF [Zimbabwe African National Union Patriotic Front, ZANLA's parent political party]. . . .
>
> . . . [T]here are "very serious anxieties" among Zimbabweans in South Africa, mainly because of concern that mass deportations will be the next step.[71]
>
> — *SW Radio Africa* (Zimbabwe), September 2013

Of course, the PRC has maintained close ties with South Africa as well. In fact, the number of visits back and forth from 2000 to 2003 (after Nelson Mandela stepped down as president) are staggering. All manner of things were discussed, including how better to administer cities and provinces. As of 2003, there were 15 pairs of Chinese and South African provinces or cities in "sister" relationships. Among the many agreements signed was one "Strengthening the Cooperation between the Police of the People's Republic of China and the Republic of South Africa." At least twice in 2000, delegations from the Communist Party of China (CPC) came to South Africa at the bequest of the ANC (ruling party of South Africa). During both visits, the head of the delegation met not only with the vice chairman of congress and vice president of South Africa, but also with the general secretary of South Africa's Communist Party. In April 2001, the chairman of the National Committee of the Chinese People's Political Consultative Conference (CPPCC) paid a visit to South Africa. Under discussion was more cooperation between the CPPCC and National Assembly of South Africa. The CPPCC chairman declared that the Chinese people "wish to exchange experience . . . in seeking the national [South Africa's] *rejuvenation*."[72] At some point, such a "rejuvenation" will make the amount of personal freedom about the same in both countries. In 2014, *Freedom House* was still showing the PRC as "Not Free."[73]

As of 27 September 2013, South Africa was still being ruled by a Tripartite Alliance between ANC, COSATU, and its Communist Party. While governmental scandals revolved around extracting minerals, citizens were still drinking polluted water, living in homes with sewerage running through them, and being "shot at when they protest."[74] Such things might be construed as a loss of human rights.

Zambia

In 1964, President Kaunda had initially imposed single-party Socialism on Zambia, where his United National Independence Party (UNIP) was the only legal political party within a "one-party participatory democracy." Then, a constitutional change in 1991 allowed for a multi-party system and change of leadership.[75] The Movement for Multi-party Democracy (MMD) that won that election was later accused of being heavily Chinese funded. However, it had promised to liberate the economy and introduce a free-market system.[76]

> The [upcoming] election will be Zambia's fifth since the advent of multi-party democracy in 1991 when Kenneth Kaunda's United National Independence Party was ousted by the MMD. . . .
>
> . . . [I]n the run-up to the polls, questions are being asked . . . if Chinese money is bankrolling the incumbent presidential candidate Rupiah Banda and his party the . . . (MMD).
>
> Beyond the claims that the Banda-branded lollipops being given out to potential voters by the MMD were made in China, the sheer scale of the ruling party's campaign has raised many eyebrows about funding sources.[77]
>
> – *BBC News,* 18 September 2011

Along with all the political maneuvering came a great deal of Chinese investment—enough to make a *de facto* takeover of Zambia likely. This nation is, after all, right next to Angola and Zimbabwe. A three-state Chinese satellite cluster would greatly facilitate Copper Belt exploitation. Unfortunately, all the best transportation corridors seem to run through Zambia.

Although China's relationship with Zambia dates back to the building of the Zambia to Tanzania Railway in the 1970's, it is in the last 10 years that Sino-Zambian trade has really taken off, growing from just $100m (£63m) in 2000 to $2.8bn last year. . . .

China's main area of interest is mining, having bought up on the cheap a number of copper, cobalt and nickel mines, which had been mothballed by Western investors when commodity prices fell.

Beyond mining and manufacturing, there is also growing Chinese presence within Zambia's retail sector, from imported textiles and electronics, to chickens farmed locally and sold in city markets. . . .

. . . [T]here have been repeated allegations—and in some cases hard evidence—of poor labour conditions and low salaries in Chinese-run mines and factories.[78]

— *BBC News,* 18 September 2011

China. . . has invested heavily in Zambia. . . . Census [to] date suggests about 100,000 Chinese live in the country, and about 500 firms are active in sectors across the economy.[79]

— *BBC Country Profile,* 1 August 2014

Southern Africa As a Whole

Clearly, the Communist Chinese have been doing everything within their power to gain control over at least one of the countries that play host to Africa's rich Copper Belt. The other (the DRC) will be discussed shortly. South Africa also has a strategically important mineral—namely, uranium. Might the PRC also be interested in it? Before that issue can be fully explored, one must get to the bottom of the extent to which Mao's "Red Guard" movement may have spread to Africa.

4 China's "Cultural Revolution" in Africa

- Did Mao's internal reform movement spread to Africa?
- What were its more brutal aspects?

Mao's "Red Guards" had terrorized China's population.

(Source: Courtesy of Wikipedia Encyclopedia, s.v. "Red Guards," public domain image from Chinese schoolbook with designtator "800px-Red_Guards.jpg")

China's Cultural Revolution Did Extend beyond Its Borders

Many of southern Africa's regimes are only remembered as being formerly Marxist, but several were initially Maoist. Maoism is an anti-revisionist form of Marxism/Leninism that differs through a more rural and agrarian focus.

> Mao substituted the dormant power of the [rural] peasantry . . . for [that of] the urban *proletariat* that [traditional Marxists hoped would overthrow the bourgeoisie and] China largely lacked. The Maoist faith in . . . the peasants' . . .

> value [over] intellectual elites fueled . . . [China's] Cultural Revolution of the 1960's and 70's. . . . Maoism was embraced by insurgent guerrilla groups worldwide; under the Khmer Rouge it became Cambodia's national ideology.[1]
>
> — *Merriam Webster Dictionary*

Most modern-day Americans are only vaguely aware of the degree of suffering within China during its "Cultural Revolution" from 1966 to 1975. (See Figure 4.1.) Up to nine million of its own citizens died as a direct result.[2] Some 200,000 intellectuals alone were forced to move from China's cities to remote areas of its countryside. Forced to live in caves and lacking the survival skills of a rural peasant, many subsequently perished.[3]

The Cultural Revolution was an anti-revisionist campaign to preserve "true" Communist ideology. To pursue it, Mao was willing to resort to violent class struggle to purge any capitalist or traditional inclinations from Chinese society. Culturally disposed to bottom-up reform, Mao enlisted the help of the nation's vast student body. At mass rallies in Beijing, his delegated representative—PLA Mar-

Figure 4.1: Chairman Mao Was behind the Cultural Revolution

(Source: Courtesy of Wikipedia Encyclopedia, s.v. "Cultural Revolution [fair use image published by the PRC govt., 'Cultural Revolution poster.jpg']"

Figure 4.2: Angry Students Began Roaming the Streets
(Source: Courtesy of Wikipedia Encyclopedia, s.v. "Cultural Revolution," fair use image originally from PRC govt. with designator "Struggle_session_poster_1.jpg")

shal Lin Biao—took center stage to denounce everyone impeding the "progress of the revolution." Then, similar rallies took place all over the country. Soon, loosely controlled groups of teenaged "Red Guards" were actively searching out counter-revolutionaries. Told initially to get rid of everything old (customs, culture, habits, and ideas), the emboldened youth wearing red arm bands were eventually to zero in on the ordinary citizenry. Because many of their groups were subsequently joined by small CPC "work teams," their degree of destructiveness initially varied. (See Figure 4.2.) However, this authority vested in the Red Guards by Mao himself was soon to create major problems.

At some point the Guards started carrying weapons. On 22 August 1966, a central directive was issued to stop police intervention in Red Guard activities.[4] Mao's praise for the rebellion was effectively an endorsement of all Red Guard actions, which then grew increasingly violent.[5] Public security in China deteriorated rapidly as central officials lifted the restraints on violent behavior.[6] The national police chief, said it was "no big deal" if Red Guards were beating "bad people" to death.[7] The police relayed his remarks to the Guards, and they responded accordingly.[8] In the course of about two weeks, the violence had left some 100 teachers, school officials, and educated cadres dead in Beijing's western district alone. The number injured was "too large to be calculated."[9] Having Mao's *Little Red Book* of quotations and the CPC work teams as its only structure, the "Red Guard" movement soon spun out of control. Eventually, much of Chinese society would be affected including CPC headquarters. It would be at least two years before the PLA would be asked to intervene.

During the peak of the ensuing "witch hunt," the Guards conducted "struggle sessions," in which abuse and public humiliation were heaped upon anyone accused of capitalistic thoughts. Such sessions often included physical violence, and many of the accused either died or ended up for years in reeducation camps. In effect, all of the educated and professional residents of the PRC had been targeted for reeducation. Those not killed outright were dispersed across the Chinese countryside to toil on farms or work in labor camps.[10]

Over this most active part of the Cultural Revolution, millions of Chinese citizens were to suffer a wide range of abuses. Besides murder, such abuses included the following: public humiliation, arbitrary imprisonment, torture, sustained harassment, seizure of property, and forcible displacement. The world would not soon forget this gruesome way in which Mao had achieved an internal catharsis, for it can also be used to subjugate other nations.

Which of China's Neighbors Were First Affected

Only now coming to light are how many "Red-Guard-like" excesses were experienced by other countries being "helped" by China during its own Cultural Revolution.

First, came their influence over what used to be the independent kingdom of Tibet. In the 1960's and 1970's, thousands of Tibetans are believed to have been killed through repression and martial law.[11]

> "September 9th [1965]: The Tibet Autonomous Region [of China] is formally established. The Cultural Revolution

Map 4.1: Cambodia
(Source: Courtesy of General Libraries, University of Texas at Austin, from their website for map designator "cambodia_sm_2014.gif")

begins, destroying 90% of the remaining monasteries and outlawing most Tibetan cultural customs and religion.[12]

– *PBS's Frontline,* October 2014

Then, near the end of the Cultural Revolution within China came a metastasis of that same obscene methodology throughout a regional surrogate. (See Map 4.1.) Cambodia's genocide from

1975 to 1979 occurred while the Khmer Rouge regime was being fully supported from the PRC. It was no coincidence when millions of Cambodians were placed in detention centers and forced-labor camps under non-sustainable living conditions. As many as three million (almost half the population) either were either killed outright or died in those centers and camps.[13] A direct account of this abomination has recently surfaced.

> [T]he Tuol Sleng Genocide Museum in Phnom Penh, the capital of Cambodia, . . . is located in a former . . . school that the Communist government of the Khmer Rouge turned into . . . a center for detention. . . . 20,000 people were killed at Tuol Sleng. All told, an estimated 2 million Cambodians were murdered in the Khmer Rouge reign of terror.
>
> . . . [Siphal] was 15 years old when his school was seized by the Khmer Rouge. . . . He was . . . sentenced to hard labor at an agricultural camp. . . .
>
> In the camp, Siphal says, there were 1,000 workers, but only 75 survived. Thanks to his ability to fish . . . Siphal lived. "They only gave us a little portion of rice a day," he says.[14]
>
> — Memories of the Maryknoll priests' driver in present-day Cambodia

China's Cultural Revolution Then Spreads to Africa

Soon, what have since come to be known as the "Red-Guard" insurgencies occurred in southern Africa. Because the Dark Continent was on the opposite side of the earth from Mainland China, few Western journalists initially noticed the similarities in method between Mao's internal cleanup campaign and Africa's various "freedom struggles." The student movement against low-level officialdom had spread to workers and peasants within China, so it was highly compatible with the community aspects of Maoist guerrilla warfare. Unfortunately, that and other components of China's Cultural Revolution were to result in a number of mass atrocities in Africa as well.

At Mozambique, whole tribes were transplaced by the Chinese-backed FRELIMO to work at communal villages and collective farms. Then, as many as 75,000 people may have perished in those reeducation centers.[15] There were "Red Guards" present in large numbers in Mozambique—707 at one camp alone.[16] While probably just Chinese-trained indigenous fighters, they may still have been practicing the Cultural Revolution ways of "building popular support."

Within Zimbabwe, there were "land reforms" in which hundreds of thousands of city dwellers were forcibly removed by the PRC-backed ZANU-PF regime. Very possibly, it also had reeducation centers. Near the town of Bulawayo in the southwestern portion of the country is evidence of an early 1980's massacre of over 20,000 people.[17] As late as 2000, the ruling party of Zimbabwe was using Red Guard tactics to control its population.

> Zimbabwe's self-styled war veterans and mobs of ruling ZANU-PF party youths are using classic tactics of mass intimidation to cow their political opponents.
>
> They come at night on hijacked tractors and trailers, driving into farm workers' compounds, beating them, lecturing them on the evils of the opposition Movement for Democratic Change (MDC) and the perfection of ZANU-PF.
>
> Then, in the style of the Red Guards of the Chinese Cultural Revolution, they force the beaten workers to go with them to the next farm to repeat the process, according to farm staff.[18]
>
> — *IOL News* (South Africa), 25 April 2000

Throughout Tanzania, there was a move toward collective farming that looked very much like a Cultural Revolution tool. There were Red Guards from the PRC present throughout the building of the TANZAM Railway.[19] As early as 1967, President Nyerere had issued a "Socialism and Rural Development" declaration that proposed the creation of *"Ujamaa"* villages. It said members of the rural population were too spread out in their individual attempts to make an agrarian living, and that they would do better by moving together to farm communally.

> In 1973, the infamous Operation *Vijiji* (Villagization) was [actually] carried through. The operation, termed one of the greatest social experiments in post-colonial Africa, entailed forced relocation of hundreds of thousands, perhaps millions, of people. The government wanted people to live

> in *Ujamaa* (Socialist) villages to facilitate services and communal farming ("Land Law Reforms in Tanzania," Fimbo, Dar es Salaam Univ. Press, 2004).[20]
>
> — Christian Mechelsen Institute (Norway)

Since the demise of the Soviet Union, Angola has come more and more under China's wing as well. From the start, its Marxist government had "people's tribunals" and "labor camps."[21] To what extent the increasing Chinese influence has led to more a Mao-like catharsis, no one really knows. Still, there are distinct hints of it.

> In Luanda, Angola's capital, the government has forcibly and violently evicted thousands of people living in informal housing areas with little or no notice. . . .
>
> This report focuses on 18 mass evictions carried out by the government between 2002 and 2006. . . . In total, more than 3,000 houses were destroyed and many small-scale cultivated land plots were seized, affecting some 20,000 people.
>
> By documenting forced evictions that occurred between 2002 and 2006, this report provides evidence that such evictions were neither sporadic nor isolated events in Luanda. The forced evictions represent a pattern of abusive conduct on the part of the Angolan government that has not significantly changed over the past several years or been fully addressed.[22]
>
> — *Human Rights Watch,* October 2014

Zambia with Its Strategically Vital Copper Belt

Zambia may have been influenced twice by China's Cultural Revolution—directly at first (like everyone else) and just recently out of unfortunate habit. Kenneth Kaunda, as the first elected president of independent Zambia in 1964, had maintained a warm working relationship with the PRC. That's what made the TANZAM railway possible. His regime had also seized land for agricultural reform.[23] Though large numbers of people may not have been killed at detention centers, many were thrown off their land and deprived of any way of making a living.

> Late 1960's-1970's—Key enterprises nationalized. Private land nationalized in an unsuccessful agricultural improvement program.[24]
>
> — *BBC Country Profile* (Zambia Timeline)

Now, 40 years later, something similar to Red-Guard-like activity is coming from the political party that had originally displaced Zambia's Chinese-backed government.

In 2011, Patriotic Front (PF) candidate Michael Sata became Zambia's new president in a very close election against former (pro-Chinese) president and MMD candidate Rupiah Banda.[25] Then, through "cadres,"[26] the PF began to act very much like the CPC that had used teenagers to "purge" its own citizenry in Mainland China.

> On September 6 [2013] in Mkaika, Banda [the former president's son] was attacked by PF "cadres" (young men armed with machetes, sticks, and axes). Police were present but did not prevent the attack. . . .
>
> On June 12, PF supporters poured beer over prominent government critic Father Frank Bwalya. . . . There were other instances of PF supporters accosting government critics. . . .
>
> On September 18, PF supporters blocked and beat opposition UPND leader Hakainde Hichilema. . . .
>
> On May 31, a group of suspected PF supporters entered a Lusaka church and assaulted religious leaders, journalists, and civil society members attending a peaceful prayer protest against the government's removal of subsidies on maize meal and fuel.[27]
>
> — *Lusaka Times* (Zambia), 7 April 2014

While Sata may have unseated the MMD candidate and been openly opposed to the lousy working conditions in Chinese mines, he still had an MMD background and was used to MMD methods and semantics.

> For us in the PF, winning the elections was just the first milestone of the revolution to transform Zambia.[28]
>
> — Official Patriotic Front website

Sata had started out in politics as "municipal councilor" and governor of Lusaka under first President Kaunda. Then, he resigned from Kaunda's UNIP in 1991 to join the newly formed (and Chinese-backed) MMD. There, he subsequently served as MMD minister of local government, labor, and health, and later as "minister without portfolio," the third-highest post in MMD government. In 2001, Sata formed the PF, only to lose that year's election and those for 2006 and 2008 to the MMD. Though no Communist himself, Sata was still used to the Chinese way of doing things.[29]

As of early October 2014, President Sata was finishing out the five-year term he had won in 2011. Within Zambia were still detention centers at which opposition party personnel were sometimes held without sufficient cause.[30]

Thus, one might say that certain "shortcuts" from China's Cultural Revolution had become part of Zambia's political culture, even though the ruling party no longer liked Communists. That's the unfortunate nature of Cultural Revolution shortcuts. They quickly become the gift that keeps on giving.

Africa's Most Recent Example of "Red-Guard" Activity

Sudan sports a "revolutionary regime" like those in Iran and China. But unlike Iran, Sudan has been getting Chinese advice for many years on how best to run its governmental agencies.[31] In 2009, the Chinese Foreign Ministry admitted to long-term "bilateral economic, political and military relations" with the country of Sudan.[32]

Instead of a Revolutionary Guard Corps, Khartoum would have a Popular Defense Force (PDF) to insure that the Islamic revolution had reached every part of its defense establishment. A semi-military wing of Sudan's ruling party, this PDF would be "formed from Sudanese citizens."[33] More than just a supplement to regular army units, it then helped to organize and train tribal militias in rebellious regions (like the *Janjaweed* in Darfur). It has been particularly active along Sudan's disputed southern border.[34] There, mostly in South Kordofan province, the PDF appears to have permitted more Red-Guard-like brutality than the IRGC ever did within Iran or any of its foreign targets. In South Kordofan alone, according to *Time Magazine,* the PDF has contributed to the "genocide" of up to two million people.[35]

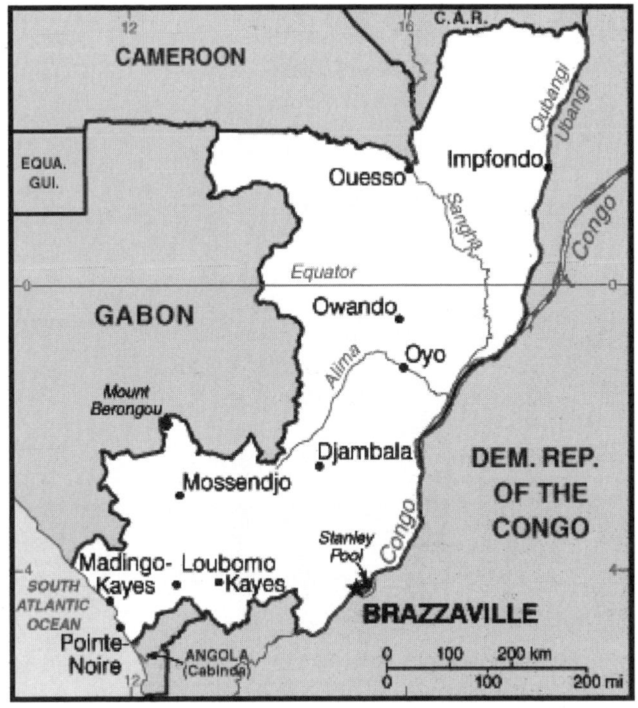

Map 4.2: Congo Republic (Brazzaville)
(Source: Courtesy of General Libraries, University of Texas at Austin, from their website for map designator "congo_republic_sm_2013.gif")

Chinese Influence over Other Parts of the Dark Continent

The Soviet Union had provided military aid to several northeast-African nations before its breakup in 1990. Which country then took over its interests is not hard to imagine.

The Congo Republic and DRC are both rich in petroleum. The Congo Republic is just north of Angola. (See Map 4.2.) After all that fighting next door, Brazzaville ended up with a Marxist regime. One might expect initial Soviet influence, but that's not what the research shows.

A Lengthy Liaison with the Congo Republic

According to the CIA, a quarter century of experimentation with

Figure 4.3: Congolese Paratrooper
(Source: Courtesy Orion Books, from *Uniforms of Elite Forces*, ©1982, Plate 32 [No. 95])

Marxism was abandoned in the Congo Republic in 1990, and then a democratically elected government took over in 1992. A brief civil war in 1997 restored former Marxist President Denis Sassou-Nguesso to power, and ushered in a period of ethnic and political unrest. Southern-based rebel groups agreed to a final peace accord in March 2003, but the resulting calm seemed tenuous at best.[36] Was there more to the story?

The Republic of the Congo (Brazzaville) is one of sub-Saharan Africa's major oil producers (with 1.6 billion barrels in crude oil reserves alone), so one suspects considerable Chinese interest after the demise of the Soviet Union. But a little research shows such interest to predate not only the civil war, but also the 1990 elections.

Since diplomatic relations between the PRC and Congo Republic were first established in 1964, its leaders have exchanged formal visits no fewer than 22 times. They have also signed four separate agreements on "cultural cooperation," with the last one occurring in 2004.[37] One must therefore wonder if there may have been any Chinese military support for this regime during the Congolese civil war.

In 1997, Angolan troops aided pro-Sassou-Nguesso forces to capture Brazzaville, forcing the duly-elected President Pascal Lissouba to abdicate his office. When this occurred, the Soviet Union had been discontinued for seven years. (See Figure 4.3.) In other words, Angola had already adopted China as its new Communist mentor, and its army was—for all practical purposes—a Chinese proxy.

During March 2002, Denis Sassou-Nguesso had little trouble winning the presidential elections after his principal rivals were "barred from the contest."[38] In 2009, Sassou-Nguesso won a second seven-year term in office. As of 2014, *Freedom House* still lists his "republic" as "Not Free." It gives, as its reason, the continuing repression of opposition parties and independent media outlets.[39]

Somalia's Dual Background

In 1970, Mohamed Siad Barre proclaimed a Socialist state in Somalia, paving the way for close relations with the U.S.S.R. (Union of Soviet Socialist Republics). In 1977, with the help of Soviet arms, Somalia attempted to seize the Ogaden region of Ethiopia. It was defeated thanks to Soviet and Cuban backing for Ethiopia, which had also turned Marxist.[40] But, the U.S.S.R. was not the only Communist power interested in Somalia. Situated near the end of the ancient trade route from Asia, Somalia's instability made it the perfect entry point to the Dark Continent for the heroin headed westward to its biggest market. (See Map 4.3.)

> China and Somalia established diplomatic relations on December 14, 1960. From 1960 to 1990, bilateral ties between the two countries had witnessed a smooth and steady advancement. . . .
>
> During the period from 1960 to 1990, many [some 14] Somalia leading officials visited China. . . .
>
> In 1991 when the Siad government was overthrown, Somalia was bogged down into a separatist situation. . . . [But] the two countries have still maintained diplomatic

relations. Ever since the outbreak of the Somalia civil war, the Chinese Government has been closely concerned about the situation. . . . Since January 2003, China has begun to act as the U.N. Security Council coordinator on the Somalia issue.[41]

— Chinese Foreign Ministry, 10 October 2006

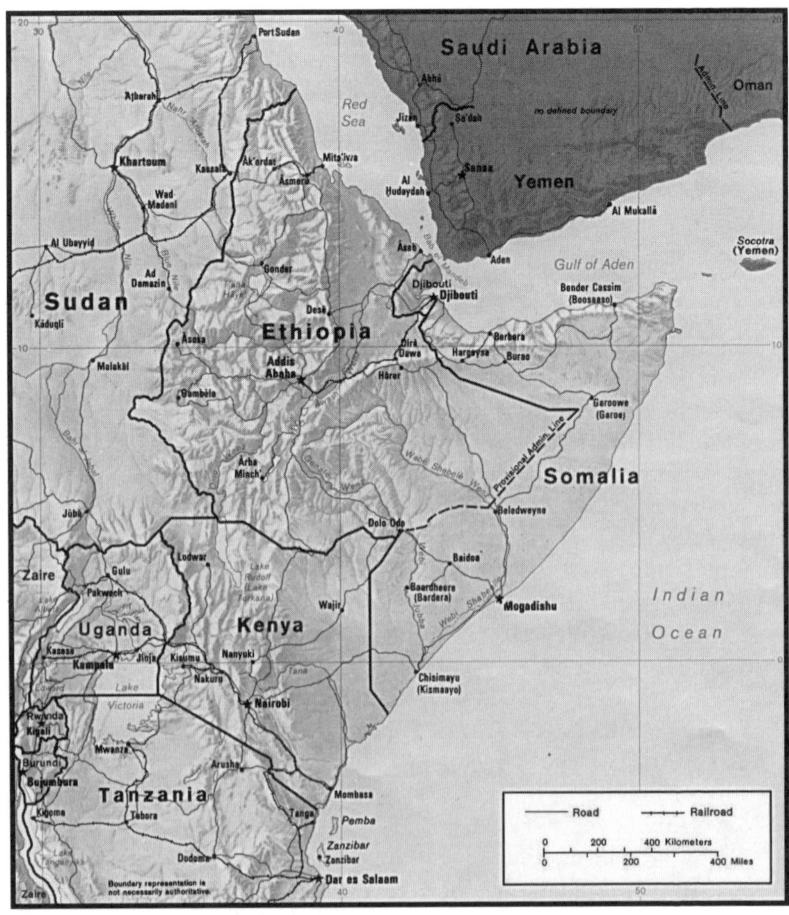

Map 4.3: Somalia at the Horn of Africa

(Source: Courtesy of General Libraries, University of Texas at Austin, from their website for map designator "horn_of_africa.jpg")

Nor Are Ethiopia and Eritrea Any Strangers to the PRC

Haile Selassie's reign over Ethiopia ended in September 1974, when a Soviet-backed Marxist–Leninist military junta, called the "Derg," deposed him. Since the demise of the Soviet Union, PRC influence has increased. By 2008, 70% of all infrastructure construction projects in Ethiopia were being carried out by Chinese construction companies.[42]

Prior to 1991, Eritrea had been a part of Ethiopia. While the Eritrean People's Liberation Front (EPLF) was getting material support from the Soviet Union, its predecessor had a different mentor. (The EPLF had emerged from Eritrean Liberation Front [ELF] splinter groups in the early 1970's.[43])

> China assisted the Eritrean Liberation Front (ELF) with weapons and military training until 1972, when Ethiopian recognition of Beijing as the legitimate Chinese government led to China's abandonment of the Eritrean struggle.[44]
>
> — *Foreign Intervention in Africa,* by E. Schmidt

From 1998 to 2000, Eritrea and Ethiopia then fought a war in which both sides were militarily equipped by the PRC.[45] One might therefore conclude that China is extremely interested in the Horn of Africa. Only at issue is why? For natural-resource delivery, it does not heavily depend on the Suez Canal.

More PRC Influence in Unexpected Places

China has for 50 years attempted to exploit the "Copper Belt" that runs through the DRC and Zambia. But, it has lately been quite active in the nations just to the east of there—Rwanda and Burundi.

Rwanda

Rwanda was one of the two tiny countries to challenge the pro-Communist Kabila regime in the DRC. Now, there is a Chinese building boom underway in this central African state that smells very much like a "non-military" takeover of its natural resources,

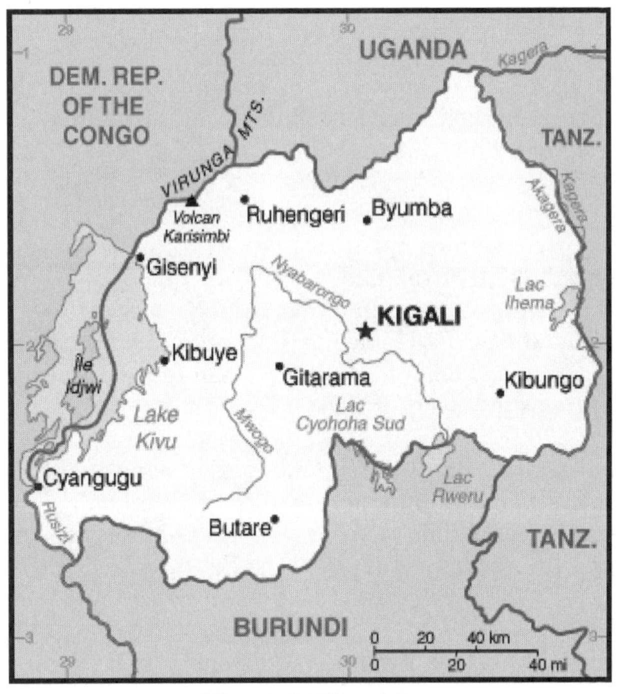

Map 4.4: Rwanda
(Source: Courtesy of General Libraries, University of Texas at Austin, from their website for map designator "rwanda_sm_2014.gif")

industrial base, and eventually its politics. (See Map 4.4.) Such a thing would be far less tragic if a former Rwandan regime hadn't shown so little regard for human rights in 1994.

> Chinese investment in Africa has increased at an unprecedented level during the past two decades. Known as the "weapon of mass construction," China's footprint in Rwanda is no exception.[46]
>
> — *AllAfrica News,* 14 February 2014

China Star Construction Co. Ltd, a subsidiary of FoShan China Star Steel Structure Co. Ltd, has already built nine factories in Rwanda and is planning to build five more.[47] Only in theory will

Figure 4.4: U.N. Unable to Stop the Rwandan Genocide
(Source: "School Days," by SGT.[Ret.] J.T.Manuszak ©, U.S. Army Ctr. of Mil. Hist., from url: http://www.history.army.mil/art/Somalia/Manuszak_Somalia_files/image007.jpg)

Rwanda's citizens benefit. Local construction companies feel they can no longer compete. According to a local engineer, most of big building and roads construction projects are being executed by Chinese contractors. He explained that Chinese companies win big tenders through a combination of lower construction costs and vast technical and financial backup. They can offer lower prices because they get most of their materials and equipment from China.[48] They also use Chinese immigrants for workers.

It's difficult to compete with Chinese companies that have constant access to low cost capital. The origin of their financial capacities is their home banks which provide them with loans at a very low rate of interest. Wei Heng, the operations manager at

China star construction Co. Ltd, claims that his company has been receiving 8% loans from Chinese banks. Another engineer claims the Chinese companies will use every possible means to win a tender, even bribery.[49]

This recent upsurge in PRC interest in Rwanda could be due to some of the DRC's mineral deposits extending below ground into that tiny country. The Global Mining Institute does say that gold, cassiterite (tin ore), and wolframite (tungsten ore) are available there.[50] That makes Rwanda one of the few sources of tungsten outside of China, and the mining presence of Xiamen Tungsten Co., Ltd. fully understandable.[51] Without tungsten, Western military projectiles would have far less penetrating power.

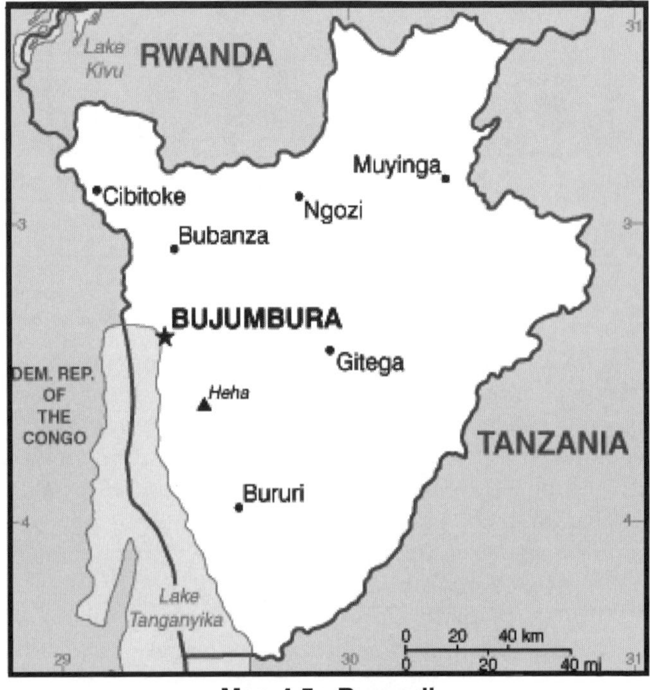

Map 4.5: Burundi

(Source: Courtesy of General Libraries, University of Texas at Austin, from their website for map designator "burundi_sm_2014.gif")

With all that foreign assistance, Rwanda should now be a thriving and happy place. Right? Wrong. It is government crackdowns against not only opposition parties, but any critical voice that has earned Rwanda a "Not Free" rating from *Freedom House* in 2014.[52]

Thus, one is inexorably drawn to a nightmarish part of Rwandan history. That Hutu rampage of 1994 did resemble a Red Guard cleansing that had spun out of control. Group evil knows no bounds for depravity. According to the movie "Hotel Rwanda," the machetes with which almost a million Tutsis were hacked to death had just come from China.[53] Still, it was France that was openly backing the Hutu regime, and a U.N. mission to Rwanda that had taken no action. So, no direct Chinese involvement with the massacre was ever alleged. While the PRC has been known to destabilize targeted countries, it would never resort to genocide. (See Figure 4.4.) As after the Chinese "assistance" to Sudan, genocides just sometimes occur.

Burundi

It's within Rwanda's tiny neighbor to the south—Burundi—that a full assortment of "Copper Belt" minerals can be found. (See Map 4.5.) This tiny country has access to nickel, uranium, rare-earth oxides, cobalt, copper, platinum, vanadium, niobium, tantalum, gold, tin, and tungsten.[54] That may be why the PRC is now footing the bill for a new presidential palace and hydropower dam on the Ruzibazi River.[55]

China is also building a new railroad from Mombasa (Kenya) through Nairobi and then on to Uganda, Rwanda, and Burundi. In all probability, this highly expensive venture is not just an act of friendship.

Groundwork Now Laid for Some Serious Research

Much of the brutality of China's Cultural Revolution has certainly come to Africa. But, as a political tool, it can be easily made to look like long-standing inter-tribal hatred. Then, the West will deem it unavoidable. Might all of the most recent refinements to the Maoist expansionist method have finally resulted in a "relatively peaceful" way of taking over an entire continent? The next few chapters will explore this very distinct possibility in depth.

5 The PRC's Building and Immigration Program

- How many Chinese construction projects are there in Africa?
- Why all the Chinese emigration to Africa?

Mao's First Premier—Zhou Enlai—visited Tanzania in 1965.

(Source: Wikipedia Encyclopedia, s.v. "Zhou Enlai," under provisions of GNU Free Documentation License, image designator "1924_Zhou_Enlai.jpg," © n.d.))

What's Wrong with So Much Chinese Construction?

From a Bedford Falls perspective, the many PRC foreign-aid projects in Africa's "developing nations" may seem like unselfish philanthropy. But China is not like America. It doesn't give away money (or what it can buy) for other countries to use any way they want. It always specifies a precise purpose. To make sure that purpose happens, it stations long-term observers inside the recipient nation. Along a strategically vital transportation artery, it will minimally have workers from the PRC-owned company that has been picked to do the work.

China's Ulterior Motives

Since the early 1990's, the PRC's main diplomatic push within the Dark Continent has been a "one-China" foreign policy at the U.N. for all member states. Every manner of incentive has been tried: loans, buying credit, debt reduction, ending rebel aid, presidential palaces, limousine fleets, hydro-power plants, electricity lines, highways, hospitals, textile mills, handicraft training, sugar refineries, cement plants, sports stadiums, agro-veterinary projects, etc. Whether simple business venture or infrastructure project, most such schemes have entailed joint ownership with predominantly Chinese equipment and workers. In almost every country, the building plan has included improvement to its transportation system. This mutual thread between neighboring states may be just the easiest way to extract the Dark Continent's mineral and petroleum resources.

As For the Most Mineral-Rich Nation

The majority of the multiple-element Copper Belt lies within the DRC. After Angola's civil war, the DRC became the most highly contested nation in Africa. Since 1998, some 5.4 million DRC citizens have lost their lives there to "interfactional" fighting.[1] Those wounded, tortured, or raped are, of course, many times that number. That's a lot of human suffering, and it's still going on. Perhaps, the West needs to look a little harder at who or what has been fanning those flames, and why.

Most of that interfactional fighting has occurred along the DRC's eastern border. While this region is generally known for its copper and cobalt, it also has uranium and rare earths. More easily to acquire those resources, China has been refurbishing the Benguela Railroad that runs from the Angolan seaport of Lobito to the DRC-Zambia border region.[2] In June 2008, it also managed to trade a 1,000-mile road from Zambia to the northeastern DRC for all the minerals it can extract in the foreseeable future. It and the DRC government were to form a joint mining company in which only a third is DRC owned. The Kinshasa government would then foot its part of the construction bill by allowing China to take natural resources for free.[3] As this incredible "arrangement" was trade oriented, Washington failed to see that President Kabila had been manipulated. Nor does it suspect China of keeping the eastern DRC intentionally destabilized to discourage Western business interests.

> Congo and China are forming a massive mining company . . . with Congo owning 32% and China . . . 68%.
>
> The Chinese are putting up all the money. . . .
>
> But the money isn't free—it will [be] . . . loans. . . . Congo will pay back China with copper, cobalt and road tolls.[4]
>
> — *National Public Radio (NPR),* 30 July 2008

To pursue this possibility of strategic deception, one has only to look a few hundred miles to the north—at the Darfur region of Sudan. There, the PRC wants oil and no Western competition. As such, it provides "small arms for petroleum" and U.N. protection to the Islamist regime behind Darfur's genocide.

The Congo's eastern mining-region is also rife with ethnic rivalries. Here, the Congolese Army has secretly allied itself with the *Forces Democratiques de Liberation du Rwanda (FDLR)* to suppress what it calls a Tutsi rebellion. The two have even run joint raids on Tutsi villages.[5] Within the *FDLR* is the same *Interahamwe* that committed Rwanda's horrendous genocide. To fund this "militia ally," the Congolese Army further allows it to control much of the trade in tin, tungsten, and coltan.[6] Thus, one starts to see an unhappy similarity between the Arab *Janjaweed* of Sudan and the Hutu *FDLR* of the DRC. And in both places, the same aspiring superpower is nonchalantly waiting in the wings to monopolize the most important natural resources. If those 5.4 million lost DRC souls were separated into ethnic categories, many might qualify for separate "genocides" in the same general location. One would almost certainly be of more Tutsis.

As early as November 2008, troops from China's most militarily proficient African proxy (Angola) were helping DRC forces to defend Goma at the center of this affected region.[7] Also coming were troops from China's most blatant surrogate, Zimbabwe.[8] Of late, the U.N. has gotten more involved there as well, but this is not the U.N. of the Korean War era. Within Africa, Chinese allies provide the U.N. with most of its combat troops. The ramifications of this will be further discussed in the next chapter.

Part of a Disturbing Trend

Within Africa as a whole, the PRC's expansionary activity has followed several variants since most of the fighting stopped. For Zimbabwe, it involves openly bolstering a failed state with only a few natural resources. At Nigeria, Chinese oil companies patiently wait while non-Muslim rebels discourage Western competitors.[9] In Sudan and Angola, so many Chinese immigrants have been arriving as to alter their very foundations.[10] While the obvious link is mineral or oil removal, there have been political ramifications. The PRC has a "revolutionary" government that still considers some form of rebellion vital to the progress of developing nations. To many African leaders, China's ongoing good will feels more like sabotage or invasion.

> [A]long with the infrastructure come Chinese laborers and companies. . . . In addition, cheap Chinese goods . . . have flooded African markets, wiping out competition, crippling local enterprises, closing factories and adding to widespread unemployment.[11]
>
> – *NPR,* 28 July 2008

> Michael Sata, nicknamed King Cobra, is Zambia's feisty opposition leader. . . . Sata speaks of exploitation.
>
> "Today, the Chinese are not here as investors, they are here as invaders," Sata says.[12]
>
> – *NPR,* 1 August 2008

> Adama Gaye, a Senegalese author and commentator, says Chinese merchants were the vanguard of Beijing's [strategy]. . . .
>
> The Chinese merchants, he says, were "the advance force that has allowed opening . . . territories, . . . they were followed . . . by the big companies and . . . political leaders."[13]
>
> – *NPR,* 1 August 2008

Where Lots of People and Money Are Combined

In the PRC's obvious quest for global "hegemony," it has made good use of two of its most abundant assets: (1) a mushrooming population; and (2) a huge cash surplus. As China's principal source of many "strategic minerals," Africa has experienced both forms of influx.

Some of the Chinese money has gone directly into loans, debt reduction, and purchasing credit. Perhaps the biggest overall assistance package was to oil-rich Angola: (1) a two-billion-dollar line of credit in 2005; and then (2) six and a half billion more in loans for infrastructure rebuilding.[14] Of course, not all recipients have been as popular as Dos Santos. Guinea's highly despotic and corrupt former government was bolstered by a Chinese four-billion-dollar bailout in 2009.[15] The vast majority of PRC gifts have had their exact purpose specified—like for a natural-resource removal conduit. Also stipulated are the use of Chinese companies and equipment. Thus, many such arrangements have come with their own Chinese "security personnel." Wherever there are former PLA members, the Pentagon should be more interested.

It's through these "civilian" enterprises that the PRC's other unique asset—a citizen excess—ultimately comes into play on the Dark Continent. Hundreds of thousands of Chinese laborers and shop owners have already descended on Sudan—enough to forever change its economic and political fabric. An equal number may have ended up in Angola, though only 70,000 were officially registered as working there in 2010.[16] That's because many arrived as a part of a Chinese construction project, but then never left. One wonders how much of an intelligence-gathering or politics-altering role they may still have in their new home. After all, their family move to Africa had undoubtedly been government directed and then partially subsidized. If any of those construction companies could now be proven to be secret extensions of the PLA, their overall purpose in Angola would become far more suspect. All Asian Communist governments share the same three-part heritage: (1) outsmarting their opposition through deception; (2) operating from the bottom up; and (3) then winning wars with as little actual fighting as possible.

As of 2005, the international news media had reported large numbers of Chinese contract workers in the following countries: (1) Sudan; (2) Eritrea; (3) Djibouti; (4) Nigeria; (5) Angola; and (6) Zimbabwe.[17] Those in Zimbabwe come as no surprise, but the ones in some of the other places do. While the Nigerian contingent can be easily explained by all that petroleum, those at the Red Sea entrance must either be to guard a shipping chokepoint or overland conduit.

China's Foreign Construction Market

The PRC now has a wide array of state-owned corporations working overseas at building bridges, roads, railroads, pipelines, and other facets of any good resource-extraction corridor. These corporations have been especially busy in Africa. Most such projects have been funded by both the host-country and China. In return for all the construction expenditures, the PRC has often been getting special oil or mineral extraction privileges.

As late as 1997, there may have been as many as 15,000 Chinese civilian enterprises still run by the PLA. There were those only to provide the PLA with financial support, those that had helped to refurbish China's own infrastructure, and others in various defense industries. Of the first variety, hundreds must have been operating internationally. Whether or not on purpose, many then proceeded to flood strategically contested regions with so many Chinese-made products as to run all local industries out of business. (Cheap Chinese goods were still undermining Cameroonian industry as late as 2008.[18]) This, in turn, created an economic dependency on the PRC from each affected country. That dependency was soon to be exploited.

Corporate Extensions of the PLA

The PLA was supposed to have divested itself of all civilian business interests by the year 2000. But, because previous Beijing directives to do so had failed, it is still suspected of exceptions.[19] With deception so integral a part of Asia's military heritage, this should come as no big shock to anyone. As repeatedly noted, China still considers Third-World revolution to be part of its progress. Revolution (in all of its forms) most easily takes root in a volatile environment. Where Chinese peacekeepers are not authorized, who better to create a "strategic" presence than a PLA-run enterprise with its own security personnel?

Of course, any of the PRC's "state-run" companies would also have former soldiers as security guards. Whether any still have a PLA mission may never be discovered. What is known is that the PRC's principal spy agencies do something in Africa that their Western counterparts never have. They focus almost entirely on economic intelligence. In addition, all state-owned companies would likely be required to follow the same strategic agenda as their national defense establishment.[20]

Two of the Biggest Suspects

For many years, both China Ocean Shipping Company (COSCO) (ocean-going vessels) and Hutchison Whampoa (port facilities) were heavily suspected of being PLA business extensions. Unfortunately, only the former has ever been officially accused.

> "Although presented as a commercial entity, COSCO is actually an arm of the Chinese [Communist] military establishment. . . ," states a 1998 special report written by the House Task Force on Terrorism and Unconventional Warfare.[21]
>
> — *Newsmax,* 27 February 2003

More Candidates

The PLA has undoubtedly had other civilian "appendages," but one of the most interesting is China National Electronics Import and Export Corporation (CEIEC). In an increasingly electronic age, such a corporation could pose a significant risk.

> Although China officially denied that it installed the fiber-optic air defense network inside Afghanistan, the Pentagon is certain that China sold the military system to the Taliban. . . .
>
> The military command network in Afghanistan is described by Pentagon analysts as similar to the fiber-optic air defense system installed in [Saddam Hussein's] Iraq by China. . . .
>
> The fiber-optic network in Afghanistan has more than just a common thread with the Iraqi air defense system.

> The Chinese company CEIEC that built and installed the new system for the Taliban is also a known arms manufacturer, owned and operated by the People's Liberation Army. According to an official Defense Intelligence Agency (DIA) document, CEIEC is the prime maker of electronics for the Chinese army. The DIA documents state that virtually all CEIEC products are military in nature, including "cryptographic system," "mine detection equipment," "fiber and laser optics," "communications technology" and "radars."[22]
>
> — *Newsmax,* 20 October 2001

To confirm the threat posed by CEIEC, one had only to visit its website in 2005. In an introductory video, a CEIEC spokesman announced that the company specialized in defense electronics, ship building, world trade, and overseas engineering. Among its ongoing engineering projects were hydro-power dams and electric grids. Then, in what has become all-too-common PLA rhetoric, the company's president proclaimed, "The process of economic globalization is inevitable." After many decades of "hoodwinking" the West, Chinese officials may have become somewhat arrogant themselves. Appearing over and over in the video was the same Chinese metaphoric cartoon—a tiny seed growing into a large tree. Its lyrics were not as comforting—"one seed, one world."[23] The proverbial seed is, of course, the PRC's global agenda. All CPC members still see China as the center of the civilized world. The CEIEC's current website makes it look like a private firm.

Another civilian enterprise—China Railway Construction Corporation (CRCC) may have been the former "railway arm of the People's Liberation Army." As of 2005, it was the world's sixth biggest construction contractor, with projects in over 60 countries.[24] "During the 1970's (long before China became rich), the PLA had built—at great cost—the Karakoram Highway between Xinjiang and northern Pakistan."[25] More recently, the CRCC has fabricated the high-altitude and extremely challenging Qinghai-Tibetan railway that became operational in July 2006.[26] This may help to explain why China Railway Shisiju Group Corporation (CRSSG) was building China's transportation corridor across Afghanistan to the Iranian oil fields. At the top of CRSSG's home page is a CRCC logo.[27] It takes the form of an elongated globe with CRCC inscribed across its entire breadth. Obviously implied is that CRSSG is a subsidiary of the once PLA-operated CRCC.

The History of PLA Business Involvement

At the birth of the PRC in 1949, China's only large civilian enterprises were owned by government agencies, and its national infrastructure was in shambles. Then, its military was give the job of economic rejuvenation—through building railroads and factories, reclaiming of wasteland, digging irrigation canals, establishing state farms, and participating in disaster relief. Having accepted this mostly non-martial role, the PLA devoted many of its structural elements—like its Engineering Corps, Railway Engineering Corps, Capital Construction Engineering Corps, Signal Corps, and Production and Construction Corps—to nothing other than local infrastructure enhancement. It continued with this type of work into the mid-1980's, with many of its soldiers being concurrently trained in various civilian occupations.[28]

Through a Socialist desire for military self-sufficiency, China's ruling party had allowed the PLA to create enough civilian enterprises to financially support its own requirements. The PLA soon became semi-autonomous, making China's civilian leaders nervous. After the PLA fared poorly in the Sino-Vietnamese War of 1979, those leaders decided to shrink its size to free up more resources for economic development. This put even more pressure on the PLA to support itself.[29] It may have also given its generals the idea of using international construction as a way of accomplishing an increasingly global security mission.

Then, Deng Xiaoping began to decrease his military's participation in national-level politics. Further to streamline the PLA, he is supposed to have "civilianized" its Railway Engineering Corps and the Capital Construction Engineering Corps.[30] Yet, as late as the mid-1990's, the PLA still had extensive commercial holdings in non-military areas, such as real estate. By the turn of the century, it was to have no more companies without a clear military purpose. Yet, other firms may have been deemed helpful to "peaceful" foreign expansion. Their management structure would remained unchanged, with their leaders simply retiring from active military service to run an ostensibly private enterprise.[31]

The PLA's Current Commercial Interface

As with many other things in China, the PLA's supposed banishment from the business world may have been an intentional ploy by the CPC. Where national defense is involved in America, aren't all manner of secrets possible?

> The [Chinese] People's Liberation Army must have one of the most extensive military industrial complexes in the world, employing some 700,000 employees in about 10,000 enterprises. . . . [I]n the 1980's . . . Deng Xiaoping's policy of economic reform forced the military more or less to finance its own modernization, due to a relative decline in the official budget. By conversion of part of its industries to civilian production, the [Chinese] Army was able to supplement its income. . . . In 1998, the Party demanded that the PLA withdraw from non-military commercial activities, but it remains unclear to what extent this order has been heeded.[32]
>
> — Internat. Inst. of Social History, December 2009

In fact, there's reliable proof this Central Committee directive may have gone unheeded in some cases. The PLA was still facing more costs than its governmental allotment could cover. To help make up the difference, it may have actually expanded a few of its existing business arrangements with *Sun Yee On*—the Hong Kong triad with the largest overseas operation. When combined with COSCO shipping, that link to organized crime would have greatly expanded the PLA's already existent smuggling network. In ways that construction projects never could, it also gave the PLA a way to undermine its only remaining opposition—America.

> In Shanghai, . . . the People's Liberation Army owns a string of nightclubs with the Sun Yee On triad society.[33]
>
> — *The New Republic,* 14 and 21 July, 1997

> [D]uring the divestment process [after 1998], the PLA's reputation suffered . . . when revelations about the involvement of military enterprises in smuggling . . . came to light. The military transferred large numbers of businesses to local governments, closed others, and, in some cases, handed them over to families of PLA officers. Thousands more . . . remained in military control.[34]
>
> — Council on Foreign Relations, September 2010

Still Active Corporate Extensions of the PLA

In 2005, one internet encyclopedia was showing 75 Chinese corporations to be government owned, with no indication of which might still belong to the PLA. COSCO, CRCC, China Metallurgical Group Corporation (MCC), and various oil exploration companies were all included on this list, but not Hutchison Whampoa, CEIEC, China State Construction Engineering Corporation (CSCEC), and China Road and Bridge Corporation (CRBC).[35] This internet list was obviously incomplete, because the last two were clearly shown by their websites to be state owned. Like CRBC, CSCEC was probably part of the PLA. CSCEC is now China's biggest international general contractor—with projects in more places than can be easily summarized. CRBC has offices in Angola, Burundi, Cameroon, CAR, Chad, DRC, Congo Republic, Côte D'Ivore, Equatorial Guinea, Ethiopia, Gabon, Kenya, and up to eight other African nations.[36]

Only for Hutchison Whampoa and CEIEC is there no mention anywhere of state-ownership. Hutchison builds port facilities in over 54 countries (and at both ends of the Panama Canal),[37] and CEIEC works on advanced electronics. In 2005, Hutchison Whampoa's chairman was using the same chilling metaphor at his website as the chairman of CEIEC had at his: "[International infrastructure assistance projects] are the country's [China's] roots. And like a tree, the deeper its roots, the more flourishing its branches and foliage [to more easily cover the world]."[38]

Other Infrastructure Builders

In the hybrid economy of a Communist state, why couldn't any company, whether state-owned or private, still help the PLA with its overseas strategy? If neither bragged about the cooperation, who in the West would know? Just as the PLA once turned to infrastructure enhancement to consolidate its homeland, it may now be using the same approach to a fledgling province.

China Communications Construction Company Limited (CCCCLTD) can also be determined from its website to do "infrastructure construction." More focused on "lines of communication" than telephones, it works on ports, roads, railways, bridges, and tunnels. It's logo is an elongated earth fully covered with CCCCLTD projects. The website also lists CRBC and China Harbor Engineering Company (CHEC) as subsidiaries. Founded in 1979, both CRBC and CHEC must have been part of the PLA.[39]

The PLA's former Railway Engineering Corps (now China Railway Group [CRECG]) does a great deal of infrastructure building around the world as well. While CCCCLTD and CRECG are both owned by the State Council,[40] they may still be contributing to the PLA's expansion plan.

The Companies Most Closely to Watch in Africa

CRBC is now constructing the Kenya to Copper-Belt-adjacent Burundi railroad in Africa.[41] While it was busy repairing the 2010 flood damage to the Karakoram Highway, its parent nation took over *de facto* control of a big part of Pakistani occupied Kashmir.[42] On the CRBC's official website, the Secretary of Party Committee (company's CPC representative) asserts the following: "In the . . . global competition, it [CRBC] gives birth to an enterprise culture of hardworking, fighting and dedication."[43] Fighting is what armies do, not civilian corporations.

Within West Africa, it is the CRCC—the PLA's former railway arm—that has been refurbishing the old railroad from Angola's seaside city of Benguela to the DRC-Zambian border (and CRECG completing the road between Zambia and the northeastern DRC). CRBC only has responsibility for the highway between the town of Benguela and port of Lobito. Still, that puts CRBC right in the middle of three of China's most important resource conduits. (See Figure 5.1.) One can only wonder why this same company—or another CCCCLTD subsidiary—has been helping to build the Oakland Bay Bridge.[44]

The PLA is known to have constructed all Chinese portions of the Karakoram Highway in the early 1970's. Because of the same time frame, it is just as likely to have helped with the TANZAM railway in East Africa as with the Pakistani portions of the Karakoram. More than one researcher has the PLA's Railway Engineering Corps—predecessor to modern-day CRECG—helping to build the TANZAM.[45]

The former Ministry of Railways' foreign-aid department and now CRCC subsidiary—CCECC—sometimes competes with the CRBC for the same building contracts in Africa. Since 2012, the

CCECC has worked on the $4 billion, 740-km electric railway that connects Addis Ababa (Ethiopia) and Djibouti, as well as the $5.6 billion Chad railway network and other rail lines in Libya and Mauritania. In May 2014, it also acquired a $13 billion coastal railway project from the Nigerian government. Its parent company (CRCC) has already built a railroad in Saudi Arabia.[46] Thus, CRCC, CRBC, and CRECG may all be pursuing the same PRC strategy, while only appearing to be in competition with one another. CRCC seems to prefer operating in the North African Muslim countries where much of the oil is, whereas CRBC and CRECG have mostly worked in mineral-rich Central Africa. A chart in Chapter 21 will further detail their zones of influence.

Most of the PLA's former corporations seem to have been taken over by the State Council. However, there is some evidence of shared ownership between governmental entities. CRCC shows up on the current list of State Council owned businesses (now totalling 117), as does COSCO, CSCEC, CRECG, and CCCCLTD (parent to CRBC and CHEC). Only missing from that list is CEIEC. Besides advanced electronics, this company works on railway electrification, signaling systems, rolling stock (electric trains), and railway facilities. It

Figure 5.1: Early Mining Operation
(Source: Courtesy of Wikipedia Encyclopedia, s.v. "Mining," public domain image from "The Loyal West in the Times of the Rebellion," by Barber and Howe [1865])

has "cooperation relationships" with over 160 countries or regions worldwide, with its main African offices in Angola, Egypt, Algeria, and Ethiopia.[47] All of this heavily suggests PLA ownership.

Some non-engineering corporations are probably secretly owned by the PLA as well. The following excerpt points to a few possibilities.

> China Poly Group is a commercial arm of the . . . (PLA) General Staff Department. The PLA General Logistics Department operates China Xinxing. The PLA General Political Department owns and operates China Carrie. And the PLA Navy runs China Songhai.[48]
>
> — *Multinational Monitor,* 1997

None of these four companies (or their modern-day sequels) show up on the list of State-owned Assets Supervision and Administration Commission (SASAC) companies. China Xinxing Import and Export Corporation seems the most active. A military trading enterprise, China Xinxing maintains "business cooperation in more than 40 African countries."[49]

The Full Extent of China's Infrastructure Offensive

Chinese firms have been building many things throughout Africa. Most of the biggest will ultimately facilitate oil or mineral removal. Large-scale mining takes electricity and transportation. That electricity must be first generated at hydro or thermal plants and then transmitted to the resource removal site along a power grid. Then, the petroleum or ore is transported to the nearest ocean by pipeline, railroad, or truck.

> China is presently involved in infrastructure project(s) in 35 African countries. A concentration of projects is . . . in Angola, Nigeria and the Sudan. However, China is planning a new range of projects in other countries, especially in the DRC. The country's activities have been divided fairly evenly among . . . power generation (especially hydropower), and transport (especially railroads).[50]
>
> — Japanese Trade Organization, October 2014

In places where big PRC loans have not been as forthcoming as Angola, Nigeria, or Sudan, Chinese companies have simply entered into joint funding agreements with local counterparts.

> Overall, about 70% . . . of the value of contracts won by Chinese firms under multilateral projects was accounted for by just four countries: Ethiopia, Mozambique, Tanzania, and the DRC.[51]
>
> — Japanese Trade Organization, October 2014

There are Chinese-assisted hydropower dams being built in Ghana, Nigeria, Sudan, Kenya, Mozambique, Zambia, Gabon, the DRC, and Guinea. Resource-removal concessions are helping to fund such projects in Ghana, the DRC, and Guinea. Under construction in Sudan, Nigeria, Ghana, and Botswana are jointly owned thermal power stations.

Most noticeable are Africa's new railroads. In recent years, the PRC has made financing commitments of $4 billion dollars for railway construction alone. Involved is the rehabilitation or construction of roughly 3000 kilometers of rail line. The largest deals have been in Nigeria, Gabon, and Mauritania. There are other tracks being laid in Libya.[52]

Of course, the Communist Chinese have been building roads throughout the Dark Continent as well. There are over 18 projects involving more than 1,400 kilometers of highway.[53] Here appears a familiar name.

> Road building has been an especially important activity in Angola, Botswana and Ethiopia. By far the most active Chinese road construction firm was the . . . (CRBC).[54]
>
> — Japanese Trade Organization, October 2014

That puts the CRBC at work on big transportation conduits in nine African countries: Angola, Zambia, Kenya, Ethiopia, Tanzania, Uganda, Rwanda, Burundi, and Botswana. Its website also makes mention of building a new highway between Mali's two most important cities. In addition, CRBC mans offices in 12 other African nations: Gabon, Mauritania, Equatorial Guinea, Ivory Coast, Malawi, South Sudan, Togo, Niger, Congo Republic, Mozambique, and Guinea.[55]

Always Something in Return for Chinese Help

Angola's $2 billion-dollar line of credit in 2005 was backed by an agreement to supply the PRC with 10,000 barrels of local crude oil every day for the next 17 years. Tied to this "loan" was also a stipulation that most (70%) construction contracts be awarded to Chinese state-owned enterprises of PRC government choosing. Since then, there have been several equally large Chinese loans to Angola—for strictly infrastructure. Currently, over 100 Chinese companies are active there, with almost 70,000 Chinese workers employed on different projects around the country. Among other things, CRBC is rebuilding the road between the cities of Uige and Maquela do Zombo.[56]

Since 2001, China has also provided $1.3 billion dollars for infrastructure improvement to Sudan. The early projects were all in the power sector. In December 2008, developmental contracts in the amount of $1.5 billion dollars were concluded between the two countries. These projects included a power station, oil pipeline, and the Dibaybat-Malakal road.[57] In return, China almost certainly received oil "privileges."

China's engagement in Nigeria amounts to a total of $5.4 billion dollars. Nigeria's first loan in 2005 for power station construction was oil-backed. In return for its initial cost, China could purchase 30,000 barrels of crude oil a day for renewable one-year periods.[58] In July 2006, China received four oil blocks (two in the Lake Chad Basin and two in the Niger Delta) and a controlling stake in the Kaduna refinery from the Nigerian government in return for investing in a new hydropower plant at Mambila.

Then, there was the monumental deal between China and the DRC in June 2008 that exchanged vast quantities of minerals for a 1,000 mile road between the Zambian border and northeastern DRC. That road was to run up through the mining district, roughly paralleling the DRC border, from Kasumbalesa to Kisangani in Oriente Province on the Congo River. This was not the first trade of minerals for something else between the two nations. There was even an "arms for metals" arrangement at one point. In September 2007, another "resources-for-infrastructure" agreement was signed between two Chinese state construction companies and the DRC's state copper company. The Chinese partners had promised $9 (soon to become $6) billion worth of roads, railways, hospitals, schools, dams, and mine development. In return, the DRC government had pledged up to 10 million tons of copper and hundreds of thousands of tons of cobalt.[59] This transaction may have been the precursor to the big road deal. If so, state-owned companies had done the initial negotiating on governmental foreign policy.

Through similar "deals," China has secured direct equity in Zambia's vast copper, coal, and manganese reserves. In addition, it has purchased "stakes" to the yield of various other mining operations.[60]

Only China's Initial Interest Is in Resource Removal

Backed by almost unlimited sums of governmental money, state-owned Chinese corporations haven't had to play by the same rules as other businesses. Though copper and cobalt prices have fallen in recent years, China remains committed to extracting these strategically vital resources from the Dark Continent at whatever loss in revenue. At Chinese mines in Zambia and DRC, there has simply been retrenchment. Within Guinea, plans to develop aluminium mines in exchange for the construction of dams, roads and bridges have only been temporarily delayed.[61] Chinese investors have also delayed plans to conclude a $3 billion-dollar investment in Gabon's Belinga iron ore deposit.[62]

Despite such setbacks, Chinese enterprises have still come out ahead. Declining asset values for foreign mining and petroleum companies have permitted their easy buy-out. In exchange for cash injections by Chinese corporations, others have had to relinquish part of their extraction concession limits.[63]

The Overall Scope of This Peaceful "Invasion"

As in the days of the "Red Guard" uprisings, China's ultimate intention is to "communize" as many governments as it can. Subsequent chapters will discuss the extremes to which it may be willing to achieve that end. Make no mistake, military force is among them.

Now, with China's armed forces and state-owned enterprises both pushing its "One World" foreign policy, Western observers should not be surprised to see cooperation between them on the Dark Continent. China sent at least 4,000 troops to Sudan in 2000 to protect the oil pipeline it had just built.[64] As of 2006, it had some 1700 PLA peacekeepers in Africa.[65] Now, the PLA navy has become more active in local waters. It has lately had three ships off the coast of Somalia to protect Chinese commerce, and one went so far as Libya to rescue PRC workers. That navy will be there not only to safeguard trade routes, but also to protect a 1900% increase in the number of Chinese immigrants.

> The [PLA] navy . . . [is] the guardian of China's ever-expanding economic interests. These range from . . . (seeing most of the South China Sea as an exclusive economic zone) to protecting . . . Chinese shipping, preserving the country's access to . . . raw materials . . . , and safeguarding the soaring numbers of Chinese citizens who work abroad (about 5m today, but expected to rise to 100m by 2020). . . .
>
> [In 2011], one of those vessels was sent to the Mediterranean to assist in evacuating 35,000 Chinese workers from Libya.[66]
>
> — *The Economist,* 7 April 2012

Some 95 million new voters could drastically alter the internal politics and foreign policy of many of Africa's less populous nations. Of its 54 member states, 42 have less than 30 million citizens, and 33 have less than 16 million.[67] In the latter category are some big oil providers: Tunisia, Libya, South Sudan, Congo Republic, Tunisia, Namibia, and Equatorial Guinea. Also of tiny size are the following mineral producers: Gabon, Guinea, Namibia, Zimbabwe, Zambia, Burundi, Rwanda, and Madagaskar.

The expanding role of the Chinese navy around the Dark Continent is now more apparent. But what of all the PRC peacekeepers in U.N. missions? How do they fit into this increasingly complex picture?

Peacekeepers Wherever There Is Instability

- What skills do Chinese peacekeepers normally have?
- Why are there so many of these soldiers in Africa?

China now regularly deploys U.N. peacekeepers to Africa.

(Source: Wikipedia Encyclopedia, s.v. "Flag of the United Nations," public-domain image from Bast64 [2009] with designator "Flag_of_the_United_Nations.svg")

There's More Than One Way to Project Military Power

To assist beleaguered nations, the Pentagon has traditionally opted for standoff airstrikes over "boots on the ground." Wherever authorized, the latter follow a standard progression: initially (1) local-force advisers/trainers; then (2) supporting-arms forward observers; and only as a last resort (3) actual combat units. Not all countries operate this way. Two of world's most expansionist—the PRC and Iran—actually prefer a ground presence. While the PRC achieves it through U.N. peacekeepers or building-project security guards, Iran will station a single squad of IRGC special operators in each foreign neighborhood. That squad's job is not only to maintain order, but also to insure a "proper" political cadre. Iran has dispatched such widely dispersed forces to three countries so far: Lebanon, Yemen, and Iraq.

As both China and Iran have "revolutionary governments" that like to operate from the bottom up, one suspects those PRC peacekeepers and corporate guards of doing more than just forestalling rebel activity.

The Visible PLA Footprint

Only on occasion will the PRC risk uniformed troops on foreign soil. So far, a flood along Pakistan's Karakoram Highway and possibility of attacks on a Sudanese pipeline have offered the best excuses for same. Elsewhere within Africa, the TANZAM and Benguela railroads may at some point provide another, as may China's new highway into the northeastern DRC. At the end of 2014, the PRC had about 1700 peacekeepers in Africa. Some of its non-combat personnel were already stationed near that new DRC road—in the U.N. mission base camp south of Goma.[1] Though theoretically working for the U.N., those Chinese specialists have a lot of spare time on their hands.

Uniformed PRC Troops As Construction Project Security

During August of the year 2000, Britain's *Sunday Telegraph* reported a "huge influx" of Chinese soldiers into Sudan to help with that nation's war in the south. Four years later, the *Washington Times* lowered the estimate to 4,000 and said those troops were there to protect the Chinese-built pipeline.[2] The latter version is more probably correct, because 11,000 Chinese soldiers were reportedly sent to Gilgit-Balistan (in Pakistani-occupied Kashmir) when the Karakoram Highway was damaged by a 2010 flood. Many subsequently remained there.[3] A few of India's biggest newspapers immediately questioned the claim. Then, *Rediff News* pointed out that it really didn't matter whether there were any uniformed troops present, because many of the projects had "PLA construction crews."[4]

Extent of the PRC's Dark Continent Peacekeeping Effort

China's reasons for so many peacekeepers in Africa should not be expected to match those for a Western nation. Beijing has lately been following a "One World" foreign policy. Besides providing the PLA with overseas outposts, peacekeeping missions can often be exchanged for host country favors.

> Beijing has contributed at a higher level to U.N. Peacekeeping Operations [UNPKO's] in states where it has economic interests.
>
> . . . China not only selectively chooses its PKOs, but in doing so takes advantage of a multilateral institution to favorably advance its own interests.[5]
>
> — *The Diplomat* (Tokyo), May 2014

> In 2006, it [the PLA] provided over 1,600 personnel to peacekeeping operations in Africa—about 70% . . . of its global peacekeeping efforts [Gill, Huang, and Morrison, *China's Expanding Role in Africa,* 21.]. . . .
>
> . . . China is transforming the PLA into a global force and is looking for opportunities to use it. . . .
>
> . . . the PLA . . . seeks an expanded role in African peacekeeping operations.[6]
>
> — *Joint Forces Quarterly,* 2009

Possible Secondary Mission for All Those Chinese Troops

Chinese leaders have been hinting at using peacekeepers as part of a global strategy for years. They could greatly help the PLA with its new "active-defense" role. This role entails "counteracting" U.S. hegemony worldwide.

> In 2004 Hu Jintao, China's president, said the PLA should be able to undertake "new historic missions". Some of these involve U.N. peacekeeping. In recent years China has been the biggest contributor of peacekeeping troops among the permanent five members of the Security Council.[7]
>
> — *The Economist,* 7 April 2012

According to the well-respected *Economist,* peacekeepers have been one of the host-government inducements to "fast-track" resource removal. There have been PRC peacekeepers in Sudan, the DRC, and Liberia for precisely that purpose.[8] Thus, one wonders how many of the CPC's other peacekeeping missions have ulterior motives.

> As of April 2012, [U.N.] missions with some PRC presence include Western Sahara . . . , the Democratic Republic of Congo . . . , Darfur . . . , Sudan . . . , South Sudan . . . , Côte d'Ivoire . . . , and Liberia.[9]
>
> — *Second Line of Defense* (Arlington, VA), 2013

The *BBC* claims that up to 600 PRC troops were offered to the U.N. for peacekeeping duty in Mali.[10] One thus wonders if China may also be joining the U.N.'s CAR mission. If Sino-peacekeepers were only in such places to stop the fighting, they would all have infantry backgrounds. But, they don't. Along with many engineers are a considerable number of law enforcement personnel. This would suggest getting somehow involved with the economic and political processes of those countries.

> According to the ministry [of public security], China has sent more than 1,700 [military] police for U.N. peacekeeping missions to Timor Leste, Bosnia and Herzegovina, Kosovo, Liberia, Afghanistan, Haiti, and Sudan since January 2000.[11]
>
> — *Global Times* (Beijing), 12 November 2011

According to the same article, as many as 900 more Chinese policemen may be going to South Sudan. The U.N. has yet to be told about this, because its latest statistics only reflect 172 Chinese peacekeeper police worldwide.[12]

Military Advisors

The PRC also sends military advisers to many of Africa's most resource-abundant countries, such as Nigeria and Angola.[13] The number of recipients of such advisers is expected to rise as the

Chinese military attempts—through instruction of local forces—to protect the increasing number of Chinese business ventures and employees.

Defense Attachés and Military Visits

The PRC also has almost two dozen military attachés in the 54 African countries.[14] This is an increase of seven over the 2006 total, with 75% of those nations having their own attachés in Beijing. By every indication, the PRC intends to further increase its Dark Continent attaché presence.[15]

As of 2009, there were no fewer than 34 high- and functional-level exchange visits in progress between the PLA and Africa's national militaries.[16]

Arms with Little, If Any, Intention of Creating Stability

The PRC is now thought to be the largest exporter of weaponry to the Dark Continent. According to Amnesty International, "recipient countries . . . have tended to be developing countries with poor human-rights records." Within Africa, they include Algeria, Angola, DRC, Guinea, Egypt, Kenya, Libya, Sudan, and Zimbabwe.[17] The prestigious *Washington Post* reports China now "flooding sub-Saharan Africa with . . . cheap assault rifles and ammunition." It further states that such items have surfaced in a number of places where the U.N. has been trying to restrict their sale. Such active war zones stretch from the DRC to Côte D'Ivoire, Somalia, and Sudan.[18] As with China's other business transactions in Africa, financial profit does not seem to be the ultimate goal. A few fairly reputable military publications see the PRC's arms sales as intentionally fomenting violence.

> Despite China's insistence that its weapons are not fueling regional conflict or instability, there is evidence to the contrary. In fact, most Chinese FMS [Foreign Military Sales] over the past 15 years are going to some of the least stable areas of Africa, including Zimbabwe, Congo, and Sudan.[19]
>
> — *Joint Forces Quarterly,* 2009

The PRC was able to supersede the U.N. embargo on arms shipments to the Darfur Region of Sudan by selling them to the government supporting the *Janjaweed*—namely, Khartoum. In 2008 and 2009, the PRC added $34 million worth of artillery, tanks, and armored vehicles to the $1.8 million in small arms it had already peddled to Sudan. The PRC has also profited from a few "equal-opportunity" arms deals. The most highly publicized was during the 1998-2000 Ethiopia-Eritrea border conflict. There, it blatantly bypassed U.N. arms embargoes to sell $1 billion worth of arms to both sides at once.[20]

Since 2000, Beijing has sold armaments and other military equipment to as many as half (27) of Africa's total (54) of countries. Such arrangements with Sudan, Angola, Burundi, Equatorial Guinea, Eritrea, Ethiopia, Nigeria, Tanzania, and Zimbabwe have, in some cases, been interdependent on oil deals. Unfortunately, regimes with poor human rights records have had just as much access to the ordnance.[21]

Linking arms sales to intentional instability in Africa is a difficult proposition because so many nations have been marketing their military wares there. Even South Africa now has a thriving arms industry.[22] Still some very reputable sources have long equated small-arms availability with more local repression. That's why there's an international treaty now floating around to restrict their sale.

> It is increasingly clear that the proliferation of light weapons is a destabilizing force throughout the world. Pistols, rifles, machine guns, grenades, light mortars, and light artillery [e.g., recoilless rifles] are the weapons used most often in repressing civilian populations.[23]
>
> — *Foreign Affairs*

According to the Norwegian Initiative on Small-Arms Transfers, China has—since 2000—sold small quantities of light weaponry to Benin, Botswana, Burkina Faso, Cameroon, Djibouti, Egypt, Libya, Mozambique, and Zambia. It has sold larger amounts to Ethiopia, Kenya, Namibia, Niger, South Africa, Sudan, Tanzania, Uganda, and Zimbabwe.[24] While China has repeatedly claimed that such ordnance is to help those countries to defend themselves, its collective impact on the continent's overall security has been quite the opposite.

Some of these arms have gone to willing surrogates and others to unsuspecting instruments of Chinese foreign policy. China was Zimbabwe's primary supplier of arms when that southern African nation sent troops to the DRC in 1998 in support of Laurent Kabila. Other Dark Continent states have transferred such weaponry to rebel groups that serve their interests in neighboring countries or local militias that help to maintain order at home.[25] In this way, any direct trail of evidence back to the PRC of arms transactions that have been intentionally made to foment trouble is cleverly severed.

Chad Offers the Latest Example of Military Proxy Building

Chad is one of Africa's biggest oil producers. In 2007, China purchased the rights to a large oil exploration zone in Chad. Many Chinese benefits were to follow—including work on some key infrastructure projects, like roads and railroads. A large portion of Chinese oil royalties is now being invested in arming and training the Chadian army. As a result, Chad's military is now considered to be one of the best equipped in sub-Saharan Africa. Of late, this country has also been able to finance at least two costly foreign interventions. It continues to maintain a large military presence next door in the highly volatile CAR. It has also helped France to quell Islamist separatists in Mali.[26]

How Many Other Proxies Does China Have in Africa?

There have been Chinese-backed militias in Africa before, but now there seem to be entire national armies that are occasionally willing to pursue PRC interests. Those of Zimbabwe, Angola, Namibia, Chad, and Sudan militarily intervened in the DRC between 1998 and 2002,[27] with the Zimbabwean contingent staying all four years.[28] (See Map 6.1.) Chad just recently sent forces to the CAR and Mali.[29] Beijing has been supplying every one of these intercessor nations with arms.[30]

If peacekeeping is now one of the ways in which China can further its own foreign policy, then one should not be surprised to see troops from PRC allies working for the U.N. Of late, there are

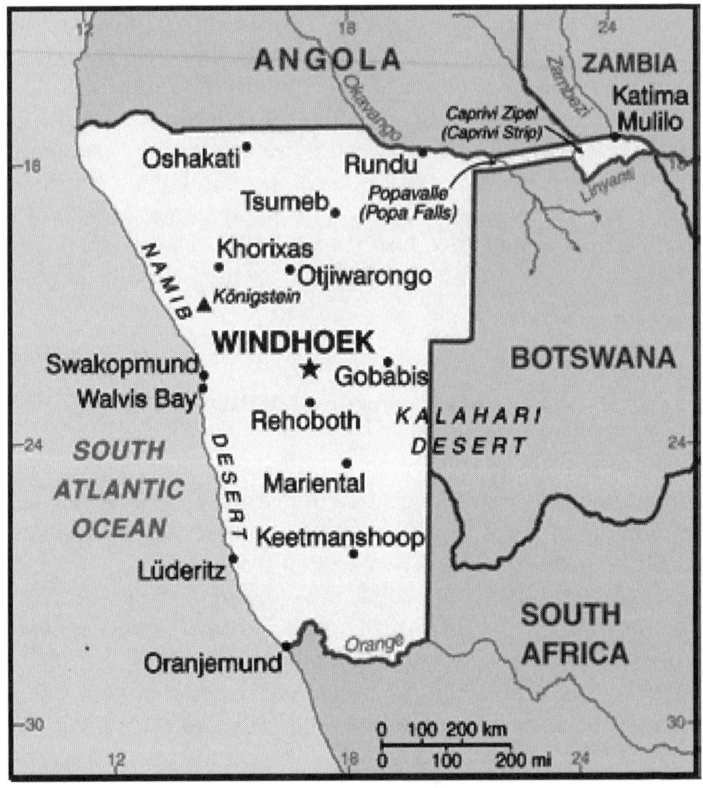

Map 6.1: Namibia May Soon Have Military Proxy Status
(Source: Courtesy of General Libraries, University of Texas at Austin, from their website for map designator "namibia_sm_2014.gif")

South African peacekeepers in the DRC and Sudan,[31] after being deployed for a while to Burundi.[32] One cannot help but notice the natural resources at these sites.

In 2014, Rwanda provided 5667 troops to U.N. peacekeeping operations around the world, while Tanzania gave 2253, South Africa 2251, Chad 1091, Zimbabwe 48, and Namibia 73. Most African soldiers were presumably sent to Dark Continent missions.[33] Yet, the U.N.'s new Intervention Brigade for the Eastern DRC contains no Rwandans.[34]

In early 2013, an increasingly PRC-oriented South Africa was so bold as to dispatch some combat troops unilaterally to the CAR to try to bolster the incumbent regime.[35] Over the years, South Africa has also provided election advice/security to various countries. That makes her new small-arms-manufacturing industry particularly troubling.

Revealing Comments from China's Ambassador to Namibia

The PRC's "transformation" of Africa may have started over 50 years ago, but it is still ongoing. No longer as openly martial as before, it has since come largely to depend upon perverted variations of democracy and capitalism. So far, Washington has either been fooled by this ploy or simply chosen to ignore it. As a direct result, its ability to provide long-term security to America has been gradually ebbing. Appeasement didn't work in 1938, and it won't work now.

In an unguarded moment, the Chinese ambassador to Namibia has revealed not only that country's little known Chinese history, but also its "so far obscured" Chinese future.

> During 1960's and 1970's, the Chinese military camps in Tanzania equipped the new-born "People's Liberation Army of Namibia" with arms and guerrilla tactics . . . and helped [the] Namibian people to win the . . . independence struggle. Since the establishment of [formal] diplomatic ties between our two countries on 22 March 1990, the second day after the independence of Namibia, we have treated each other as comrade[s]. . . .
>
> Besides the economic assistance with no political preconditions, the Chinese government encourages Chinese enterprises . . . to invest in Namibia. By setting up joint ventures, . . . China helps improve the economic competitiveness of Namibia. In 2013, we witnessed the ground breaking of Husab Mine of Swakop Uranium that is the largest entity investment project of China in Africa with 5 billion U.S. dollars in total. . . . After the completion of construction

in October 2015, it will become the second largest uranium mine in the world.[36]

— Chinese Ambassador to Namibia, 2014

One has to wonder if this admission of a resource-oriented Chinese 50-year continuum could also be present in other countries around the Dark Continent. It may be time to start itemizing the new ways in which the PRC has started to dominate this resource-rich region.

Communist China's New Modus Operandi

- How did China formerly expand its sphere of control?
- Which new ways are now being attempted in Africa?

PRC sees itself as the center of the civilized world.

(Source: Wikipedia Encyclopedia, s.v. "China," public-domain image from Steinsplitter with designator "800px-Flag_of_the_Peoples_Republic_of_China.png")

Other Type of Research Will Be Necessary

What regularly passes for "conventional wisdom" inside the Beltway is actually just a politically correct and "top-down" (Western) way of looking at things. For assessing any Eastern threat, it has definite limitations.

All citizens of the PRC are from a "bottom-up" culture that predates Communism by thousands of years. Though their current government may be highly autocratic at the top, its various agencies are still "culturally predisposed" toward getting things done from the bottom up. Properly to explore Chinese expansion in Africa, one must therefore use a form of research that will consider all the tiny and obscure elements that might collectively accomplish that expansion.

So, as promised in the Preface, this work's conclusions about Africa will be derived from a nontraditional—more law-enforcement-like—approach to intelligence gathering. Instead of accepting at face value what the Mainland Chinese and Levant Islamists have been reportedly doing there, it will look for hidden components to their methodology. Both like to take over a region through incremental involvement at the village or neighborhood level, so many tiny—and seemingly mundane—clues must be collected. Those that then mesh with the suspect's previous worldwide record of expansion will be further pursued.

How the PRC used to get its way in Africa should be apparent from the last few chapters. Before attempting to gather more contemporary evidence, one must clearly identify any subsequent refinements to this *modus operandi*. Then, the modern-day clues may reveal not only China's ongoing plan for the Dark Continent, but also the world.

First the Givens

That China has become more active globally needs no further proof. While the U.S. news media has been strangely silent on this subject, foreign journalists have been talking about this change to "Sino-foreign-policy" for years. The PRC's old way of spreading its ideology through armed insurrection seems almost at an end. In its place has blossomed pseudo-philanthropy. Only Americans in their 70's remember the more militaristic approach in any place other than the Chinese border region. Yet, as demonstrated by Chapters 3 and 4, there were others. Across the full breadth of southern Africa, Chinese proxies applied military force for decades (starting around 1965).

Now, the entire planet seems to be the target of Chinese "good will," with enough benevolent meddling in South America alone to fill another volume. The PRC doesn't want to militarily conquer the world, just bring most of its nations under economic, and then political, domination. The retrieval of Taiwan used to be its foremost objective. As of mid-2014, only Burkina Faso, Swaziland, and Sao Tome and Principe within Africa still recognized Taiwan.[1] Now, more than just a "one-China policy in the U.N." will be the price extracted from any country on the Dark Continent foolish enough to accept PRC assistance.

All the while, the U.S. government has been seemingly unconcerned with this change in Chinese foreign policy. Either the PRC's more subtle ways of subverting another nation has eluded its "radar," or the full extent of its own monetary obligations to China have dulled its perceptions.

The PRC has had the same ruling party for nearly 70 years. That means its "new" Dark Continent strategy may just be a 4th Generation Warfare (4GW) refinement to what Mao's first premier got rolling in Tanzania in 1965. Largely fought across a wide nonmartial spectrum, 4GW is very difficult for highly compartmentalized Western governments to counter.

The Chinese-built TANZAM railroad terminated at the Zambian end of the Copper Belt. From the start, it must have been bringing minerals out to ship back to China after carrying guerrillas in to alter the region's political climate. What that rail line now transports out is probably still ore (just in smaller quantities), but what it shuttles in may be Chinese immigrants and goods. Their ultimate role would be much the same as the rebels—eventually to Communize the local electorates.

China's Previous *Modus Operandi*

As was evident in Vietnam, southern Africa, and then later on Peru,[2] China formerly spread its brand of Communism to other nations through armed insurrection. Wasn't that Mao's area of expertise—how, through rural uprising, to take over an area? The CPC still sees revolution as a prerequisite to international progress, but why must all revolutions look like the armed overthrow of an incumbent government, or even be violent? To see how China's expansionist methodology has changed, one must only take a closer look at African history.

At the end of the "Red-Guard" insurgencies of the 1970's in southern Africa, the PRC took full advantage of the indigenous population's lack of sophistication and security at the polls.[3] Then, Communist-backed "freedom fighters" handily won the U.N.-brokered elections in Mozambique, Zimbabwe, Angola, and South Africa. Only the first and last of these nation states have since managed to avoid one-party rule. Yet, both still have left-leaning parties in power. In 2014, a former Communist was elected to his second term as president of South Africa.[4]

> [The] (ANC) has veered sharply to the left and will go into elections . . . with a manifesto largely dictated by the country's Communist party. . . .
>
> Under Jacob Zuma, its new leader, it has quietly adopted a radical platform of social policies.[5]
>
> — *The Times* (U.K.), 25 January 2009

Most troubling is the fact that South Africa seems no longer content with minding its own business. Since 2002, it has been pursuing a wide-sweeping "plan for African rebirth" among its various neighbors. Some of those "neighbors" are farther away than others. Within the quite distant DRC, it was Nelson Mandela who finally convinced Laurent Kabila and all intervening nations to sign the 1999 peace accord.[6] China had already been sending more than just peacekeepers to the DRC; it also had "election observers" there.[7] Then South Africa began to combine its own peacekeeping role with that of election "training" for the DRC's outlying villages. According to Human Rights Watch, there are major problems with such an approach to voting verification. "The institutions that are organizing the elections are politicized" themselves.[8]

China's Evolving Methodology

The PRC has always tried to help African nations with their ways of governance. Then, it discovered how to do so more subtly than the voter intimidation that took the place of Red-Guard revolt. Before each election, left-leaning candidates would get campaign funding of unspecified origin.[9] If there were already a Socialist party in power, it received regime-saving loans,[10] presidential palaces,[11] and inter-agency contact teams from the CPC.[12]

So, China's "new" formula for subjugating the Dark Continent is simply a less direct way of "Communizing" governments while siphoning off their wealth. There is no more need for armed overthrows, because the PRC has created regimes that feel obligated to cooperate. The whole process is so benign and gradual that the West doesn't notice the damage.

Perhaps, Africa was to be the test site for an "ally-generating" formula that could be applied anywhere in the world, even to a longtime nemesis—like America herself. Because the leader of the "Free World" would normally base his or her decisions on capitalistic or democratic mores, this new formula for PRC expansion would appear to obey both types.

The Likely Details of This New *Modus Operandi*

With Muslim extremism as a diversion, China has become far more sophisticated in its countering of U.S. "hegemony" worldwide. Only after economic and political manipulation have failed will it resort to organized violence. Through the teachings of Sun Tzu, it has learned how to add new victims to its fold of "favored nations" without ever evoking any Western ire. Because of the separation of responsibilities within the U.S. government, the PRC has only to employ some form off non-martial warfare to achieve its goals.[13] Currently at China's disposal are the following obscure instruments for Communist expansion: (1) non-traceable funding from the local trafficking in narcotics; (2) political advisers from regional proxies; and (3) a worldwide network of state-owned corporations. For the really tough objectives in its lengthening "String of Pearls," it can always resort to societal destabilization. Normally, China's so-called national assistance wreaks enough of its own havoc. One has only to study Zimbabwe (formerly Rhodesia) to see what can happen to a country that has been befriended by the PRC. Its remaining population may have been better off under Apartheid.

The most common PRC scenario is first to flood a country with enough low-priced manufactured goods to run its local industries out of business. As its overall economy is ruined, that country becomes more dependent on Chinese aid (and its political price). Then comes a massive flow of immigrants, mostly of the day laborer, shop owner, and factory worker variety. All must live where Beijing directs, so most probably had their long moves to the Dark Continent subsidized. To make ends meet, many may then collect "sales-worthy" information for the local contacts of Chinese agencies.

Among those thousands of "extra-alert" immigrants have undoubtedly been intelligence agents and community organizers. In essence, the economic and political foundations of all targeted nations are being gradually altered at the neighborhood and village level. The eventual result will be a more PRC-like central government—one fully supportive of Chinese foreign policy.

China can now combine a wide range of non-lethal strategies for what will still amount to a political end game. Most intriguing are the excuses for first entering the country. The PRC sent large numbers of uniformed military personnel to Pakistani-occupied Kashmir following a 2010 flood and avalanche that damaged the Karakoram Highway. This is the strategically vital road that carries Iranian oil back to China.[14] While ostensibly providing security to Chinese construction crews, those PLA soldiers may never have left. Now China is said to have *de-facto* control over what was formerly the Pakistani-governed territory of Gilgit-Baltistan.[15] Of course, there may also have been some form of remuneration. In 1963, China

Figure 7.1: There Are Leopards from Asia Too
(Source: Corel Gallery Clipart, Animal Totem "04C079.")

openly "bought" the Trans-Karakoram Tract (of Indian-claimed territory) from Pakistan.[16] So, not only disaster relief, but also outright purchase must be considered two of China's "softer" forms of invasion. (See Figure 7.1.)

In 2000, China also deployed thousands of unformed troops to Sudan to protect a new pipeline it was building from the war-torn central portion of the country to Port Sudan.[17] So, at some point, Chinese troops (not necessarily in uniform) may also be present at the TANZAM or Benguela railways, China's new road into the northeastern DRC, or even some of the Chinese-owned mining operations.

Less Obvious Particulars of the New Method

Around China's immediate periphery, Chinese aid workers have been actively watching for Western counterparts to try to influence local politics. That's probably because all have been themselves tasked with a secondary mission of creating or expanding local Communist cadres.

To discredit an incumbent regime, the Chinese have also been known to intentionally rile up its population. While local demonstrations used to be their favorite way, now there is evidence of something much more insidious. Along with any drug deluge would come a huge increase in violent crime. This would in turn distract government agencies from properly safeguarding against political improprieties.

Last, but not least, is actual election tampering. Of all the South American countries now sporting leftist regimes, many had been visited by political advisers from Cuba.[18] Just because China's government is totalitarian does not mean its operatives haven't discovered how to win a democratic election. Mostly required is money. Right before the first Zimbabwe elections in 1980, there was a rumor intentionally spread that the ballot boxes would later reveal how each villager had voted.[19] Fearing retribution, many cast their ballots for the Communist candidate. And then, there is the little matter of campaign funding from undisclosed sources. How much advertising, rides to the polls, and vote buying might be possible from the political party with access to local drug-trafficking revenue?

China's "End Game"

The PRC has tried hard to make its subjugation of Africa seem to follow all the Western standards of democracy and free enterprise. Nor does any "thus modified" government appear to be pro-Communist. Ethiopia provides an example of just how obscure such a process can be. To most American researchers, Ethiopia is nothing more than a traditional U.S. ally. A closer look reveals a country that is only a parliamentary democracy on paper. In actuality, the Ethiopian People's Revolutionary Democratic Front (EPRDF) controls all but a handful of seats in the 547-member parliament, and thus dictates who ends up as president and prime minister. This long-time ruling party of Ethiopia still suppresses political dissent with Red-Guard-like beatings.[20] But, because of Ethiopia's Soviet background, it has seldom been associated with China. Yet, its current government may be just as friendly with Beijing as those in southern Africa.

The similarities in political situation between Ethiopia and South Africa are striking. They may offer a preview of what awaits all nations in Africa. While appearing to be federal republics and parliamentary democracies, they will become carefully controlled Socialist states. All the while, the American people will be none the wiser to their own government's loss of leverage in the region.

And Now On to the Research of More Recent Events

Within this framework of an updated *modus operandi,* one can now piece together tiny bits of open-source evidence to try to flesh out China's current take-over strategies for Africa. Most interesting will be any direct cooperation with Islamists, funding of local initiatives through drug proceeds, and intentional destabilization of targeted countries. With politicization as the ultimate goal, all such strategies must appear to be something other than what they actually are—"death by a thousand razor cuts."

> By June 2012, China had invested 45 billion dollars in Africa, including over 15 billion dollars of direct investment. Meanwhile, over 2,000 Chinese companies are operating in 50 African countries.[21]
>
> — *Xinhua News,* 29 March 2013

Any study of Dark Continent exploitation by foreign elements must necessarily address all the Salafists from the Middle East. With their support, local Muslim radicals have been spreading discord throughout Africa's northern half for quite a while.

Part Three

Caliphate Formation

"It is possible to live in peace." — Mahatma Gandhi

(Source: Mahatma Gandhi, as quotes at www.wagingpeace.org.)

African Parts of Former Muslim Empire

- Which African nations were part of old Islamic Empire?
- Where are new caliphates now forming?

African areas of old Muslim Empire were near a sea or river.

(Source: FM 90-3 [1982], p. 2-5)

The Original Muslim Empire

What has become known as the "Ancient Muslim Empire" was—during much of its existence—really just a series of interconnecting kingdoms. Initially at its center was the caliphate of the official successors to the Prophet Muhammad (Abu Bakr, Umar I, Uthman, and Ali), with its capital at Damascus. The rule of these first four caliphs would spread from the Middle East to Africa during a "golden age of pure Islam." Then began a shift in power over their vast Empire and its various parts to other dynasties. By 661, Mua'wiyah I—a member of Uthman's Umayyad clan—had wrested

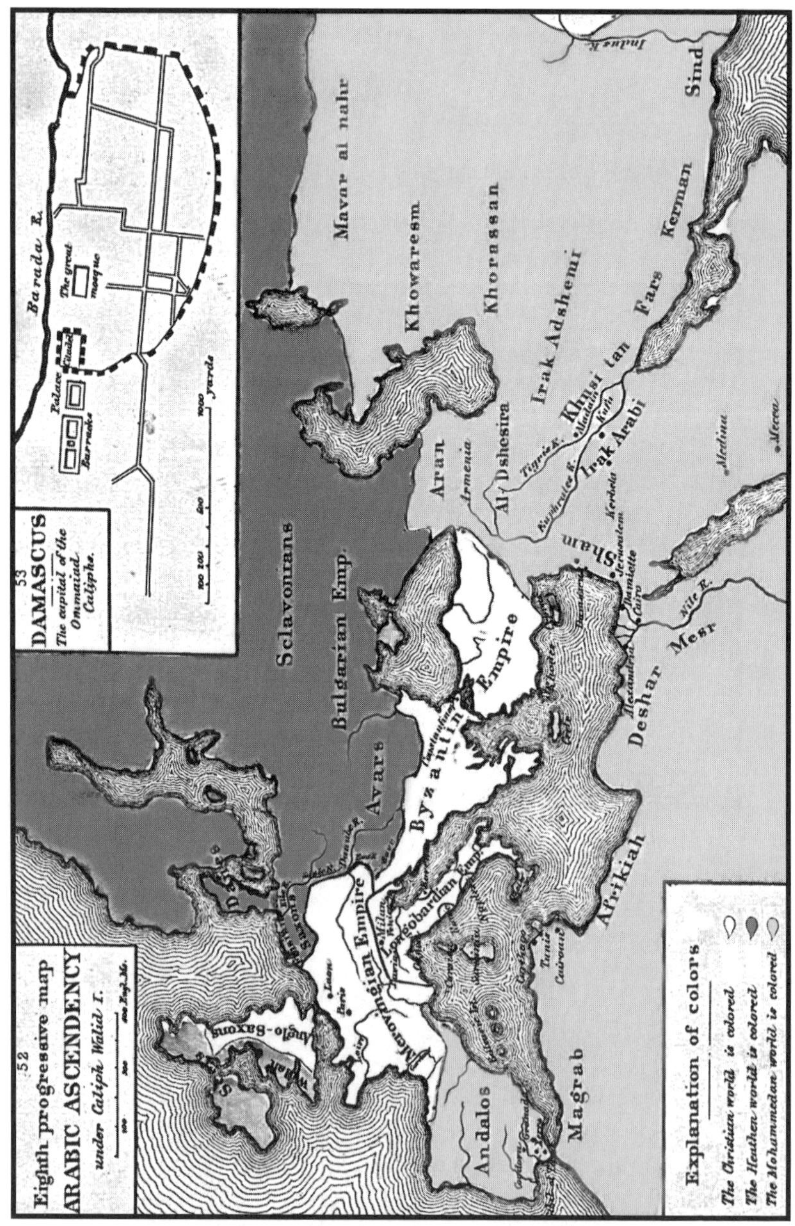

Map 8.1: The Ancient Muslim Empire

(Source: Courtesy of General Libraries, University of Texas at Austin, from their website for map designator "arabic—ascendency 1884.jpg")

Figure 8.1: What May Be Muslim Empire Ruins at Samarra
(Source: DA Pam 550-31 [1990], coverart)

control of the original caliphate from Ali. (Ali would subsequently become the first Shiite Imam.) Mua'wiyah's reign would mark the beginning of the "Umayyad Caliphate" that would run the Empire until 750. (See Map 8.1.) Then began a complicated struggle for dominion across its entire expanse.[1]

Which Dark Continent Areas Became Part of That Empire?

Generally speaking, everything north and east of the Sahara Desert became part of the "Muslim Empire" that thrived between 636 and 1099. In reality, only those African areas that lay along the lower Nile River, upper Red Sea, and Mediterranean came under full Arab control. That Arab conquest had begun four years after the death of Muhammad and lasted more than four centuries. Caliphs first ruled the entire Empire from Damascus, then Baghdad (or Samarra), and finally Egypt.[2] (See Figure 8.1.)

Figure 8.2: The "Light" of Islam Had Spread across Africa
(Source: Wikipedia Encyclopedia, s.v. "Abbasid Caliphate," public-domain image from Cassim by Maxfield Parrish [1909] with designator "Ali-Baba.jpg")

Umar (634-644) continued the wars of occupation that had been started by the first caliph, Abu Bakr (Muhammad's father-in-law). Heading westward into Egypt, Umar had conquered it by 642. Then, under Uthman (644-656), this "foreign invasion" continued into Libya.[3] Finally, under the (Sunni) Umayyad Caliphate (661-750), Arab armies moved on to what is now Tunisia, Algeria, and Morocco.[4] At no time did this African part of the Muslim Empire extend very far down into what is now Sudan, Chad, Niger, Mali, Mauritania, or Western Sahara. (Look again at Map 8.1, and then see Figures 8.2 and 8.3.) Next to run this expanded Empire were the Sunni Abbasids.

Egypt

After assuming authority over the Muslim Empire from the Umayyads around 750, the Abbasids moved its capital to Baghdad. Some 200 years passed, and then—within Egypt—Abbasid rule was interrupted when Shiite Fatimids took over the country. (Their Shia identity dated back to the followers of fourth Sunni

Figure 8.3: Empire Had Followed Upper Red Sea Shoreline

(Source: Wikipedia Encyclopedia, s.v. "Saladin," public-domain image from "The Holy Land . . .," from drawings by David Roberts [1845] with designator "Isle of Graia3.jpg")

caliph Ali.) Egypt soon became the center of a powerful kingdom that, by the end of the tenth century, still included most of coastal North Africa.

At first, the Fatimids were tolerant of non-Muslims. Then, the third Fatimid caliph, al-Hakim (996–1020), departed from this policy of tolerance during the second half of his reign. Due to this and other reasons, the Fatimid dynasty began to weaken at the end of the 11th century. With its end, "orthodox" (Sunni) Islam once again became the official religion of Egypt; and Saladin—the famous victor over the Crusaders—its leader.[5] Unfortunately, much of the kingdom's control west of Egypt had already been ceded to others.[6]

Saladin and his successors would renew the discriminatory decrees against non-Muslims, but neither actively persecuted them. Those successors, the Sunni Ayyubids, would then rule Egypt until 1250.[7]

In 1261, following the destruction of Baghdad by the Mongols, the Abbasid line of rulers recentered their dwindling kingdom around the now Mamluk capital of Cairo. The Mamluks had been an army of largely Turkish composition formed by the Abbasids to defend their territory.[8] Under the Ayyubids, a few Mamluk generals had amassed considerable power in Egypt. They then used that power to reinstall the Abbasid dynasty that was to rule that region from 1261 to 1511. Their rule was finally displaced by the Sunni Ottomans.[9]

Libya

As far back as the 8th Century, the Abbasid rulers of the Muslim Empire had been forced to cede much of their authority over Maghreb (the Atlas Mountains and coastal plains of Morocco, Algeria, Tunisia, and Libya) to their predecessor—the Umayyads. Those same Umayyads were then to create their own separate caliphate in Spain.[10]

Tunisia

The 8th Century Abbasids had also given up control over Ifriqiya (Tunisia and eastern Algeria) to the Aghlabids.[11] Some 11 Aghlabid emirs were to rule this area from 800 to 909. After breaking a rebellion of Arab soldiers, Ziyadat Allah I (817–838) sent them to conquer Sicily, which would remain in Arab hands for two centuries.[12] Long before the birth of Jesus, Tunisia had been the center of Phoenician expansion into the Western Mediterranean. What was once ancient Carthage is now a suburb of Tunis.

Morocco

By the end of the 8th Century, the Abbasids had also handed over the Berber part of Morocco to the Idrisids.[13] The Idrisid dynasty was eventually crushed between the Umayyad powers in Cordoba and the Fatimid leaders in Cairo. The last of the Idrisid rulers was subsequently killed while a prisoner of the Umayyads in 985.[14]

Ancient Muslim Empire's Overall Impact on the Region

That part of North Africa that abuts the Mediterranean and northern Red Sea would—from the time of the Muslim Empire—be traditionally Sunni. Egypt had been ruled by Shiites for a while during the Empire period, but its army had restored Sunni dominance. Because of the desolate terrain and Nile River cataracts between Egypt and Sudan, these two neighboring countries would never share a mutual heritage. Nor would Egyptian developments have much affect on the lands beyond Sudan—Eritrea, Djibouti, Ethiopia, and Somalia.

This geographical barrier would later come into play when the anti-Western Muslim Brotherhood was born in Egypt around 1928, became outlawed there, but then took over Sudan's politics in the late 1980's.[15] Soon, *al-Qaeda's* top leaders were in Sudan helping that country to foment Islamist revolt throughout North Africa. While *al-Qaeda* was eventually evicted from Sudan around 1996, many of its military trainers may have ended up in Somalia. Ethiopia and its former territory of Eritrea went to war in 1998. But, no attempt at a Muslim state in Somalia or Eritrea can be to re-acquire Empire status.

Salafist Interest in Northeastern Africa

- Has a new Muslim Empire been already attempted?
- In which country was it centered?

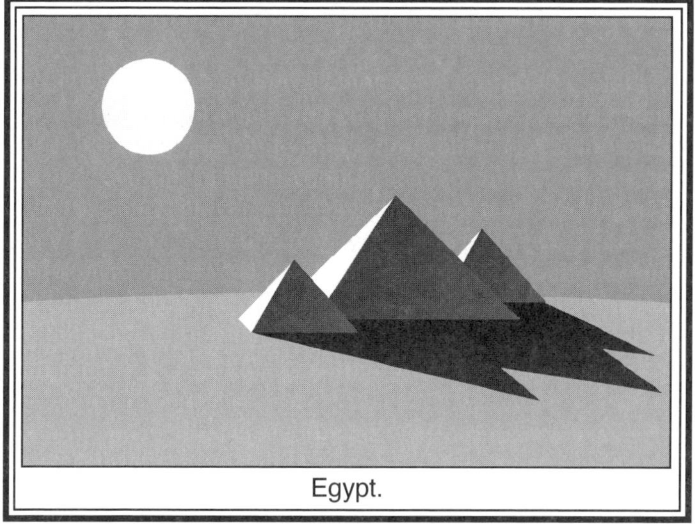

Egypt.

(Source: Corel Gallery, Corel Landmarks #26A017)

Only within Egypt Could Former Empire Be Reestablished

Several events in Cairo over the years have likely signaled someone's intention to reestablish the African part of the Ancient Muslim Empire. When the anti-Western Muslim Brotherhood was born near there in 1928, its leaders undoubtedly had that in mind. Their outlook was fundamentalist Sunni *wahhabist*. *Wahhabism* claims to purify and restore the original form of Islam. As a strictly Sunni movement, the Muslim Brotherhood could have reinstated the former caliphate.[1] But, throughout most of its existence, the Muslim Brotherhood has been banned from Egyptian politics.

Figure 9.1: Egyptian Paratrooper
(Source: Courtesy of Orion Books, from *World Army Uniforms since 1939*, © 1975, 1980, 1981, 1983 by Blandford Press Ltd., Part II, Plate 110)

Only a Fleeting Moment of Success in Cairo

From 2012 to 2013, the Muslim Brotherhood did finally manage to control Egypt by way of its presidential elections. Only through that country's military establishment was the more pro-Western *status quo* finally restored. (See Figure 9.1.)

More Opportunity in Sudan

Prior to this brief voting victory in Egypt, most of the Muslim Brotherhood's political power had been in Sudan. Though never part of the Ancient Muslim Empire, that country had made a concerted effort in the late 20th Century to spread fundamentalist Islam throughout the region.[2] Whether it ever intended a Sunni caliphate is not clear, because of its government leaders' *salafist* tendency to cooperate with fundamentalist Shiites (like those from

Iran and Lebanese *Hezbollah).* Still, from late 1991 to 1996, Sudan had played host to *al-Qaeda's* organizational hierarchy. Therefore, all the important prerequisites for a Sunni caliphate had been in place.

It was through an alliance of militant organizations in the 1990's that Khartoum had tried to destabilize Eritrea,[3] Algeria,[4] Egypt, and Tunisia.[5] This alliance went by a number of names. The first and most recognizable was the Popular Arab and Islamic Conference (PAIC). The last was the INF (Islamic National Front).[6] Its similarity in title to Sudan's ruling-party—the National Islamic Front (NIF)—has proven confusing to many. All that must now be remembered is that PAIC answered to the NIF, and not the other way around.[7]

The NIF had initially arisen out of the Sudanese chapter of the Muslim Brotherhood. That chapter's head, Hassan al-Turabi, became NIF's official founder. While initially out of favor with the Nimeiri regime, he was named its attorney general in 1977 as a conciliatory gesture. From that office, al-Turabi helped other Brotherhood members to acquire positions of economic and political influence. Then, he again fell from official grace. "In 1989, a military coup brought to power a regime that was . . . a tool of the NIF."[8]

Though still quite suitable for Sunni caliphate formation, Sudan shows no such inclination of late. Its former *al-Qaeda* residents have moved on to other places—most notably Somalia.[9] After showing some expansionary interest in neighboring Chad,[10] Sudan has been mostly preoccupied with the unrest in its own Darfur and southern regions. No one knows to what extent China may have discouraged Khartoum's dream of a caliphate. Only clear is that Sudan has for quite some time functioned as a veritable Chinese surrogate. Along with several formerly Communist nations, Sudan militarily intervened in the DRC between 1998 and 2002.[11] Then, in 2000, it allowed thousands of Communist Chinese troops—with no U.N. affiliation—onto its own soil.[12] Its army still receives arms (and probably training) from the PRC. Additionally, it has experienced a massive influx of Chinese immigrants.[13]

Sudan's Next-Door Neighbor to the West

Somewhat surprisingly, it is another adjacent nation—Chad—

that possesses one of the best equipped and most active armies in North Africa. That army has recently taken part in two foreign operations—one in the Central African Republic (CAR) and the other in Mali.[14] Alongside Sudan, Chad had also militarily intervened in the DRC between 1998 and 2002.[15] Thus, it has always had some affiliation with the Communist camp. Like Sudan, it has gotten military equipment and training from the PRC.[16] But then, Chad now produces more oil than both of the Sudans put together. That makes it just as appealing to China.

Unlike Sudan and Chad, the really big oil producers—Libya and Algeria—were part of the Ancient Muslim Empire. (Look back at Table 1.1.) Their internal struggles will be discussed in the next chapter.

New Caliphates Elsewhere in North Africa

Besides *al-Shabaab* in Somalia, the are other *al-Qaeda* affiliates in the region: (1) EIJM in Eritrea; and (2) *Gama'at al-Islamiya* in Egypt.[17] Despite an ongoing string of armed-militant attacks on Egyptian forces in the Sinai Peninsula since the ouster of the Muslim Brotherhood president, Egypt seems unlikely to host a new caliphate. *Ansar Beit al Maqdis,* an affiliate of the Islamic State of Iraq and Syria (ISIS), has been taking the credit for these Sinai incursions.[18]

There have been so many attacks by *al-Qaeda* affiliates in Kenya and Tanzania, that one might expect some kind of joint effort between *al-Shabaab* and *al-Qaeda* in the Arabian Peninsula (AQAP) to establish a continental-boundary-spanning Islamic state. Certain advantages would accrue from controlling both sides of the Suez Canal entrance. Perhaps Osama bin Laden had bigger plans for Somalia than was previously thought. In May 2014, the *al-Shabaab*-occupied area of Somalia was being called the "Islamic Emirate of Somalia." (Look back at Map 1.5 more closely.)

> There has been far more al-Qaeda activity in East Africa and the Horn [of Africa] than in any other part of sub-Saharan [region]. . . .
>
> Al-Qaeda cells almost certainly exist today in all the countries of East Africa and . . . the al-Qaeda threat may well be increasing. . . . The recent defeat of the Islamic Courts

in Somalia [a rival administration] may have disrupted the plans of the jihadists . . . , but . . . [here] political stability is ephemeral. . . . This is a time to pursue long-term solutions to root [out] causes rather than . . . short-term tactical victories.[19]

— *Horn Affairs,* 2013

The Red Sea and Gulf of Aden Are Not Very Wide

At some point, other events in tiny Yemen—at the western end

Map 9.1: Modern-Day Islamists May Be Interested in Suez
(Source: Courtesy of General Libraries, University of Texas at Austin, from their website for map designator "n_africa_mid_east_pol_95.jpg")

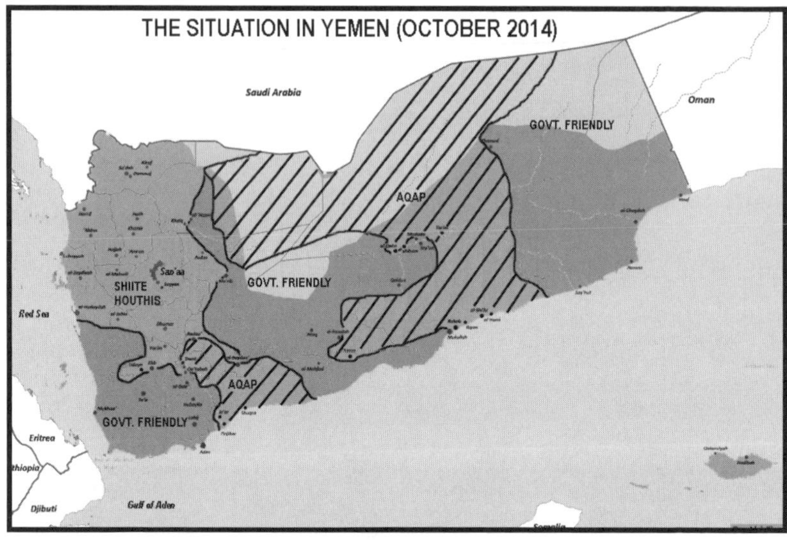

Map 9.2: Shiite Houthi Rebels Gaining Ground
(Source: General Libraries, Univ. of Texas at Austin, from their website, based on map designator "https://archicivilians.files.wordpress.com/2014/10/yemeni-map1.png")

of the Arabian Peninsula—may affect those in Eritrea or Somalia. After all, those two nations are only 30 and 90 miles away from Yemen, respectively. (See Map 9.1.) Since September 2014, Yemen's capital of Sanaa has been under the control of Shiite Houthi rebels. (See Map 9.2.) On 22 January 2015, its president, cabinet, and prime minister became so embattled that they reportedly abdicated their positions.[20] None of this would make much difference to the Dark Continent, if the Houthi rebels had not been trying to reestablish a former Shiite imamate.

The northern Houthis are not particularly fond of the eastern AQAP faction that has done so many bad things to America. Yet, examples abound of cooperation between fundamentalist Sunnis and Shiites in other parts of the Middle East. To make matters worse, the Iranian Crescent now extends all the way from Iraq to Suez—with Alawites (a Shiite offshoot) still in control of Syria, *Hezbollah* now running Lebanon,[21] and a *Hezbollah*-supported *Hamas* currently governing Gaza.[22] Thus, Iran's interest in proxies on both sides of the southern approaches to the Suez Canal might be considerable.

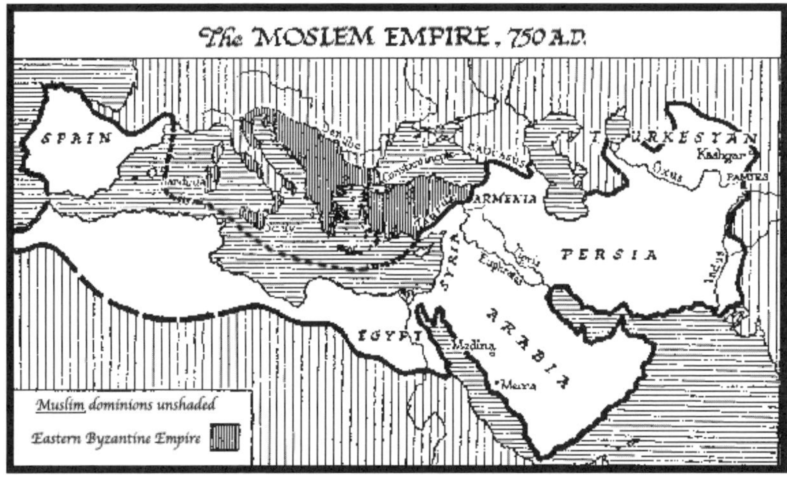

Map 9.3: The Ancient Muslim Empire at Its Largest
(Source: Courtesy of fordam.edu/halsall, at Medieval Sourcebook, from H.G. Wells, *A Short History of the World* (London: 1922), map designator "islam2map.tif")

Any such plan would necessarily involve a very friendly Eritrea. Eritrea has too small a Shiite population to ever willingly be part of an imamate, so the necessary governmental approval would have to be achieved through some means other than popular consent.

Iran Helping to Restore Yemen's Former Imamate

In the early 1960's, Egyptian-backed Yemeni army officers terminated that country's 1,000-year Shia imamate to establish the modern Yemeni republic. Prior to that imamate, this area had been part of the Ancient Muslim Empire with its capital in Syria and Iraq.[23] (See Map 9.3.)

When Republican troops seized Sanaa, the Imam fled to Yemen's northern mountains (around Sadda) to conduct a counteroffensive. Iran then began to support the Saada rebels, though Yemen's Zaydi Shias are doctrinally different from Iran's Twelver Shias. On occasion, these Saada rebels may have also accepted support from Lebanese *Hezbollah* and *al-Qaeda*. There's an easy explanation for the apparent dichotomy in allegiance. Lying directly along the ancient trade route from Asia to Africa, this region has long played host to drug smugglers.[24] (See Map 9.4.) Criminal enterprises generally pay little attention to religious differences.

Lebanese *Hezbollah's* Involvement

In February 2010, one of America's best respected nongovernmental intelligence sources announced that *Hezbollah* was withdrawing its 400-man contingent from Northern Yemen in response to an IRGC directive. That contingent's 160 casualties implied direct contact with the Saudis along the Yemeni border,[25] possibly while an assault battalion. During *Hezbollah's* early years in Lebanon, it would occasionally conduct an attack for Palestinian proxies to emulate. Yet, only one thing is certain, *Hezbollah* personnel had been directly involved in the Yemeni fighting.

> *Hezbollah* sources have told STRATFOR that they have troops actively engaged in combat in Yemen.[26]
> – *STRATFOR Weekly,* 3 February 2010

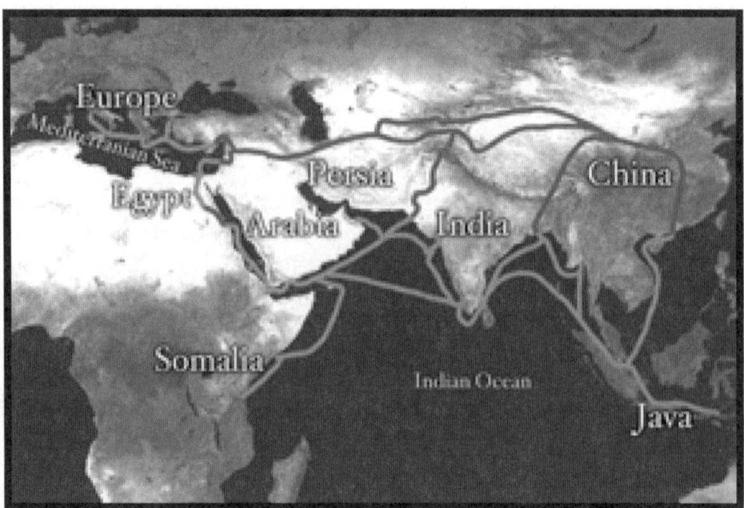

Map 9.4: Ancient "Silk Route" through Yemen and Somalia
(Source: Wikipedia.org, s.v. "Somalia," under provisions of GNU Free Documentation License, map designator "Silk_route.jpg," from NASA/Goddard Space Flight Center)

At the time, any doubt as to *Hezbollah's* combat presence in Yemen could be quickly dispelled by viewing its new Turkish website. Sporting a *Hezbollah* flag on the main page, what may have been an *Islami Davet* supplement contained images of *Hezbollah* fighters with Houthi rebels.[27] Whether or not the Yemeni *"Baseej"* were being led by *Hezbollah* personnel, they were almost certainly being trained by them. The following quote reveals where—on the African continent—much of that training may have taken place.

> Yemen's state-controlled press claims Houthi rebels have been trained in an Iranian-run camp across the Red Sea in Eritrea. Yemen's president . . . says members of Lebanon's Iran-backed *Hezbullah* militia are teaching them.[28]
>
> — *The Economist,* 19 November 2009

In 2009, the Yemeni army launched an offensive against the Shia rebels in Yemen's northern Sa'ada Province. Yet, even after a shaky cease-fire between the two in January 2010,[29] the rebels' zone of control still extended nearly to the Yemeni capita of Sanaa. (See Map 9.5.)

Yemen Actually Had Three Rebellions in Progress

When considered together, Maps 9.2 and 9.5 reveal another interesting development in Yemen. The long-time Marxist secessionists and AQAP seem now to be allied.

After populist demonstrations unseated the autocratic leaders of Tunisia and Egypt in early 2011, others occurred in Yemen.[30] Within Yemen, however, it was far from clear which of the three anti-government factions was mostly to blame. On 17 February 2011, two people were killed during riots in the southern port city of Aden.[31] Aden just happens to be at the center of Yemen's Marxist Secessionist region. (See Map 9.5.)

Prior to 1990, the Republic of Yemen had been in the north, whereas only the People's Democratic Republic of Yemen (PDRY or "South Yemen") had been in the south and bordering on the Gulf of Aden. The PDRY was a Marxist State with close ties to all Communist powers at the time. It extended from the area's only major port—Aden—all the way to the Omani border. With little

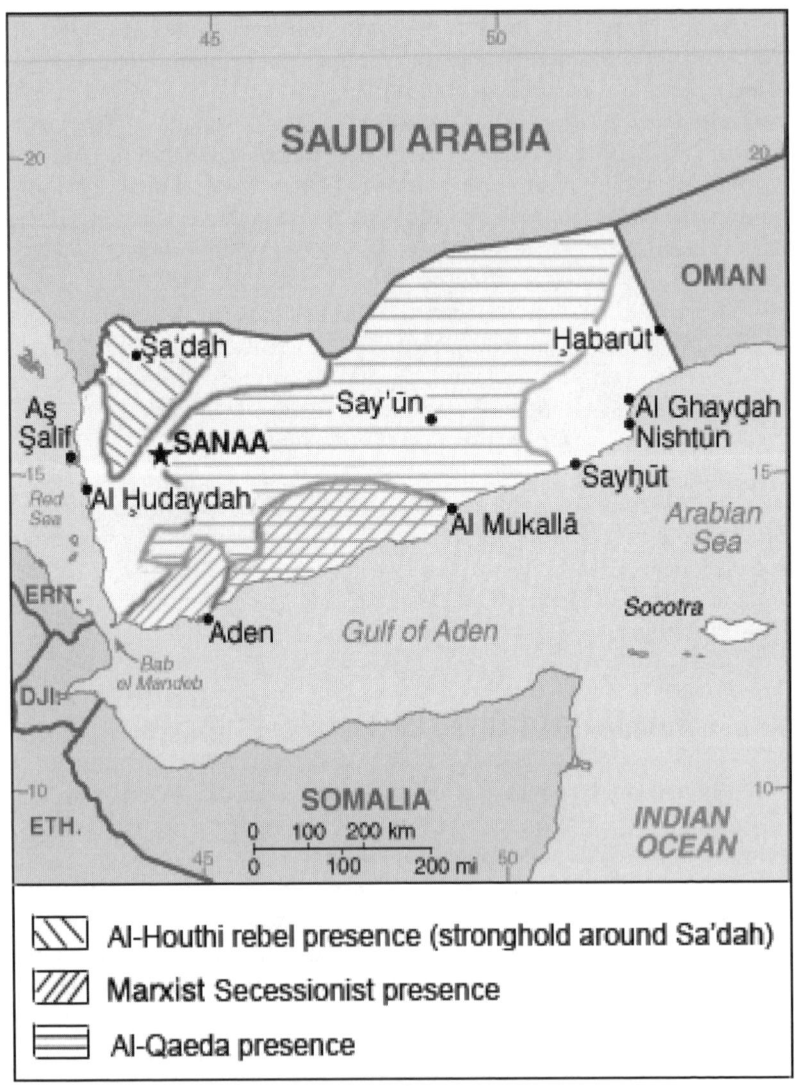

Map 9.5: Yemen's Various Factional Areas in May 2010
(Source: Map based on "Yemen Conflict Map," by Zimmerman, Frist, & Harnisch, CriticalThreats.org, 12 May 2010; Univ. of Texas at Austin map "yemen_sm_2010.gif")

industrial or agricultural income,[32] it may have welcomed gratuities from the smuggling that regularly occurred along its portion of the ancient trade route between Asia and Africa. After the PDRY was incorporated into Yemen in 1990, its Socialist elements remained both restive and cash deprived. The *al-Qaeda*-supported eastern Sunni tribes had similar problems.

As the Sunni extremists and Marxists seem now to be cooperating, they may both want enough autonomy to monitor all coastal trade. There's a certain Asian nation that would feel right at home in this Marxist environment. It would like nothing better than a loosely governed Yemen, like in the nations of the African Sahel. If it were trafficking in Afghan opiates bound for America, it would also want an *al-Qaeda* affiliate doing the smuggling (as do so in the Sahel). A Shiite imamate in the area would be of little hindrance to *al-Qaeda,* as long as that imamate didn't control the entire Yemeni coast. It might even act as a deterrent to Western interference.

Iran's Interest in the Dark Continent

Possibly to recruit *Baseej* soldiery for its proxy wars in Iraq, the Levant, and Yemen, the IRGC and its Lebanese prodigy—*Hezbollah*—have remained active in various parts of northern Africa, particularly Sudan. Any extension of a Shiite Yemeni imamate onto the Horn of Africa would be highly improbable, however. While Eritrea's dictatorial regime has allowed Iran to train such *Baseej* on its soil and maintain a military presence in the port city of Assab,[33] it is not a Muslim theocracy. In fact, over half of its population are Christian. The only other place for an African extension of a Yemeni Shiite imamate would be Somalia, and Sunni *al-Qaeda* has already spoken for most of that country.

Through funding and military trainers to Sudan, Iran had been promoting Islamist uprisings throughout oil-and-mineral-rich East Africa for years—most notably, Kenya, Uganda, Tanzania, Somalia, and Ethiopia.[34] Ayatollah Khomeini had called for a global revolution by both Shiites and Sunnis in 1979.[35] "By early 1995, Iranian funding [had] enabled the . . . [Sudanese NIF] and *al-Qaeda* to establish twenty-three training camps [for rebels of various nations] throughout Sudan." At some of the *al-Qaeda* camps were *Hezbollah* and IRCG trainers.[36] Many of these camps stayed open after *al-Qaeda* left Sudan in 1996.[37]

The government of Sudan has since become a revolutionary "republic," under much the same model as Tehran or Beijing before it. The PDF is now Sudan's parallel army and trusted power base.[38] In some ways, the role of the PDF inside Sudan mirrors that of the IRGC within Iranian borders.[39]

Yet, Iran has not been operating unilaterally in the region. "The military co-operation of the Muslim Brotherhood and *Hezbullah* [go] back to the 1980's." Their "closeness" has been confirmed by Sheikh Bilal, an aide to *Hezbollah's* long-time leader, Hassan Nasrallah.[40] To support Iran's revolutionary ambitions in Iraq and elsewhere, the Muslim Brotherhood may still be recruiting *jihadists*—of both Muslim persuasions—all across North Africa.

How Iran's Foreign Policy Is Administered

There are small detachments of IRGC's vaunted Quds Force throughout Africa's northern half. Some may be gathering intelligence, while others are almost certainly promoting local revolution.[41]

> On October 27, 2008, the deputy commander of the Basij [or Baseej] became the first top Guard leader to publicly acknowledge that Iran supplies weapons (and possibly advice) to "liberation armies."[42]
>
> — Congressional Research, 26 October 2010

> There are [Quds Force] Directorates for . . . Egypt, Tunisia, Algeria, Sudan, and Morocco.[43]
>
> —Ctr. for Strat. & Internat. Studies, August 2007

Besides promoting more *sharia* law in Africa, Iran also has an interest in its natural resources. Tanzanian officials intercepted a huge shipment of smuggled uranium 238 in the autumn of 2005. Bound for smelting in Kazakhstan and delivery to Bandar Abbas (in Iran), this weapons-grade ore had come from the Shinkolobwe mine of the DRC's Katanga Province.[44] Iran's nuclear ambitions may still be linked to some of that area's rebel activity.

Hezbollah's presence in West Africa derives from a different set of motives. It has largely to do with badly needed funding from a long-time cocaine conduit from Colombia to Europe.

10 Islamist Initiatives in Northwest Africa

- Whatever happend to Libya after Gadhafi's demise?
- To what extent are al-Qaeda affiliates involved?

Western side of the mighty Sahara.

(Source: FM 90-3 (1982), p. 2-5)

Libya's Unfolding Nightmare

On 20 January 2015, Americans in Libya were warned by the U.S. State Department to leave.[1] (See Map 10.1.) One week later, a luxury hotel in Tripoli was assaulted by gunmen wearing explosive vests after a car bomb detonated in its parking lot. An initially *Hezbollah* (and then *al-Qaeda)* way of attacking had finally reached northwestern Africa. While popular with foreigners, this hotel also housed Omar al-Hassi—prime minister of Tripoli's new rival government. When local supporters of ISIS took credit for the attack, inveterate Libya watchers were left scratching their heads. Such

Map 10.1: Libya

(Source: Courtesy of General Libraries, University of Texas at Austin, from their website for map designator "libya_sm_2014.gif")

a thing was certainly possible, because a militant group in Derna (a coastal town between Benghazi and Tobruk) had been publicly declaring allegiance to Abu Bakr al-Baghdadi since October 2014. But why would ISIS endanger the leader of an already Islamist regime? Perhaps, it was to warn him against consorting with too many Western businessmen. In mid-February, the same ISIS affiliate that had attacked the hotel beheaded 21 Coptic Christians from Egypt on a beach near Tripoli, thereby invoking Egyptian air strikes against Derna.[2]

What Had Come of the Air War to Oust Gadhafi?

By early 2011, the Arab Spring had spread to Libya. Moammar Gadhafi's brutal crackdown on protesters triggered a civil war that prompted U.N. air and naval intervention on behalf of the rebels. After months of seesaw fighting, the Gadhafi regime was finally replaced by a transitional government. Within a year, Libyans had elected their first "General National

Congress" (GNC). It, in turn, installed Ali Zeidan as prime minister. Then, Abdullah al-Thani was assigned to the post on 14 March 2014. Two months later, a former Libyan general who had lived in the U.S. for many years came mysteriously onto the scene. His name was Khalifa Hiftar. Claiming to be opposed to all fundamentalist militants, he seized Tripoli, suspended the GNC, and launched a drive to push all extremists from Benghazi. He believed the Muslim Brotherhood had been exercising too much control over the GNC. Who subsequently functioned as prime minister is not completely clear. It could have been Ahmed Maiteeq, or a temporarily retained al-Thani. In August 2014, an Islamist-backed force launched Operation Libya Dawn to "liberate" the capital from Hiftar's control. After forcing al-Thani to flee to a small city near the Egyptian border, it restored the GNC. As Tripoli's newest occupiers were setting up their own assembly and cabinet, the internationally recognized parliament (or House of Representatives)—that had been elected to replace the GNC during Hiftar's tenure—moved to Tobruk at Libya's eastern end for safety.[3]

Meanwhile in Tripoli, Omar al-Hassi became prime minister of the replacement—and decidedly Islamist—regime. Though he and Tripoli's other self-proclaimed rulers had never been recognized by the U.N., they took over ministries, oil facilities, airports, and much of the western and central portions of the country.[4] Since the former (Hiftar-installed) administration had been fighting Islamist factions in Benghazi, most of the oil-rich eastern part of Libya may still be under its (and al-Thani's) control. Yet, Islamist brigades continue to battle Hiftar-friendly units around Benghazi.

That makes two competing governments (one still under duress) within what is starting to look very much like a "failed state." No one really knows to what extent, if any, *Ansar al-Sharia* (the U.S. consulate attack suspect) is linked with the new Tripoli rulers. On the surface, there is no affiliation. Though *Ansar al-Sharia* is composed of former rebels from several east-Libyan militias *(Abu Obayda bin al-Jarah,* the Malik, and 17 February Brigades), it still has its roots in Tunisia. That's the tiny nation just to the west of Tripoli. (Look at Map 10.1 again.) Within Libya, *Ansar al-Shariah* operates mostly around Benghazi and denies any presence elsewhere. Operation Libya Dawn had been launched by rebels from Misrata and Islamists of the "Libya Revolutionary Operation's Room" (LROR). At one time, the LROR had been officially tasked by the GNC with protecting Tripoli. It was stripped of that mission after some of its members kidnapped Prime Minister Zeidan in October 2013. A branch of the LROR had also been sent to Benghazi to deal with that city's deteriorating security. Then in August 2014, the LROR returned to Tripoli as a part of Operation Libya Dawn.[5]

Before that Arab Spring, there had been only two opposition groups in western Libya—"Libyan Islamic Fighting Group (LIFG)" and the Muslim Brotherhood. The LIFG was an alleged *al-Qaeda* affiliate that sought to establish an Islamic State. It may have turned into the al-Watan Party, whereas the Muslim Brotherhood is now represented by the Justice and Construction Party (JCP). Prime Minister Zeidan had been a vehement critic of the Muslim Brotherhood. Thus, that Brotherhood may now be quite influential inside the LROR and new Tripoli regime. It is not uncommon for anti-Islamist Libyans to claim that the Brotherhood is working in league with *al-Qaeda* or *Ansar al-Sharia.*[6] In the developing world power struggles often fluctuate between violent and nonviolent processes. Thus, eastern Libya may be in considerable danger of becoming part of a new Tripoli-based Islamic state. Libya was, after all, the first western conquest after the Ancient Muslim Empire's move into Egypt.

Regional *al-Qaeda* Strengthened by Gadhafi's Departure?

After Gadhafi's ouster, much of his mercenary army fled south with all of their weaponry. Some 2,000 returned to their native countries of Mali, Niger, Mauritania, and Nigeria. Within Mali, the return from Libya of well-armed Taureg fighters led to local Taureg separatists launching a new rebellion against the Malian government in January 2012. A mutiny by Mali's out-gunned and frustrated soldiers then turned into a *coup d'etat,* when they stormed the Presidential Palace in March. This erased more than two decades of democratic rule. AQIM has since announced that it too acquired thousands of Gadhafi's weapons.[7]

Right after the *coup,* Mali's military effectively controlled only the southern part of that country. Three weeks later, Dioncounda Traore—head of its National Assembly—nevertheless took over as interim president.[8] Then, in January 2013, 4500 French troops helped the Malian government to break the "Islamist" rebels' 10-month grip on the northern part of the country—an area renamed the "Islamic State of Azawad." Prior to that offensive, the French had developed friendly relations with local Tuareg chieftains. As a result, Tuareg MNLA separatists abandoned their *al-Qaeda* allies. That made AQIM and recent augments, like *Ansar Dine,*[9] the most significant Islamist opposition in Mali.

To What Extent Is *al-Qaeda* Now Active in the Region?

As early as 2011, an increase in *al-Qaeda* activity had been noted all across the southern Sahara from Somalia to West Africa. Specifically affected were Niger, Algeria, Mali, and Mauritania.[10] Those are some of the places suspected of being along northern branches of an east-west transcontinental drug corridor. Doing (or protecting) the actual smuggling are rebel factions closely linked to *al-Qaeda*: (1) *al-Shabaab* in Somalia; (2) *Boko Haram* in the southern portions of Niger and Mali;[11] and (3) AQIM in Algeria and the northern parts of Mali and Mauritania.[12] That may be how they now acquire much of their funding. Weapons are likely being smuggled along the same routes.

What of Tunisia?

Tunisia may be the only country in North Africa to benefit from the Arab Spring. (See Map 10.2.) By late January 2011, a "national unity government" had been formed. Elections for the new Constituent Assembly were held in late October 2011. Two months later, that Assembly chose human-rights activist Moncef Marzouki as interim president. It then spent a couple of years drafting and ratifying a new constitution. Presidential and parliamentary elections for a permanent government took place in December 2014. Beji Caid Essebsi, a self-proclaimed technocrat was subsequently installed as president.[13] Of late, Tunisia has been experiencing some militant activity. Over a dozen Tunisian troops were killed by Muslim radicals near the Algerian border in July 2014. In response, Tunis has placed "restrictions on certain mosques and imams."[14]

Algeria and Morocco

There was no Arab Spring change of power in either Algeria

Map 10.2: Tunisia

(Source: Courtesy of General Libraries, University of Texas at Austin, from their website for map designator "tunisia_sm_2014.gif")

or Morocco. (See Maps 10.3 and 10.4.) In April 2014, an ailing Abdelaziz Bouteflika was elected to a fourth term as president of Algeria. He had first taken office in 1999 when that country was still embroiled in a civil war between its military and Islamist militants.[15]

In early 2011, King Mohammed VI of Morocco responded to the region's pro-democracy protests by implementing various reforms. They included a new constitution—passed by popular referendum—that gave additional powers to the parliament and prime minister. However, Morocco was to remain a constitutional monarchy. In November 2012, the Justice and Development Party—a moderate Islamist party—won the largest number of seats in the parliamentary elections, making it the first Islamist party to lead the Moroccan government. In other countries, similar political party titles have sometimes implied the Muslim Brotherhood. Although Morocco is not the U.N.-recognized "administering power" for the Western Sahara, it still exercises *de facto* control over 80% of that territory. Since 1991, the U.N. has monitored a cease fire and continued to conduct negotiations between Morocco and the Polisario Front.[16]

Western Sahara

Western Sahara is a disputed territory at the northwestern corner of the Dark Continent. It is bordered by Mauritania on the south and Morocco on the north. (See Map 10.5.) After Spain with-

Map 10.3: Algeria

(Source: Courtesy of General Libraries, University of Texas at Austin, from their website for map designator "algeria_sm_2014.gif")

Map 10.4: Morocco

(Source: Courtesy of General Libraries, University of Texas at Austin, from their website for map designator "morocco_sm_2014.gif")

drew from its former colony of Spanish Sahara in 1976, Morocco annexed the northern two-thirds of what subsequently became Western Sahara. In 1979, Morocco claimed the remaining third after Mauritania's withdrawal from it.

Then, a guerrilla war broke out with the Polisario Front contesting Morocco's sovereignty over the region. This war ended in 1991 with a cease-fire and U.N. peacekeeping operation. As part of that effort, the U.N. sought to offer a choice to local residents between independence (as favored by the Polisario Front) and integration into Morocco. Its proposed referendum never took place due to lack of agreement over voter eligibility.

A 1,700-mile-long defensive sand berm had been built by the Moroccans from 1980 to 1987. Running the length of the territory, it now separates the opposing forces with Morocco controlling roughly

80% of the land west of the berm. Due to occasional demonstrations by Western Sahara's native Sahrawi population, Morocco maintains a heavy security presence there.

Several neighboring states have now rejected the Moroccan administration in Western Sahara and extended diplomatic recognition to the "Sahrawi Arab Democratic Republic" represented by the Polisario Front in exile in Algeria.[17] Western Sahara may lie along the cocaine smuggling route from Guinea Bissau to Spain.[18] Some of those drugs go by fast boat to Morocco, while others cross Mauritania by vehicular convoy.[19] Because the only paved road follows the coast in this region, some part of Western Sahara may be involved in the trafficking. The other northern drug branch runs up from Niger to Algeria's Mediterranean coastline. (That will be shown in Chapter 13.)

Map 10.5: Territory of Western Sahara

(Source: Courtesy of General Libraries, University of Texas at Austin, from their website for map designator "western_sahara_sm_2014.gif")

The Relative Threat Posed by the Salafists

The Islamists may seem more active in the northern portion of Africa than the Communists are in its south, but only because of their more violent methodology. Without a doubt, the Chinese also have designs on the petroleum-rich North, and the *jihadists* on Central and West Africa. But, before any more intelligence can be gathered, an update to the Islamists' *modus operandi* must be assembled. Without the latest "take" on how both suspects prefer to operate, additional clues on Africa's subtle subversion will be hard to identify.

11 Any Changes to the Muslim Method

- What binds the ISIS-flag-carrying factions together?
- What sources of income do they share?

ISIS flag flown by AQAP, AQIM, al-Shabaab, Boko Haram

(Source: Wikipedia Encyclopedia, s.v. "ISIL," public-domain image from Yascine [2013] with designator "800px-AQMI_Flag.png")

2015 Started Out with a New Feel to It

In February 2015, Western researchers began to sense a new metastasized version of the so-far-undefeated Islamist expansionary method. News of January's events had started to sink in. Apparently in progress was a widespread attempt at another Muslim Empire. Too slow for modern-day *jihadists* must have been the way *al-Qaeda* and the Sudanese Muslim Brotherhood had tried to spread sharia law—through WIFJ and PAIC alliances. Now there was ISIS—a makeshift movement that anyone could join. Besides ISIS's near takeover of Iraq, other Islamist factions had made sizable gains in

Yemen, Nigeria, Libya, and Morocco. That's far too many places to have opposition progress, if the old "domino theory" were to apply to any group other than Communists.

After materializing from nowhere, ISIS had quickly moved to the outskirts of Baghdad. That caught most Western strategists by surprise. While all could vaguely relate to the power of "swarm" tactics, they still lacked the cultural background to fully value that much loss in overall control. To them and most other Americans, ISIS was an anomaly—a bottom-up Islamist entity with the combined attributes of a criminal enterprise and rebel army. Whereas *Hezbollah* and *al-Qaeda* had previously relied on piecemeal attacks by semi-autonomous proxies to gradually amass political power, ISIS seemed to be doing everything backwards. First, it declared itself a fully functioning Islamist state. Then, it immediately started spending the proceeds from captured oil fields, using the ammunition and equipment of vanquished foes, and receiving more than enough reinforcements from media recruiting. But, what really set ISIS apart from any other modern-day invader was its attempt—through heinous barbarity—to discourage any further opposition. It started out with the mass executions of hundreds, if not thousands, of opposing ground troops. Then, it descended into the absolute depths of depravity with the horrific ceremonial beheading or burning of pilots, journalists, and aid workers.

The attention of most Americans was riveted on the Levant. Sadly, things of a similar nature had been happening elsewhere. The Iranian Crescent had reached all the way to Yemen, with Shiite rebels taking over the capital and threatening to restore an imamate. The *al-Qaeda* affiliate in Somalia had been attacking "soft targets" in Kenya and calling its Somali heartland an "Islamic Emirate." An Islamist party now controlled the Moroccan parliament for the first time. An Islamist force had taken over the whole western end of Libya to include its capital. There were Islamist rebels still active in Egypt, Algeria, Niger, Chad, Mali, Mauritania, and Nigeria. In fact, those in Nigeria had been doing so well as to also declare themselves an Islamist state. Of all these various setbacks to African peace and tranquility, that in Nigeria was the most troubling.

Events in Nigeria

According to Associated Press (AP), *Boko Haram* had declared an Islamic caliphate in northeastern Nigeria as early as August 2014.[1] However, it was events of January 2015 that prompted the *New York Times* to confirm the claim. (See Map 11.1.)

> While much of the world has been focused on the rise of the Islamic State [of Iraq and Syria], another proto-Islamic state has been waging a campaign of terror while dreaming of a caliphate in Nigeria.[2]
>
> — *New York Times,* 15 January 2015

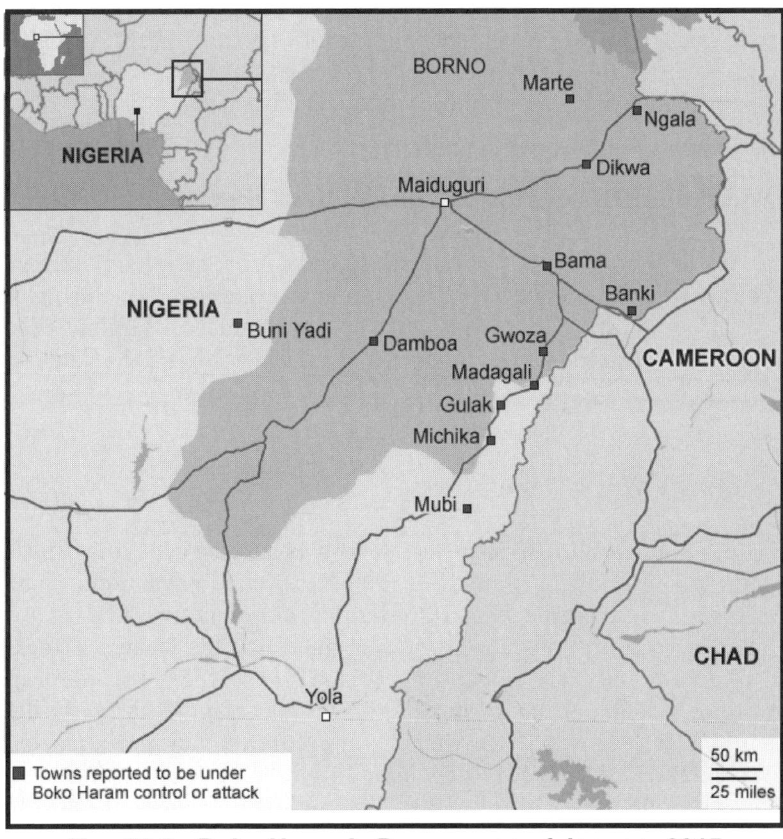

Map 11.1: Boko Haram's Progress as of January 2015
(Source: Courtesy of General Libraries, University of Texas at Austin, from their website for BBC map designator "_80356846_nigeria_boko_haram_v7.gif")

During the week of 5 January, the villages of Baga and Doron Baga were razed by *Boko Haram,* killing some 2500 residents.[3] Prior to that time, most of the U.S. news media reports had been about *Boko Haram's* successive kidnappings of girls and taunting of the Western World to do something about it. Then, *Boko Haram* appeared to intensify its efforts to take over the region. On 1 February, Nigerian Army defenders of the area's biggest city (with two million residents)—Maiduguri—were just barely able to fend off the third assault in a week from Islamic extremists. During this latest attack, the extremists had advanced on four different fronts at once.[4] About the same time, *Boko Haram* started attacking border villages in Cameroon, prompting the AU to authorize neighboring countries to help fight the spreading Islamic onslaught. The Chadian military responded with both ground and air forces, supposedly driving the rebels from several previously held towns.[5] By comparing Map 11.1 to an earlier *BBC* version, one could see that *Boko Haram* had been expanding its area of occupation in every direction.

Concurrent Events Far to the North of Nigeria

While the powerful faction that seized a large swath of territory around Tripoli to form a rival Libyan government in the Spring of 2014 was not an ISIS affiliate, it was nevertheless Islamist. (See Map 11.2.) Unlike Nigeria, Libya had been part of the ancient Muslim Empire. That should be of major concern to Washington.

America's Worst Nightmare

Ever since *Unrestricted Warfare* was released by the PLA's principal publishing house in 1999,[6] the U.S. government has been on formal notice that its organization structure and procedures have been creating automatic openings for foreign attack. Though not directly alleged by this Chinese treatise, much of America's problem has been in her "firepower-and-technology-dependent" way of war. This way of war creates so much trepidation and collateral damage that the population being helped often gets disenchanted with its "deliverer." Add to this the constant effort to kill opposition leaders through drone missile attacks, and one begins to see why ISIS has been so successful.

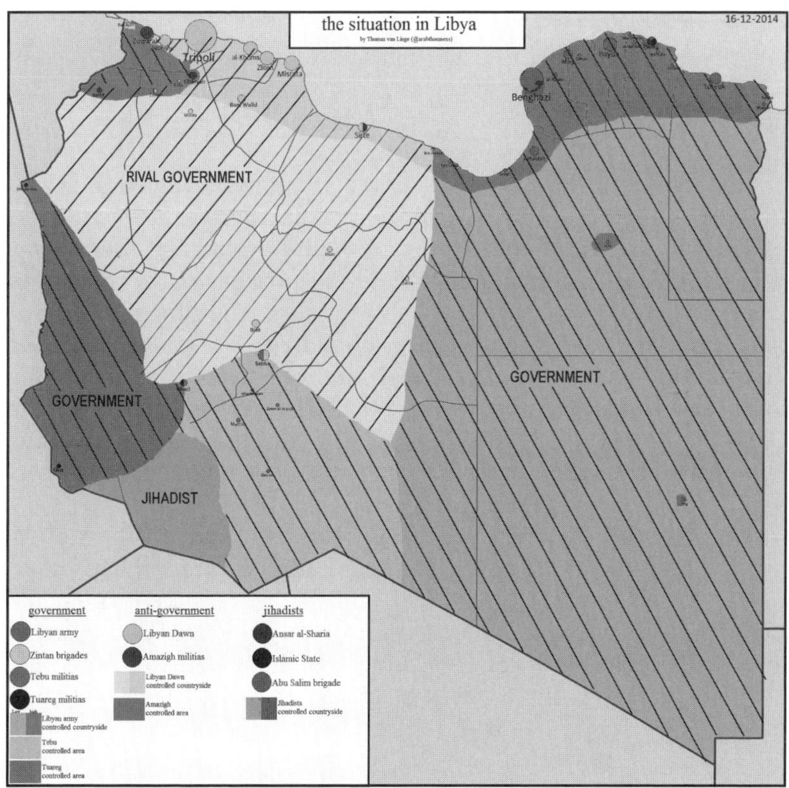

Map 11.2: Libya Dawn's Holdings on 16 December 2014
(Source: Courtesy of General Libraries, University of Texas at Austin, from their website, based on Thomas van Linge map with designator "kyhcrE0.png")

There is an equally valid style of fighting in which top leaders play a relatively insignificant role. Throughout history, it has gone by any number of names—*ninja* warfare, Stormtrooper warfare, Maoist warfare, light-infantry warfare, common-sense warfare, maneuver warfare, asymmetric warfare, unconventional warfare, and most recently the martial arena of 4GW. That ISIS is not sophisticated enough to fully fathom its possibilities suggests a hidden adviser. For ISIS, this adviser is not likely to be Iran. While Iran has supported various Sunni rebel groups over the years, it has never done so while actively fighting one.[7]

Some ISIS behavior is not new. Other militant Islamic factions have quickly started to collect taxes and deliver governmental services to just occupied regions. Others have armed themselves with captured arsenals.[8] And still others have developed long-term income from criminal activity—most notably drug smuggler protection. But the extent to which the original Levant version of ISIS has delved into other forms of criminal activity has only been matched by a non-Islamic Nigerian group—MEND.[9] Like MEND, ISIS has been looting banks, stealing petroleum, and kidnapping civilians for ransom.[10] A *modus-operandi*-oriented policeman might suspect a mutual adviser. (There will be more on MEND later.)

A clear precedent for ISIS has been the sophistication of its public affairs effort. It has all but dominated the digital battlefield by several means: (1) 46,000 ISIS-linked Twitter accounts; (2) using memes and emojis to interest future recruits over the internet; and (3) al-Hayat-produced short videos, an hour-long film, and nine *Dabiq* magazine issues.[11] With all of this, ISIS has undeniably had help.

Possibly to evoke more of the West's self-defeating "aerial-surveillance-and-bombardment strategy," ISIS has now resorted to ultraviolent propaganda. Fully to exploit the 21st-Century media and social-networking outlets,[12] it has lately arrived at capturing and then publicly killing Christians.[13]

The part the West should have expected, but didn't, is that—with enough money—ragtag misfits cannot only buy the world's best hand-held weaponry, but also experts on the above-mentioned alternative warfare style.

> "ISIS is a movement that would be hiding in caves if it did not have a professional cadre of trained, internationally recruited, professional light infantry."[14]
>
> — *Time Magazine,* 9 March 2015

The hiring of advanced weaponry and tactics experts is well within the reasoning capability of misguided misfits, but a thoroughly advanced propaganda campaign isn't. (See Figure 11.1.)

In essence, ISIS has experienced none of the growing pains of a new outfit. It started out as a fully functioning caliphate, and has since grown to considerable size. Besides AQAP, AQIM, *al-Shabaab,* and *Boko Haram* flying its flag,[15] many others have pledged their allegiance. They are as follows: (1) *Ansar Beit al-Maqdis* in the Sinai portion of Egypt; (2) various militant factions around Derna, Libya; (3) *Ansar al-Sharia* (Yemen); (4) *Abu Sayyaf* in the Philippines; and (5) the Caucus Emirate in Chechnya.[16]

ISIS's "high-tech" recruiting campaign has garnered many new *jihadists* for its ongoing "wars of liberation" in Syria and Iraq. Most of the other militant factions have been using ISIS as an "umbrella organization." While creating the impression of more personal strength than actually exists, their well-publicized affiliation with ISIS has resulted in less of a chance of local retribution.

As an established caliphate, ISIS also provides food, shelter, and "educational alternatives" to the Sunni faithful.[17] In the wave

Figure 11.1: Harmless Minarets Evoke Images of Other Things

(Source: Corel Gallery Clipart, Miscellaneous, Totem, designator "31F035")

of Western bombardment that is sure to follow its latest excesses, ISIS will then try to portray itself as the Sunnis' "savior." All the while, the West's focus will be riveted—almost exclusively—on ISIS, just as it was on *al-Qaeda* following the horrific Twin Towers attack. Any other challenges to national security will be largely ignored.

Gravity of the ISIS Threat

After ISIS's widespread propaganda campaign, this many vows of allegiance from "elsewhere-located" militant factions has worried many Americans. They have also found quite alarming the 60 simultaneous attacks by a probable ISIS affiliate against Egypt's military's checkpoints in the Sinai on 1 July 2015 (following the assassination of that country's chief prosecutor).[18] Cairo, after all, was a capital of the Ancient Muslim Empire. But what must now be remembered is that this latest attempt at a worldwide "caliphate" is much less structured than what Osama bin Laden and the Sudanese Muslim Brotherhood unsuccessfully attempted in the 1990's. Without *fatwas* or strategy conferences, how much actual cohesion could the new coalition have?

While ISIS's Levant contingent has become fairly good at seizing open and poorly defended terrain, its worldwide footprint is nothing more than an imaginary network. No number of empty threats against U.S. or European malls is going to change that. Playing off the West's fear of Muslims is exactly what an East Asian expansionist element would do as a feint to obscure its own nonmartial intentions. Still, various Islamic factions have been trying to "further undermine an already decadent West" through drugs, so that part of their attack will be discussed next. As might be expected, those fringe Muslims have not been pursuing this objective unilaterally.

Part Four

Africa's Cross-Continent Drug Conduit

"Corruption ought not to be an inevitable product of democracy."
— Mahatma Gandhi

(Source: Attributed to Mahatma Gandhi.)

12 Afghan Opiate Entrance to Africa

- Where are the opiates that enter East Africa headed?
- From the poppies of what country do most come?

Coast of Somalia is most likely delivery point.

(Source: DA Pamphlet 550-33 [1989], cover)

The Stark Reality of Narcotics Smuggling

Among the world's most profitable trade commodities is heroin. Up to 90% of it still comes from Afghan poppies,[1] and its biggest market is the U.S. America enjoys a capitalistic system that continues to allow campaign contributions from undisclosed sources. As such, she experiences a certain amount of drug-related political pressure. In recent years, this pressure may have become so intense that certain agencies are reluctant to draw attention to recurring holes in her armor. Further to pursue this possibility, one must look back into history.

Near the end of the Soviet-Afghan War (1988), the head of the Drug Enforcement Administration (DEA) told the U.S. Senate Intelligence Committee that drug labs along Afghanistan's southern border were producing more than half of the heroin sold on U.S. streets. Such a reality would have taken a sophisticated smuggling network between Baluchistan and America. Then, the CIA upped the estimate to 60% with the following route specifics: (1) 11 "one-ton" heroin storage vaults in the Sohrab Goth neighborhood of Karachi; (2) three tons of heroin awaiting shipment to the U.S. or Western Europe at any give time from that port city; and (3) most heroin heading westward by boat.[2]

Some semblance of an Afghan heroin conduit must still exist (with its final leg coming through Mexico), because the National Drug Threat Assessment (NDTA) for 2011 describes the following:

- The abuse of . . . heroin . . . appears to be increasing.
- Mexican-based transnational criminal organizations dominate the supply, trafficking, and wholesale distribution of most illicit drugs in the United States.
- The Southwest Border remains the primary gateway for moving illicit drugs into the United States.
- Overall drug availability is increasing.[3]

— Specific Findings of the NDTA for 2011

The 2013 NDTA Summary also shows more heroin reaching America, but then strangely "speculates" that a larger Mexican poppy crop and more Mexican cartel distribution are responsible. Must those cartels only refine, smuggle, and sell the harvest of their own fields? Does Mexico really grow enough poppies to make such a claim possible? Or, have hard-to-establish Mexican production/distribution estimates just been conveniently linked to the greater supply of U.S. heroin?

> Heroin availability continued to increase in 2012, *most likely due* to an increase in Mexican heroin production and Mexican traffickers expanding into the eastern and midwest U.S. markets. . . . The amount of heroin seized at the Southwest Border increased significantly between 2008 and 2012 and this, along with other indicators, points to increased smuggling of both Mexican-produced heroin and South American-produced heroin through Mexico.

> According to National Seizure System (NSS) data, the amount of heroin seized each year at the Southwest Border increased 232% . . . from 2008 (558.8 kilograms) to 2012 (1,855 kilograms). The increase in . . . seizures *appears to correspond* with increasing levels of production of Mexican heroin and the expansion of Mexican heroin traffickers into new U.S. markets. [Italics added.] [4]
>
> – *2013 NDTA Summary*

After fully discussing the Mexican, Colombian, East Asian, Dominican, and Cuban Transnational Criminal Organizations (TCOs), the NDTA for 2011 then makes a very revealing statement about the link between the TCOs in Asia and those in West Africa.

> [West] African TCOs have an international reach and smuggle . . . primarily Southwest Asian heroin, to the United States. They operate in many major U.S. cities, including New York City, Baltimore, Washington (D.C.), Atlanta, Detroit, Chicago, and Houston. They also smuggle Southeast Asian heroin ("Ghana," *CIA World Factbook,* June 2011; "Heroin Movement Worldwide," CIA, Dec. 2008). These organizations mainly use human couriers who swallow the drugs, hide them on their body, or conceal them within their luggage. They also smuggle heroin to the United States in mail parcels and air freight [5]
>
> – *NDTA (for) 2011*

That the West Africans have been using human couriers to move the world's two largest supplies of opium (Afghan and Golden Triangle) to America does not automatically infer a "piecemeal" approach. Several Ivory Coast nations may be part of a major opiate conduit that runs from the Golden Triangle and Pakistan, through the Middle East, across the Sub-Sahara, down into Venezuela or Brazil, and then up through Central America to the U.S. A cocaine smuggling route has existed between Venezuela and West Africa for years.[6] Why couldn't the same transportation network be carrying illicit cargo in the opposite direction? Has anyone conclusively proven that all heroin flooding the U.S. is from Colombian and Mexican poppies? In May 2011, one Texas police officer claimed that chemical tests had shown most heroin arriving from Mexico to be of Afghan origin.[7]

Even the "politically careful" U.N. has strongly alluded to Afghan heroin reaching the U.S. through West Africa. As any drug deluge would severely destabilize its intended target, America's national defense agencies need to get more interested in this difference of opinion.

After a Possible Whitewash

Like certain unnamed governments, the U.N. has now become obsessed with "political correctness." It tries never to say anything the least bit embarrassing about a regular Security Council member. As such, its research on drug trafficking (with all of the inevitable payoffs) is often a little sketchy. The U.N. freely admits to Afghan heroin reaching Africa. What it has been reluctant to say is that much of that heroin on the Dark Continent may be headed for the U.S. instead of Europe. Only within the details of a few public disclosures does that annoying reality begin to take shape.

While the U.N.'s drug threat assessment for 2013 never actually admits to heroin from Afghanistan moving across Africa, it heavily implies it.

> The local [East African] market is estimated to consume at least 2.5 tons of pure heroin per year, worth some US$160 million in local markets. The volumes trafficked to the region appear to be much larger, as much as 22 tons, suggesting substantial transshipment [to somewhere else]. Eastern Africa is a known transit area for heroin destined for South Africa and West Africa.[8]
>
> — *U.N. Office on Drugs and Crime (UNODC) Threat Assessment,* September 2013

The amount of Afghan heroin being trafficked through East Africa [Somalia, Kenya, Tanzania] has recently increased dramatically.

> In 2010, that [the degree of heroin smuggling] began to change. A series of larger seizures were made indicating that large volumes of Afghan heroin were entering the [Northeast African] region by sea from Iran and Pakistan.

> Between 2010 and 2012, more heroin was seized than in the previous 20 years.[9]
> — *UNODC Threat Assessment,* September 2013

While South Africa might have been the destination for all 20 tons of missing Afghan heroin, local supply statistics fail to bear this out.

> [East] Africa is a known transit area for heroin destined for South Africa, but there have been no indications of sudden increase in demand in this well-monitored market.[10]
> — *UNODC Threat Assessment,* September 2013

Of particular interest, the U.N. seems to think that smuggler *"dhows"* have been sailing all the way from Pakistan to the Dark Continent: (1) across the Gulf of Oman; and then (2) via the Indian Ocean to Kenya and Tanzania (to avoid the Somali pirates). Another possibility is that those *dhows* have been moving along the Yemeni coast to drop-off their cargos where no national authority is likely to bother them—at the Somali shoreline. Such a route would more fully benefit from the extremist presence and looser government controls along the way. A Western thinker might instead expect air-cargo shipments from the Emirates. (See Map 12.1 and Figure 12.1.)

> It appears that the primary method of trafficking is *dhows,* the modern version of the traditional sailing craft. They depart from the Makran Coast, a strip of desert coastline that crosses from Pakistan to Iran along the coast of the Arabian Sea and the Gulf of Oman. Air couriering also takes place.[11]
> — *UNODC Threat Assessment,* September 2013

U.N. researchers still suspect a certain amount of help in the drug smuggling from Somali radicals.

> Members of *al Shabaab* have been linked to . . . a Tanzanian Islamist group reportedly linked to heroin trafficking.[12]
> — *UNODC Threat Assessment,* September 2013

The most recent Dark Continent seizures of illicit drugs have

Map 12.1: U.N.-Surmised "Coastal" Delivery Route

(Source: Courtesy of General Libraries, University of Texas at Austin, from their website, for map designator "txu-oclc-192062619-middle_east_pol_2008.jpg

Figure 12.1: The Traditional Way of Coast Hopping
(Source: DA PAM 550-175 [September, 1988], cover)

mostly been at sea, but none immediately off the Somali beaches. They have instead been in the coastal areas of Kenya and Tanzania.

All of the large seizures made since 2010 appear to have involved maritime transport, although the type of vessel used was often unclear at the time the seizure was made. But their timing tracks the movement of the *dhows,* which travel south with the Kaskazi monsoon trade winds, blowing from December to mid-March. Four out of the five recent large seizures made in the region were made during this period.

According to local law enforcement agencies, the point

> of entry for the drugs has varied over time. Initially, the port of Tanga in northern Tanzania appears to have been favored. . . . The largest confirmed seizure (211 kg) was in Lindi, close to the border with Mozambique, in January 2012. The drugs are then transported by land to destination markets in . . . Tanzania and Kenya. . . .
>
> It is also possible that some heroin enters the region by container, and that containers may be used to import *yet undetected loads* outside the monsoon season. Containers could also be used to move drugs inland, as at least one seizure in the past has indicated. . . .
>
> If large volumes of heroin are transiting Eastern Africa on the way to Europe or the U.S., though, they have proceeded almost entirely undetected.[13]
>
> — *UNODC Threat Assessment,* September 2013

The DEA's Position As of 2012

The DEA is a highly reputable organization of fully dedicated personnel. As do most U.S. intelligence agencies, it looks the hardest at (further investigates) that which tends to support American foreign policy. And, like any "top-down" bureaucracy, it doesn't always follow-up on the suspicions of lowly field agents. The most painful example of this come from a sister organization just prior to 9/11.[14]

Within the following testimony supposedly lies a summary of Afghan heroin smuggling to the U.S. from Africa. But, upon closer examination, one can see that only the West African crime families are mentioned and the full quantity of heroin reaching America never actually revealed.

> [Southwest Asian (SWA)] heroin is principally smuggled by West African criminal groups from Pakistan through Iran and other Middle Eastern countries on to East Africa then to West Africa. Kenya, Tanzania, South Africa, Nigeria and Ghana are the principal transit zones in East and West Africa. The heroin is transported from the source zone in maritime containers, small wooden fishing vessels called *dhows,* air cargo, luggage and body-carried by couriers for eventual shipment to the U.S. and Europe. The United

> States still represents only a small fraction of the global market for SWA.[15]
>
> – DEA Senate Testimony, May 2012

Heroin is only implied at the end of the last sentence, never actually indicated. What if a Colombian cartel were smuggling cocaine north, dealing directly with Dawood Ibrahim in Karachi, and then using his *al-Qaeda* affiliates to move large quantities of Southeast Asian heroin across Africa to Venezuela? That would make the first part of the DEA's assessment still true (just noncomprehensive), and the last sentence only an innocent "typo." *Webster's Dictionary* defines the word "market" as the gathering of people for buying and selling. Without ending in the word "heroin," that last sentence only says that few U.S. citizens would want to purchase any Afghan commodity.

The largest market for 90% of the world's supply of opiates is now, and will always be, America. Only at issue is how much of that supply is still reaching U.S. customers. As with alcohol during Prohibition, no amount of governmental interdiction (or spin) will put a complete stop to it. And only a tiny portion of that 90% could do immense damage on the streets of Chicago.

The DEA's apparent (albeit unintentional) denial of dangerous quantities of SWA heroin still arriving in America would be more credible, if the same testimony had not warned of Nigerian syndicates making "crystal meth" for shipment to the Far East.[16] While such a thing is certainly possible, it would make little difference to the U.S. or anyone else. China is the world's largest supplier of precursors for methamphetamine.[17] As such, the Far East already has more than enough of its own supply of crystal meth.

Then There's the White House Assessment

As late as July 2014, the White House was still suggesting that most of the heroin on U.S. streets was from a larger poppy crop in Mexico and Colombia. It was as if a hopeful trend had been suddenly turned into hard fact by combining it with a geographical coincidence.

> During the 1990's, Latin America evolved as the primary supplier of heroin to the United States, with Mexican heroin

> most prevalent west of the Mississippi and Colombian heroin most prevalent east of it.[18]
>
> — Office of National Drug Control Policy, July 2014

Along with the SWA and Golden Triangle variety, both types of Western Hemisphere heroin have probably been purchased by the Mexican cartels, smuggled across the U.S. border, and then distributed by their affiliated gangs.[19] How could the consumption areas for Mexican and Colombian opiates now be so perfectly demarcated? Nowhere on the White House website is there any mention of the Afghan "white stuff" still reaching America. Yet, the supply of heroin on U.S. streets had greatly increased by August 2013.[20] Afghanistan was continuing to provide 90% of the world's total supply—thanks to a bumper crop every year since the U.S. arrived in 2002 (including the years of opium blight from 2007 to 2009).[21] This White House failure to adequately explain the worsening situation may have had its origins in May 2009, when the head of the Office of National Drug Control Policy officially announced that the traditional "War on Drugs" was over (with the new focus on how to limit the abuse of prescription medicines).[22]

The Statistical Inconsistency

Of late, it has been widely reported that U.S. neighborhoods are awash with inexpensive bags of white heroin.[23] In 1990, 60% of all street powder was coming from poppies grown in Southern Afghanistan.[24] Now, the American people are being told that only Colombian and Mexican plants are to blame for their current epidemic. All the while, the CIA continues to maintain that Latin America grows only 1% of the world's total supply of opium.[25] How could a 1% opium source have stolen all the heroin business from the 90% source? There are two possibilities: (1) fully refined SWA heroin has been crossing the oceans in larger quantities than officially admitted; or (2) less refined Afghan opiates have been further processed in the Western Hemisphere. How else could the world's largest heroin market be now flooded?

> "Most [narcotics] traffickers do their morphine refining close to the poppy fields, since compact morphine bricks are

> much easier to smuggle than [bulky] bundles of pungent, jelly-like opium," writes Alfred W. McCoy in *The Politics of Heroin. . . .*
>
> . . . The modern [heroin-producing] technique entails a complicated series of steps in a good [state-of-the-art] laboratory.[26]
>
> — *PBS's Frontline,* "The Opium Kings"

If raw opium from the 1% Western Hemisphere source is being turned into white powder on this side of the "pond," then why couldn't morphine bricks from Afghanistan and the Golden Triangle be as well? Can the chemists analyzing all heroin seizures along U.S. borders fully distinguish between "Asian-grown" and "Mexican-or Colombian-grown" product? What if all Asian-grown heroin were being laced with the other variety to further obscure a back-door African pipeline? There are many questions that the American public is still dying to have answered.

No Freelance Operation

Because drug smuggling is so highly profitable, there are invariably criminal enterprises involved—if for no other reason than to take a cut of the proceeds. Thus, the flow of Afghan heroin into Somalia and then across the sub-Sahara may have been conducted by *al Shabaab, Boko Haraam,* and other Muslim radical factions, but it is likely coordinated by local syndicates and overseen by an international crime family. According to a well-respected source of U.K. defense news, all Horn of Africa governments are well aware that "terrorist groups [in the region] rely . . . on the proceeds of smuggling (drugs . . .) and a network of transnational organized crime to fund their activities."[27] Sadly, a foreign government may be involved as well.

Beijngs's Link to Organized Crime

When the Chinese got Hong Kong from the British in 1997, they were worried its Taiwan-affiliated triads would make trouble. Soon, they realized that—as criminal enterprises—those triads could be "bought." And that's precisely what happened to the biggest.

> So he [Deng Xiaoping] bought them: the *Sun Yee On,* the largest Hong Kong triad society, no longer requires initiates to pledge allegiance to Taiwan; now it is to the People's Republic of China that they swear.[28]
>
> — *The New Republic,* July 1997

By this point in time, the Chinese Premiere had been thinking for almost fifteen years about how to harness the Hong Kong triads. After adding Hong Kong to the PRC, he was first interested in how those triads could help to fund his regime. Then, he must have realized the role they could play in foreign policy.

> Of all of the treacherous aspects of Hong Kong's reunification with China, the most treacherous—and the least noticed—is . . . a cooperation pact between the triad societies and the Communist Party. This dreadful alliance, of the world's largest criminal underground and the world's last great totalitarian power, has received surprisingly little attention in this country [America], even though the U.S. Justice Department has identified triad racketeering as a significant global threat.[29]
>
> — *The New Republic,* July 1997

Soon, the PLA was making money off the triad with the biggest overseas operation *(Sun Yee On)*, and very possibly thinking about how to use it against the PRC's only remaining opposition to global domination.[30]

> [The triads'] powerful influence is felt worldwide in counterfeiting, arms dealing, alien smuggling and money laundering. Hong Kong is a key transit point for the Southeast Asian heroin and methamphetamine that pour into the United States, and triads play a key role in the drugs' transshipment.[31]
>
> — *The New Republic,* July 1997

13 Middle of the Smuggling Corridor

- Which nations do the drugs cross after leaving Somalia?
- How is the transit of Ethiopia accomplished?

Most African borders are porous where trade is concerned.

(Source: DA Pamphlet 550-36 [1991], p. 75)

Countries through Which the Afghan Heroin Must Pass

According to a recent UNODC route map, a large quantity of Afghan heroin comes into East Africa on its way to the U.S.[1] How it then crosses the Dark Continent may be more evident to someone who lives there. A longtime resident of Khartoum describes a much more relaxed system of personal movement between countries—with a border fee often the only requirement.[2] This would greatly facilitate smuggling and help to obscure any pattern.

The region is attractive to international drug trafficking syn-

> dicates as they are quick to exploit non-existent or ineffective border (land, sea and air) controls, limited cross border and regional cooperation as well as serious deficiencies in the criminal justice systems. Hence, the low seizure figures are more an indication that few resources are allocated to drug control and that international border controls are weak, than a sign that no drugs are being trafficked through the region.[3]
>
> — UNODC, "East African Drug Smuggling Patterns"

A Different Type of Research Will Again Be Necessary

If the exact trace of this narcotics "pipeline" across Africa were easy to establish, INTERPOL (International Criminal Police Organization) and various nations would have already blocked it. Thus, one cannot expect to arrive at the precise route through some standard research method. To solve an extremely difficult crime, police detectives will often establish the most likely scenarios and then attempt to rule out all but one. Here, a series of gradually refined hypotheses will be needed to zero in on route particulars. The end result will still be a guess, but it will be a progressively refined guess. Africa will be crisscrossed three times from where the opiates probably enter its east coast, each with more attention to their means of transit and other factors. (See Figure 13.1.) With each pass, a more concise smuggling path should become apparent.

The first guess at drug route location will be made—while moving from east to west—through mostly CIA assessments of each nation's degree of narcotics trafficking. The next will be from west to east, while referring to U.S. State Department, DEA, and U.N. reports. Then, the final and closest approximation of drug route location will be made while moving from Red Sea to Atlantic again to see if enough rebels or corrupt officials are present for transpo/protection. (See Map 13.1.)

Where the Drugs Go First from Somalia

As suggested by the last chapter, the vast majority of Afghan opiates would most logically come into East Africa through the semi-failed state of Somalia.

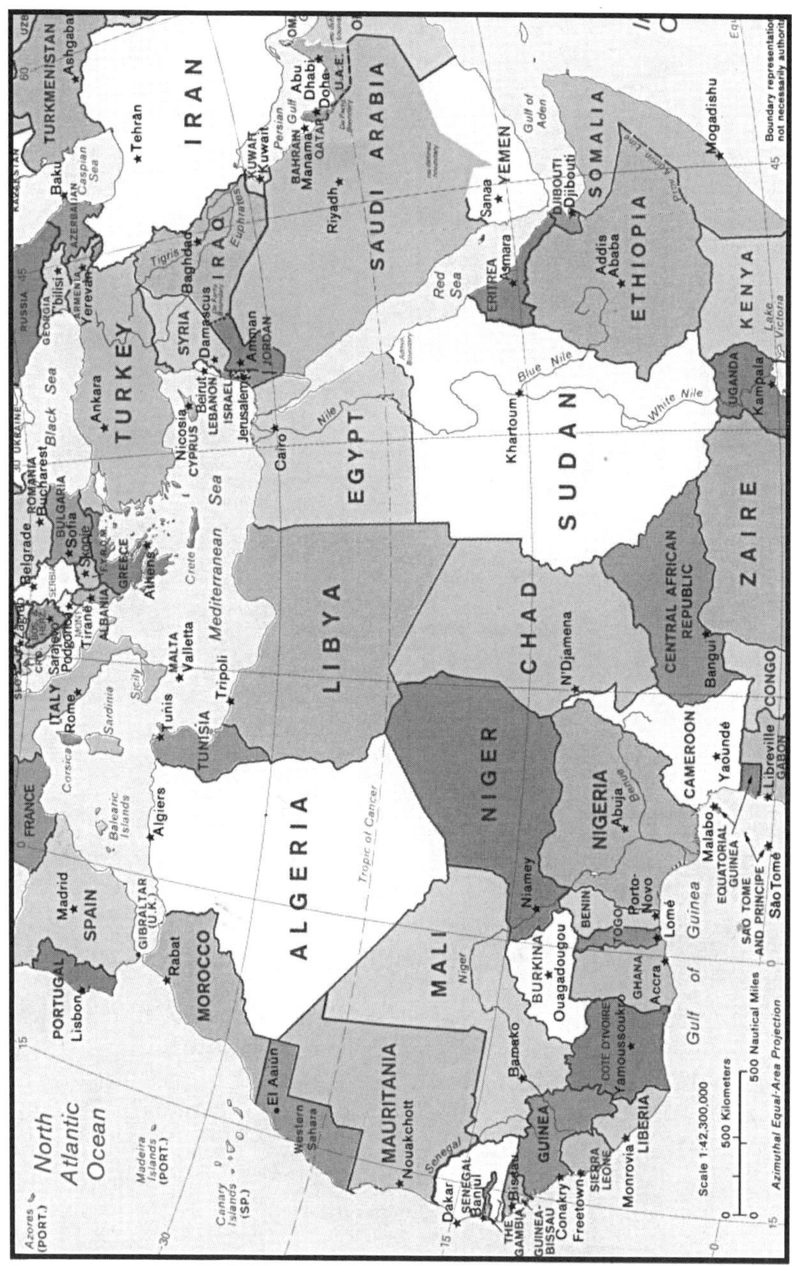

Map 13.1: Full Expanse of the East-West Drug Route

(Source: Courtesy of General Libraries, University of Texas at Austin, from their website for map designator "n_africa_mid_east_pol.95.jpg")

Figure 13.1: Baobab Tree in Zone between Desert and Jungle
(Source: FM 5-103 [1985], p. 4-39)

> Anecdotal evidence suggests that Somalia, currently in the process of establishing a central authority, is host to widespread . . . drug . . . trafficking.[4]
> — UNODC, "East African Drug Smuggling Patterns"

After Somalia, that heroin (or lesser-refined morphine bricks) would have to cross either Ethiopia or Kenya. While the CIA admits to problems in both, Ethiopia provides a more likely path because of its lawless Ogaden region, road network, and proximity to Sudan.

> Ethiopia—transit hub for heroin originating in Southwest and Southeast Asia and destined for Europe.[5]
> — *CIA World Factbook*

> Kenya—transit country for South Asian heroin destined

> for Europe and North America; . . . relatively high levels of narcotics-associated activities.[6]
>
> — *CIA World Factbook*

Next must come either Sudan or Uganda. Northern and southern Sudan are both unstable enough to be good candidates, but only Uganda has been officially associated with narcotics passage. Nevertheless, the below excerpt suggests only a branch corridor down into Uganda, Kenya, and Tanzania from the main east-west conduit through Ethiopia. (Look back at Map 13.1.)

> Uganda—Increased seizures [in East Africa] with Nigerian connections bound for Uganda, Tanzania, and Kenya through Ethiopia have been noted.[7]
>
> — UNODC, "East African Drug Smuggling Patterns"

To the west of Sudan, Nigeria is the first country to have been officially linked to a heroin conduit by the CIA. Much of Nigeria's northern portion is no longer under government control.

> Nigeria—a transit point for heroin and cocaine intended for European . . . and North American markets.[8]
>
> — *CIA World Factbook*

Then would come either Burkina Faso and Mali or all the little countries along the Gulf of Guinea and Ivory Coast. For Burkina Faso, the CIA admits "illicit cross-border activities." For Mali, it notes only a high rate of human trafficking and northern segments under Islamic militant control until just recently.[9] While the Ivory Coast countries register more direct hits, they may only contain alternate feeder branches for the South American cocaine entering the main east-west conduit. The other possibility is a coastal drug shuttle.

> Benin—transshipment point used by traffickers for cocaine destined for Western Europe.[10]
>
> — *CIA World Factbook* in 2008

> Togo— transit hub for Nigerian heroin and cocaine traffickers.[11]
>
> — *CIA World Factbook*

> Ghana—major transit hub for Southwest and Southeast Asian heroin and, to a lesser extent, South American cocaine destined for Europe and the U.S.[12]
>
> — *CIA World Factbook*

> Côte d'Ivoire—utility as a narcotic transshipment point to Europe reduced by ongoing political instability.[13]
>
> — *CIA World Factbook* in 2008

> Liberia—transshipment point for Southeast and Southwest Asian heroin and South American cocaine for the European and U.S. markets.[14]
>
> — *CIA World Factbook*

Most often mentioned as the main entrance portal for South American cocaine at Africa's far western end is Guinea-Bissau.[15] As such, it would also be the most likely departure point for Afghan heroin headed eventually to the U.S.

> Guinea-Bissau—increasingly important transit country for South American cocaine en route to Europe; enabling environment for trafficker operations thanks to pervasive corruption; trafficking in narcotics is probably the most lucrative economic activity. The combination of limited economic prospects, a weak and faction-ridden government, and favorable geography have made this West African country a way station for drugs bound for Europe.[16]
>
> — *CIA World Factbook*

> Guinea-Bissau . . . has become transshipment point for Latin American drugs [no destination specified]. . . . Guinea-Bissau is also a major hub for cocaine smuggled from Latin America to Europe. Several senior military figures are alleged to be involved in the trafficking of narcotics, prompting fears that the drugs trade could further destabilise an already volatile country.[17]
>
> — *BBC Country Profile*

Guinea-Bissau's northern neighbor—Senegal—may be an integral part of the transcontinental conduit's Atlantic end or just the first stop on a northern branch into Europe.

> Senegal—transshipment point for Southwest and Southeast Asian heroin and South American cocaine moving to Europe and North America.[18]
>
> — *CIA World Factbook*

Further Hints from the African Pipeline's Atlantic End

In mid-July 2014, France decided to spread its military forces from Mali to three other countries: Chad, Mauritania, and Burkina Faso. By so doing, it hoped to do two things: (1) disrupt the flow of weaponry and drugs that had been supporting militant factions; and (2) block the militants' access to Libya and the Atlantic.[19] Implicit in the French choice of new sites was the likely passage of South American cocaine along at least two pathways into Europe: (1) one immediately north out of Guinea-Bissau through Mauritania; and (2) another eastward through Burkina Faso and Mali *en route* to some other northward segment. The choice of Chad for further troop deployment suggests an eastward extension of this same smuggling corridor from Mali. Of course, another country lies in the way—namely, Niger. Within southern Niger and northern Nigeria, national governments would have to curtail any smuggling activity by *Boko Haram* on their own. The French have their own law-enforcement intelligence network. As such, they were undoubtedly aware that Afghan heroin was moving westward along this same route to join the northward flow of cocaine into Europe.

Key to a More Concise Guess at the East-West Pathway

The Sahel Region (Sahel Acacia Savannah) has traditionally provided the easiest trade routes across Africa. Sparsely vegetated and mostly flat, it offers the best alternative to the shifting sands of the Sahara and heavy woodlands to its south. Stretching the full breadth of Africa from the Atlantic Ocean to Red Sea, it would give "trans-continental" narcotics smugglers the option of temporarily deviating from their regular route to avoid interdiction. (See Map 13.2.)

Not surprisingly, the only good east-west road across Africa follows the southern edge of the Sahel. While not fully paved, Trans-

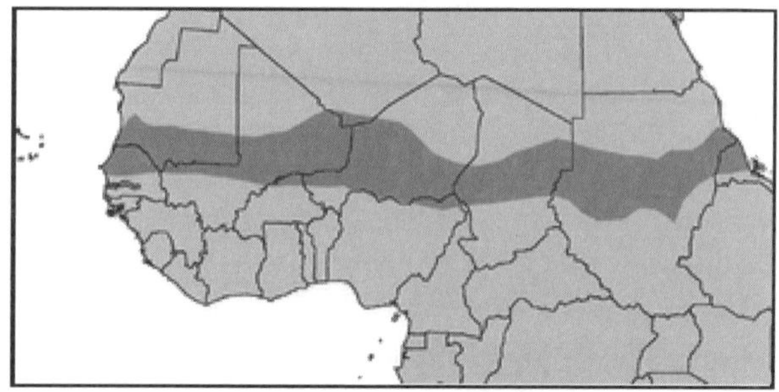

Map 13.2: The "Sahel"

(Source: Wikipedia Encyclopedia, s.v. "Sahel," under provisions of GNU Free Documentation License, map designator "320px-Sahel_Map-Africa_rough.png," © n.d.)

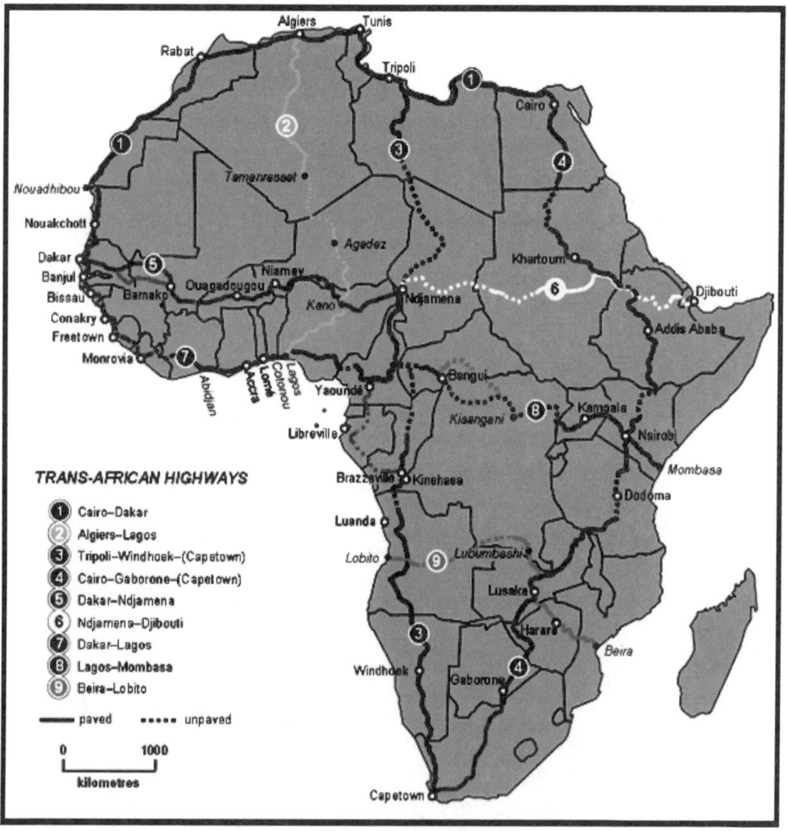

Algiers
Tunis
Rabat
Tripoli
Cairo
Tamanrasset
Nouadhibou
Nouakchott
Agadez
Dakar
Banjul
Bissau
Bamako
Ouagadougou
Niamey
Kano
Ndjamena
Khartoum
Djibouti
Addis Ababa
Conakry
Freetown
Monrovia
Abidjan
Accra
Lomé
Cotonou
Lagos
Yaoundé
Bangui
Kisangani
Kampala
Nairobi
Libreville
Mombasa
Brazzaville
Kinshasa
Dodoma
Luanda
Lobito
Lubumbashi
Lusaka
Harare
Beira
Windhoek
Gaborone
Capetown

TRANS-AFRICAN HIGHWAYS
1 Cairo–Dakar
2 Algiers–Lagos
3 Tripoli–Windhoek–(Capetown)
4 Cairo–Gaborone–(Capetown)
5 Dakar–Ndjamena
6 Ndjamena–Djibouti
7 Dakar–Lagos
8 Lagos–Mombasa
9 Beira–Lobito
paved
unpaved
0
1000
kilometres

Map 13.3: Trans-African Road Network

(Source: Wikipedia Encyclopedia, s.v. "Trans-Arican Highway Network," under provisions of GNU Free Doc. Lic., designator "Map_of_Trans-African_Highways.PNG," © n.d.)

African Highway 5 (and then 6) runs all the way from Senegal to Djibouti. No self-respecting drug runner would stick strictly to this road, but the Sahel topography allows him to simply drive around any suspicious areas. Smugglers overflying the region could also use this roadway as a navigational aid. (See Map 13.3.)

This Lateral Conduit's Most Western Offshoot into Europe

To the north of Guinea-Bissau lies a well-documented cocaine corridor into southern Spain. While the drug runners have been paying for, and receiving, safe passage from resident militants and corrupt officials, their ultimate "boss" must still be an organized crime element. Not every study makes this clear, however.

> When shipments from Latin America reach the coast of Guinea-Bissau, the cocaine is broken into smaller consignments that are then sent [north] . . . to the Mediterranean coast. . . . [They] travel . . . across regions controlled by a network of terrorists associated with al-Qaeda in the Islamic Maghreb. . . . The associated al-Qaeda cells . . . receive a sort of fee when the smugglers cross their territories, in Mauritania. [See Map 13.4.] [20]
>
> — Pulitzer Center, 19 June 2009

The DEA has been recently suggesting that this same northbound cocaine conduit may also branch off toward the U.S. Such a thing would require a major compromise of European-shipping-container protocols. In effect, the Colombian cocaine would be joining a westward flow of Afghan heroin from the Mediterranean, instead of Afghan heroin joining the more logical flow of Colombian cocaine through Central America. A DEA news bulletin hints at the more likely of these two scenarios—the latter.

> [The] DEA . . . announced . . . charges against . . . head of the Guinea-Bissau Armed Forces, for conspiring to provide aid to . . . *"FARC [Fuerzas Armadas Revolucionarias de Colombia]"* . . . by storing *FARC*-owned cocaine in West Africa; conspiring to sell . . . surface-to-air missiles to be used to protect *FARC* cocaine processing operations in Colombia against

Map 13.4 Mauritania

(Source: Courtesy of General Libraries, University of Texas at Austin, from their website for map designator "mauritania_sm_2013.tif")

> U.S. military forces; and conspiring to import narcotics into the United States.[21]
>
> — *DEA News Bulletin,* 18 April 2013

Of course, some of that South American cocaine may be entering Africa through the tiny countries that line the Ivory Coast, with a bit being diverted into U.S. cities as an intentional feint. Drug routes are like wartime infiltration lanes. They often contain alternate pathways in the same general vicinity. For any particularly risky segment, aircraft would take the place of ground transportation. (See Figure 13.2.)

> During the last decade, drug trafficking organizations based in South America have increasingly used countries along or near the West African coast as trans-shipment hubs for importing massive quantities of cocaine to be later

Figure 13.2: Some Legs Possible by Small Plane
(Source: FM 5-103 [1985], p. 4-39)

distributed in Europe or elsewhere within Africa. Through a combination of privately owned aircraft and maritime vessels, these organizations, predominantly based in Colombia and Venezuela, have transported hundreds of tons of cocaine, worth billions of dollars, to places such as Guinea Bissau, Guinea Conakry, Sierra Leone, Togo, Mali, Ghana, Nigeria, and Liberia. . . .

. . . The CS [confidential source] advised the defendants that a portion of the cocaine paid to the CS would be transported from Liberia to Ghana, from where it would be imported into New York.[22]

— *DEA News Bulletin,* 1 June 2010

This Lateral Pipeline's Other Southern Portal

The other main entrance to the east-west pipeline from the south would not be through well-governed Ghana, but more probably through the relatively lawless countries of Benin and Togo. (See Map 13.5.) They lie between Ghana and Nigeria. The Bight of Benin (on the Atlantic) is known to be the other main entry portal onto the Dark Continent for South American cocaine.[23]

Organized crime groups from Togo, Nigeria, Ghana, and Burkina Faso, involved in the shipment of . . . drugs, are a problem in Benin, presumably due to the lack of port and border security. . . .

While neighboring countries are making a concerted effort to fight the drug trade, the traffickers are using Benin to traffic drugs from South America into the United States and Europe.[24]

— "Benin Crime Report," U.S. Dept. of State, 2012

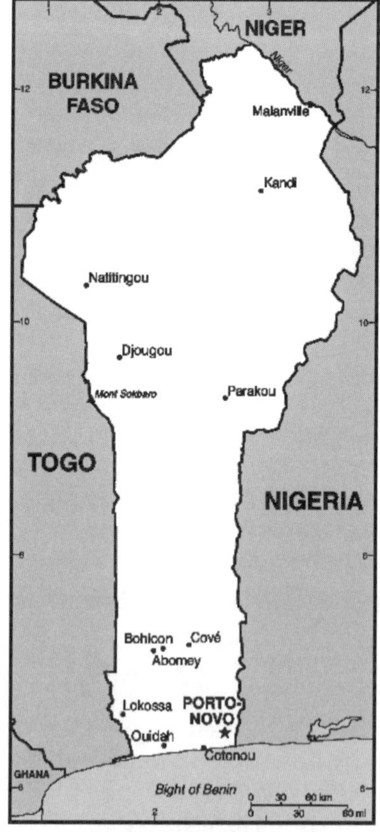

Map 13.5: Benin

(Source: Courtesy of General Libraries, University of Texas at Austin, from their website for map designator "benin_sm_2014.gif")

> Drug Trafficking Organizations (DTO) and Transnational Organized Crime (TOC) groups continue to exploit the vulnerabilities of Benin's ports of entry through illicit activities to include . . . drug trafficking. The porous borders, lack of law enforcement resources, and convenience of an international airport and port (particularly one that services several inland countries such as Burkina Faso and Niger) provide vulnerabilities for organized crime groups to exploit. . . .
>
> Drug trafficking continues to be on the rise in West Africa. Local law enforcement agencies lack the capacity and training to control organized groups. . . . DTOs utilize Benin as transit point for trafficking cocaine, heroin and most recently methamphetamine precursors from Latin America, Pakistan, and Afghanistan into other African destinations, Europe, and Southeast Asia.[25]
>
> — "Benin Crime Report," U.S. Dept. of State, 2014

> While neighboring countries . . . fight the drug trade, traffickers are using Togo to traffic drugs from a direct flight from Brazil to Lomé into other parts of the Sahel and Europe.[26]
>
> — "Togo Crime Report," U.S. Dept. of State, 2014

Such Drugs Do Not Go Directly North into Europe

The east-west conduit's central branch into Europe would not be a northward extension of the Benin or Togo ocean outlet. It would probably be east of there. After briefly entering Niger, it would dip down into Nigeria at Kano so as to intersect with the only paved highway across the Sahara to the Mediterranean Sea (at Algiers). (Look back at Map 13.3.) Despite all of the interdiction efforts in Afghanistan and Pakistan, most of its illicit opiates have continued to flow by main road to Karachi (through easily concealable packets).[27] Thus, one might expect the same mode of shipment in Africa. The U.S. Department of State confirms the likelihood of a major drug route branch running northward through Niger.

> Niger is currently rated HIGH for crime. It adjoins seven countries, which makes closely monitoring its borders nearly impossible. [See Map 13.6.] Its central location and the

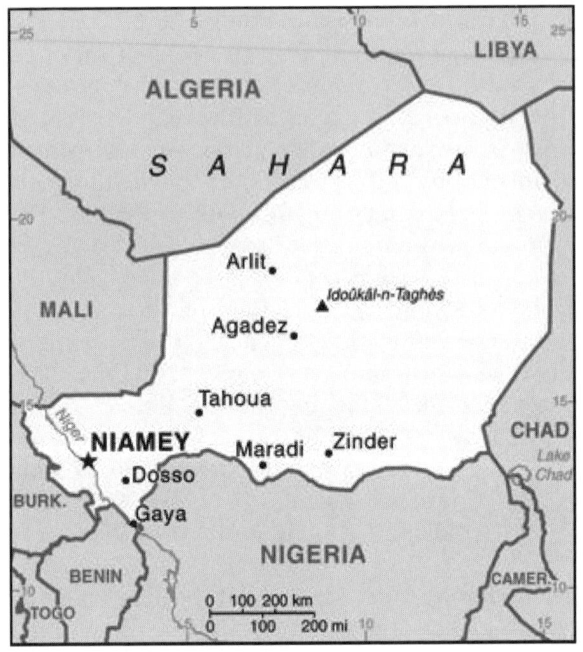

Map 13.6: Niger

(Source: Courtesy of General Libraries, University of Texas at Austin, from their website for map designator "niger_sm_2014.gif")

vast open Sahara Desert in the north facilitate the transit of criminals, weapons, migrants, contraband, and illegal drugs. . . .

. . . With its large, lengthy, and porous borders with seven countries, Niger has long been a transit route for smugglers. In the northern part of the country, the Sahara Desert, the nomadic Taureg have facilitated trade, including smuggling of contraband such as . . . illegal drugs. . . . Since the 2011 war in Libya, Niger has seen a rise in smuggling activity and there have been repeated clashes between smugglers and Nigerien [Niger's] security forces. . . .

. . . Niger is considered a transit country for the smuggling of illegal drugs from other West African countries to Europe.[28]

— "Niger Crime Report," U.S. Dept. of State, 2012

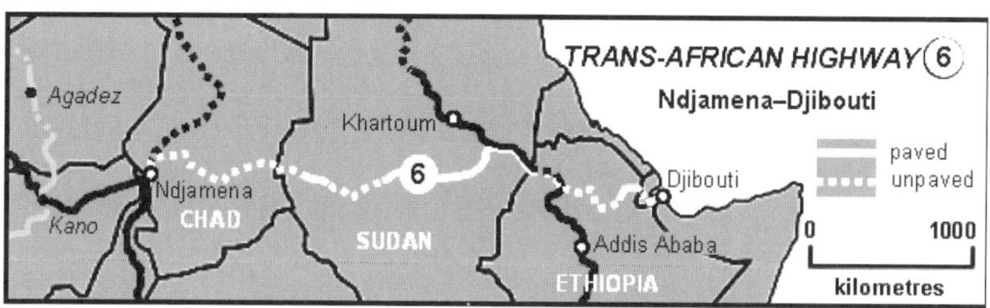

Map 13.7: Trans-African Highway 5 Turns into Highway 6
(Source: Wikipedia Encyclopedia, s.v. "Ndjamena-Djibouti Highway," under provisions of GNU Free Doc. License, designator "Ndjamena-Djibouti_Highway.png," © n.d.)

While further investigating where this north-bound branch springs from the east-west conduit, one discovers unhappy evidence that a back-door heroin route into the U.S. may have existed for many years. Also confirmed is that Kano is the first likely place for the drugs to move northward into Europe. (See Map 13.7.)

> General Bamaiyi . . . paraded a convicted drug courier before the assembled Kano state officials. . . [after] burning of 700 kg of cannabis, heroin and cocaine seized in Kano state, northern Nigeria. . . .
>
> . . . For years Nigeria has been known as a transit point for drugs entering the U.S. and Europe.[29]
>
> — *The Independent* (U.K.), 1995

On that northern leg across the mighty Sahara, *Boko Haram* would turn over drug load protection to AQIM *(al-Qaeda* in the Islamic Maghreb). Which organized-crime faction may now own those drugs is not clear, nor does it really matter. The cocaine may still be owned by a Colombian cartel, Lebanese syndicate, or Nigerian mob. The opiates may still belong to an Asian family.

> South American cartels and local allies are exploiting institutional . . . weaknesses to turn Central Africa into a transit hub on their "cocaine route" to Europe. . . .

Map 13.8: Chad

(Source: Courtesy of General Libraries, University of Texas at Austin, from their website for map designator "chad_sm_2013.tif")

DEA, said in a report . . . new players, including . . . [AQIM] and . . . Boko Haram, were getting increasingly involved in cocaine trafficking to raise money for their activities.[30]

— *Voice of America News,* 8 September 2012

Organized crime groups involved in drug . . . smuggling continued to be the main organized crime problems. . . .

Drug smuggling is part of the larger phenomenon of cross-border smuggling and general lawlessness in . . . Alge-

> ria's border regions. Algerian officials believe that branches of AQIM operating in the far south of Algeria, near the borders with Mali and Mauritania, exert significant influence over smuggling cocaine from South America. Several media reports link Colombian drug cartels to AQIM, claiming that AQIM provides protection for narcotics shipments headed into Europe.[31]
>
> — "Algeria Crime Report," U.S. Dept. of State, 2013

The Main Drug Route East of Niger

The big country directly to the east of Niger is Chad. It must contain part of the east-west drug route, because the French have diverted some of their troops there. (See Map 13.8.)

> Drugs are sometimes smuggled through Chad along trading routes that traverse the north.[32]
>
> — "Chad Crime Report," U.S. Dept. of State, 2013

The Hardest Part of the Puzzle—Ethiopia and Somalia

(Look back at Map 13.7 and then at Map 13.9.) The same east-west "Sahel" highway that has so far seemed to mark the drug route now intersects the road from Khartoum to Addis Ababa and then heads off toward Djibouti on the Red Sea. Smugglers would steer clear of the Ethiopian capital's heavy security blanket. Their most likely pathway into Somalia would be southeast by road through the ivory-smuggling hub of Harar and then across the lawless Ogaden Region.

If those drug traffickers kept to the main road, the first Somali border town they would encounter would be Beledweyne. But, Beledweyne has recently come under Somali government control. This was not always the case, however. A pictorial display from the Spring of 2011 shows an *al-Shabaab* region that stretched all way from most of the Somali coast to either side of Beledweyne. (See Map 13.10.) It also reveals a strange finger-like "nonaligned" corridor that ran from the north end of *al-Shabaab* territory to the Ethiopian border just north of Cadaado (a Somali town northeast of Beledwyne).[33]

In 2011, *al-Shabaab* controlled Somalia's shoreline all the way from Ras Kamboni at the Kenyan border to just short of Hobyo. A late 2014 revision to that same map shows *al-Shabaab's* coastal holdings shrunken to a 100-mile stretch between Hobyo and just

Map 13.9: The Back Roads into Beledweyne
(Source: Courtesy of General Libraries, University of Texas at Austin, from their website for map designator "txu-pclmaps-oclc-11302687-ethiopia_pol-1979.jpg")

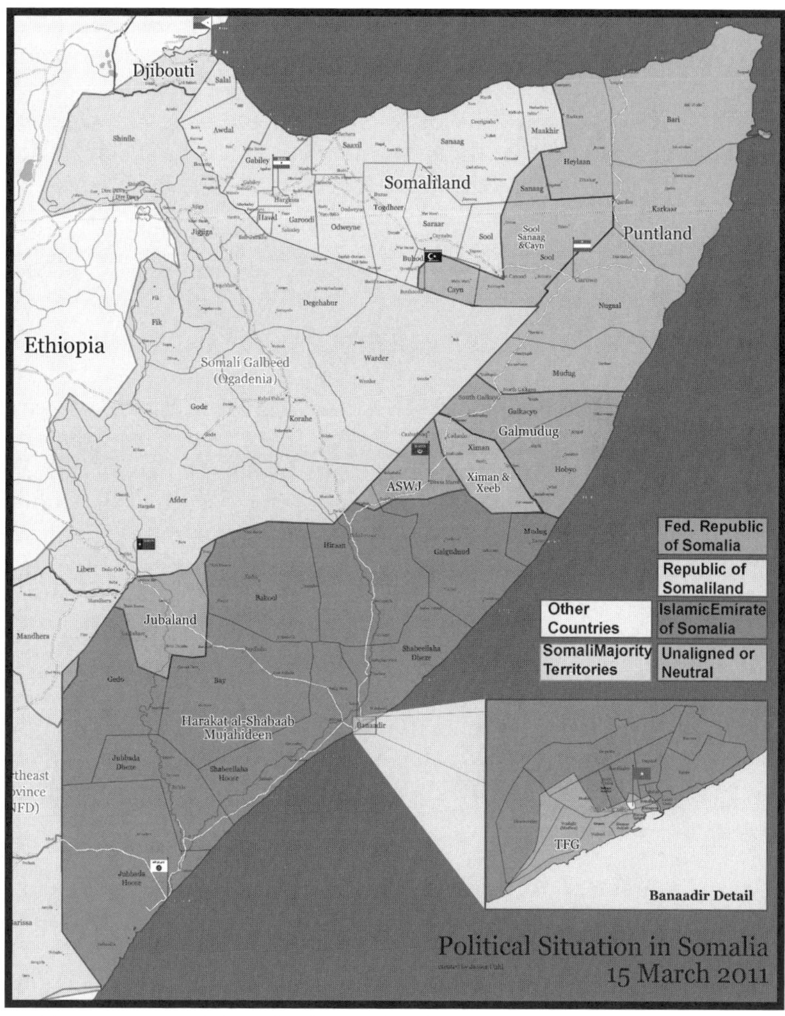

Map 13.10: Al-Qaeda-Controlled Territory as of March 2011
(Source: Wikipedia Encyclopedia, s.v. "Somalia," under prov. of GNU Free Doc. Lic., designator "20110324011204!Somalia_map_states_regions_districts.png," by J. Dahl ©; as retrieved in November 2014 from this url: http://upload.wikimedia.org/wikipedia/commons/archive/9/9f/20110324011204!Somalia_map_states_regions_districts.png)

south of Mareeg.[34] (Look back at Map 1.5.) This just happens to be where the above-mentioned nonaligned finger originated. Even though both former "pathways of least resistance" into Ethiopia are now supposedly under Somali government occupation, either may mark the current smuggling route. Are not all smuggling lanes within the "Lower 48" also theoretically under U.S. government control?

By whichever route the drug loads are reaching the Ogaden, *al-Shabaab* would escort them to where another ethnic Somali faction—the ONLF—could take over. All other groups likely to provide transpo/protection to the Afghan pre-heroin, as it moves westward from Ethiopia, would have *al-Qaeda* affiliations.

One More Pass to See If Enough Militants Are Available

As Trans-African Highway 6 moves westward, it crosses present-day Sudan north of its border with South Sudan and then its Darfur Region. So, Khartoum or one of its Islamist proxies—like the *Janaweed*—may be in on the drug smuggling. Or, the illicit activity may be by the anti-government Sudan Revolutionary Front, to which the highly Islamist Justice and Equality Movement (JEM) and Sudan People's Liberation Movement-North (SPLM-N) both belong. This Revolutionary Front operates across the entire breadth of the country.[35]

Next in line is Chad. It also has Muslim rebel factions. As of 2007, the three most significant of these were the United Front for Democratic Change (FUDC), Arab-dominated UFDD, and Rally of Democratic Forces (RaFD).[36] At present, UFDD seems most active.

Then comes Niger. Tuareg tribesmen are thought by the U.S. State Department to be smuggling drugs there.[37] But, Niger's Tuaregs are not in open rebellion like those in Mali. They live in the north, whereas Trans-African Highway 5 runs along Niger's southern border. There, *Boko Haram* could easily cross over from Nigeria to control the east-west conduit. Thus, Niger's Tuaregs must only be helping with its northern branch into Algeria. Their better-armed Malian brethren, with know ties to AQIM,[38] would be there as well.

After southern Niger comes Burkina Faso. While not known to have an Islamic insurgency, it is still suspected by the French of being on the main drug corridor. There are Udalan Tuaregs in Burkina Faso,[39] but they are not widely enough dispersed to be doing the smuggling. More likely, an "expeditionary" element of Nigeria's *Boko Haram* is again the culprit.

> *Boko Haram* also has significant connections to several other African countries: Burkina Faso, where *Boko Haram* recruits have reportedly trained.[40]
> — *American Foreign Policy Council Report*

Next in the suspected string of drug corridor countries is Mali. (See Map 13.11.) Within Mali, the MNLA appears now to be the strongest insurgent faction.[41] Operating out of northern Mali, MNLA is mostly composed of Tuaregs and has previous links to AQIM. *Ansar Dine* is Taureg as well and has now merged with the MNLA.[42] Because Trans-African Highway 5 runs across southern Mali on its way to the Atlantic, MNLA may only be helping with northern Niger's drug branch into Europe. Still, both the French

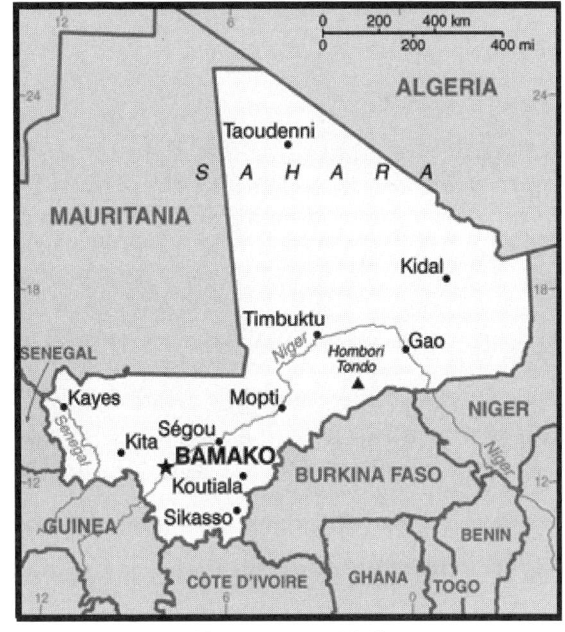

Map 13.11: Mali

(Source: Courtesy of General Libraries, University of Texas at Austin, from their website for map designator "mali_sm_2013.tif")

Map 13.12: Guinea
(Source: Courtesy of General Libraries, University of Texas at Austin, from their website for map designator "guinea_sm_2013.tif")

and the DEA must agree that some South American cocaine has been passing through Mali. So, someone other than MNLA must be aiding with its east-west shipment. MUJAO exists within that country, as does AQIM, *Boko Haram,* and *Ansar al-Sharia* (Mali).[43] But, MUJAO, AQIM, and *Ansar al-Sharia* (Mali) all operate out of northern part of Mali, so *Boko Haram* is once again the odds-on favorite for protecting/running the east-west narcotics pipeline through its southern part.

Trans-African Highway 5 then proceeds on through Guinea on its way to Senegal. How the drugs then make it to Guinea-Bissau's shoreline must wait for a later chapter. (See Map 13.12.)

How the Afghan Opiates Subsequently Get to America

One "law-enforcement" way to arrive at the details of a trans-Atlantic leg of a heroin pipeline from West Africa to the U.S. would be to rule out any arrangement that couldn't handle enough overall quantity or exploit existing security gaps. In other words, such a pipeline must carry massive amounts of product without making any new footprint.

In May 2015, Washington finally admitted that Venezuela—with the help of its regime leaders—had become a transitory hub for drugs headed to the U.S.[44] But, Colombian cocaine headed for America has no need to go through Venezuela. It just moves by sea-borne shuttle up the West Coast of Central America.[45] So, Venezuela must be a transitory hub for drugs coming from somewhere else—like Africa.

> [When] U.S. and Colombian authorities began closing smuggling routes through the Caribbean in the late 1980's and 1990's, Colombian criminals began smuggling cocaine and heroin through the Central American isthmus and Pacific routes. Both . . . led them to Mexico. . . .
>
> Since the Colombians began selling cocaine at the wholesale level to Mexican organized crime, rival factions have battled over control of the downstream revenue, largely dictated by points of entry into the United States, such as Nuevo Laredo, and points of reception from Colombia, such as Acapulco. . . .
>
> Acapulco is a straight shot north from Buenaventura, Colombia, the country's largest Pacific port. Many of Colombia's drug trafficking organizations, including the . . . *(F.A.R.C.),* used the Buenaventura port to smuggle loads of pure cocaine north. The lack of coastal patrols along the Central American isthmus facilitates the route. Speed boats regularly take illicit products north to Acapulco, where they are loaded onto trucks destined for Nuevo Laredo. . . .
>
> . . . Acapulco happens to be the most logical reception point for both [Mexican] cartels because it avoids the better patrolled waters that surround Mexico's Yucatan peninsula in the Caribbean.[46]
>
> — *Power and Interest News Report,* August 2006

As late as 2008, the *CIA World Factbook* was listing almost every Central American country as a "trans-shipment point for South American cocaine."[47] Its 2015 sequel still states that "[Mexico]

Figure 13.3: COSCO Freighter on Its Way Back to Venezuela
(Source: Drawing based on Corel Gallery Clipart, Totem Ship #37C019, © Posterity Press)

continues as the primary transshipment country for U.S.-bound cocaine from South America, with an estimated 95% of annual cocaine movements toward the U.S. stopping in Mexico."[48]

Thus, the whole idea of South American cocaine more easily reaching America through Africa is ridiculous. U.S.-bound Asian opiates are not "piggybacking" with Colombian cocaine from the southern Mediterranean. They have to be arriving via Venezuela from West Africa.

Thousands of airline "mules" and packages from the Ivory Coast countries might incrementally get the job done, if the U.S. authorities were not already alert to the scheme. The shipping-container theory is the most promising "bulk" option, because most drugs crossing the Mexican border appear to be doing so by truck-borne container.[49] But, there is one other bulk possibility. A hasty swap of cocaine for heroin (or morphine bricks) off the coast of Guinea-Bissau or Benin could amount a fairly sizable load. (See Figure 13.3.) With it, there would be no risky trip across the Sahara, no new concealment procedures at Mediterranean ports, and no additional circumvention of U.S. border security. In other words, large quantities could be delivered without any further footprint.

14 The West Coast — Portal to America

- Which West African nations are drug-smuggling hubs?
- Is the eastbound cocaine conduit also bringing heroin west?

Guinea-Bissau offers a huge archipelago of coastal islands.

(Source: Courtesy of Sorman Information and Media, from Soldf: Soldaten i falt, © 2001 by Forsvarsmakten and Wolfgang Bartsch, Stockholm, p. 31)

How Much Heroin Has Been Reaching the U.S. via Africa?

Chapter 12 has shown large quantities of Afghan opiates moving westward through Africa. Only at issue is whether a sizable portion is then crossing the Atlantic to America. The official U.S. position is that almost all goes north to Europe. Afghan heroin has traditionally entered Europe through Iran and Turkey. Why would a more circuitous route into Europe even be necessary? Criminal behavior is like warfare. All manner of deception is possible. An alternate route into Europe would be perfect cover for a hidden pipeline to the U.S.

The Most Probable Way West

Guinea-Bissau—Guinea's tiny neighbor—used to be the key transfer point for South American cocaine headed to Europe. (See Map 14.1). Now, there is evidence of cocaine entering West Africa through any number of places from Gambia to Guinea and Ghana to Cameroon.[1]

> [Drug] shipments to . . . West Africa gained in importance between 2004 and 2007, resulting in the emergence of two key trans-shipment hubs: one centered on Guinea-Bissau and Guinea, stretching to Cape Verde, Gambia and Senegal; and one centered in the Bight of Benin, which spans from Ghana to Nigeria. Colombian traffickers often transport the cocaine by "mother ships" towards the West African coast before off-loading it to smaller vessels. Some of it proceeds onward by sea to Spain and Portugal while some is left as payment to West Africans for their assistance–as much as 30% of the shipment (SOCA, *U.K. Threat Assessment of Organised Crime, 2009/10*). The West Africans then traffic this on their own behalf, often by commercial air couriers. Shipments are also sent in modified small aircraft from . . . Venezuela or Brazil to various West African destinations (ibid.; U.K. Home Affairs Committee, "The Cocaine Trade").[2]
>
> — *U.N. World Drug Report (for) 2010*

Still probable, however, are two principal cocaine corridors into what used to be *Afrique*. For each, the actual entry points might slightly vary to avoid a pattern. As interdiction efforts have increased, the mode of transportation may have occasionally been altered as well. By whatever combination, the South American cocaine continues to flow.

> [For Europe-bound cocaine,] both maritime seizures and airport seizures on flights originating in West Africa virtually disappeared at the end of 2008. Some [incoming] trans-Atlantic traffic may have shifted to private aircraft, however. In November 2009, a Boeing 727 jet was found alight in Central Mali. It is believed that the plane departed

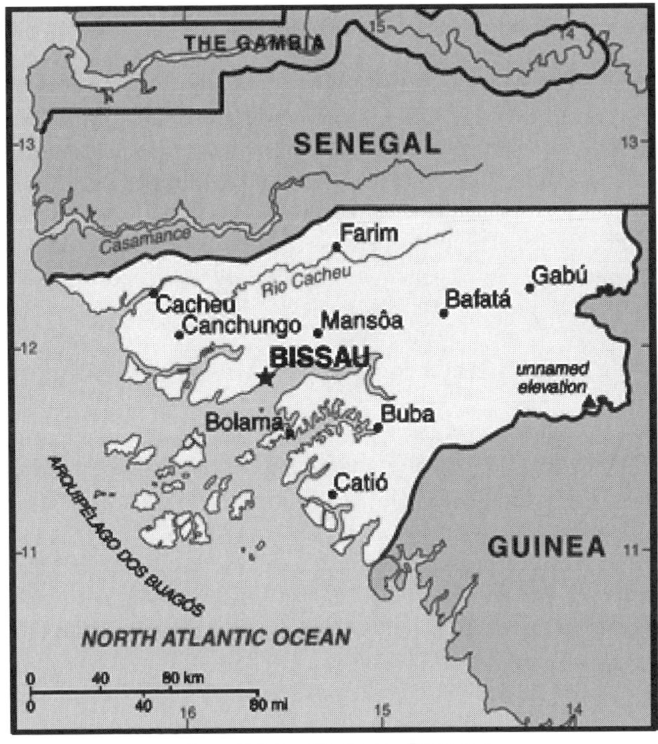

Map 14.1: Guinea-Bissau
(Source: Courtesy of General Libraries, University of Texas at Austin, from their website for map designator "guinea_bissau_sm_2014.gif")

> from . . . Venezuela and that it was carrying cocaine. . . . [C]ocaine trafficking via West Africa may have started to increase again in late 2009.[3]
>
> — *U.N. World Drug Report (for) 2010*

The most logical way for a large quantity of Afghan opiates to be reaching America through West Africa is backwards along the same shipping network that brought in the cocaine. It could be crossing the Atlantic in the form of fully refined heroin or just compact morphine bricks. Such bricks could then be turned into white powder anywhere from Venezuela to Mexico. That process might adequately disguise the place of origin.

Before Any Asian Narcotics Leave the Dark Continent

Before any more research on how the Afghan opiates are getting from Route 5 onto Venezuela-bound boats, there must be a discussion on what role international organized crime or intrigue might play. While it's possible that morphine bricks are simply being resold to each successive recipient as they cross the Dark Continent, most crime and foreign-policy experts would expect an overseer of their entire passage.

Islamist Factions Have Been Doing the Actual Smuggling

Over the years, several Islamist factions have been acquiring much of their funding through some aspect of the drug trade. Others have simply facilitated the trafficking to undermine the West.

> Islam forbids the use of opium . . . but the [Afghan] militants now justify the drug production by saying it's not for domestic consumption but rather to sell abroad as part of a holy war against the West.[4]
>
> — *McClatchy News Service,* 10 May 2009

> In the mid-1980's, the *Hezbollah's* use of the illicit drug trade as a funding source and a weapon against the West was sanctioned by an official *fatwa* (religious edict) issued by *Hezbollah:* We are making these drugs for Satan America and the Jews. If we cannot kill them with guns, we will kill them with drugs.[5]
>
> — *Funding Evil,* by Rachel Ehrenfield, 2005

Organized Crime Is Definitely Involved

Such an Islamist strategy to sabotage the West could never be realized without the help of organized crime. More than skilled drug runners are necessary. Just as important are enough corrupted officials to look the other way.

> Since the 9/11 attacks, West Africa has been directly connected to the global anti-western *jihadist* ambitions of Osama bin

> Laden. *Al-Qaeda* made logistical inroads into West Africa, seeking to radicalize regional Islamist sentiment and to benefit from the pervasive influence of organized crime.[6]
>
> — Pulitzer Center, 19 June 2009

While this link to organized crime is not always acknowledged, most radical Shiite and Sunni factions would not be as easily cooperating without a mutual mob contact. Just as no one doubts the existence of criminal syndicates in the narcotics-trading center for all of Latin America, neither should they doubt it at Guinea-Bissau or Benin.

> Reports by INTERPOL and United Nations agencies detail evidence that cocaine traded through West Africa accounts for a considerable portion of the income of *Hezbollah* and *Hamas,* the Islamist movements based respectively in Lebanon and the Gaza Strip. These reports say *Hezbollah* uses the Lebanese Shi'a expatriate population in South America and West Africa to guarantee an efficient connection between the two continents.
>
> In Latin America, both *Hezbollah* and *Hamas* are particularly active in Ciudad del Este, on the "tri-border area" where Argentina, Brazil and Paraguay converge. This freewheeling border town is famous for cocaine trafficking, piracy and contraband goods, which are often smuggled across the Parana River into Brazil. Guinea Bissau is a strategically unique *trait d'union* between Latin America and Europe.[7]
>
> — Pulitzer Center, 19 June 2009

> For nearly a decade, the presence of *Hezbollah, Hamas,* [and] Islamic Group of Egypt . . . have converged with organized crime groups in the triple-border area [of Brazil, Paraguay, and Argentina].[8]
>
> — *Inside al-Qaeda,* by Rohan Gunaratna

Because *Hezbollah* has been so frequently associated with the cocaine conduit into Guinea-Bissau, a Lebanese cartel may be operating that nation's drug hub. Or, it may be run by *Hezbollah* itself (now designated a full-fledged TCO by the U.S. government).[9] The third possibility is an illicit "corporate extension" of *Hezbollah*, just as the IRGC has business entities. However, the Benin cocaine portal would be most likely managed by the Nigerian syndicate. Then, along any leg of the connecting road system to Europe (from either portal), local rebels would be hired to provide drug-load protection. (See Figure 14.1.)

> When shipments from Latin America reach the coast of Guinea-Bissau, the cocaine is broken into smaller consignments that are then sent by fast boats to the coast of Morocco and Senegal or moved in trucks through Mauritania and across the Sahara to the Mediterranean coast. Convoys of heavily armed four-wheel-drive vehicles travel through the Sahel, across regions controlled by a network of terrorists associated with al-Qaeda in the Islamic Maghreb [AQIM]. The Lebanese network based in Bissau makes business at the source, directly with the *FARC,* on behalf of *Hezbollah.* The associated *al-Qaeda* cells, based in the Sahel, receive a sort of fee when the smugglers cross their territories, in Mauritania.[10]
>
> — Pulitzer Center, 19 June 2009

Chapter 13's approximation of the trans-Sahara drug routes appears to be confirmed by the following news report. However,

Figure 14.1: Only Organized-Crime Families Use "Fast Boats"
(Source: Corel Gallery Clipart, Ship Totem "37C037")

the DEA's prediction of shipping-container involvement may only hold true for drug loads crossing the Mediterranean *en route* to Europe.

> From west African coastal states such as Guinea-Bissau, the drugs pass through Mauritania, Mali and Niger before ending up in Libya or Egypt. From there, law enforcement officials suspect the drugs are hidden in containers on board cargo ships, which are less likely to be searched than those from Latin America.[11]
>
> — *The Guardian Observer* (U.K.), November 2009

Which crime families subsequently handle distribution of the narcotics inside the European Union is not clear. Nor is where—along the inbound lanes—those families originally purchase the product.

There May Be Some International Intrigue Here As Well

What the above-named sources have thus far said is this: first (1) doctrinally opposed Muslim radicals have come to rely on the same drug conduit; then (2) Communist rebels have been protecting that conduit's South American segments. That's too many oranges, lemons, and kumquats to be coincidently sharing the same fruit salad. Such an improbable mix generally means an international chef seeking anonymity. Might a Far Eastern criminal syndicate be holding dissimilar pieces together within South Asia, Africa, and Latin America so that its parent nation could obscurely destabilize its only remaining opposition to worldwide domination? After all, bottom-up collective effort is the trademark of all Asian organizations.

Within the Middle East, Iran has been sponsoring both Shiite *Hezbollah* and Sunni *Hamas*. Bin Laden has met with *Hezbollah* operations chief Mughniyeh, and *al-Qaeda* operatives have trained at *Hezbollah* camps in Lebanon's Bekaa Valley.[12] But neither Iran nor any Sunni nation has a powerful enough organized-crime family to run such a widespread operation. That dubious honor now belongs to only a few nationalities—most notably the Russians and Mainland Chinese.

All the while, the insurgent faction protecting the most vital legs of the narcotics conduit in South America has become more Maoist than Marxist.[13] That tends to favor an Oriental choice for conduit coordinator.

Because the Hong Kong triad with the largest overseas operation has sworn allegiance to the PRC,[14] the ruling party of China may have now asked it—for strategic reasons—to oversee (and refine) an already existent smuggling network. To do so, even a powerful triad would still need the assistance of local cartels and revolutionaries.

The Role of Most Militants in the Trafficking

Hezbollah and *FARC* fighters may be helping to provide security at the Guinea-Bissau smuggling hub, but an organized-crime element must still coordinate all incoming and outgoing loads. That element would most likely be from Lebanon. While periodically swapping cocaine for weapons, *FARC* has mostly provided drug route protection within South America.

> Now they [the *FARC]* tax every stage of the drug business [within their area of operations], from the chemicals needed to process the hardy coca bush into cocaine . . . , right up to charging for the processed drugs to be flown from illegal airstrips they control.[15]
>
> — *BBC News,* September 2003

The links between the Colombian *FARC* and Lebanese are, by no means, new.

> [L]inks between crime syndicates in Ciudad del Este and the *FARC* reportedly date . . . from the mid-1990's. . . . Of three known *FARC* havens in Brazil, the biggest . . . is . . . only 100 miles (161 kilometers) north of Foz do Iguacu. . . . It is . . . on a 6,000-hectare ranch belonging to businessman Ahmad Mohamad, a Lebanese naturalized in Paraguay and arrested by Brazil's Federal Police in September 2002 [Godoy, "As Farc usam Brasil . . . ," *O Estado de Sao Paulo,* 1 March 2003].[16]
>
> — Fed. Research Div., Lib. of Congress, July 2003

The Relationship between Different Criminal Entities

While Colombian drug cartels may move cocaine eastward along the same approximate latitude to West Africa, some other crime family must then take over its further shipment. Just as the Mexican cartels now purchase all cocaine loads from their Colombian counterparts, so probably would another syndicate purchase them in West Africa.

Within a drug transit hub as lucrative as Guinea-Bissau, little actual smuggling would occur without the expressed permission of a global player more powerful than the Colombians, Lebanese, or Nigerians. As in the Triple-Border Region of South America,[17] there must be a transnational entity to which all other traffickers donate a portion of their proceeds. At any given location, this publicity-shy "top dog" can be difficult to identify. That's why many researchers fail to mention him.

> An international network led by Latin American drug cartels and the Lebanese Islamist group *Hezbollah* has chosen West Africa . . . as the nexus for illegal trade in cocaine, oil, counterfeit medicines. . . . [P]rofits fuel terrorist activities worldwide.[18]
>
> — Pulitzer Center, 19 June 2009

Even with *Hezbollah's* help, the Colombian cartels could not be running the whole operation in West Africa. Nor could the Nigerian syndicate be controlling what happens in Europe or east of Somalia. Most likely, the drug hierarchy in Guinea-Bissau mirrors that in the venerable drug-trading center at Ciudad del Este, Paraguay. *Sun Yee On*—the triad known to be working for the PRC—has been spotted there.[19] It would still need Colombian cartels to deliver the product to the coast, or possibly a little farther. For a trans-Atlantic crossing, it could always call on COSCO. But, along any cross-country legs within South America and other continents, there would still be corrupt officials or local rebels (whether Communist or Islamist) to safeguard the loads. Inside Africa, many of those protection fees might end up with *al-Qaeda*. There has been a symbiotic relationship between Communists and Islamists for a very long time.

> Argentinian *(sic)* intelligence submitted a report in 1999 confirming that "agents of the *al-Qaeda* organization . . . had

> been identified in the triple border area" (Montoya, "War on Terrorism Reaches Paraguay's Triple Border," *Jane's Intelligence Review,* December 2001, 12). An official Argentine report added . . . Muslims politicized and radicalized by *Hezbollah* were providing finance to *al-Qaeda* (ibid.). . . .
>
> . . . Islamist groups active in Latin America are also establishing [drug-trafficking] links with organized crime groups in East Asia. . . . [Members of] the Chinese mafia (14-K Triad, Pak Lung Fu [and others]) have . . . been detected in the triple border area (ibid., 14).[20]
>
> — *Inside al-Qaeda,* by Rohan Gunaratna

Which Syndicate Runs the East Asian Legs of the Conduit?

When the Colombian cocaine reaches Karachi, Pakistan, Dawood Ibrahim would be the local drug lord who would act on behalf of *al-Qaeda.* He also handles most of the outgoing shipments of Afghan opiates.[21] Of late, there has been more cooperation between Dawood and *Boko Haram.* Mr. Ibrahim would like to flood West-friendly India with cocaine,[22] and probably to send some of his vast supply of Afghan pre-heroin back along the same transportation network that brought in the cocaine. *Boko Haram,* a direct *al-Qaeda* affiliate, is undoubtedly aware that some Afghan opiates have been making it across the African Sahel on their way to Europe and America since the mid-1990's.[23] They would be foolish to not now try to capitalize on this money-making opportunity.

A certain amount of Golden Triangle heroin also passes through the Karachi and Emirates region on its way westward. Neither Ibrahim, nor the Lebanese, Nigerians, Colombians, or Mexicans would be in overall "charge" of a two-way drug pipeline that encircled the planet, despite all of their interactions with one another. Most of the world's supply of illicit drugs comes from Asia, so a far-reaching Oriental syndicate would most probably oversee its passage to market. All smaller crime families in the narcotic's chain of custody would then behave more like semi-autonomous subcontractors to that top Oriental syndicate. As long as they regularly gave a cut of their drug transfer proceeds to the Oriental entity, they would be left alone to coordinate all "pipeline-operating" details among themselves.

Where Official Corruption Plays a Role

Trade in illicit narcotics generates such immense sums of money that high-level payoffs are to be expected. Within the free-wheeling countries of West Africa, such payoffs easily result in governmental collusion.

> [A]s of April 2010, the armed forces of Guinea-Bissau are controlled by people designated as drug traffickers . . . by the U.S. Government. . . . Guinea-Bissau is not unique in this respect. In Guinea, the presidential guard . . . appears to have been involved in drug trafficking. . . . After the disruptions in Guinea-Bissau and Guinea, it appears this hub relocated to the Gambia. . . . [W]ith state authorities dominating the trade in some countries, . . . there is little evidence of insurgents dealing in the drug. There have been allegations that rebels in the north of Mali and Niger, as well as political militants in Algeria, have been involved in trans-Saharan trafficking.[24]
>
> — *U.N. World Drug Report (for) 2010*

Guinea now has a new president. But, from what he has been saying about Conakry's previous regime (the one awarded a multibillion-dollar Chinese bailout in 2009 [25]), some of the governments in neighboring countries may now be under same international drug-smuggling pressures as his predecessors in Guinea. This would make cleaning up any morphine base portal to America extremely challenging. Wherever too much government corruption exists, criminal activity becomes business as usual.

> Alpha Condé, who took over in Guinea three years ago on a pledge to end nearly half a century of corrupt, despotic rule, said the French operation to cleanse Islamists from lawless northern Mali in January had stopped smugglers using the area to transit cocaine.
>
> While he had personally backed the French action, he claimed it had led to the traffickers refocusing their attention on neighbors like Guinea, where the entire government ended up on the traffickers' payroll five years ago.[26]
>
> — *The Telegraph* (U.K.), 15 June 2013

Might Internal Strife Be Just Another Corporate Strategy?

The most obvious drug route influences have already been discussed. Yet, there are one or two more. Major drug conduits tend to occur in volatile regions. This unfortunate reality leads to a question. Has the passage of narcotics made those places less stable, or do drug traffickers stir up popular dissent to make interdiction less likely?

The UNODC has said that "the countries of West Africa need help . . . to resist transnational organized crime" and "the region will continue to face serious . . . threats to governance and stability as long as transnational contraband markets are not addressed."[27] Such a statement implies a direct connection between the instability and cross-nation drug passage. If the PRC did not have a heritage of military deception and Hong Kong triad in its employ, no one would wonder about someone intentionally fomenting trouble in the Sahel to obscure smuggling. Yet, Communist China has displayed an inordinate amount of interest in the heavily Muslim and still chaotic Sudan region. Perhaps, not all of that interest is with petroleum. Sudan is the next country over from the most likely heroin entry point—Somalia. Whether or not such a direct connection exists, one would still be hard pressed to attribute all the Sahel lawlessness west of Sudan to natural causes. Within Asia, conspiracies are more often the rule than the exception.

> Of the 25 countries with the highest risks of instability globally, nine were in West Africa: Niger, Mali, Sierra Leone, Liberia, Mauritania, Guinea-Bissau, Côte d'Ivoire and Benin (Hewitt et al, "Peace and Conflict 2010," Ctr. for Internat. Development and Conflict Mgt.) [28]
>
> — *U.N. World Drug Report (for) 2010*

How Hard Is It for Drugs to Cross Africa?

The Dark Continent is not the same as other parts of the globe. After bypassing the normal "embassy visa procedure" to visit Sudan in 2006, a world traveler had the difference explained to him by a local hotel owner (and permission coordinator).[29] Within Africa, one can often enter a different country by just showing up at the border with money in hand. Within such a loosely controlled environment, Afghan narcotics would have little trouble moving across the Sahel and then down onto the Ivory Coast. From there, they would only go one place.

> Venezuela is a key transit country for drug shipments . . . to the United States.[30]
> — *Insightcrime.org*, September 2012

At some point *en route* to America, the Afghan opiates must be purchased by Mexican cartels. As with the Golden Triangle heroin and Colombian cocaine, this change of ownership most likely occurs in Central America. All drugs of "foreign-origin" are then smuggled into the U.S. by Mexican cartels, along with what has been locally grown and refined. The Mexicans, while not wishing to outright own any drugs not yet in their territory, may still monitor the progress of inbound shipments.

> "Mexican narcotraffickers operate like multinational emissaries "to establish contacts . . . that can deal with the Turkish and Indian criminal organizations . . . to facilitate the . . . sale of drugs," specifically heroin.[31]
> — Autonomous Technical Institute of Mexico

The Most Probable Chain of Custody

In all likelihood, Mexican cartels get the Afghan opiates from Colombian cartels, who have in turn obtained them from Lebanese or Nigerian syndicates at Guinea-Bissau and the Bight of Benin. Within either drug hub, the product may have been outright purchased by the Colombians or simply swapped for an equal value of cocaine. Before reaching these West African portals, the Lebanese probably bought the opiates from the Nigerians, and the Nigerians from a Pakistani crime family.

While the Lebanese may administer their branch of the drug conduit all the way to Spain, the Nigerians' control over their segments probably ends at Algiers and the Indian Ocean. So well connected with *al-Qaeda* is the Karachi syndicate that it could easily maintain ownership of the morphine base all the way to Somalia.

That a Mexican cartel might "advance purchase" a drug load in India or Pakistan and then expect it to be safely delivered to their Central American doorstep is highly unlikely. No self-respecting criminal enterprise would ever relinquish control over a paid acquisition. The actual purchase must come closer to home. That takes intermediate owners.

A Closer Look at Nigerian Organized Crime

As implied by the Chapter 12 excerpt from the *NDTA for 2011,* the Nigerian TCO is either more influential than most U.S. citizens suspect or has a powerful mentor. Well documented for years has been the cooperation between Hong Kong's triads and Mexico's cartels.[32] Why couldn't those same triads forge a few links with the biggest TCO in West Africa as well. The fact that the Nigerians have been "assisting" opiates from both Southeast and Southwest Asia to reach their biggest markets would certainly suggest such a relationship.

> African criminal enterprises have developed quickly since the 1980's. . . . Easier international travel, expanded world trade, and financial transactions that cross national borders have enabled them to branch out of local . . . crime to . . . develop criminal networks within more prosperous . . . regions. . . .
>
> Nigerian criminal enterprises are the most significant of these groups and operate in more than 80 other countries of the world. They are among the most aggressive and expansionist [of the] international criminal groups and are primarily engaged in drug trafficking and financial frauds.
>
> The most profitable activity of the Nigerian groups is drug trafficking: delivering heroin from Southeast and Southwest Asia into Europe and the U.S. . . . Large populations of ethnic Nigerians in India, Pakistan, and Thailand have given these enterprises direct access to 90% . . . of the world's heroin production.[33]
>
> — *Federal Bureau of Investigation (FBI) Report* (still on its website as of July 2014)

Often associated with the Nigerian syndicate are the people

of Igbo origin—one of the largest ethnic groupings in Africa. Most are Christian and live in the southern part of the country. It was mainly Igbo separatists who had formed the short-lived country of Biafra at the southeastern end of Nigeria during its tragic civil war from 1967 to 1970.[34]

> In West Africa, the [drug] traffickers appear to be primarily Nigerian, although they may hold residence . . . in any West African country. Nigerians from the southeast of the country, particularly of the Igbo ethnic group, are especially implicated.[35]
>
> — *Transnat. Organized Crime in Western Africa*
> UNODC, 2013

Heroin of Afghan Origin Is Still Reaching the U.S.

Like large rivers, sizable drug conduits change their course and sometimes even a means of conveyance, but they do not go completely away. When the Golden Triangle heroin flow to New York City via Vancouver (British Columbia) became too heavily interdicted by Canadian and U.S. authorities, it was simply diverted to Mexico. In other words, Golden Triangle product was still getting to New York City, just by a different path. Similarly, if 60% of the heroin on U.S. streets was coming from southern Afghanistan in 1990,[36] a significant portion of America's street heroin is still being produced from Afghan poppies. That's the inescapable lesson from the Prohibition period. Any U.S. government claim that this SWA opiate corridor has now been completely shut down is just another example of bureaucratic optimism, political spin, or worse.

The most logical location for the latest variant to this perpetual SWA pipeline is through West Africa and then across the Atlantic to Venezuela or Brazil. After all, South America is—at its closest point—only 1800 miles from Liberia. (See Map 14.2.) Of all the locales for a major drug conduit, open ocean offers the least danger of interdiction. Enforcement agencies must not automatically assume all drugs are reaching the Mediterranean before heading west.

> West Africa is increasingly being used by drug traffickers as a transit point for drug[s] bound for Europe from Latin America. . . .

> Additionally . . . heroin is being trafficked through the region. Originating from Asia, primarily channeled through East Africa, its final destination is Europe and also North America.[37]
>
> — *West Africa Coast Initiative,* UNODC, 2014

If the UNODC is willing to admit that Asian heroin (or a less refined version of it) is coming to North America through West Africa, then that is what's happening. The extent of its flow is anybody's guess, but it is probably large. According to the U.N., South American "cocaine worth $1.25 billion passes through West Africa every year" going the other direction. With that much money changing hands, the *Geopolitical Monitor's* claim that "international criminal organizations have gained a foothold in the region" needs no further proof.[38] In fact, the U.N.'s new *West Africa Coast Initiative* has as its basic premise that one or more "transnational organized-crime" elements are now present there.[39] Such groups would be involved with both commodities, and their most influential member overseeing an "integrated effort." Because some opiates moving through West Africa come from Southeast Asia, that most influential member is likely to be the Hong Kong triad with the largest overseas operation—*Sun Yee On.*

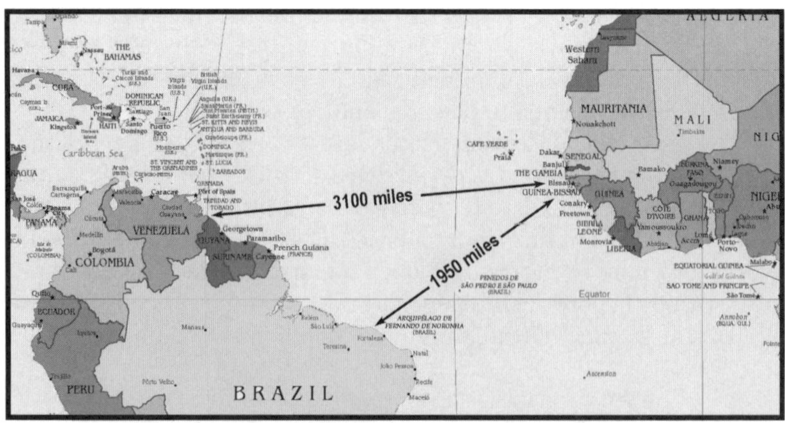

Map 14.2: Proximity of the Two Continents
(Source: Courtesy of General Libraries, University of Texas at Austin, from map designator "world_pol_2013.jpg")

Likely Trace of the West African Opiate Pipeline

While trying to counter a wily organized-crime element, one must make (and continually refine) projections of any drug conduit. Map 14.3 depicts the collective input of this research so far with regard to pipeline location. Such estimates are only approximate of course, but still valuable. They could not only assist with interdiction, but make closer scrutiny possible.

A criminal-insight nonprofit believes this "alternate" narcotics highway across Africa to have two separate branches northward into Europe: (1) one through Guinea-Bissau and its neighbors bound for southern Spain; and (2) another via Ghana and its tiny neighbors headed for northern Spain, France, and Italy.[40] In all likelihood, the Lebanese crime family monitors the day-to-date functioning of the former, and its Nigerian counterpart the latter. Still to be determined is how the Afghan opiates get from Trans-African High-

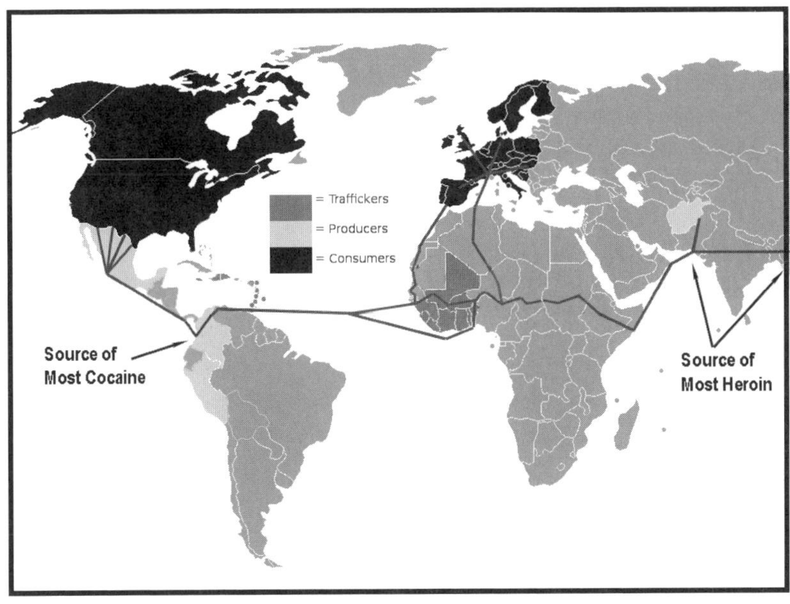

Map 14.3: Approximate Trace of "Dual-Purpose" Drug Conduit
(Source: Modification of public-domain map from Wikipedia Encyclopedia, s.v. "West Africa Coast Initiative," with image designator "Drugtrade.png")

Figure 14.2: Reason for U.S. Squad Augment at Police Outposts
(Source: http:// search.usa.gov public-domain image from url: www.quartermaster.army.mil/oqmg/professional_bulletin/2005/Spring05/Images/299th%20Spt%20Bn.jpg)

way 5 to Guinea-Bissau's island archipelago. In this part of West Africa, the governmental agencies of more than one country may be assisting with the transfer.

All Heroin Network's Are Multi-Faceted

For Asian opiates (from both sources), these projected pathways would provide a back door into both Europe and America. The front door for Afghan heroin into Europe has traditionally been through Iran or Turkey (where it had been fully refined), and then some of that finished product made it to America from there. The front door for Golden Triangle heroin to the U.S. has lately been across the Pacific and subsequently in through Mexico.

On 24 June 2015, one of America's most reliable news media outlets—NPR—finally admitted that much of the recent influx of heroin into this country was not from Colombian or Mexican poppies, but from Afghan poppies. It said much of the addictive white powder was coming to the U.S. via Europe's traditional Turkish portal, with the final transit being accomplished through a glut of trucks at the Bulgarian border.[41] There may be some truth to the claim, because more trucks have routinely arrived at the Mexican border than can be adequately searched.[42] NPR went on to say that two-thirds of Europe's total supply of heroin was arriving this way, with only a third of that being forwarded to America.[43] This means a full third of Europe's heroin may be coming from the trans-African conduit's northern branches, while an indeterminate quantity of partially refined opiate more easily passes from its western end to Venezuela, and then on to Mexico.

A Blessing in Disguise?

If the White House is comfortable with that much morphine base crossing Africa on its way to Central America for further refinement and U.S. distribution, it need take no further action. If the White House would rather limit this destabilizing influence on American society while enhancing the security of over 20 African nations, it now has a way. (See Figure 14.2.) Without some kind of local security assistance, many of those nations will eventually fall under Islamist or Communist control. How tiny American infantry contingents could safely accomplish both missions at once will be discussed in the appendix. First, other forms of Communist and Islamist cooperation in Africa must be explored.

Part Five

Cooperation between Expansionist Entities

"Remember that all through history, there have been tyrants and murderers, and for a time, they seem invincible. But in the end, they always fall. Always." — Mahatma Gandhi

(Source: Mahatma Gandhi, from www.goodreads.com/quotes.)

15 Where Both Factions Work Together

- Which goals do the two expansionist elements share?
- Might they be working as allies against the West?

Infidel PLA soldiers and Salafists easily coexist in Sudan.

(Source: Courtesy of Orion Books, from *World Army Uniforms since 1939*, © 1975, 1980, 1981, 1983 by Blandford Press, Part II, Plates 81 and 124)

The Most Obvious Liaison

As demonstrated by Chapters 12 through 14, Chinese and Islamist elements have been working together in Africa to undermine the U.S. and Europe through a flood of Afghan heroin. An assortment of fundamentalist Muslim factions (both Sunni and Shiite) have been facilitating the flow of drugs across the Sahel and then down into Venezuela, while a Hong Kong triad is likely assisting with the liaison between them, the Karachi syndicate, and Colombian cartels. Among the Islamic groups most often implicated in this smuggling are *al-Shabaab, Boko Haram, AQIM,* and *Hezbollah.*

Similarities in Method

Just because the Communists and Salafists have been using the same 4GW methodology to confound Washington does not automatically infer joint conspiracy. Narcotics trafficking generates so much money that both may be cooperating simply to realize bigger profits. Several militant Muslim factions have been supporting themselves for years through drug route "transpo" and protection. But so too have two of the most successful guerrilla outfits in South America—*FARC* and the Shining Path (both now Maoist in ideology).[1] Throughout the Western Hemisphere, the PRC prefers to influence elections through locally-generated funds that cannot be subsequently traced.[2] Drug trade involvement provides such a source.

While most expansionist ploys may have been developed by Beijing's first few Communist regimes, many were later adopted by other "revolutionary" governments (like those in Iran and Sudan). Some have since undergone 4GW refinement. In 1999, the PLA Publishing House's *Unrestricted Warfare* listed all security challenges the U.S. government might have trouble handling. Among them were "illegal drug trade" and "out-of-contol immigration."[3] To influence the voting base of a country, would all immigrants have to be of Chinese origin? Just prior to the 2005 election of Iraqi Prime Minister al-Maliki (from the radical Shiite *Dawa* party), there were counterfeit ballots, campaign currency, and Iranian "voters" entering Iraq in large numbers.[4] At that point in history, the eventual fracturing of Iraq became inevitable. While fundamentalist Iran would eventually be blamed, it had—almost certainly—not invented the trick.

Most Chinese immigrants to Africa will similarly push for Sinocentric national policies and Socialistic leaders. But, a tremendous influx of Chinese workers has not only happened to the relatively secular countries of Eritrea, Djibouti, Nigeria, Angola, and Zimbabwe, it has also occurred in highly Islamist Sudan.[5] There, while a Muslim Brotherhood launched regime continues to support fundamentalist militants throughout the region, the PLA has been protecting that regime's best source of income—namely, its oil industry. The PRC receives much needed energy, and in return Sudan gets military hardware and U.N. protection for its rogue behavior. The two countries have been pursuing such supposedly separate agendas for many years without the least evidence of animosity between them. Those who would dwell too heavily on religious differences might never acknowledge the danger.

So, whether coordinated or not, there exists a mutual effort between Chinese and Islamists to upstage and undermine the West. It's most obvious along the African network for Afghan heroin delivery to Europe and America. Sudan lies along the initial stages of that network. So, another Chinese ally farther along the same network may provide clues as to the Sino-Sudanese relationship—particularly if that ally were to have its own oil.

Best Example of Such a Tryst

As China is the recurring partner in these symbiotic-relationships, one need not stick to the Dark Continent for a procedural model. At the point where the trans-African drug shipments enter South America is a fairly religious country with up to a million Chinese workers already in its oil-producing region.[6] It also has tens of thousands of other Communist transplants (from Cuba) in its governmental hierarchy. That country is, of course, Venezuela. The following U.S. State Department assessment reveals "popular defense units" and tiny "Bolivarian Circle groups" promoting a Chinese version of revolution. That's because Cuba—the regional purveyor of Communism—accepted the PRC as its mentor following the demise of the Soviet Union in 1991.[7]

> As of February 2005, Cuba . . . had 20,000 doctors, dentists, teachers, and sports trainers in Venezuela, mainly working in poor pro-Chavez neighborhoods of Caracas. Fidel Castro pledged in early 2005 that the number of Cubans would increase to 30,000 by the end of the year. In 2004, President Chavez reportedly posted dozens of Cuban "advisers" to the internal security and immigration agencies of the [Venezuelan] Ministry of Interior and Justice, other key ministries, and the Central Bank. . . .
>
> . . . [The] Chavez government has sought to develop military relations with [Communist] China. . . . China's defense minister visited Venezuela for the first time in September 2001. . . . Some Cuban advisers reportedly have

been posted in [Venezuelan] . . . Military Intelligence . . . and some Cuban military advisers reportedly are engaged in training the [Venezuelan] military. . . .

. . . The Chavez government apparently now sees the United States as its principal adversary. Now closely allied with Fidel Castro Ruz of Cuba, President Chavez reportedly has ordered Venezuela's armed forces to implement a new Cuban-style strategy in which the top priority is preparing to fight a war of resistance against an invasion by the United States. . . . "Popular defense units" of 50 to 500 civilians are to be established in workplaces and on farms. . . .

. . . In addition to the official security forces, Chavez has distributed weapons to the estimated 10,000 members of the Bolivarian Circles, independently organized groups of Chavez supporters at the grassroots *[sic]* level of Venezuelan society. These groups are modeled on Cuba's Committees for the Defense of the Revolution [CDR] and operate in groups of between seven and 11 people.[8]

– *Lib. of Congress Country Profile,* March 2005

To fully assess the degree of Chinese influence on Venezuela, one must first understand the meaning of "CDR."

A CDR unit was set up on each square block throughout all urban areas [of Cuba], and equivalent counterparts were located in rural areas. The CDRs act as the eyes and ears of the regime at the most personal level; they are designed as a "neighborhood watch" in which neighbors are both the watching and the watched. The police tap into . . . CDR officials' personal assessments of the revolutionary commitment of each individual within the jurisdiction. . . .

. . . *[T]he Cuban social and criminal justice systems are more similar to those of Chinese communism than of Soviet communism.* After the revolution, the national revolutionary militia, the police, and the Committee for the Defense of the Revolution (CDR) were responsible for maintaining law and order. [Italics added.] [9]

– *Global Security*

By August 2008, the Venezuelan defense apparatus had been

thoroughly infiltrated by Cubans,[10] and local estimates of governmental "volunteers" from Cuba had risen to 100,000.[11] Chavez's Bolivarian Circle groups had obviously been modeled after Cuban CDRs to ensure his population's acceptance of the Communist revolution. As such, their initial activity resembled that of the Chinese Red Guard movement. Only missing were the reeducation centers and mass killings. Similarly, Venezuela's Popular Defense Units (UDPs) must have been similar to Cuba's "national revolutionary militia." They worked hand and hand with the Bolivarian Circle groups to maintain law and order.

> The [UDP] groups wear civilian clothing with military patches and drill without weapons. . . .
>
> . . . Chavez said the new military reserves will number more than 1.5 million and the rest of the population will be recruited [and trained by them] to help defend the country in guerrilla warfare. . . .
>
> Venezuela's new military doctrine . . . prescribed the use of "reserves" to augment national security. . . . "[P]opular commands" [were] made up of "basic action units" in charge of community defense, supplies, communications, and intelligence collection. . . .
>
> The government may tap the *Frente Francisco de Miranda (FFM)* youth movement to fill out its [UDP] reserve forces. . . . [T]he *FFM* is a quasi-military, Chavez-affiliated youth movement, noted for serving as a political and military training school for radicalized Venezuelan youths.[12]
>
> — *Global Security*

Clearly, Venezuela's defense establishment had been loosely patterned after that of China. If that of Sudan were similar, then PRC exchange visits may have had more to do with its particulars than Iran. Still, most Western journalists would rather compare the PDF to IRGC. What they forget is that fundamentalist Sunnis will not normally emulate fundamentalist Shiites.

What Makes the Sudanese PDF Different from the IRGC

Though formed as the "semi-military" wing of Sudan's ruling party when General al-Bashir took over the country in 1989, the

Sudanese PDF was originally made up of civilians. Just as with Mao's Red Guards, their job was to insure that the ruling party's agenda was being followed by everyone. Specifically, the Sudanese PDF was to "train citizens on military and civil capabilities, [and] raise security awareness and military discipline among them, in order to act as a back-up force [to the military]."[13] Though strictly Islamist, the PDF's members were not "*sharia* police." Their role would eventually evolve into mobilizing, equipping, and funding militia auxiliaries.[14] When pro-government militias were being "guided" by the PDF in the Darfur and Southern Kordofan regions of Sudan, separate genocides resulted.[15] (See Figure 15.1.) That sounds more like Red Guard excesses in China and Cambodia than anything the IRGC ever perpetrated. The IRCG did help to launch Lebanese *Hezbollah* and still supports *Hamas,* but neither it nor any of its proxies has yet to be accused of genocide. Therefore, one can make a good case for the PDF never being patterned after the IRCG.

IRGC members were former anti-Shah guerrillas who were to be Ayatollah Khomeini's "guardians of the [Islamic] revolution." Their multifaceted role would be as follows: (1) dislodge opposition factions and restore order to the cities and countryside; (2) provide internal security to expand the Ayatollah's control; and (3) prosecute the war with Iraq.[16]

To keep an eye on (and counterbalance) the Iranian Armed Forces, the IRCG became an integral part of almost every unit.[17] The Shah's "top-down" military system was to be changed into one in which every soldier's allegiance would be not to his commander, but rather the Islamic State. From throughout Iranian society, the IRCG was to recruit and train a 20-million-man-strong military auxiliary called the *Baseej*.[18] As such, it would provide most of the frontline fighters for the war with Iraq. Besides recruiting and training junior infantrymen, the IRCG may have been the first "revolutionary" component in history to enforce religious doctrine while maintaining political stability. (Communist countries don't allow religion.)

> In rural regions . . . [IRGC] Guard bases located in individual small towns. In more urbanized areas . . . a subordinate headquarters, which may even be a storefront . . . overseas further subdivisions of the city ("Duties . . . of

> Guard," *Kayhan,* 167). The intention and result is that the Guard [more easily] achieves maximum penetration of the civilian population. . . .
>
> . . . [T]he Guard's role in maintaining internal order and enforcing Islamic law distinguishes it from other revolutionary armed forces, especially those of Communist regimes.[19]
>
> — *Warriors of Islam,* by Kenneth Katzman

The PDF More Closely Follows the Chinese Model

The role of the PDF in Sudanese society has never been as multifaceted and pervasive as that of the IRGC in Iranian society. In recent years, the PDF's influence has been limited to providing

Figure 15.1: Khartoum-Supported Janjaweed in Darfur
(Source: Corel Gallery Clipart, Man Totem "28V005" and Holiday Corel "21A038")

military reservists and recruiting, equipping, and training tribal proxies. All the while, it has done very little enforcing of religious doctrine.

The IRCG, on the other hand, still has semi-autonomous detachments in every Iranian village and neighborhood. From deep inside Iranian society, it continues to enforce Islamic law, collect intelligence, quell antigovernment sentiment, and stand ready to provide soldiers for a "people's army." That's why the Sudanese PDF's way of doing things—and its shameful by-product in Darfur and Southern Kordofan—more closely resembles Maoist behavior. It may well have taken its inspiration from Chinese government exchange visits to Sudan.

Proof of That Close a Relationship between the Countries

In the early 1990's when al-Turabi of the Muslim Brotherhood was helping to run Sudan, that country and Iran were friends, and al-Turabi opposed to Communism. But former general Omar al-Bashir was the actual president of Sudan at the time, and had been since a military coup in 1989. After al-Turabi was expelled from the al-Bashir government, the links between Sudan and China began to strengthen. Al-Bashir is still in power. In a recent state visit to China, here's how the formally charged war criminal was greeted by the Chinese premier.

> "Mr. Bashir, . . . we welcome you," said Mr. Hu [Jintao], who added that he hoped to continue the "traditionally friendly relations" between the two countries. . . .
>
> . . . For years, Sudan has supplied roughly seven per cent of China's oil needs—the equivalent of half its daily output—in exchange for financial and military support.[20]
>
> — *The Telegraph* (U.K.), June 2011

After confirming the same depth of this long-term relationship between the two countries in a 2009 interview, Sudan's president actually divulged a few of its details.

> From the first day, our [the Sudanese] policy was clear: To look eastward, toward China . . .

> We believe that the Chinese expansion [into Sudan] was natural because we filled the space left by Western governments . . . with China. . . . The success of the Sudanese experiment in dealing with China without political conditions or pressures encouraged other African countries to look toward China.[21]
>
> — al-Bashir, in *Time Magazine* interview, 2009

Obviously, any Chinese influence on al-Bashir's governmental procedures and policies had been highly discreet. The staggering number of interagency exchange visits between the PRC and South Africa from 2000 to 2003 suggests that's how the change had been accomplished in Sudan as well.[22] It was so piecemeal and incremental that al-Bashir never realized it was happening. China had simply begun to apply the methods of a "bottom-up" culture to its international affairs. The "motivator" in this subtle transformation had been more Chinese business and aid.

> In May 2006, the Sudanese Minister for Industry . . . received a delegation of Chinese companies to discuss investments in Sudan's secondary sector [businesses other than oil]. Military ties were strengthened as well. . . . This charm offensive [by China] partially stemmed from the political aspiration to maintain influence [over Sudan].[23]
>
> — *Sudan Tribune,* August 2007

With this subtle Chinese influence on Khartoum came changes to Sudan's foreign policy, and what would subsequently transpire along its borders. That something would be two widely separated genocides.

> Sudan and China established diplomatic relations on January 4, 1959 and have since become strongly close global allies.
>
> The People's Republic of China is Sudan's biggest trade partner. Sudan imports low cost items as well as armaments from China. China and Sudan enjoy a very robust and productive relationship in the fields of diplomacy, economic trade, and political stratagems.[24]
>
> — Sudanese Embassy in Washington, D.C, 2015

An Indirect But Brutal PRC Strategy Starts to Take Shape

Most of the PRC's 4GW refinements to its expansionist agenda for the Dark Continent seem now apparent. Such ploys would work best where Western corporations were worried about safety, and their parent countries about Islamic extremism.

While vowing not to interfere with each targeted country's internal processes, the PRC then alters that country's political base through immigration, sways its governmental decisions through inter-agency cooperation, and influences its elections through non-traceable campaign funding. No separate maneuver is strong enough to result in a pro-Chinese regime, but their combination over a number of years is that powerful. To manipulate the elections, Chinese operatives most likely rely on local revenues from petroleum, minerals, or narcotics. Such revenues tend to be greater where there is no Western presence. That's why China has so often befriended rogue nations in the past and continues to encourage chronic disorder in others.

Whether the objective country is Islamic or not makes little difference to the Chinese. However, in an Islamic, partially Islamic, or *al-Qaeda*-threatened country, any suspected extremist activity would provide a ready-made diversion to all PRC manipulation.

16 Intentional Instability

- What might be gained by destabilizing another nation?
- Is there any evidence of this type of subversion in Africa?

Not every country seeks progress through tranquility.

(Source: Corel Gallery Clipart, Holiday, Image Club image "21B004")

Which Adversary Would Attempt Such a Thing?

While Islamists and Communists both try to discredit the regimes of targeted nations, only one seeks chronic disorder. (See Figure 16.1.) The Islamists will quickly replicate all governmental services at the local level. This may temporarily confuse people. But, it is the Asian Communists, who as 4GW and Maneuver Warfare (MW) masters, know how to capitalize on constant chaos. They have learned from Vietnam and other forays that any uncertainty presents an almost insurmountable challenge to the West's "structure-seeking" preference for 2nd-Generation-Warfare (2GW).

Western corporations tend to shy away from dangerous locations. Previous chapters have shown the PRC's current "One Globe" strategy to be largely business oriented within Africa. Thus, it is perfectly logical for the PRC to permit some instability within their economically targeted areas. Instability creates the opportunity for peacekeepers, corporate security guards, and—as in Sudan in 2000—even the occasional expeditionary force. The PRC's two most strategically important objectives in Africa provide telling examples—Sudan for oil, and the DRC for minerals. Haven't both nations been suffering from chronic discord despite the U.N.'s best efforts to assuage it?

How might societal turmoil be intentionally promulgated? Several ideas come immediately to mind: (1) arms and training for all warring elements; (2) the occasional atrocity; and (3) a PRC-supported government proxy or rebel force.

What about Rwanda's Backing of M23?

The M23 is an eastern DRC rebel group of mostly Tutsi composition. Many of its members are former defectors from the DRC army. In November 2013, the M23 was driven out of the strategically vital town of Goma and then forced to surrender by a DRC military contingent backed by a special U.N. Intervention Brigade. Because M23 has always been supported by Rwanda,[1] one wonders why the PRC has lately been so "charitable" (with a new palace, etc.) to Rwanda. Might China have just abandoned M23 while previously doing things to encourage it? Such actions are certainly possible, but any hard proof of the PRC keeping the world's most coveted mineral region too dangerous for Western enterprise is not likely. Here's how the area's opposing factions have previously gotten access to Chinese weaponry.

> Chinese arms have appeared frequently in the eastern Congo and Rwanda. According to the Stockholm International Peace Research Institute (SIPRI), the Rwandan army, Hutu militias and the opposition Rwandan Patriotic Front (RPF) [Tutsis] used Chinese weapons. . . . The Rwandan government reportedly purchased them from independent arms dealers. Those used by the RPF came from Ugandan

Figure 16.1: Hunger More Frightening Than Communism
(Source: DA Pamphlet 550-33 [1989])

government stocks. The Hutu militias obtained them from stocks sold initially to the DRC and Seychelles.[2]
— Jamestown Foundation, 2009

A recent U.N. report claims that Rwanda and Uganda had both sent small arms, heavy artillery, military supplies, and new recruits to M23.[3] Kigali may have believed itself helping DRC Tutsis to counter the same *FDLR* Hutus who had committed its own genocide. But, a powerful mentor may have also benefited. This war in the eastern DRC is now, and always has been, about minerals. As long as the region remains unstable, China will continue to have free rein over their extraction. But neither Rwanda nor Uganda are particularly interested in them, despite Western news media insinuations to the contrary. Those tiny nations are more worried about the murderous factions that continually run cross-border raids from the DRC. Around Goma, the coveted minerals and oppressed Tutsis merely share the same space.

> The Congolese army has been fighting various Rwandan-backed rebel factions for at least 15 years in a brutal war over the country's vast mineral resources.[4]
>
> — *CBC News* (Canada), 23 July 2013

China's Opinion of M23

Joseph Kabila's DRC army may be North Korean trained and all troops in the U.N. Intervention Force from Chinese allies (South

Figure 16.2: Rape Has Become a Weapon of War in the DRC
(Source: Corel Gallery Clipart, Woman, Miscellaneous, Totem, designator "47P006")

Africa, Tanzania, and Malawi),[5] but this doesn't mean that the PRC is diametrically opposed to M23. Didn't the Chinese government support both antagonists in the Ethiopia-Eritrea War? [6] Unfortunately, whoever encourages both sides during a vicious conflict becomes indirectly responsible for any atrocities that either may commit. (See Figure 16.2.)

M23's Background

The M23 is a rebel militia formed on 4 April 2012 after hundreds of Tutsi DRC soldiers deserted, citing poor conditions in the army and the government's unwillingness to honor all facets of a "23 March 2009" peace agreement. That agreement had been between the Kinshasa regime and M23's predecessor—the National Congress for the Defence of the People (CNDP). Most of those deserters were former CNDP fighters who had been absorbed into the DRC army as part of this agreement. Many of their friends were not offered amnesty as promised.[7]

That agreement was signed in Goma. That's because Goma is at the heart of the DRC region where both government and Hutu *FDLR* forces have long been guilty of looting and physical abuse against Tutsi residents.[8] That's right. This is the same *FDLR* to which the *Interahamwe*—those guilty of Rwanda's 1994 genocide—still belong. The Kinshasa regime has traditionally been PRC backed. It was also Communist China that provided the *Interahamwe* with its final "instrument of mass destruction" (all the machetes).[9] Thus, one now wonders whether the two anti-Tutsi campaigns are somehow connected.

Because of the DRC government's apparent lack of pressure against *FDLR* rebels and their own army's excesses in the region, M23's occupation of Goma in 2012 seemed—to many residents—as an improvement to their personal security. Facing accusations of unsavory behavior by M23's leader,[10] the DRC army wanted Goma back. It was then that the U.N. Intervention Force—made up of China's closest African allies—helped the DRC army to dislodge M23 from Goma and finally push it across the Ugandan border.

Does the PRC have something against Tutsis? Or does it simply find the ongoing animosity between Hutu and Tutsi beneficial? The answer to that question may lie in another part of Africa where two separate genocides have already occurred.

Latest Source of Instability in the Oil-Rich Sudan Region

Since early 2014, there has been a new civil war raging in the Eastern Sub-Sahara. This one is between South Sudanese President Salva Kiir's SPLM (Sudan People's Liberation Movement) government and the rebels of former vice president Riek Machar. Machar has been accusing China of "conflicting roles" in the dispute—namely, playing both ends against the middle. The PRC has been selling vast quantities of small arms to South Sudan in deference to U.S. and European Union (E.U.) arms embargoes while concurrently pushing—as a member of the Security Council—for peace. The cash-strapped government of South Sudan has been forced to use oil as collateral for this Chinese aid.[11]

Unfortunately, the government of South Sudan is now guilty of setting villages on fire and attacking civilians in its ongoing campaign against the rebels of its former vice president.[12] That means China's new infantry peacekeeping battalion in South Sudan may end up bolstering a repressive regime.[13]

Where the Ultimate Problem May Lie

The PRC and Iran both have "revolutionary" governments. In other words, their leaders consider rebellion to be a prerequisite of every nation's growth. As such, they may not equate armed insurrection with instability, or peace with progress. Instead, they could view the constant strife within the DRC's Copper Belt and Sudan's Abyei Oil region as nothing more than the natural growing pains of several developing nations. That this strife just happens to favor whichever world power is still willing to do business there is just a happy coincidence.

17 The Jihadist Threat as a Diversion

- Do Asians often wait for a diversion before attacking?
- How might such a diversion be manifested in Africa?

Somali pirates have distracted West from smuggling route.

(Source: Courtesy of Michael Leahy from the cover of "Terrorist Trail," © 2006)

Background Perspective

To bring a chronic offender to justice, a criminal investigator will often establish a *modus operandi* from that offender's past history. Then, he will try—through that person's recent behavior—to predict his next move. Whether or not the CPC is still capable of mass murder, it has been striving for economic and political domination over every part of the world. Away from its borders, it has only risked a ground expeditionary force twice of late—both to protect a source of petroleum. That's because its new way of usurping regional power through "philanthropic assistance" has been working just fine. In fact, all that technological improvement to its own weaponry may be nothing more than a holding action to keep the West from noticing its far more subtle main attack.

Only within Asia do the victims of PRC expansion suspect how lethal such a flood of obligatory benevolence can become. The government of Taiwan certainly realizes it. Isolating Taiwan, with the intention of eventually bringing it back under Beijing's control, has been at the center of China's foreign policy for decades. There is no reason to expect any change to this policy. Yet, with Sun-Tzu-savy Taiwan, no amount of "charm-laden" subversion is likely to achieve that goal. At some point, China will have to invade Taiwan. To do so, it will need a major diversion in a distant region. That region is likely to be the Middle East.

That ISIS has been all but begging for a large Western expeditionary force to confront in the Levant thus becomes quite suspicious. Other radical factions have taken credit for the actions of every nearby malcontent. But, ISIS's public relations blitz has so far amassed allegiance from not only South Asia, but also North Africa. Horrifically killing large numbers of pro-Western hostages did not evoke the desired response, so in mid-March 2015 what were supposedly ISIS affiliates upped the ante. First, one attacked Western tourists at museum in Tunisia (thereby disrupting the travel market). Then, another killed a large number of "mosque-goers" in Yemen (widening the rift between Sunni and Shiite). Most revealing was when ISIS next posted an on-line "hit list" for 100 U.S. service personnel.[1] It did not just want a Western ground invasion, it wanted one from the U.S. In late June, ISIS renewed the first two parts of this invitation with a massacre of 38 beach occupants in Tunisia and 27 Shiite worshippers in Kuwait. By including up to 30 Britons, the former prompted an exodus of thousands of European tourists from North Africa's most stable country.[2] Then, further escalating the third part of a very suspicious string of aggravations, a man of Arabic heritage shoots and kills four U.S. Marine recruiters in Chattanooga, TN, on 16 July 2015.[3]

A Key Part of Any Such Enticement Must Be Yemen

Because Yemen is only 30 miles from Africa, the Yemeni incident deserves a closer look. In early 2015, the new president of that country—Abed Rabbo Mansour Hadi—was forced to abandon its capital of Sanaa by Shiite Houthi rebels. He took up residence in the former capital of Marxist South Yemen—the port city of Aden. Shortly thereafter, forces loyal to the previous (and Houthi friendly) president Ali Abdullah Saleh, attacked Aden's international airport and the palace containing Hadi. The very next day, an ISIS element—not previously active in Yemen—took credit for mosque bombings in Sanaa that killed 137 Shiite worshippers. Hadi soon fled from Aden by boat for Saudi Arabia. Then, an Arab coalition—with Saudi Arabia at its head—started an aerial bombardment of the Houthis and resupply of ground forces still trying to defend Aden. All the while, AQAP was gobbling up more territory to the east of there.[4] Had ISIS (or whoever has been conducting its public-affairs campaign) taken advantage of the situation to evoke more of a military response from the West?

Map 17.1: Failed-State Neighbors
(Source: Courtesy of General Libraries, University of Texas at Austin, from their website for map designator "aden.jpg")

However it had occurred, the same Yemen to which the U.S. had dedicated so much effort against AQAP, was now another failed state like Somalia. But Somalia was just across the Gulf of Aden from it. (See Map 17.1.) As of 23 March 2015, there were no U.S. government personnel in either. In effect, the bottleneck along an age-old smuggling conduit was free of interference.

It is with this global perspective in mind, that one can now return to the situation in Africa. There, any action of an ISIS affiliate must now be viewed as an opportunity for the PRC to further consolidate its already considerable gains. No direct Chinese advice or assistance would be necessary for such ISIS affiliate activities to constitute a diversion for further PRC expansion.

Has Anyone in Washington Been Watching the African Trend?

That China has helped to create a chronic state of animosity between North and South in oil-rich Sudan should now be evident. The most petroleum-abundant nation in Africa is Nigeria. (See Map 17.2.) Might China have somehow provoked the growing rift been northern and southern portions of that nation as well? While of different Abrahamic religions, those predominantly Muslim and Christian populations used to happily alternate between winning the national elections.[5] Then, what about ongoing events in the third most prolific oil producer in Africa—Libya? Through what appears to be nothing more than a power struggle between competing Muslim factions, that country now has rival governments.

In all three environments, Western corporations would not want to operate. When nations of immense strategic value keep getting split in half with such a result, one suspects a little East Asian influence.

> If his forces are united, separate them. If sovereign and subject are in accord, put division between them.[6]
>
> — Sun Tzu

> All warfare is based on deception. . . . [W]hen using our forces, we must appear inactive.[7]
>
> — Sun Tzu

The Sudanese example of divisive PRC expansionism was ini-

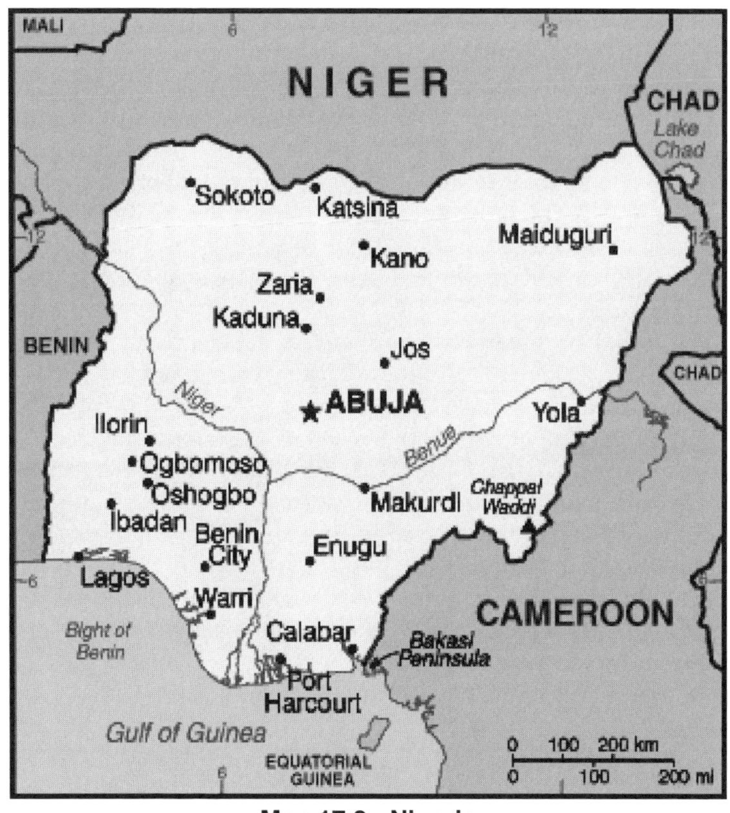

Map 17.2: Nigeria
(Source: Courtesy of General Libraries, University of Texas at Austin, from their website for map designator "nigeria_sm_2013.tif")

tially addressed in Chapter 2. That the government of South Sudan now has two competing components (with China helping both) will be detailed in Chapter 18. The same syndrome in Libya has been covered by Chapter 11. So, the current chapter will deal only with the possible Chinese partitioning of Africa's greatest energy resource—Nigeria. There too, chronic *jihadist* activity—to include the occasional bombing incident in its capital of Abuja—would tend to scare away Western business interests.

Needless to say, Islamist activity in Africa need not be directly instigated or even abetted by the PRC for it successfully to divert Western attention from China's expansionary progress.

When *Boko Haram* "Invaded" Nearby Nations in Early 2015

Chapter 13 has shown that *Boko Haram* has been transporting/protecting drug shipments through more than just northern Nigeria for quite some time. (See Figure 17.1.) This Islamist rebel faction's early 2015 cross-border forays into neighboring countries did not mark its first presence there. *Boko Haram* has been taking refuge, training, transiting, and recruiting in western Chad, northern Cameroon, southern Niger, Burkina Faso, and southern Mali for years.[8]

The Sahel highway just happens to run through N'djamena (Chad), Kano (Nigeria), Niamey (Niger), Ouagadougou (Burkina Faso), and Bamako (Mali). (Look back at Map 13.3.) Initially, it encounters Fotokol at the northern end of Cameroon and then Maiduguri in Nigeria. (See Maps 17.3 and 17.4.) That's why in early 2015, *Boko Haram* tried so hard to capture both cities. Thus, *Boko Haram* may be more interested in its main source of income—the drug trade along Trans-Africa Route 5—than any caliphate aspiration. One wonders how many drug-trafficking "mentors" *Boko Haram* really has. Here's what the Cameroon Army discovered in Fotokol in the autumn of 2014.

Figure 17.1: Boko Haram Controls Edge of the Sahel
(Source: DA Pamphlet 550-36 [1991], p. 37)

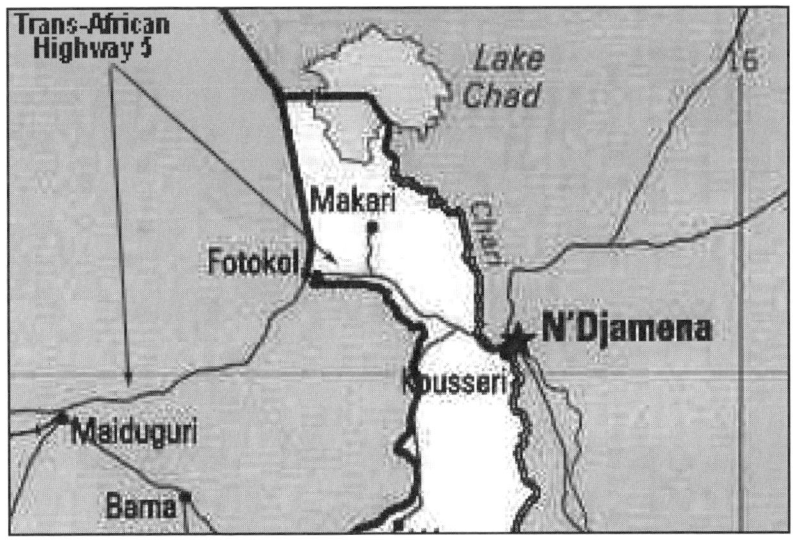

Map 17.3: Militants Trying to Control Trans-African Highway 5
(Source: Library of Congress, tiny excerpt from CIA map designator "base 802575 (R02413) 7-98," as retrieved from this url: http://africa.updmedia.com/cameroon_3.php")

> The Cameroon army announced yesterday that they have arrested the Mayor of Fotokol, Ramat Moussa and 300 Boko Haram fighters. The army revealed that huge stocks of Boko Haram weapons were found at the mayor's residence including Chinese made weaponry.[9]
>
> — *Udumakalu Word Press* (Nigeria), October 2014

Boko Haram has, on occasion, strayed into Chad during what *Reuters* calls a "five-year drive to create an Islamist state." Chad—the most proficient army in the region, with suspected links to the PRC—has lately become more involved. While the authorization source is unclear, Chad already had military posts in Fotokol, Cameroon, when that town was attacked by *Boko Haram* in early February 2015. Chinese expansion watchers were then concerned when the AU decided to create a N'djamena-based force of 8,750 troops from Chad, Nigeria, Cameroon, Niger, and Benin to fight the militants. That implies Chadian control over what Nigerian troops do in their own territory. (See Figure 17.2.) This Chadian-foriegn-policy-oriented force would be authorized to cross all regional boundaries at

Figure 17.2: Nigerian Infantry Sergeant
(Sources: Courtesy of Orion Books, from *World Army Uniforms since 1939* © 1975, 1980, 1981 by Blandford Press, Ltd., Part II, Plate 90)

will.[10] That Benin had been added to the coalition tends to confirm a cocaine corridor up its full length from the Gulf of Guinea. Such a corridor would almost certainly involve *Boko Haram*.

In late June 2015, Chad's capital of N'DJamena suffered its first suicide bombing. The three-part attack on police facilities killed dozens of people, with *Boko Haram* the prime suspect. Then, in early July, *Boko Haram* gunned down nearly 100 praying Muslims in Kukawa (a Nigerian town near the Chadian border), after killing another 48 men nearby. Kukawa is the southern terminal of the old trans-Saharan trade route to Tripoli.[11]

Boko Haram's History

The 200 teenaged school girls seized by *Boko Haram* in April 2014 were not its first female hostages. Because of the seizure's proximity to a major smuggling hub (for humans as well as com-

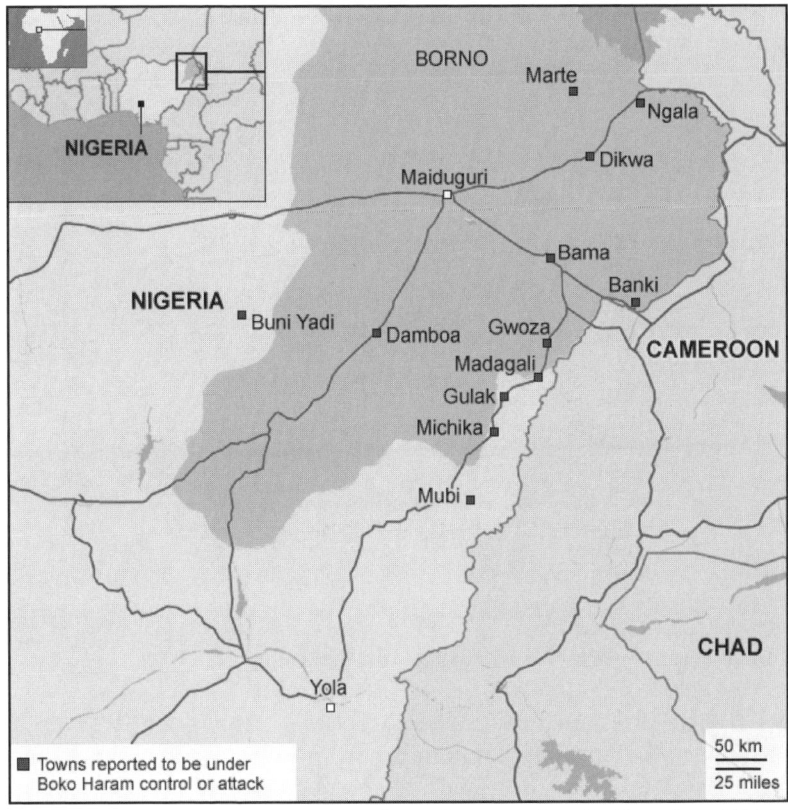

Map 17.4: Towns under Attack or Occupation in October 2014
(Source: Courtesy of General Libraries, University of Texas at Austin, from their website for BBC map designator "_78361184_nigeria_boko_haram_v4.gif")

modities), this should come as no surprise to anyone. In May, *Boko Haram's* leader Abubakar Shekau promised to sell 276 girls into slavery.[12] That's 76 more than were taken in April.

Founded in 2002, *Boko Haram* initially focused on opposing Western education. In the Hausa language, *Boko Haram* means "Western education is forbidden." It launched military operations in 2009 to create an Islamic state. Since an emergency was declared for Borno, Adamawa, and Yobe states of Nigeria in May of 2013, *Boko Haram* has taken many women and children hostage. Somewhat suspiciously, the Nigerian government has held most of its negotiations with this extremist group in Chad.[13]

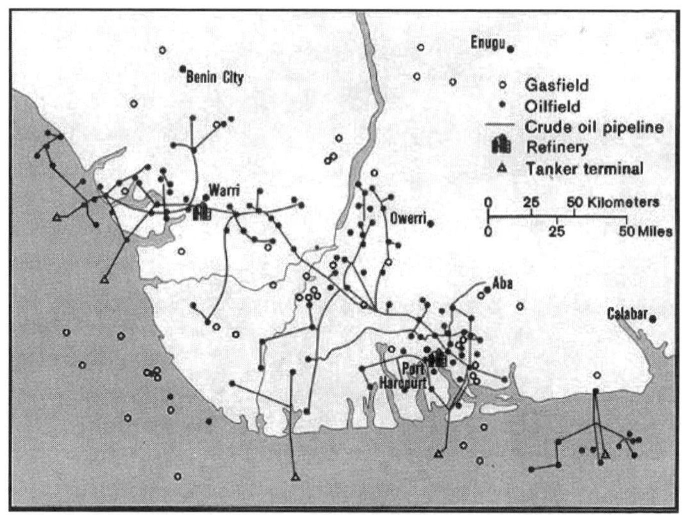

Map 17.5: Nigeria's Petroleum Assets
(Source: Courtesy of General Libraries, University of Texas at Austin, from their website for map designator "nigeria_gas_1979.jpg")

Then There's MEND in Southern Nigeria

By 18 April 2006, attacks by purportedly Muslim militants had cut Nigeria's oil production in half—down to 1.1 million barrels per day. (See Map 17.5.) It was MEND behind much of this violence in the Nigerian port areas. As of 7 June 2006, one U.S. oil executive had been killed, three dozen oil workers from the U.S. and other countries kidnapped, and two pipelines bombed—triggering an international increase in the price of oil.[14] As Nigeria has the largest petroleum reserves in Africa, what happens there is vital to U.S. security. (Look back at Table 1.1.)

Actually, MEND is mostly Christian in make-up, though at least in part funded by Muslims. It also has a Muslim leader—the currently jailed Alhaji Mujahid Asari-Dokubo. While Asari-Dokubo is an outspoken admirer of Osama bin Laden, *al-Qaeda* may not be his only mentor. Chapter 14 has already shown the connection between Muslim smugglers and the PRC. MEND's main financial supporter is a smuggling suspect.

> [A] possible link with al-Qaeda might be former Bayelsa state governor, Depriye Alamieyeseigha, [is] MEND's main

> financial supporter, who is . . . suspected of . . . smuggling arms and of enjoying close links with Osama bin Laden.[15]
> — Project for the Research of Islamist Movements

For a while, the MEND activity in southern Nigeria had cut the flow of oil to America in half. Because of the open warfare between Muslims and Christians in that country's north, MEND is often associated with *al-Qaeda*. But what has oil to do with *sharia* law? MEND has primarily gone after Western oil interests. It has kidnapped U.S. workers and destroyed U.S. facilities. While its jailed leader is a professed admirer of Osama bin Laden, its members are non-Muslim. In a 2007 *National Geographic,* its fighters are pictured with brand new Yamaha outboard motors and Eastern-bloc weapons.[16] One could reasonably conclude that a rich Asian oil magnate has helped to equip it. Yet, most Western observers dangerously assume that its only benefactor is Islamist.

> MEND emerged independent of either the Wahhabi Shari'ah movement in northern Nigeria or the Nigerian Taliban that first appeared in Yobe state in December 2003. . . . Its members are mainly Catholics, though Asari [its jailed leader] is an exception.[17]
> — Project for the Research of Islamist Movements

Should the big American oil companies find operating in Nigeria too risky, Chinese oil companies are all set to move in according to *ABC News.*[18] Thus, another roundabout way of the PRC assuming control over a region starts to take shape. Against a backdrop of Muslim separatism, that way may be to discourage Western influence through the activity of pseudo-Islamic rebels.

Latest Reports of MEND Activity

MEND, though suspected of the first Abuja car bombing (in 2010), initially had no Islamist agenda. Instead, it was a loose mix of armed gangs that Niger Delta politicians had created to use as private armies and rig elections. While professing to want more oil benefits for the Delta population, MEND has been conducting various criminal rackets, like the kidnapping of civilians for ransom and theft of large quantities of crude oil from pipelines. As with Hong

Kong's biggest triad, that means MEND's services are for hire. Only part of MEND has disarmed as a result of the 2009 government amnesty offer or observed its 2010 cease-fire. The rest of MEND is continuing to operate. After attacking a military patrol boat in early 2014, MEND threatened to reduce Nigerian oil production to zero by 2015 and "drive off our land, all thieving oil companies."[19]

There's No Direct Link between MEND and *Boko Haram*

Subsequent car bombings have occurred in Nigeria's capital of Abuja. One was in August 2011 outside the U.N. compound, and another in May 2014, days before the city was to host the World Economic Forum on Africa. In both cases, *Boko Haram*—and not MEND—was suspected.[20] But, *Boko Haram* has yet to claim any attack on the oil-producing areas of southern Nigeria.[21]

While nominally supporting other regional separatist initiatives (like AQIM's near takeover of northern Mali), *Boko Haram* wants mostly to create an Islamic state in the northeastern corner of Nigeria. It has expressed global ambitions and even a desire for a presence in the U.S., but that presence would not be as a militant faction. More likely, it would be as the facilitator of the ongoing drug deluge. Thus, any plan to take over all of Nigeria may be ex-

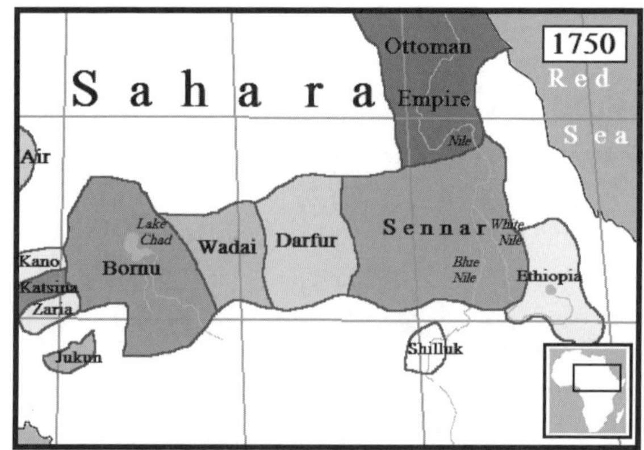

Map 17.6: The Bornu Empire
(Source: Wikipedia Encyclopedia, s.v. "Bornu Empire," image from Gabagool in April 2009 © with designator "CentralEastAfrica1750.png")

tremely long-term for *Boko Haram*. That's why it has pushed into the strategic transit corridor at the borders of Chad, Niger, and Cameroon, instead of attacking to the south.

After ISIS declared a caliphate in June 2014, *Boko Haram* leader Shekau pledged his support for ISIS and adopted the same banner as ISIS. In August, he announced his own caliphate with the expressed intention of expanding it to the territorial limits of the 14th to 19th Century "Bornu Empire."[22] (See Map 17.6.) That empire was a self-proclaimed Muslim emirate that included Nigeria's present-day Borno state and narrow portions of Chad, Niger, and Cameroon. Prior to the Bornu Empire had been the Kanem-Bornu Empire. Apparently, Lake Chad has always marked the junction between a north-south trans-Saharan trade route and one crossing the continent from east to west through the Sahel. In fact, the recently attacked Kukawa had been the capital of that empire.[23] Commerce (whether legitimate or otherwise) along those routes had somehow provided enough revenue to sustain the Kanem-Bornu Empire. (See Figure 17.3.)

Figure 17.3: Warriors of the Earlier Kanem-Bornu Empire
(Source: Wikipedia Encyclopedia, s.v. "Bornu Empire," public-domain image from Barth's Travels & Discoveries [1857] with designator "Group_of_Kanem-Bu_warriors.jpg")

The Presidential Elections of Early 2015

All 12 northern states of Nigeria have practiced *sharia* law since 2000,[24] but they don't allow its harsher punishments. Thus, the winning of the late March 2015 presidential election by the Muslim candidate will be of little help to *Boko Haram's* caliphate. If that candidate and former head of state—Muhammadu Buhari—were to apply his anti-corruption and military background, he could greatly inhibit that radical faction. Unfortunately, such an agenda becomes far more difficult near a major drug conduit.

> [H]e [Buhari] was [previously] removed from power by the military because his anticorruption policies were pinching certain interests within the leadership too hard [from Council on Foreign Relations book].[25]
>
> — *Time Magazine,* 16 February 2015

There is little doubt that *Boko Haram* has been transporting/protecting Afghan opiate shipments from as far east as Chad to as far west as Senegal.[26] (Look back at Map 13.1.) Only still to be determined is the degree to which corruption in the included countries has facilitated the conduit. In Senegal on the Atlantic, where Trans-Africa Route 5 terminates at the western-most transshipment hub,[27] *Boko Haram* commanders reportedly held negotiations with one of Nigerian President Goodluck Jonathan's closest advisors in late 2012.[28] That's a long way from the Nigerian war zone.

Boko Haram May Have More Than One Regional Obligation

Boko Haram launched attacks on Diffa and Bosso just across the border in Niger in February 2015, presumably to pay that nation back for participating in the AU task force.[29] While those two towns are nowhere near Trans-Africa Route 5 (the suspected drug conduit), they do lie close to the Agadem oil fields. It was for what those fields contain that Niger signed an agreement in 2008 with China National Oil and Gas Development Exploration Corporation (CNODC).[30] The CNODC is state-owned by the PRC. Those *Boko Haram* attacks would have tended to discourage any Western competition for that petroleum. And this is not the only Chinese corporation contributing to its country's foreign policy in the region.

Part Six

How the Trade and Strife Are Connected

"An eye for an eye only ends up making the whole world blind."
— Mahatma Gandhi

(Source: Mahatma Gandhi, from www.brainyquote.com.)

18 Oil & Mineral Removal _ through Aid Projects

- How might foreign aid end up harming its recipient?
- What if that aid had powerful "strings" attached?

PRC oil tanker en route from Sudan to the Straits of Malacca

(Source: Corel Gallery Clipart, Ship, Totem image "37C048")

Africa's Strategic Importance

In 2012, the British Geological Survey listed the minerals in short supply in the Western world as follows: antimony, beryllium, cobalt, fluorspar, gallium, germanium, graphite, indium, magnesium, niobium, platinum group, rare earth elements, tantalum, and tungsten. Many are vital to the U.S. defense industry. For some, Africa provides the only abundant source outside of China—tungsten and cobalt for example. Both are used for advanced electronics and high-strength alloys. That makes what goes on in Africa extremely important to America's security.

On 22 March 2015, CBS's prestigious "60 Minutes" news program made two startling admissions about rare earth metals: (1) that China has a veritable monopoly on them; and (2) that many of the most sophisticated U.S. weapon systems depend on them.[1]

Shortfall Specifics

While 83% of all tungsten comes from China, deposits also exist in Rwanda (now mined by Xiamen Tungsten Co., Ltd.[2]) and the DRC. The Copper Belt that runs through the DRC and Zambia also yields much of the cobalt mined worldwide.[3] Then, that cobalt is shipped to China for refining. As such, the PRC remains the biggest exporter of cobalt to the U.S.[4] If America were ever to have a falling out with China, its supply of these two national defense needs would be quickly exhausted.

Besides 68% of the world's cobalt, Africa has 99% of its chromium, 85% of its platinum, 70% of its tantalite, 64% of its manganese, and 33% of its uranium. In actuality, the chromite reserves (chromium ore) of Kazakhstan (within Central Asia) would have to be added to those of South Africa and Zimbabwe to arrive at 95%.[5] Still, the world's total supply of stainless steel is mostly made from African chromium.

China has been unable to meet its own annual demand for copper, zinc, nickel, and a number of other minerals. It is reported to be almost exclusively reliant on Sub-Saharan Africa for its cobalt imports, and significantly dependent for manganese from Gabon, South Africa, and Ghana. Along with South Africa and Zimbabwe, Madagascar and Sudan provide the PRC with most of its chromite.[6]

Guinea (on Africa's northwest coast) is the world's largest exporter of bauxite—the ore from which aluminum is made.[7] The PRC's effort to get at that bauxite is indicative of the extremes to which it is willing to go to acquire certain commodities. Large quantities of illicit drugs are also passing through Guinea.

> While the rest of the world recoiled in horror at recent events in Guinea, where at least 150 pro-democracy supporters were killed and dozens of women publicly raped by government soldiers, China has sensed an opportunity to steal another march on Western competitors in Africa.

> China is preparing to throw the junta in Guinea a lifeline in the form of a multibillion-pound oil and mineral deal, financed largely by soft loans. Such policies have already served China well with rogue and discredited regimes from Angola to Sudan.[8]
>
> — *The Times* (U.K.), 13 October 2009

China's Way of Transporting Those Minerals

In every part of the globe, China's state-owned corporations have been quietly working on road, rail, pipeline, and seaport facilities with which to remove each region's mineral and petroleum wealth. Hutchison Whampoa's website now boasts 319 berths at 52 ports worldwide. While its only existing port in Africa is at Dar es Salaam (at the end of the TANZAM Railway from Zambia),[9] that may soon change. Chinese ships also frequent the harbors at Lobito (at the Angolan end of the Benguela Railway), Louala (Cameroon), Port Sudan (northern Sudan), Mombasa (Kenya), and Nacala (Mozambique). At some point, Hutchison Whampoa will almost certainly take over the day-to-day functioning of China's new deep-water megaport at Lamu, Kenya.

South Sudan's Oil

At the border between South Sudan and its former parent lies the sizable Abyei oil reserves. (See Map 18.1.) James Wani Igga is South Sudan's Vice President and Deputy Chairman of its ruling SPLM party. When he and Chinese Premier Li Keqiang met in Beijing on 1 July 2014, here's what they had to say. While Li seemed mostly interested in oil extraction, he still confirmed the "pro-Communist" leanings of that new country's ruling party (and former rebel army).

> Igga said South Sudan and China share a deep friendship, and that South Sudan is grateful for the long-term support given by the Communist Party of China (CPC) and the Chinese government for its peace, stability and economic development.

Map 18.1: South Sudan
(Source: Courtesy of General Libraries, University of Texas at Austin, from their website for map designator "south_sudan_sm_2013.tif")

South Sudan will continue to strive for its national reconciliation and peace, and will protect the safety of Chinese companies and people, he vowed.

He [Li] called on the two sides to expand cooperation in such areas as industry, finance, poverty reduction, environmental protection, cultural exchanges and security, and jointly construct networks of railways, highways and regional aviation.

> Igga echoed Li, saying the cooperation framework he proposed during his Africa visit in May encouraged countries in East Africa. The East African countries are willing to cooperate with China to promote regional transportation network construction.[10]
>
> – *Xinhua News,* 1 July 2014

Kenya's New Megaport

The PRC is now helping to build a transportation corridor from the Abyei oil fields through Juba to its new megaport at the Lamu Archipelago on Kenya's northeast coast. (See Maps 18.2 and 18.3.) Its former route through Khartoum to Port Sudan has become less convenient since South Sudan's secession from the north. However, China is not worried about the instability of this border region. If it were, it wouldn't have chosen a megaport site within 100 miles of *al-Qaeda's* longtime refuge at Ras Kamboni, Somalia. (Look more closely at Map 18.2.) The PRC simply wants another way to carry out both Sudanese and Ethiopian resources. In return for funding part of the construction, it almost certainly expects trade concessions from both countries. Such an arrangement is nothing new in Africa. In 2008, the Chinese government negotiated with Kinshasa to build a road up from the DRC's southern border to its highly volatile northeast. In return for the road's development, China received full trade access to the DRC's portion of the Copper Belt.[11]

Within the details of the new Kenyan corridor lies the Chinese corporation responsible.

> Kenya's $25.5bn [billion] Lamu Port and New Transport Corridor Development to Southern Sudan and Ethiopia (LAPSSET) includes the construction of a 32-berth port, three international airports, and a 1,500 km railway line. A new oil refinery, in nearby Bargoni, and an oil pipeline are also planned. The pipeline would run to Kenya's Eastern Province before splitting, with one branch running to South Sudan's capital, Juba, and another through Moyale in the north to Addis Ababa [Ethiopia]. A 1,730 km road network is also in the works. . . .

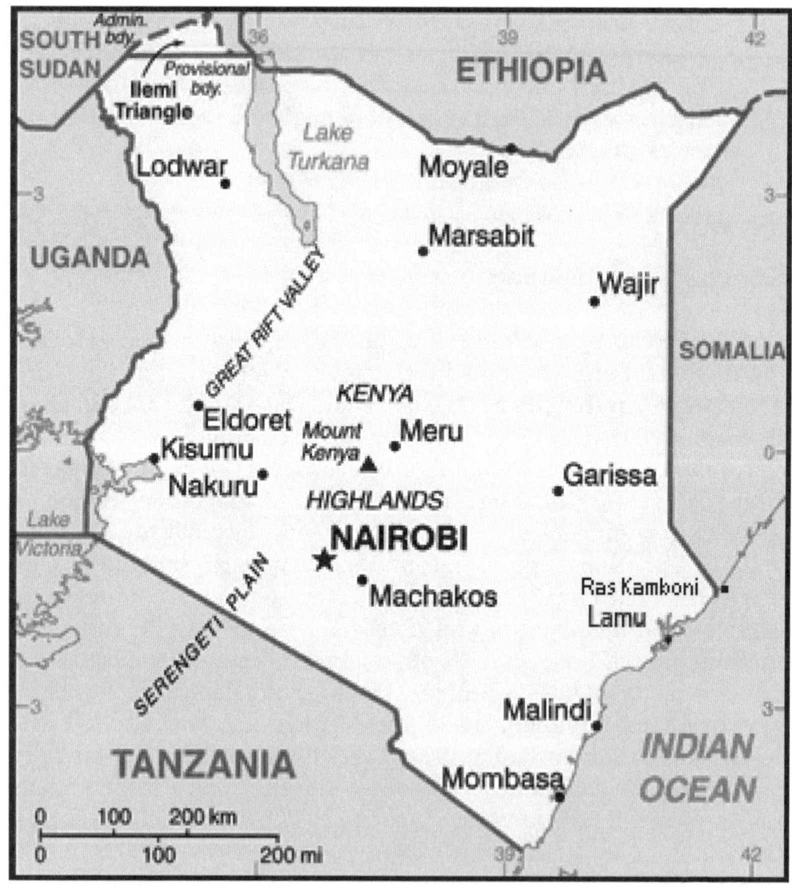

Map 18.2: New Chinese Megaport at Lamu in Kenya
(Source: Courtesy of General Libraries, University of Texas at Austin, from their website for map designator "south_sudan_sm_2013.tif")

A consortium headed by China Communications [Construction Company (CCCC)] has won tenders to build much of the mega-port, and construction is under way on the road network and associated resort cities.[12]

— *Al Jazeera News Service,* 13 October 2013

The megaport will be a few miles north of Lamu Island on a desolate stretch of African mainland.[13] That's at the east side of

Manda Bay—the deep water passage between Pate and Manda islands. (Look again at Map 18.3 and then at Map 18.4.) While the first ship was to have docked there in 2012,[14] construction got delayed due to lack of funding.

CCCC is still state owned,[15] and has CHEC and CRBC as two of its biggest subsidiaries. Because of what they do for transportation, both probably had their roots in thc PLA. In 2011, CRBC had offices in 20 African nations, 10 East Asian nations, eight Central Asian nations, and three Middle Eastern nations.[16] Now, it has a total of 50 offices. Many are in strategically contested regions. While CRBC repaired the 2010 flood damage to the Karakoram Highway, control over big part of Pakistani occupied Kashmir was effectively usurped by China.[17]

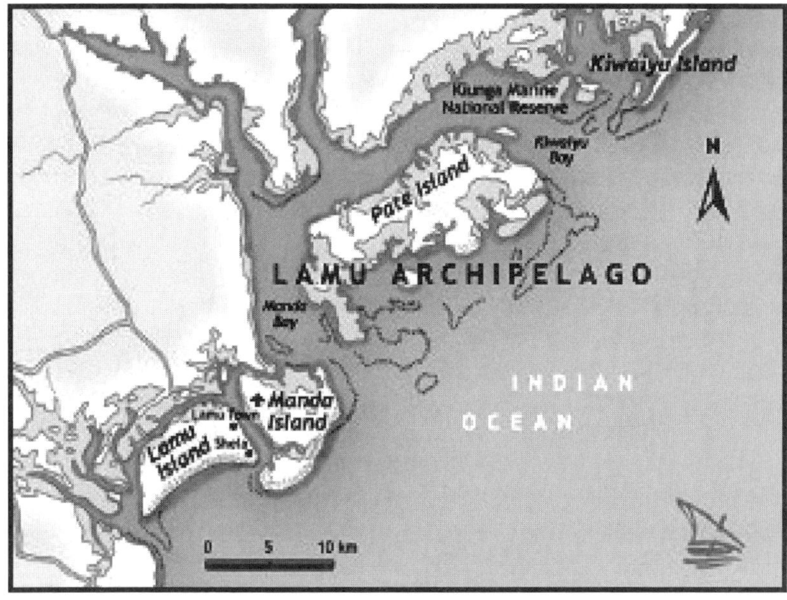

Map 18.3: The Lamu Archipelago
(Source: Courtesy of Lamu Holiday Homes, Kenya, with the following image designator "lamu-archipelago-bild1.jpg," ©)

"Bottom-Up" Societies Operate Differently

As American explorers Lewis and Clark did with the Indians they encountered, might the Chinese construction companies be negotiating their own "safe-passage" agreements with local tribal militias? In June 2014, *al Shabaab* gunmen bypassed Lamu to attack the town of Mpeketoni just to its south.[18] Then, in July, they attacked Hindi (right next to Mpeketoni) and freed a member of the earlier raid from the Gamba Police Station at Garsen.[19] An interesting pattern had begun to emerge. Through it all, the new port facility has not been touched. Might that imply some sort of *detente* between China and the *al-Qaeda* affiliate? Of course, PRC

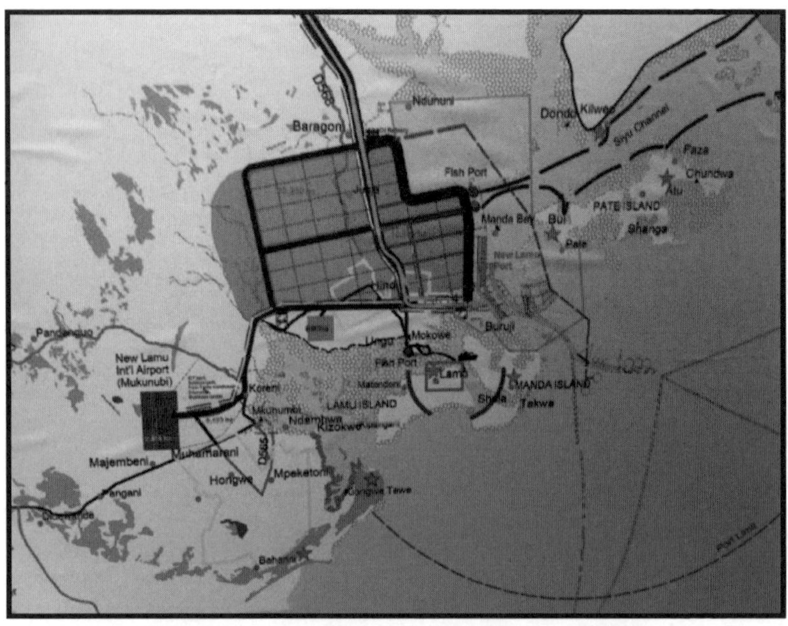

Map 18.4: Planned Extent of Lamu Facility

(Source: Courtesy of Lamu Port Properties, from map entitled "Lamu Port Urban Area Vision 2030" at its website (http://lamuportproperties.kbo.co.ke),© 2012)

Figure 18.1: Kenyan Paratrooper
(Source: Courtesy Orion Books, from *Uniforms of Elite Forces*, ©1982, Plate 3, No. 93)

construction crews often come with their own security detachment, and both Kenyan and Ethiopian troops had been in the area. (See Figure 18.1.) But, would that have deterred *al-Shabaab* suicide squads?

While the new port was to have been partially operational in 2012, the actual construction of its first three berths did not start until June 2014.[20] If the only problem had been lack of funding, one wonders why the Chinese didn't just make up the difference.

In September of 2011, a British national and her husband had been killed in terrorist raid on Kiwayu (a tiny island at the northeastern end of the Lamu Archipelago). Six months later, this same woman was released by a pirate gang. Then, Kenyan troops entered Somalia in response to the kidnapping and other cross-border raids by *al-Shabaab*. That's when *al-Shabaab* vowed to take revenge.[21] Such a thing might have required additional negotiations between the Chinese construction companies and Somalians regarding Lamu. Since that time, the new superport has remained totally unscathed. Map 18.5 shows the precise locations of all terrorist activity in its vicinity.

When a crime is committed, one looks for a motive. *Al-Shabaab* could have randomly attacked Mpeketoni and Hindi, or done so to discourage foreign investment in the land around the new port.

> Most of them [the properties] are on sale and searches can be done at Mpeketoni Lands Office. . . . There are also lawyers in . . . Mpeketoni and Hindi township who can do searches and other due diligence processes for prospective purchasers.[22]
>
> — Lamu Port Agency website

The kidnapping of the two Brits would certainly support the collusion hypothesis. MEND has been kidnapping to limit Western oil company interest in Nigeria. Whether or not a nonaggression pact had been reached between the Chinese and *al-Shabaab* should eventually become evident from how often the new transportation hub is attacked. As of October 2015, *al-Shabaab* had run a number of other high visibility attacks in Kenya, but none were anywhere near the new superport. (See Map 18.6.)

Not the Only PRC Project in East Africa

China is also building a new railroad from Mombasa to Nairobi and then on to Uganda, Rwanda, and Burundi—to more easily extract their resources. (See Map 18.7.) CRBC is the key player in this effort as well. Its web page describes such activity as part of the PRC's "'Go Global' strategy."[23] Because the U.S. government separately delegates all economic and military responsibilities, it sees no danger in this hoarding of vital defense needs.

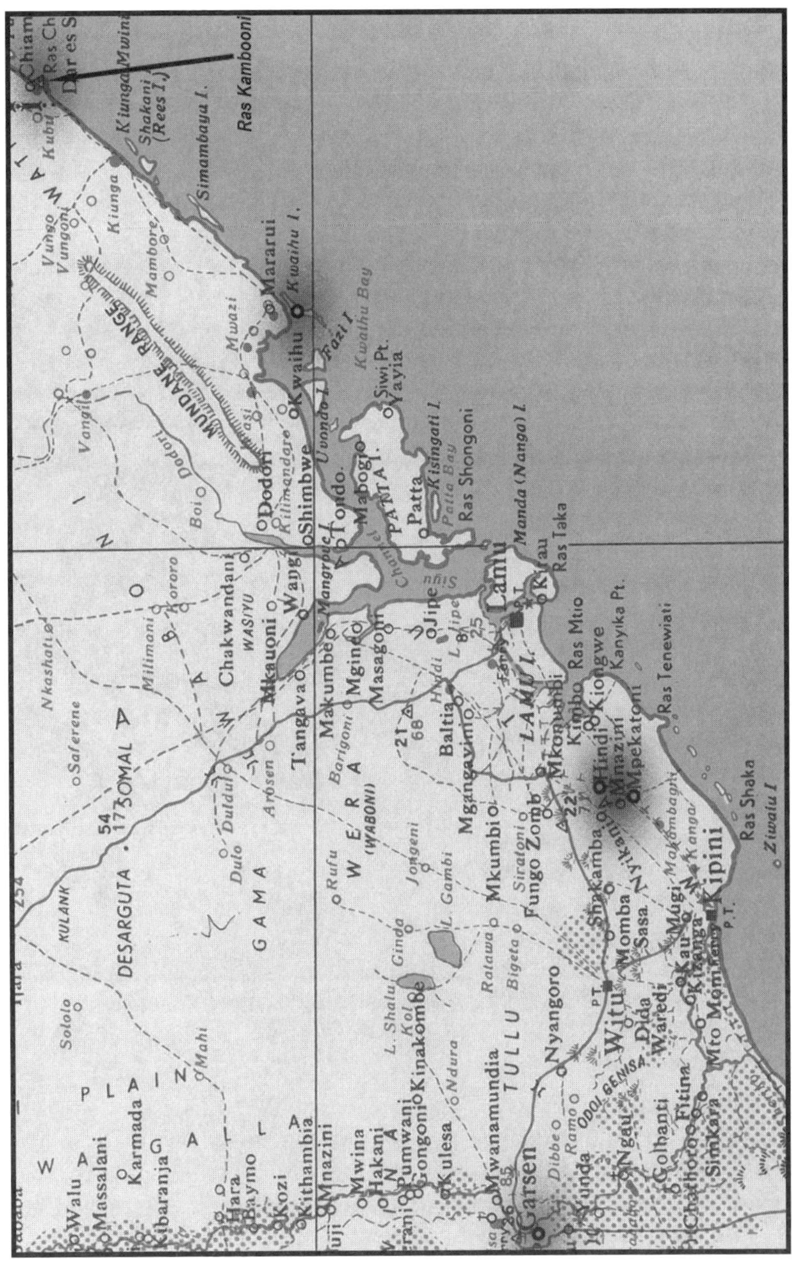

Map 18.5: Al-Shabaab Activity around Lamu

(Source: Courtesy of General Libraries, University of Texas at Austin, from their website for map designator "txu-oclc-6654394-sa-37-38-2nd-ed.jpg")

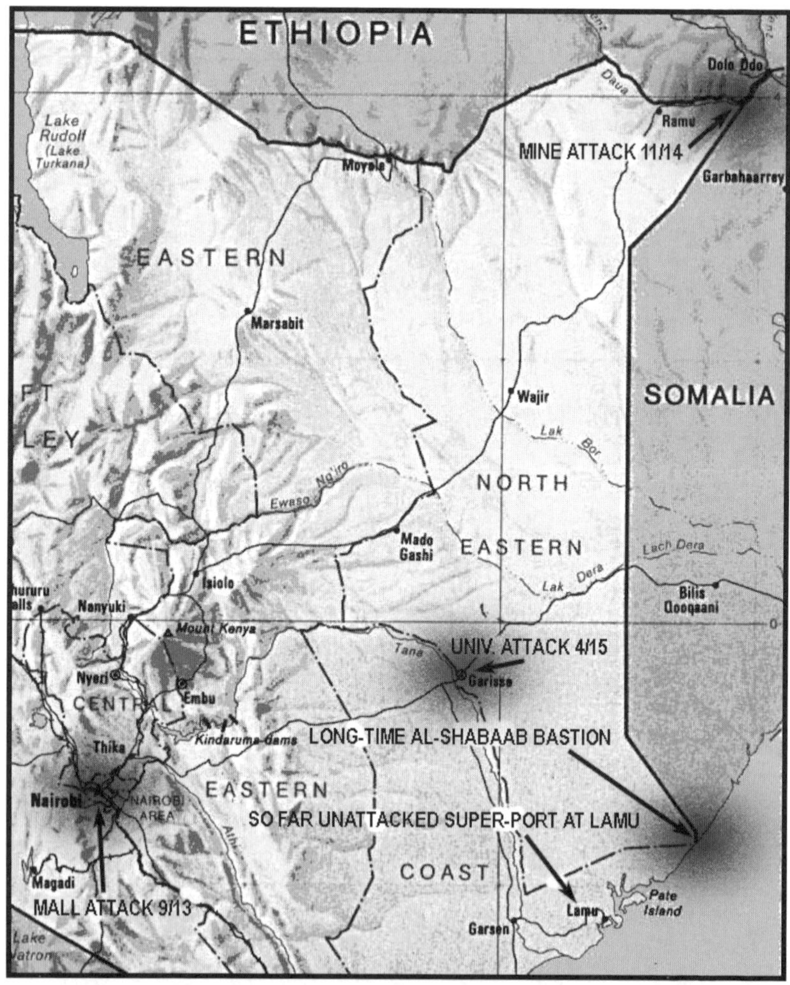

Map 18.6: Al-Shabaab Activity Elsewhere in Kenya
(Source: Courtesy of General Libraries, University of Texas at Austin, from their website for map designator "kenya_rel_1988.jpg")

The PRC has additionally been helping the government of Mozambique to build a deep-water port and rail line at Nacala to more easily extract the coal from Moatize in Tete Province.[24]

At present, China only has one other major rail project in East Africa. Being built by CCECC is an electrified line between Addis Ababa and Djibouti.[25]

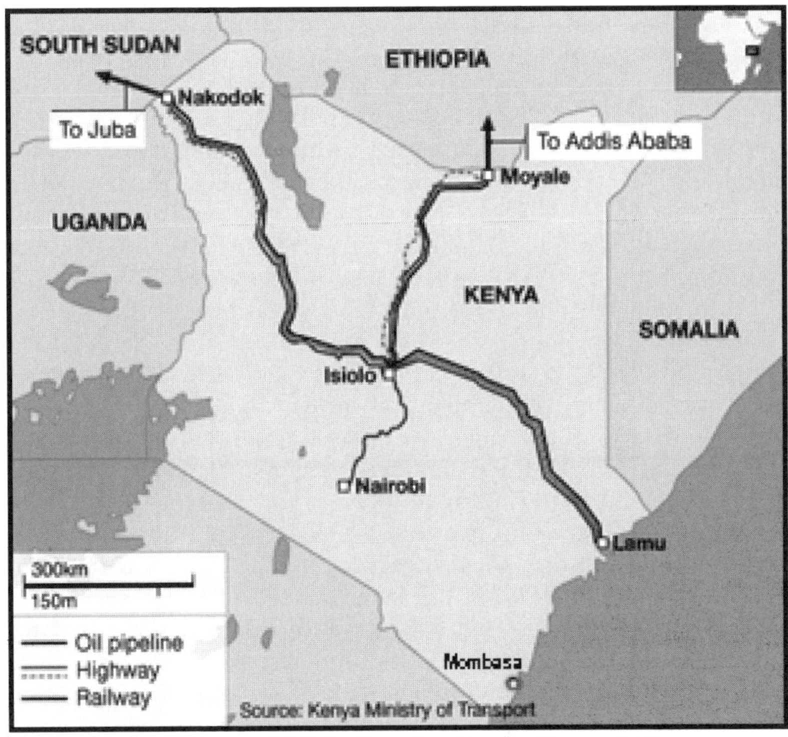

Map 18.7: LAPSSET's Precise Route through Kenya
(Source: Courtesy of Kenya Ministry of Transport via BBC news story with image designator "_58831456_kenya_infrastructure_464.gif")

All these "foreign-aid" projects don't just have philanthropy as their intention.

> [T]his money comes with strings attached—it must be spent [by the African governments] on Chinese goods or Chinese-built infrastructure and the projects are often run by Chinese staff and with Chinese resources [equipment].[26]
>
> – *Smart Rail World,* 29 November 2013

Then There's Africa's West Coast

Also to be operational in June 2014 was Cameroon's new port of Kribi near Duoala. Well situated on the Gulf of Guinea, it will play a key role in the export of iron ore, aluminum, and other commodities from landlocked Chad, the CAR, and DRC. Tugs powerful enough to move the largest ships have already been supplied by the Chinese government. This deep-water port, begun in 2012, has cost an estimated $1 billion. Eximbank China provided 85% with the remaining 15% coming from Cameroon's government. The new port's construction was by CHEC.[27] From Louala, there will eventually be a transportation corridor that stretches all the way across Africa at its narrowest part. It will tie into LAPSSET at Juba.[28]

In Angola, the PRC has also been upgrading the port of Lobito, and gradually extending the Benguela Railway into the mineral-rich (and still volatile) Katanga Province of the DRC. This province alone provided more than half of the world's cobalt supplies in 2013. It is also rich in copper, gold, manganese, uranium, tin, tungsten, and iron ore.[29] From the end of this Benguela Railway extension will run the new road from Kasumbalesa (at the southeast corner of Katanga) to Kisangani in the north.[30] *En route,* it bisects other rich mining districts. Within them is 70% of the world's supply of coltan (from which tantalum is extracted, a key component in advanced electronics). That coltan comes from the Kivu regions on either side of Goma. That's the same city from which the new U.N. Intervention Brigade composed of troops from China's closest African allies recently helped the DRC army to evicted the anti-*Interahamwe* M23.[31] (See Map 18.8.) Anywhere near Goma, the Chinese corporate entities would need "safe passage" agreements from more than one warring faction. With enough money in hand, such a thing might not be all that hard to arrange.

Fully evident from the road deal is how China has been able to upstage the West (replace Western hegemony) throughout Africa. The PRC has been trading infrastructure for resource extraction privileges. Meanwhile, all Western companies must closely adhere to the DRC's mining code, and then pay taxes and royalties on whatever they take out.

> Congo and China are forming a massive mining company called Socomin, with Congo owning 32% . . . and China owning 68%. . . .
>
> The Chinese are putting up all the money to build the [mining] facility, and . . . to build the rail lines and roads that . . . get the ore back to China. . . .

> But the money isn't free—it will take the form of loans to the Congolese government. Congo will pay back China with copper, cobalt and road tolls until China recovers its investment.[32]
>
> — *NPR News,* 30 July 2008

While Chinese Communist construction companies often come with their own security detachments, any PLA troops in a targeted country are normally U.N. peacekeepers. (Over 300 Chinese military personnel now fulfill this role in the DRC—some in its highly volatile northeast.[33]) But, there is another possibility for direct military involvement. It almost always comes with local government concessions.

> [T]he Government of the Democratic Republic of the Congo has made a deal with the Democratic People's Republic of Korea [North Korea], which trains troops of the Democratic Republic of the Congo and in exchange, it is believed, has received a mining concession around Shinkolobwe, very rich in uranium. The Americans in the past extracted uranium from this mine.[34]
>
> — *U.N. Secretary General Letter,* 12 April 2001

This same U.N. study goes on to draw some rather interesting conclusions about corporate involvement in the ongoing conflicts of the eastern DRC.

> The conflict in the Democratic Republic of the Congo has become mainly about access, control and trade of five key mineral resources: coltan, diamonds, copper, cobalt, and gold. . . .
>
> Exploitation of the natural resources of the Democratic Republic of the Congo by foreign armies has become systematic and systemic. . . .
>
> The role of the private sector in the exploitation of natural resources and the continuation of the war has been vital. A number of companies have been involved and have fuelled the war directly, trading arms for natural resources. Others have facilitated access to financial resources, which are used to purchase weapons. Companies trading minerals, which

Map 18.8: Chinese Extraction Routes for DRC Resources
(Source: Courtesy of General Libraries, University of Texas at Austin, from their website for map designator "congo_demrep_sm_2013.tif")

the [U.N.] Panel considered to be "the engine of the conflict in the Democratic Republic of the Congo" have prepared the field for illegal mining activities in the country. . . .

Top military commanders from various countries [not necessarily African] . . . needed . . . this conflict for . . . allowing access to [the] wealth.[35]

— *U.N. Secretary General Letter,* 12 April 2001

19 China's Sun-Tzu-Like Agenda

- How Westernized has modern-day China really become?
- What are its global ambitions?

Sun Tzu knew how to win wars without actually fighting.

(Source: Corel Print House, People, "Royalman")

PRC Now Deeply Committed to "Globalization"

Mainland China's current government is just as anti-democratic and atheistic as it was during the Korean War. That's why the *CIA World Factbook* still calls it a "Communist state." In 1999, two Chinese Colonels wrote a book entitled *Unrestricted Warfare* for the PLA's official publishing house. This book was quickly translated by a CIA affiliate and then widely shared over the internet within most U.S. military circles.

After repeatedly alluding to violence and chaos as being unavoidable in most parts of the world, this book advises the following: "Any of the political, economic, and diplomatic means now has sufficient strength to supplant military means."[1] What the two Chinese Army officers were really saying is this. Only where political and economic subversion fails will the PRC now have to resort to armed rebellion to bring a targeted country into the Communist camp. Being implied, of course, is something more sinister. To fully recognize it, one must remember that there had been tension between China and America ever since the only other Communist power—namely, the Soviet Union—was dissolved. As unofficial representatives of the PLA, the two Colonels were also putting a long-time rival in its place. Between then lines, the following sentiment comes through loud and clear: "We, the Chinese people are more knowledgeable and clever than you Westerners; since the inception of Communism, you have been our traditional adversaries; so, to cause you to 'lose more face,' we are now going to tell you what we are about to do to you."

As, in most Communist writing, the underlying message in *Unrestricted Warfare* has been so thoroughly immersed in disjointed explanations that the average Western reader never picks up on it. One's best chance to recognize it is at the very end of the piece. That's where those, who are always accusing Westerners of being arrogant, make the same mistake. In so doing, they reveal their holistic plan for the future of the world, knowing full well that the U.S. government so strictly separates its various responsibilities as to be somewhat hamstrung by doing so.

> China still has a "revolutionary" government. . . . As a result, . . . we have turned the entire world into a battlefield in the broad sense. . . . The occurrence of revolution in military affairs, along with other revolutions, has altered the last decade of the 20th century." . . .
>
> Although the boundaries between soldiers and non-soldiers have now been broken down, and the chasm between warfare and non-warfare nearly filled up, globalization has made all the tough problems interconnected and interlocking, and we must find a key for that. The key should be able to open all the locks, if these locks are on the front door of war. And this key must be suited to all the levels and dimensions, from war policy, strategy, and operational techniques to tactics; and it must also fit the hands of individuals, from

> politicians and generals to the common soldiers. We can think of no other more appropriate key than "unrestricted warfare."[2]
>
> — *Unrestricted Warfare*
> PLA Publishing House, 1999

The PRC's "revolutionary government" considers a certain amount of internal turmoil to be a prerequisite of progress within every nation around the world. While pursuing its various interests, the PRC thus finds a highly unstable environment to be a natural (and promising) place to work. Western companies tend to shy away from such places; and the West's preoccupation with peace often creates an opening for Chinese peacekeepers and security guards. Meanwhile, any Western troops or military contractors in the region are only concerned with purely martial challenges—often from Islamic militants. Through it all, the PRC and its various extensions (corporate or otherwise) more easily accomplish their mutual agenda.

Where Many Westerners Go Wrong in Their PRC Assessment

A commonly held belief in America is that democracy has been slowly creeping into Chinese society through more capitalistic leeway for its citizenry. Unfortunately, what might appear to be a market-oriented economy in China really isn't. Many of the big corporations are state owned, and even the small ones have mandatory CPC representation on their management staffs. Limited free enterprise at street level does not necessarily equate to widespread personal freedom, like the power to elect one's own leaders (true democracy). What the Communists have been calling "democracy" in their country titles—like the Democratic Peoples Republic of Korea—is more accurately the "will of the people" as interpreted by non-elected leaders.

Asian thought processes are quite different from those in the Western World—not necessarily better, just different. To fully see what the Chinese are up to, one should really ask the opinion of another Oriental. As the Chinese offensive appears to be mostly economic, who better to consult than the Japanese Trade Organization?

What Such an Investigation Reveals

Within the African business world, Americans and Europeans should not expect to see PRC companies pursuing strictly capitalistic objectives. Those that are not government owned are government subsidized, so they don't need to make a profit.

> [T]he challenge facing Western companies competing against Chinese natural resource companies in Africa today . . . is a mindset *(sic)* that puts Chinese national security interests before profit, because the main shareholder is the state not private individuals and companies.[3]
>
> — Japanese Trade Organization, October 2014

The ultimate aim of all such Chinese companies within Africa is going to be homeland defense. Since the demise of the only other Communist power, that welfare has largely revolved around countering all U.S. global influence. As such, the PRC welcomes a relationship with rogue nations.

> There are two stated [PRC] goals: one [1], to support the One China policy and further isolate Taiwan; and two [2], to help rebalance the hegemony of the U.S. in international relations. In its role as "anti-imperialist counterweight to the West," China has brokered diplomatic ties with resource rich countries that bear pariah status.[4]
>
> — Japanese Trade Organization, October 2014

After the CPC's record of brutality against its own population, it doesn't really care about the human-rights records of countries with which it does business. Through a professed policy of "non-interference," it more easily extracts natural resources from oppressed nations. Meanwhile, the U.S. continues to push for democracy and human dignity throughout all foreign transactions. In essence, the PRC has been taking over the world's economy by first mimicking the West, and then playing by its own set of rules.

The PLA's Part in China's Plan for the Dark Continent

The PLA is powerful, but all of its overseas "activities" must still mesh with the—ostensibly economic—foreign policy of its parent nation. Whereas PRC corporate extensions want African business partners to purchase Chinese equipment and engineers, the PLA may want African armies to pay for Chinese ordnance and instructors. The corporations do this partly to usurp each nation's political base through immigration, whereas the PLA may do this simply to discourage U.S. military aid. In years past, PLA "help" has not always led to more local stability.

> A [high level] . . . (PLA) Military Commission was established in 1998 to prepare the groundwork for a new defence policy towards the continent [Africa]. . . .
>
> The inclusion of . . . (Commander of the elite 15th Airborne Division) had to do with . . . the shifting role of African armies in peace keeping deployment operations across the continent, and the reluctance of Western countries to get involved in such operations. The "white paper" that emerged from the commission advised the Chinese government on the need to aggressively increase arms sales to African countries as well as to step up training programmes for the armed forces of Angola, Mozambique, Nigeria, Ghana, Botswana, Namibia, Zimbabwe, Congo-Brazzaville, the DRC, Cameroon, Gambia, Burundi, and Togo to counter U.S. and other Western training programmes on the continent.[5]
>
> — Japanese Trade Organization, October 2014

The chronic violence throughout much of Africa has made this a perfect way for the PLA to influence the economic (and then political) climate at key locations. This way did not always lead to peace, however. Within at least two regional conflicts, PRC arms salesmen have supplied both sides at once: (1) Ethiopia against Eritrea;[6] and (2) Sudan against South Sudan.[7] Many PRC arms industries formerly belonged to the PLA, so they may still be affiliated with it. As such, the PLA could be doing more than just doubling Chinese revenues in conflict zones. It may be intentionally discouraging Western investment. (See Figure 19.1.)

In the ongoing dispute between Sudan and South Sudan, the PLA has provided both sides with instruction on how to fight as well as how to use their weaponry. For the Sudanese military, there has minimally been training on close air strikes.[8] To the fledgling South Sudan, the PLA recently "sent military instructors to train that

Figure 19.1: Local Unrest Not All That Hard to Generate
(Source: Corel Gallery Clipart, Man, Miscellaneous, Totem "28V020.")

nation's armed forces."[9] Implied by so broad a statement is training on more than just weapon operation and maintenance. Thus, the PRC appears guilty of fanning the flames, as already alleged by the leader of South Sudan's rebel faction in Chapter 16.

Trade As Part of China's New National Defense Strategy

China's defense strategy is now global in scope. As such, trade in scarce wartime commodities is necessarily included. One of the new peacetime roles for China's intelligence community (whether from the PLA or otherwise) is to identify economic opportunities throughout the Dark Continent.

> On the intelligence side, a joint regional meeting was held between the country's various security organs . . . in late July 1999. . . .

> At the meeting, . . . [was presented] a 115 page master-plan for the period 2000 to 2003 on aspects of China's economic engagement with Africa.[10]
>
> — Japanese Trade Organization, October 2014

It's now clear that there will be an interface between the Chinese military and business interests in Africa as part of the PRC's overall defense strategy. Besides protecting natural-resource extraction routes, the PLA will be providing initial assistance to beleaguered countries as a way of developing initial rapport.

> The transport of oil will be done . . . via Chinese built, maintained, and controlled oil pipelines to Chinese built or maintained refineries, or on to ports which will enjoy some sort of security agreement with the Chinese navy [part of PLA]. . . . Loaded onto Chinese ships. . . , the oil will travel under close surveillance by the Chinese navy. . . .
>
> Ports of call . . . [for] regular stops . . . include . . . Madagascar (Majunga, Antongil Bay), Dar es Salaam [Tanzania], Maputo and Beira [Mozambique], Port Said [Egypt], Walvis Bay [Namibia], Simonstown [South Africa], Massawa and Dahlak Kebir archipelago (Eritrea), Flamingo Bay (Sudan) and Algiers and Annaba (Algeria). . . .
>
> . . . China's growing energy investments in Africa will be followed by heightened naval activity around its coastline, and . . . an increasing number of civilian and military personnel in Africa, already obvious in China's growing role in African peace-keeping missions. It is also being followed by other Chinese non-oil companies and growing numbers of Chinese diplomatic personnel . . .
>
> . . . [There is an] entry strategy at state level . . . in a number of countries, most notably Algeria, Angola, Chad, Congo-Brazzaville, Niger, Nigeria, Mauritania, and Sudan.[11]
>
> — Japanese Trade Organization, October 2014

China has not been the least bit shy about entering uncharted territory through more military involvement, on its quest for more natural resources. The long-time U.S. ally of Equatorial Guinea provides an example.

> In Equatorial Guinea, where U.S. groups dominate a surging oil business, China provided a package of military training and specialists as the precursor to getting entrenched in the country's oil industry.[12]
>
> — Japanese Trade Organization, October 2014

Only yet to be determined is the PLA's role, if any, in the flood of Afghan opiates into America through the Dark Continent. Among the PLA colonels' *Unrestricted Warfare* options is "drug warfare (obtaining sudden and huge illicit profits by spreading disaster in other countries)."[13]

20 Proof of PRC Drug Trade Involvement

- What is Beijing's part in the African drug trafficking?
- How much hard evidence of this is there?

East Asians know how secretly to move things piecemeal.

(Source: Corel Gallery Clipart, Man, Totem image "28V011")

History May Be Repeating Itself

When the PLA was told to divest itself of all civilian enterprises in 1998, it already had quite a smuggling record.[1] It also owned 400 pharmaceutical factories inside China.[2] Currently, that massive organization may not be well enough funded by its parent government to pay for all of the latest directives. While the PRC now has more money to spend, its military also has an "active-defense" role encompassing the entire planet.

Yet, the Communist Chinese regime as a whole—with all of its flaws—has been better able to keep pace with an evolving world than most Western counterparts. Though highly despotic at the top, it has still sprung from a "bottom-up" culture. As such, it suffers from less hierarchical inertia than the average Free World administration. It also more easily learns from its mistakes. That means China's preferred way of war may now be quite different from the Westernized version that led to its embarrassment in the punitive attack on North Vietnam in 1979. The PRC's latest expansionary methods may also be more sophisticated than those used in Africa and Central America during the 1980's.

From the nation that produced Sun Tzu and all of his ways of winning wars without fighting, an economics-based expansion seems likely. Then, trade in illicit narcotics could make the following possible: (1) non-traceable funding for targeted-nation discord or electioneering; (2) automatic instability of major markets; and (3) a ready-made network for intelligence gathering or runaway immigration. Of course, local subversion can also be funded through natural-resource manipulation.

PLA's Global Strategy Must Fit This New Way of Thinking

There's a considerable body of evidence to suggest that China considers trade in drugs to be just as legitimate as trade in any other commodity. That's why the *CIA World Factbook* still lists the PRC as a "major transshipment point for heroin produced in the Golden Triangle" and "source country for methamphetamine and heroin chemical precursors."[3] Even its state-owned shipping conglomerate—COSCO—has been repeatedly accused of transporting illicit narcotics.[4]

Like all countries, China makes long-range as well as short-term plans. During the 1970's and 1980's, it was helping to free Mozambique and (to a lesser degree) Angola from the Portuguese. Neither country had any rare metals of its own, but each bordered on mineral-rich Zambia. As such, both contained Copper Belt extraction routes.

The Portuguese had a third colony in Africa—Portuguese Guinea. It was eventually to become Guinea-Bissau. While it had no natural resources to speak of, it has become West Africa's biggest drug-smuggling hub. Still, the Chinese are ostensibly more interested in enough ocean outlets to fully exploit the mining districts of Central Africa: (1) Angola's port of Lobito at the end of the

Benguela Railroad; (2) Tanzania's capital of Dar es Salaam where the TANZAM Railway meets the Indian Ocean; and (3) Kenya's new port of Lamu on a new rail line into Rwanda and Burundi. But, if ore-extraction portals are that important to the Chinese, perhaps trans-shipment points for other commodities are as well. A PRC-backed rebellion in Angola and Mozambique helped to develop one trade opportunity. Might a PRC-backed rebellion in Guinea Bissau have assisted with another? A closer look at history provides the answer.

Guinea-Bissau's Strategic Importance to the PRC

Like the Islamists, the Communist Chinese may wish to destabilize their only remaining opposition to worldwide domination. A drug deluge would certainly get the job done. To pursue this line of reasoning with Guinea-Bissau, one must only prove two things: (1) that the PRC helped guerrillas to expel the Portuguese from that country; and (2) that subsequent Chinese "assistance" has helped Guinea-Bissau to turn into a narco-state. In the following excerpt, notice how closely the PRC has guided Guinea-Bissau over the years.

> Beijing had been one of Guinea-Bissau's most enthusiastic supporters in its 12 year struggle for independence from Portugal. The Chinese had trained many of Guinea-Bissau's guerrilla leaders, including the president at the time, Joao Bernardo "Nino" Viera, and had provided . . . diplomatic support. . . . [T]he party in power when the switch took place . . . had been founded on Marxist-Leninist principles and for decades had close party relations with the Chinese Communist Party.[5]
>
> — Center for Strategic and International Studies

Guinea-Bissau has no known petroleum or mineral reserves of its own. Neither does Mali, Burkina Faso, or Niger. These are nations that might depend upon Guinea-Bissau for a trans-ocean shipping outlet.[6] Yet, China has still lavished upon this former Portuguese colony an inordinate amount of attention (to include financial incentives). It would not be doing so without wanting something in return.

> In November 2006, [Mainland] China announced it was going to fund . . . a massive dam in Guinea-Bissau. . . . Other major infrastructure projects include a deep water port in Buba, . . . the rehabilitation of Guinea-Bissau's two main highways, and the construction of a bridge over the Farin River.
>
> . . . China has [also] offered to build the national parliament building, rehabilitate the presidential palace . . . , and construct a six-story central government building. . . . In August 2007, funding was announced for . . . a justice palace [as well].[7]
>
> — Center for Strategic and International Studies

All the while, the Guinea-Bissau government has been so repeatedly linked to the drug trafficking within its borders that it is said to be running a narco-state. China seems unperturbed by this. There's a reason. It has traditionally sanctioned the movement to market of this particular commodity all over the world.

> While close ties with a suspected narco-state may create some international embarrassment for the PRC, it is very unlikely that Beijing will reconsider its policy [of non-interference in local matters]. After all, as the Burma case suggests, Guinea-Bissau is not the first narco-state to be a close friend of Beijing.[8]
>
> — Center for Strategic and International Studies

Of note, the above article was written in its entirety by a Singaporean graduate of the PLA's National Defense University in Beijing.

Proof That China Facilitated Flow of Opiates across Africa

A major cocaine conduit from Venezuela to Europe has existed through Guinea-Bissau for years.[9] China could more easily bring 90% of world's supply of opium to bear on its only remaining opposition by using this same conduit in the opposite direction. Through strategic deception and paid cover-up, it could erase almost all evidence of this reverse transit. Here's how the backward movement might be discreetly accomplished. In June 2013, three African citizens and a Colombian national attempted to "swap" heroin headed to the U.S. for South American cocaine in Ghana.[10] Such an event suggests transport of that heroin back along the same shipping network that brought the cocaine to Africa. Yet, the Washington "party line" is still that only tiny quantities of Afghan heroin are reaching the U.S. via the occasional West African airline "mule." The DEA has recently alluded to a greater influx.

> Saying that drug trafficking in West Africa has become "a plague," the U.S. Drug Enforcement Administration on Wednesday announced the unsealing of charges against four suspected drug traffickers accused of attempting to secure safe passage for millions of dollars worth of [fully refined] heroin from West Africa to the United States by paying off an airport insider.[11]
>
> – *Washington Times,* 5 June 2013

One way to resolve this difference of opinion is through a mathematical analysis. As of April 2014, the amount of acreage under opium-poppy cultivation in Afghanistan had risen some 36% since 2012.[12] That country is now in danger of becoming a "full-fledged narco-state," according to the UNODC (with most of the profits going to the Taliban).[13] And in June 2015, the prestigious Woodrow Wilson Center reported Afghan opium production higher than at any time since the 1930's, with the Taliban actively forcing the farmers to grow it.[14]

Thus, any further claim by Washington that no Afghan heroin of any significance is reaching America may be nothing more than political posturing in response to a failed foreign policy. The truth of the matter is that Afghan opiates have been continually arriving in the U.S. through West Africa since at least 2010, and not just in tiny increments or fully refined form. The British news media has had less reason to "candy coat" this reality.

> There is also evidence . . . opium is making its way from Afghanistan, through the Middle East and into West Africa on its way to the consumer markets in the United States.[15]
>
> – *BBC News,* 21 June 2010

Most often blamed for this stream of Southwest Asian opiates into America has been the "infamous . . . international networks" of Nigerian organized crime.[16] However, it's highly unlikely that the Nigerians are as powerful as purported in the following U.N. assessment.

> Drug seizures and the arrest of traffickers indicated that African drug traffickers—*particularly West African networks*—are increasingly transporting Afghan heroin from Pakistan into East Africa for onward shipment to Europe and elsewhere.[17]
>
> — 2011 UNODC Report, as summarized by *Reuters*

The Nigerian mob would not be well enough endowed nor connected to be transporting—all the way to the U.S.—heroin that it had just purchased in Pakistan. The *al-Qaeda* affiliated Karachi syndicate would be more likely be moving it by *dhow* to Somalia or possibly a little farther inland to sell to the Nigerians. Then the Colombians would buy it, and finally the Mexicans. As long as the overseeing Chinese triad got a percentage of all fiscal transactions, each local element could simply market the load to the next in line. Most maintain representatives in other parts of the world to prearrange such transfers. All the while, the PLA-affiliated organized crime family from Hong Kong would still monitor the entire transit.

Loosely to administer the full extent of a worldwide drug conduit, that Hong Kong triad must be "managing it by exception." So doing would lessen its risk of ever being implicated. As long as all criminal, insurgent, and corrupt-government players satisfactorily fulfilled their respective obligations, the triad would simply collect its cut. Like all commercial enterprises, drug trafficking still requires some managerial hierarchy. But, in the narcotics "business," no street-level worker ever knows who his or her upper-echelon bosses are.

DEA History Holds Further Evidence of PRC Involvement

In the late 1980's, the DEA seemed more concerned with the influx of crack cocaine than any other narcotic. Still, it readily admitted to a heroin conduit existing from Colombia to Mexico and then into the Lower Forty-Eight. "A Guadalajara mafia was formed in Mexico with close ties to Colombian mafia, to ship heroin, marijuana, and cocaine to the United States."[18]

Then, starting in the early 1990's, the DEA started taking more notice of Southeast Asian (Golden Triangle) heroin entering America through Africa. That's how the Nigerians may have first gotten their reputation for heroin smuggling. And guess which Asian crime family was their co-conspirator—the one with most access to ocean-going "transpo."

> By 1993, Southeast Asian heroin, which was smuggled by both China and Nigeria/West Africa-based traffickers, was one of the greatest threats to the United States. At that time, roughly 68 percent of the heroin seized in the United States came from Southeast Asia's Golden Triangle—Burma, Laos, and Thailand. China-based traffickers controlled sophisticated international networks that smuggled multi-hundred kilo quantities of heroin in commercial cargo on a regular basis.[19]
>
> — *History of the DEA (1990 to 1994)*

Roughly the same entry in the DEA's 1994-1998 sequel reiterated Chinese involvement in the opiate trafficking and suggested tiny increments as the way the Nigerians were getting pure heroin into America.

> In 1994, Southeast Asian heroin, which was smuggled by ethnic China- and Nigeria-based traffickers, was [still] one of the greatest drug threats to the United States. Almost 60 percent of the heroin that came to the United States at that time originated in Southeast Asia's "Golden Triangle"—Burma, Laos, and Thailand. Those mainly responsible were ethnic Chinese traffickers who controlled sophisticated international networks that smuggled hundreds of kilograms of heroin in commercial cargo on a regular basis. In addition to the China [activity], Nigeria and West Africa-based trafficking organizations helped smuggle the heroin, typically using the "shotgun" approach to smuggling by recruiting third party couriers to travel aboard commercial airlines and smuggle from one to 10 kilograms of heroin per trip.[20]
>
> — *History of the DEA (1994 to 1998)*

Then, the DEA history for 1999 to 2003 acknowledges three very interesting things: (1) Afghanistan having 70% of world's supply of opium; (2) the Taliban earning much of its money through opiate transporting and processing; and (3) *al-Qaeda* being "involved in the financing and facilitation of heroin trafficking activities." Still, the DEA remained most worried about white heroin from Colombia.[21] No one thought to question the origins of that heroin or whether it had been refined inside Colombia from morphine base smuggled through Venezuela via the Dark Continent from Karachi.[22] From 2003 to 2008, the DEA officially admits to Afghan heroin as a means for *jihad* but seems no closer to its precise pathway to America.[23] However, no blame should be assessed. In this case, the DEA's criminal opposition had been working for the global authority on military deception.

More Recent Clues

The DEA history is now somewhat dated. While enough incremental smuggling can be powerful, today's smaller number of West African sky mules may be little more than a diversion. Because no self-respecting Hong Kong triad would abandon such a lucrative source of income, one must look for a different way that the Afghan opiates might be reaching America through West Africa. Most U.S. street heroin cannot be from Mexican or Colombian poppies. How could 1% of the world's total supply of opium have solely captured its biggest heroin market? [24]

Just as in 1989,[25] vast quantities of heroin from Afghan poppies must still be entering America. The most likely route is through West Africa, Venezuela, and finally Mexico—all under the oversight of a Hong Kong organized-crime family. That family may well be operating under a secret foreign policy directive from the Beijing regime.

> There is a well-documented history of . . . Chinese organized crime organizations working as tools of their governments. In Panama . . . there is a dangerous convergence of well-financed Chinese . . . mobs with . . . Latin American drug lords.[26]
>
> — *American Foreign Policy Council Report*

Only now, much of the "smack" coming onto U.S. streets may be from Southwest Asian morphine bricks that have been further refined in Colombia, Mexico, or somewhere in between. The CIA still lists the PRC as "a major source country for heroin and methamphetamine chemical precursors."[27] Since 2011, at least two illegal Chinese shipments of the latter type of precursor have been seized by Mexican authorities.[28] Sadly, only free-lance strategists seem to realize the conspiratorial implications with regard to U.S. security. After all, *Sun Yee On* does now work for the PLA.[29]

> The type of precursor chemicals, their bulk amounts, and their origins make this [the above seizures] a true smoking gun, said Robert Bunker. . . at the Strategic Studies Institute, U.S. Army War College.
>
> According to several sources, including *China Brief,* the shipments are tied to the Chinese Triads. . . .
>
> The nature of the [Hong Kong] Triads also ties them to the Chinese Communist Party back in their homeland, according to . . . the author of "Contracted: America's Secret Warriors."[30]
>
> — China Society International, September 2013

There is already proof of PRC crime factions shipping Golden Triangle morphine base through East Africa for further refinement nearer to its final market.

> In . . . Eastern Africa the Chinese have [a] direct line to the Golden Triangle factories of the Mekong [River region] and control the . . . morphine base business.[31]
>
> — *Gangsters Inc.,* 30 July 2014

End Result Would Be Further Destabilization of America

Many U.S. analysts view such Chinese chicanery as nothing more serious than a little "overly-ambitious" money making. But, the PRC hasn't done much to stop the flow of drugs into America, and it already has enough money. In the following quote, a Strategic Studies expert notes the overall effect on Mexico of this precursor smuggling. One might expect the same type of adversity at the final destination of what it can produce. (See Figure 20.1.)

Figure 20.1: More Drugs Lead to More Addict and Gang Violence
(Source: Courtesy of Michael Leahy from the cover of "Homeland Siege," © 2009)

> China Uncooperative in Stopping Meth Flow: [Mr.] Bunker said the Chinese precursors are smuggled to Mexican drug cartels . . . . [T]his is a crime that is feeding the drug wars, which are in turn destabilizing the country.[32]
>
> — China Society International, 3 March 2014

The current upsurge in Chicago's murder rate has probably to do with increased street gang competition for "turf" on which to sell the now more abundant drugs. Combined with the recent upsurge in the availability of cheap white heroin,[33] might commensurate gang violence throughout America's other big cities also destabilize the country as a whole? That may be what the Chinese government has in mind, for such a thing would fit in perfectly with the PLA's "Unrestricted-Warfare" guidelines.[34] A competing world power that was beset by its own internal chaos would be less likely to help other nations to resist a Chinese takeover.

Part Seven

Combatting the Main Attack

"What difference does it make to the dead, the orphans and the homeless, whether the mad destruction is wrought under the name of totalitarianism or the holy name of liberty or democracy?"
— Mahatma Gandhi

(Source: Mahatma Gandhi, "Non-Violence in Peace and War.")

21 The PRC's Overall Occupation of Africa

- Which things do Chinese spy agencies watch in Africa?
- Which countries have been targeted and by what means?

PLA soldiers have a heritage of buiding civilian infrastructure.

(Source: Probably public-domain image with designator "1950-sl_ec06.jpg" retrieved in 2009 from this url: http://timpanogos.wordpress.com/2007/09/13)

China's Espionage Aim within Africa

U.S. corporations get no business advice from governmental intelligence agencies, but their Chinese counterparts do. Other than rigging an occasional election and isolating the few countries that still have ties with Taiwan, China's spy agencies largely focus on gaining an economic advantage in Africa. Certain managerial personnel within the PRC's state-owned corporations also belong to its intelligence community.

[L]inked to China's growing energy and resource acquisi-

> tion arrangements with African countries . . . has been . . . an increasing presence of Chinese intelligence personnel on the continent. Leading the charge has been the Ministry of State Security [MSS] . . . , the PLA's Department of Military Intelligence (DMI), and the all-powerful Ministry of Commerce (MOFCOM—the de-facto head of China's economic and business intelligence gathering).[1]
>
> — Japanese Trade Organization

A Military Presence beyond Separating Warring Parties

As already detailed, there are now large numbers of Chinese peacekeepers, warfare trainers, and military attachés throughout the Dark Continent. As early as May 2013, China offered up to 500 combat soldiers for the U.N. mission to Mali. Then, in December 2014, it was allowed to send 700 combat troops to South Sudan. These two events marked a major shift in the U.N.'s Africa policy. These were the first Chinese infantrymen to take part in its peacekeeping operations.[2] After 4000 Chinese soldiers had been unilaterally deployed to Sudan to protect a new oil pipeline in 2000,[3] few Western observers still doubted the PRC's willingness to risk open ground combat for petroleum. But, Mali has no petroleum to speak of. So, something more widespread and complicated was underway.

Peacekeeping may only be the first kind of Chinese military deployment to Africa. There are a number of other excuses it could use

> China's stepped-up peacekeeping activity parallels the PLA's growing interest to expand its non-combat missions or 'military operations other than war' (MOOTW)—disaster response, humanitarian relief and counter-piracy, for example.[4]
>
> — Stockholm Internat. Peace Research Institute

Chinese Bases in Africa?

While the U.S. has routinely established military bases throughout the world, the PRC has mostly avoided such activity, except at its immediate periphery—like in Tibet, Kashmir, or the South China Sea islands. All that may be about to change, however. In March 2014, the *Washington Times* announced that China was all set to create military bases in key spots throughout Africa, in order to directly challenge the military presence of the U.S. and E.U.[5] Naval bases would be one thing, but the permanent billeting of ground personnel might signal an upsurge to the PRC's already considerable program of expansion.

The PRC has already been invited to build a navy base in the Seychelles Islands, just off the east coast of Africa.[6] (See Map 21.1.)

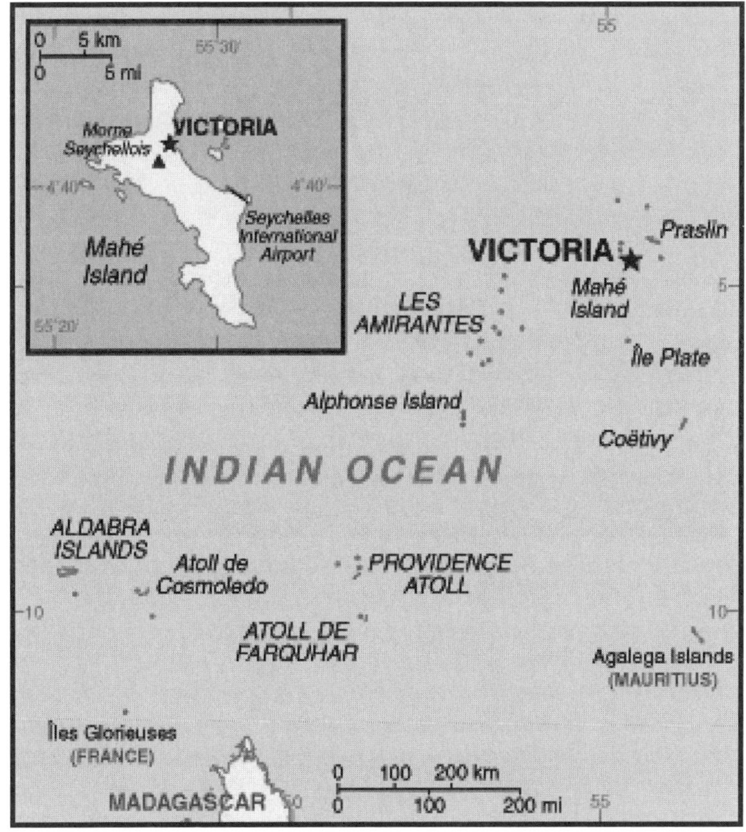

Map 21.1: China's First Navy Base in Seychelles of SADC
(Source: Courtesy of General Libraries, University of Texas at Austin, from their website for map designator "seychelles_sm_2014.gif")

Figure 21.1: The PLA Includes All Chinese Service Branches
(Source: Courtesy of Global Security (globalsecurity.org), from its "PLA History" section, © n.d., image desigator "C14053PictPowPpleArmy53.jpg")

Citing an undisclosed source in November 2014, *Namibian Times* reported Chinese interest in other Atlantic Ocean bases at Namibia (Walvis Bay), Nigeria (Lagos), and Angola (Luanda). Along the Indian Ocean, the PRC also wants bases at Djibouti, Kenya (Mombasa), Tanzania (Dar es Salaam), Mozambique, and Madagascar.

All would theoretically be for replenishment, berthing, and maintenance (of warships) to help safeguard maritime routes. While China does not claim to want U.S.-style military facilities, it hasn't ruled out "Overseas Strategic Support Bases." While a Chinese defense ministry spokesman quickly called the report "inaccurate," there is definite truth to it. On 4 January 2013, the *International Herald Leader*—a state-run newspaper under the auspices of *Xinhua News Agency*—carried similar details.[7] Such "Overseas Strategic Support Bases" could be used to preposition materiel for expeditionary ground forces. (See Figure 21.1.)

There are distinct similarities between the PRC's official reason for all the infrastructure assistance to Africa and its latest "String of Pearls" fabrication. China has been calling its Spratly Islands land reclamation project a "public service," whereas her neighbors see only an airfield from which it can enforce a territorial claim over the entire South China Sea.[8] Could a globally oriented CPC now view southern Africa as just another frontier province? If deadly force were appropriate off shore of its mainland, why not in a distant province?

Has Africa Once Again Witnessed Political Hardball?

In most Western nations, any political manipulation by China is so well hidden that most citizens never realize it. But, in other parts of the world, the Chinese aren't as careful. One well respected source has already noted China's interference with the elections in Zimbabwe and Zambia.[9] The former present of Zambia was Africa's most outspoken critic of the PRC. His final days may well mark a different side to the "friendly dragon."

On 28 October 2014, the man who had run for president of Zambia on an "anti-Chinese" platform in 2008 died in London after receiving treatment for an undisclosed illness.[10] Michael Sata had toned down his anti-Chinese rhetoric for the 2011 election in which he unseated Rupiah Banda as president (after Banda's party had been in power for 20 years). However, Sata maintained his ardor "against foreign mining companies" in the Copper Belt.[11] The new president then died in a London hospital after "a sudden onset [of] heightened heart rate."[12] Sata is rumored to have had cancer. If there was any foul play at that hospital, there is little doubt as to which world power wanted him gone. Before being elected, Sata had attacked Zambia's Chinese investors and even threatened to recognize Taiwan as the non-Communist Republic of China.[13] This would not have made PRC strategists very happy.

President Samora Machel of Mozambique—a former Chinese protege—had also died of suspicious circumstances after shifting his allegiance to the Soviet Union. He, his Russian-manned plane, and several regime members had been lured into the South African border region on a flight from Zambia home by a false radio signal imitating a landing beacon. An officer South Africa sent to investigate the crash has confirmed foul play. Mozambique is once again in the PRC camp. By latest indication, abandoned mines and offshore waters at its capital of Maputo are now being used as hazardous-waste dumps. Some of that waste must be coming from South Africa's uranium mines. With South Africa quickly approaching military proxy status with China, what that uranium can build should be of more concern to the West.[14] On sale at the Johannesburg Airport in May 2015 was a book with a disturbing title from prestigious Galago Press—*How South Africa Built Six Atom Bombs and the Abandoned Its Nuclear Weapons Program.* Within the U.S., Amazon offers a number of other books covering the same subject.[15]

Within South Africa, the human rights of certain segments of its society are reportedly in free-fall The people of color in the townships may now be free to move around the country, but they still have very little work and regularly have to endure very poor living conditions.[16] On 22 May 2015, South African police ran a series of township raids in which about 4000 people were arrested, including 1650 living in the country illegally (probably from Zimbabwe). The only official reason ever given for the nationwide crackdown was crime suppression.[17]

Finally Connecting the Dots

With an extremely clever criminal, law enforcement agencies will sometimes amass every bit of evidence (however miniscule) and then look for trends within each category. When combined those trends point toward a prime suspect. If enough hard evidence can then be found for the district attorney, formal charges are levied, and the suspect is put on trial.

U.S. national defense agencies need not be that fastidious. If

	CAMPAIGN FINANCING	ELECTION GUIDANCE	PEACEKEEPERS	CORPORATE SECURITY	MASSIVE IMMIGRATION	GOVERNANCE INSTRUCTION	DEBT FORFEIT/LARGE LOAN	FLOODING WITH PRC GOODS	MINERAL OR OIL ACCESS	AIRPORT/RAIL/ROAD BUILDING	SEAPORT/ELECTRICITY WORK	CRBC	CRCC OR CRECG	CEIEC	MINING CONCESSIONS	OIL-DRILLING CONCESSIONS	MILITARY TRAINING EMPHASIS	PROPOSED BASES
MINERAL EXTRACTION ROUTE																		
DRC			X	X			X	X	X	X		X	X		X		X	
ZAMBIA	X			X			X	X	X	X	X	X			X			
TANZANIA						X	X		X	X	X	X	X					X
RWANDA							X		X	X		X						
BURUNDI							X		X	X	X	X					X	
UGANDA							X		X	X		X						
SOUTH AFRICA/BOTSWANA						X	X		X	X	X							X
ZIMBABWE		X			X	X	X		X	X	X						X	
OIL EXTRACTION ROUTE																		
ANGOLA					X	X	X	X	X	X	X	X		X		X	X	X
CONGO REPUBLIC					X		X		X	X	X						X	
SUDAN	X		X	X	X	X	X	X	X	X	X					X	X	
SOUTH SUDAN			X				X		X	X	X	X					X	
CHAD							X		X	X			X					
ALGERIA							X		X					X				
LIBYA									X				X					
TUNISIA									X									
EGYPT									X					X				
NIGERIA				X	X		X		X	X	X		X			X	X	X
NAMIBIA							X		X	X	X	X					X	X
MOZAMBIQUE						X	X		X	X	X				X		X	X
KENYA							X		X	X	X	X						X
CAMEROON							X	X		X	X						X	
EQUATORIAL GUINEA							X		X	X	X					X		
DRUG CONDUIT																		
SOMALIA/ERITREA/DJIBOUTI					X	X	X			X	X		X					X
ETHIOPIA							X			X	X	X	X	X				
NIGER/CAR							X		X	X	X	X						
MALI			X				X			X	X	X						
BURKINA FASO/GUINEA						X	X		X	X	X				X			
GUINEA-BISSAU/SENEGAL/GAMBIA						X	X			X	X	X					X	
IVORY COAST NATIONS			X				X		X	X	X	X			X		X	
MAURITANIA/W.SAHARA			X				X			X		X	X					

Table 21.1: China's Most Heavily Targeted Countries

(All Chinese aid projects doublechecked through this url: http://china.aiddata.org)

a foreign power is suspected of denigrating America's overseas security apparatus, steps are taken to forestall actual combat. Table 21.1 is a partial record of potentially subversive Chinese "activity" in Africa. Because of the bottom-up or "death-by-a-thousand-razor-cuts" way that Asians like to attack, this table reveals a cumulative (and none-too-pleasant) reality about Africa.

Within this chart, 45 of Africa's most volatile countries have been subdivided into three categories—those China might want for mineral extraction, petroleum retrieval, or drug transit. Then, each nation is assessed from the standpoint of Chinese manipulation in the following areas: (1) voting irregularities; (2) immigration influx; (3) governance advice; (4) financial aid; (5) cheap imports; (6) mineral/oil access; (7) infrastructure building; (8) PLA-affiliated companies; (9) resource concessions; and finally (10) military plans. The countries with the highest number of hits (X's) are those of most interest to, and under the greatest influence by, the PRC. In the minerals category, DRC wins with Zambia coming in second. For petroleum, Angola and North Sudan share the prize with Nigeria close behind. There is no clear-cut winner in the drug conduit category.

In this way, one can identify not only China's primary targets within Africa, but also its preferred ways for incrementally controlling those countries. Unfortunately, the nations not as deeply involved in the petroleum, mineral, or drug trade are not listed at all. Their omission may tend to underplay the extent to which Mainland China has been interfering with Africa's remaining 10 governments.

Of course, there are other conclusions that can be drawn from such a chart. The large number of entries for the DRC means one of two things: (1) either the PRC has been trying hardest to help the African nation with the most internal chaos; or (2) the PRC has been fanning that chaos to more easily monopolize its mineral wealth. Since 1998, 5.4 million DRC residents have died from military conflict and its accompanying humanitarian crises. Some 45,000 inhabitants of that country continue to expire every month from those same causes.[18] Is it just coincidence that most of this DRC trouble has occurred in the same mining districts where China gets its strategically vital metals? Why would the ruling party of China worry about loss of life in the DRC, after having overseen the demise of so many of its own citizens during (and after) the Cultural Revolution? [19]

Figure 21.2: Could GIs Be of Any Help?
(Source: "Mogadishu, Somalia," by MSGT. ([Ret.] Peter G. Varisano, U.S. Army Center of Military History, from this url: http://www.history.army.mil/art/A&I/Mogadishu.jpg)

Of the established PRC surrogates, Angola and North Sudan each got 12 hits. With so many, those countries are unlikely to stray from the Communist camp. Neither is Zimbabwe or the unexpected Tanzania, with eight entries apiece. Election tampering in Zambia, Zimbabwe, and northern Sudan may mean China would like as much control over the first as it already has over the other two. Only partially apparent from the chart are China's probable proxy plans for Chad, Namibia, and South Africa. With that many regional allies, how easy would it be for a fledgling superpower to completely dominate the entire continent? 4GW was all but invented in China. To have any chance of winning WWIII, the Western Alliance must now somehow break the PRC's tightening grip over Africa and all of its resources. (See Figure 21.2.)

General Conclusions

Almost every non-Muslim nation of any use to the PRC for acquiring scarce commodities has been given large sums of money through open-ended grants, loans, and debt forfeiture. They have also had the rebuilding of their transportation networks largely subsidized. Such "no-visible-strings-attached" gifts have been awarded almost equally to long-standing proxies, prospective proxies, and resource-rich bystanders. Thankfully, there is a nonprofit—*Tracking Chinese Development Finance*—that does nothing but monitor such transactions. For almost every country, there is also a "China-Country Relations" entry at *Wikipedia Encyclopedia.* A closer look at every PRC aid project within Africa reveals the political/diplomatic cost of this economic assistance. Some PRC enticements—like new palaces, limousines, or "saloon" rail cars—simply cater to the whims of the ruling elite. Others, like new government buildings (particularly for foreign-affairs ministries) create a more subtle way of amending local policies and procedures.[20] All such buildings require a dedication ceremony to which the CPC counterpart should be invited. After the reception, recipient nation officials hear how their jobs are accomplished in China. Enough of this "bottom-up" advice over a number of years could result in major changes to how the recipient nation interacts with its own population and other countries. All the while, it has become gradually more beholding to (and dependent on) the PRC.

Below is a sampling of the kinds of "self-serving" Chinese projects that have been interspersed throughout the debt forgiveness and infrastructure-rebuilding initiatives. They reflect a steady diet of Chinese Communist "re-education" on how more effectively to govern one's nation. That diet is normally administered through a whole series of interagency exchange visits.

*Zimbabwe, 20949, Chinese selected Zimbabwean officials for training in China, 2010.
*South Africa, 16121, Provincial agreements to promote economic and cultural cooperation, 2004.
*Guinea-Bissau, 30634, Grant to support the Defence and Security Sector Reform Programme, 2010.
*Africa (regional), Angola, Cape Verde, Guinea-Bissau, Mozambique, Timor-Leste, 802, Training of officials and training center, 2010.

*Senegal, 2091, 90 seminars and training sessions, 2011.
*Eritrea, 30528, Cooperation between PFDJ [Eritrea's ruling party] and Communist Party of China, 2010.[21]
— *Tracking Chinese Development Finance*

Also regularly appearing on the list of Chinese foreign-aid projects throughout Africa is telecommunications work. Such a thing would not be necessary if someone weren't trying to coordinate that continent's defense. Either out of good will, or just to obscure strategic priorities, the PRC has also included a fair number of medical and agricultural entries.[22] Each separate medical visit rates its own project number, thereby causing the larger—more "self-serving"—entries to all but disappear in the pile. That's one of the ways in which important things are hidden in the East, but only veterans of Asian wars will recognize it as such.

For Those Who Still Don't See Any Problem

Americans are an honest and optimistic people. Many have a difficult time seeing how another culture might too easily equate intentional deceit with "legitimately outsmarting one's competition." With regard to the ongoing PRC immigration to Africa, most U.S. citizens think only of their own ancestors' quest for a better life. But the extent of that Chinese influx to the Dark Continent could reach as high as 100 million by 2020.[23] If that many new residents were to be concentrated in several countries that provide the PRC with much needed minerals and petroleum, they could effectively transform local politics. The total population of Sudan is only 35 million, Angola 19 million, Zambia 14 million, and Zimbabwe 13 million.

Just as immigration, foreign-aid schemes tend to evoke only warm and fuzzy feelings amongst the majority of Americans. For them, any increase in international commerce to Africa—whether in abeyance with standard protocols or not—would mean a brighter future for "developing nations." But all PRC business deals come with stipulations. Most infrastructure improvement projects must be accomplished with Chinese equipment and Chinese labor. They are not as beneficial to the host country as those involving local purchases and jobs. Others have highly unpleasant side effects—like the royalty-free extraction of oil and minerals, or the underpricing (and eventual bankrupting) of local corporations. In the end, the recipient of all this Chinese benevolence is left with much fewer natural resources and an economy that is almost totally dependent on the PRC. Business and politics are constant bedfellows. Wherever one is subverted, the other is sure to follow.

To solve a chronic problem, one must often face a "not-so-pleasant" reality. To fully appreciate the danger that the PRC now poses to Africa, one must review China's own history closer to home. This aspiring superpower has moved large numbers of its loyal Han population into Tibet and the Uyghur regions of Western China as a way of stifling any attempt at separatism or independence.[24] This way of subduing popular dissent is not new to the Chinese, nor is it an intermediate objective. Most of those Hans will enter the local business environment. As far back as 1993, a visiting Western diplomat noticed that Chinese residents "now dominate new economic activity in Tibet."[25] Once all new business opportunity in an area has been monopolized, next will come complete control over its politics, governance, and foreign policy.

As for the insinuation that the CPC may have had something to do with the excessive loss of life in Sudan and the Eastern DRC, suffice it to say that the CPC has had similar problems within its own borders. Up to nine million Chinese citizens perished from 1966 to 1975 as a direct result of the CPC's "Cultural Revolution."[26] As Chapter 4 has already shown, that same Cultural Revolution was then spread not only to Cambodia, but also to Africa. What subsequently transpired in Cambodia is a good indicator of what may have happened elsewhere. All that can now be said about the PRC's initial expansion into Africa is that their insurgent proxies committed excesses in almost every country. Best known are the massacre of over 20,000 people in a newly freed Zimbabwe,[27] death of up to 75,000 people in Mozambiquan reeducation centers,[28] and forced relocation of "perhaps millions" of people in Tanzania.[29] Now that satellite-country militias (like Sudan's *Janjaweed)* are doing most of the killing, PRC culpability is less easy to establish. Most evidence of it revolves around China indirectly arming those local militias, training them, and then doing too little to stop their various indiscretions.

With a "revolutionary" outlook on all things foreign and domestic, the CPC may see an occasional mass killing as the unfortunate price of promoting worldwide "progress." That's why it showed so little remorse for the Tiananmen Square incident. Those populist protests had been condemned by the Chinese government as being "counter-revolutionary." That China has now blossomed into a responsible friend of every country throughout the Dark Continent is the wishful thinking of those who know too little about its overall record in Africa.[30]

What makes the Chinese regime and other "revolutionary" governments different from most in the world is their complete lack of interest in bringing peace to the nations they "help." Nor do they put any human-rights pressure on the leaders of those nations. That the continuing violence and disorder in various locales creates a better business environment for the Chinese may be coincidental. But, the PRC's traditional foreign policy of trading favors for anti-Taiwan sentiment in the U.N. suggests a more sinister vision. As a permanent member of the U.N. Security Council, China has repeatedly blocked every attempt to curtail Sudanese-PDF-supported militias from committing genocides in Darfur and Southern Kordofan.[31] Thus, one may legitimately say that China has a record of not caring about the lives of the people from whom it gets natural resources.

The PRC's "infrastructure-building" and "joint-business" ventures throughout the Dark Continent may appear—on the surface—to benefit that region's various populations. But, most such ventures bring the local governments under increasing Chinese influence. Only for those Africans willing to settle for the same levels of personal freedom as in China will such an arrangement be acceptable.

What's No Longer Politically Correct to Admit

Present-day citizens of the PRC still cannot worship as they want, live where they want, or even have the number of children they want. And those are only their most obvious disabilities. Not until just recently did the CPC even think about ending its most draconian procedure. "After more than a half-century and the imprisonment of millions of people without trial, China officially moved to abolish its 're-education through labor camp system' at the end of 2013."[32] Yet, this apparent step in the right direction has turned out to be just another illusion in China's ongoing propensity for "smoke and mirrors." Here's why.

> The Communist Party established . . . [these] camps in 1955 to punish perceived enemies such as "counter-revolutionaries" and those deemed "politically unreliable," according to Amnesty International.[33]
>
> — *NPR News,* February 2014

Many such camps were hidden in plain sight at the edge of China's biggest cities. To gain admission, all one needed was an unsubstantiated allegation against his or her own character.

> Over the decades, the party [CPC] used the camps to warehouse political critics, gadflies, as well as petty criminals, drug addicts, and prostitutes. As recently as 2007, China's Ministry of Justice estimated there were about 400,000 people in the country's 310 camps.[34]
>
> — *NPR News,* February 2014

Other types of detention have now taken the place of "re-education through labor" camps in China. Thus, the self-professed "champion of developing nations" is still guilty of its own brutality.

> That doesn't mean Chinese people are now safe from extrajudicial detention. . . . [T]he government still uses mental institutions and secret jails—often converted motels—to dispatch people it doesn't like.[35]
>
> — *NPR News,* February 2014

Any nation naive enough to fall for China's new "charm" offensive, take PRC money, and then act on the ensuing governance advice, fully deserves its loss of independence. Within Africa, the Zimbabwean population is the best example of what eventually befalls a friend of the PRC.

Beltway "Business As Usual" Won't Stop the Infringement

On 15 April 2015, a widely recognized national security expert appeared before the U.S. Senate Committee on Armed Services at a hearing to discuss "China, the U.S., and the Asia-Pacific." His opening statement mostly covered how the Chinese economy has now almost overtaken that of the U.S. It concludes with a recommendation that the Committee stimulate a "vigorous debate that illuminates the risks we face" as a result of America's declining prosperity.[36]

What that Senate Armed Services Committee should instead debate is why the Pentagon seems exclusively to work on defense contracts. Some U.S. infantry squads are now instructed by well-connected, weapons-oriented, and tactically unsophisticated civilian contractors. While that might make good fiscal sense, it's no way to win a war. (See Figure 21.3.)

Then, the members of that august Committee could usefully review why so much of America's high-tech weaponry will not work without the rare metals that the PRC has already monopolized, or why the mainstream U.S. news media rarely reports Chinese expansion around the world.

Figure 21.3: Civilian-Trained Riflemen Won't Know Enough

(Source: "Pararescue," by MSG C.Vance, F.E.Warren Air Force Base Media Gallery ©, from url: http://www.warren.af.mil/shared/media/ggallery/hires/AFG-060725-004.jpg)

Finally, those distinguished U.S. senators might discuss the following: (1) why the Chinese have only to avoid a shooting war to dominate the world; (2) how their military is expert at winning without fighting; (3) how their overseas intelligence community is now focused on economic opportunism; and (4) how much trouble a Western "top-down" bureaucracy can have trying to counter an Eastern "bottom-up" threat. To many U.S. military and intelligence professionals, these things have been blatantly obvious for years. But, subject matter experts often have less influence over U.S. foreign policy, than the reform of their own organizations. That's the Committee's job, and its window for corrective action is quickly closing.

Back to the U.S. Information Gathering Proposal

The PRC threat is to world security, so Washington's seeming indifference to it must be the result of an intelligence shortfall. This book has proposed changes to how this Chinese incursion's details are collected and subsequently interpreted. Next comes a on-site test to that proposal.

22 RESEARCH PROJECTION VS. ON-SITE REALITY

- How did Zambia stack up during a May 2015 visit?
- Was the prior assessment still close enough to be useful?

Coat of Arms of an "officially Christian" main PRC target.

(Source: Wikipedia Encyclopedia, s.v. "Zambia," public-domain image from Fry1989 with designator "Coat_of_arms_of_Zambia.svg.png.")

What Again Is the New Way of Monitoring American Foes?

The proposed change to U.S. intelligence gathering is to interpret the published facts for each country based on the expansionist *modus operandi* of its most likely predator. For Zambia, that predator has been indisputably China since its independence from Belgium in 1964. This researcher traveled to Lusaka in May of 2015. While there, he visited the National Museum, talked to several low-ranking officials, read most newspapers, watched local TV, and traveled by car to the Zambian terminus of the TANZAM railway. Below are the results of that real-time assessment.

Controversial Forecasts Confirmed

Right before leaving for Lusaka, this researcher had predicted to an Africa-savy military friend that one out of every five residents of Zambia would turn out to be Chinese. Upon arrival, he was told by the first two people he asked that 20% of all Zambians are now from the PRC. That's 2.8 million, not the 100,000 that the BBC had recently determined from census figures.[1] To vote, all those immigrants have to do is take a Zambian spouse.[2]

Chapter 21 has also strongly suggested that President Sata's recent death in England while undergoing treatment for cancer may have been the result of foul play. An anonymous resident of Lusaka confirmed that a large portion of the Zambian population harbors the same suspicion.[3]

A Much Closer Election Than Previously Reported

A special election was held on 20 January 2015 to choose a president to complete Sata's term in office (until late 2016). Edgar Lungu was elected interim president. According to the CIA, Lungu of the PF Party captured 48.8% of the vote, whereas Hakainde Hichilema of the United Party for National Development (UPND) took 47.2%.[4] Local estimates made the count much closer than that. The acting manager of the National Museum reports Lungu winning by less than 1% of the vote.[5] A contract driver for Lusaka's best hotel says Lungu won by 28,000 votes out of about 7 million, or 0.4%.[6] A highly reputable source who shall remain unidentified acknowledges Chinese backing for the UPND.[7] A "People's Power Display" that still takes up the entire ground floor of the National Museum makes this claim fully believable. That display contains a number of enlarged photographs of collective farms and other Communist memorabilia from the Kaunda era.[8]

At the last moment in the political campaign, Rupiah Banda threw his support behind Lungu.[9] Banda had been Zambia's president from 2008 to 2011. He was from the MMD party that had ruled Zambia since 1991. That party had been guilty of harassment of opposition parties and abuse of state media and other resources.[10] It was also widely suspected of being financially backed by the PRC.[11] Almost immediately after this latest election, the Zambian press began to speculate as to what concessions Lungu might have made to repay Banda for the favor.[12] Within days of winning the position of president, Lungu was making a state visit to China in which President Hu Jintao afforded him all the ceremonial pomp of a world leader.[13]

Then the Bombshell Hit

On 7 May 2015, the Zambian government was accused of hiding a $192 million PRC loan to upgrade its State Security Branch. That assistance had been combined with $4.14 million for a water treatment project in Nakonde.[14] President Lungu's administration got angry at the disclosure and said that the Ministry of Finance official who had leaked the information would be summarily punished.[15] Needless to say, a Communist Chinese designed State Security system might be less protective of Zambian human rights than the existing setup.

Still, most Zambians have high hopes for Lungu. He was a personal friend of Sata and thought to have the same basic policies.[16] But policies are one thing, and resisting the almost continuous stream of temptations from a rich superpower something else. Even the much revered Sata initially saw no real problem with all the Chinese road building. It was mostly with the way Zambian workers were treated in Chinese mines that he took issue. Lungu is now faced with how best to assign royalties and taxes so that the PRC-subsidized mining operations can no longer bankrupt their Zambian counterparts.[17]

Communist-Inspired Political Party Flux

That the UPND was, in fact, a PRC organ became painfully clear within days of Lungu's PF party victory. That's when the UPND began pushing for public demonstrations to force the Zambian government to hold a referendum for authorization to rewrite the electoral provisions of its constitution before the 2016 election.[18] The UNIP party of Kenneth Kaunda's day had ultimately taken over the MMD, and one Lusaka newspaper had now begun to worry that the PF party might now be changing its platform with the addition of Banda.[19]

The UPND must have been deadly serious about that adjustment to Zambia's democratic processes. On 7 May 2015, a program aired on Lusaka TV showing how Mao had introduced "democracy" to the Shannan border region of China (to include Shanxi Province) from 1940 to 1941. Of course, the peasants of that Province had not been not fully apprised of the latest developments, so they first had to be "reeducated." Then, on the pretext of avoiding bureaucracy, Mao accomplished his "vital connection" with the people through local CPC cadres. After the reeducation process, those cadres would theoretically listen to the needs of the local citizenry and then run things in a more helpful manner.[20] Needless to say, this distorted version of democracy more often resulted in less personal freedom. But the average Zambian voter may not yet realize the price of a Communistic system.

Lungu Is Worried about the U.N.

President Lungu has publicly noted that 70% of the U.N. Security Council's agenda is on Africa, yet no African country yet holds a permanent seat on that Council.[21] Rumor has it that the Zambian population once got so incensed with U.N. Secretary General Ban Ki-moon's lecture on gay rights that he was forced to leave the country.[22] More probably, too many Zambians may have become aware of how much control the PRC now exerts over Africa's U.N. missions.

Zambia's Economy

Indirect Chinese pressure on Zambia's mining industry has resulted in more inflation as well as a number of other economic ills—like crime and corruption. Copper ingots must travel south through Lusaka in four-truck convoys to keep from getting highjacked. The airport-to-hotel trip is no longer safe by taxi. Lines at the bank-teller windows are regularly "crashed" by preferred customers. And those preferred customers seem to be getting large bundles of paper money. Still, all in all, Zambia's proud and resilient society functions extremely well.[23]

A conversation with the station master at the TANZAM railroad's Zambian end in Kapiri Mposhi revealed why truck is now the preferred way of exporting minerals from the Copper Belt. By 2012 following the drop in copper prices, the amount of ore being carried over the TANZAM to the Indian Ocean dwindled due to maintenance problems. Apparently, the tracks in Tanzania are of a slightly narrower gauge and harder to keep functional than those in Zambia. One segment in particular keeps getting swept away by mud slides. As such, the train from Dar es Salaam to Kapiri Mposhi now carries mostly passengers, a fair percentage of whom are Chinese merchants. Many may be bringing in their latest consignment of cheap Asian goods. Soon, there will be an additional rail branch from the Zambian portion of the TANZAM to Malawi, and then on to Mozambique. At that point, more Copper Belt product may be moved by train. But, at present, almost all those minerals travel by truck through Lusaka, then Zimbabwe, and then on to a South African port.[24]

Besides the ore of a few remaining mines, Zambia now has primarily food stuffs for export. Yet, a PRC company recently bought up part of Zambia's poultry industry. Whereas it takes a Zambian citizen three months to grow a chicken, it now takes the Chinese one month.[25] Unhealthy growth hormones are undoubtedly involved.

Overall Value of the Intelligence Projection

The most vital portions of the initial assessment on Zambia turned out to be correct. Zambia is still under heavy attack from the Chinese, by way of massive immigration and all other forms of political manipulation. That's because all minerals from the DRC portion of the Copper Belt may have to pass through Zambia to reach an ocean. Someone very familiar with Zambia's road system claims a new Chinese road connecting the DRC mines to the Benguela railhead actually runs through Zambia (possibly by way of Solwesi).[26] The literature strongly suggests such a road, as it does a long-planned Solwesi-Benguela rail link. That link would run from Chingola, Zambia (near Mulfulira) to the Angola-DRC border (just south of Dilolo).[27] (See Map 22.1.) As a poor road already exists between Chingola and Solwesi, its western extension may approximate that of the planned train tracks. Thus, Zambia's future endorsement of such a corridor will be absolutely essential to China's continuing exploitation of DRC resources.

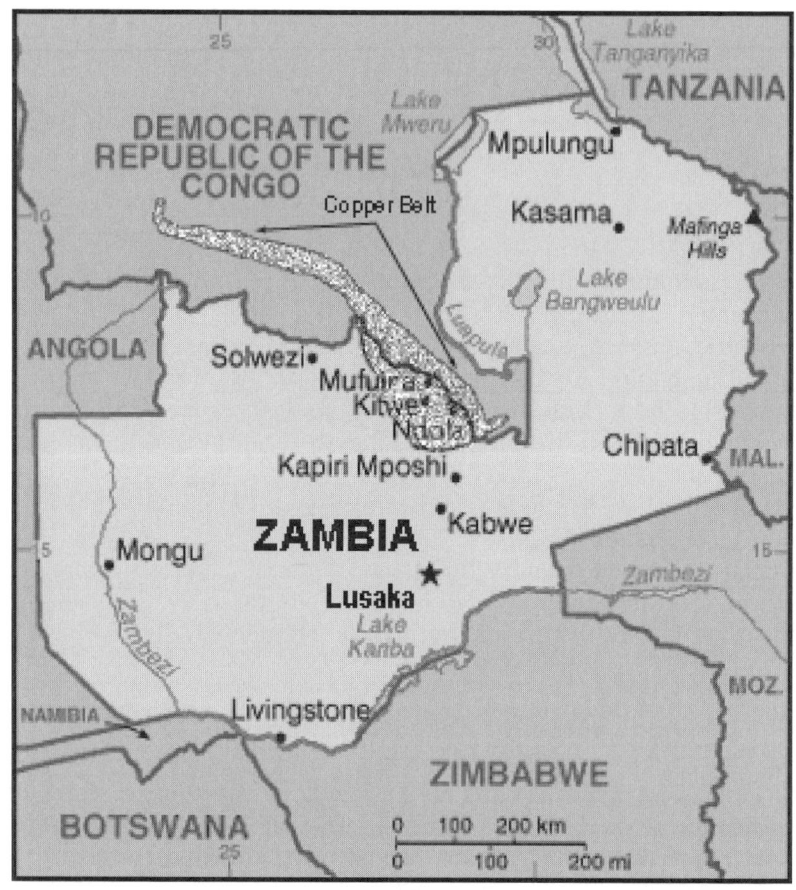

Map 22.1: DRC Minerals May Have to Leave through Zambia
(Source: Courtesy of General Libraries, University of Texas at Austin, from their website for map designator "zambia_sm_2014.gif")

> GOVERNMENT [of Zambia] has sub-contracted China Geo Corporation . . . to rehabilitate the Chingola-Solwezi Road.[28]
>
> — *Lusaka Times,* 30 January 2014

The above-mentioned company is "China Geo-Engineering Corporation International Ltd." It is not on the PRC's published list of state-owned companies.[29] With a headquarters in Beijing, it may secretly belong to (or be closely affiliated with) the PLA. How might such a link then relate to the DRC's continual bloodshed?

23 The DRC Situation Comes into Focus

- Is there ongoing Tutsi genocide in the DRC?
- Shouldn't the U.S. try to do something about it?

DRC flag is somewhat like that of North Korea.

(Source: Wikipedia Encyclopedia, s.v. "DRC," public-domain image from Zscout370 with designator "Flag_of_the_Democratic_Republic_of_the_Congo.svg.png.")

DRC Events Too Convoluted to Be by Design?

Most Americans just scratch their heads while contemplating the Congo situation. They vaguely realize that many people have died there over the last 20 years, but usually attribute all of this loss of life to "inter-factional fighting" between competing tribes. Because of the U.N.'s ongoing presence in the region, they naturally assume that everything has been done that can be. Unfortunately, the DRC plays host to not only Copper Belt minerals, but also a sizable petroleum reserve. As such, it has been just as coveted by China, as has neighboring Zambia.

It's only from a mixture of time-line details from the DRC and surrounding nations that one can start to see how PRC has been manipulating things in the Eastern Congo to its own advantage. By indirectly supporting the perpetrators of an ongoing genocide, China may have to accept much of responsibility for the chronic carnage around Goma. (Carefully read Table 23.1.) To the casual observer, it is only guilty of a little economic opportunism.

The SADC

Formed around 1992, the South African Development Community (SADC) was initially an economic alliance. Among its 15 member nations are those obvious from Map 23.1, plus the Seychelles, Mauritius, Lesotho, and Swaziland. Neither Rwanda nor Burundi is included.[1] Nelson Mandela was one of SADC's first elected chairpersons and did not personally favor direct military support of any member state. However, SADC had a subsidiary department called the "Organ on Politics, Defense, and Security." Its leader was Robert Mugabe—president of China's first full-fledged African surrogate (Zimbabwe). This "Organ" was to take the lead in the military intervention to save Kabila's DRC regime in 1997. Having endorsed Zimbabwe's elections and land reforms, Mandela did not object.[2]

> The SADC Organ on Politics Defence and Security is . . . responsible for promoting peace and security in the SADC region. It is mandated to steer and provide Member states with direction regarding matters that threaten peace, security and stability in the region.[3]
>
> — Official SADC website

China's Involvement with SADC

At some point, the PRC may have tried to join SADC (minimally as an observer), just as it did the Organization of American States (OAS) and Non-Aligned Movement (NAM) in the Caribbean region.[4] But within southern Africa, the best Communist China could manage was a great deal of "sway" over SADC's Summit and economic committees. Most of this sway was probably rooted in its massive give-away program. Every developing nation within SADC wanted its fair share. Then, most must have concluded that Mugabe was their spokesman. Two weeks after being elected chairperson of the 2014 SADC Summit, Mugabe was on his way to a state visit in China. In the not too distant future, he is also expected to be elected AU chairperson.[5]

Map 23.1: The SADC Countries

(Source: Courtesy of General Libraries, University of Texas at Austin, from their website for map designator "txu-pclmaps-oclc-792930639-africa-2011.pdf")

In the 7 May 2015 issue of *Zambia Daily Mail* is a pictorial summary of President Lungu's first 100 days in office. Within those photograph captions are some very telling one-liners. Among Lungu's "SADC visits" were "South Africa, Zimbabwe, Namibia, [and] China State Visit."[6] For whatever reason, all SADC members must now accept China as a participant.

Tribal Hatred Not the Underlying Cause of DRC Chaos

That Tutsis had helped Laurent Kabila to seize power in Kinshasa should be adequate proof that all eastern DRC violence is not from irreconcilable differences between Hutus and Tutsis. Ultimately to blame are Maoist expansion and minerals.

> In 1967 Kabila founded the People's Revolutionary Party, which established a Marxist territory in the Kivu region of eastern Zaire and managed to sustain itself through gold mining and ivory trading. When the enterprise came to an end during the 1980's, he ran a business selling gold in Dar es Salaam.
>
> In the mid-1990's, Kabila returned to Zaire and became leader of the newly formed Alliance of Democratic Forces for the Liberation of Congo-Zaire. As opposition to the dictatorial leadership of Mobutu grew, he rallied forces consisting mostly of Tutsi from eastern Zaire and marched west toward the capital city of Kinshasa, forcing Mobutu to flee the country. On May 17, 1997, Kabila installed himself as head of state and reverted the country's name to the Democratic Republic of the Congo.[7]
>
> — *Encyclopedia Britannica*

When Laurent Kabila was assassinated in 2001, his son Joseph began more discreetly to finish what his father had started.

> He [Joseph Kabila] fought as part of the rebel forces that helped his father depose Pres. Mobutu Sese Seko of Zaire in 1997. Laurent then assumed the presidency and restored the country's former name, Democratic Republic of the Congo, and Joseph was sent to China for additional military

1916-1959: Belgium takes over what will become Rwanda; it is pro-Tutsi.

1963: 20,000 Tutsis killed after Hutu uprising turns this area into Rwanda.
Many other Tutsis flee into Uganda and Zaire.

1975-1993: Mobutu's Zaire aids West in Angola fight against Communism.

1990: Tutsi RPF launches rebellion against Hutu-governed Rwanda.

1994: Rwandan genocide occurs with the death of up to one million Tutsis.
U.N. does little to stop that genocide.
Hutu perpetrators escape into Eastern Zaire and join the FDLR.
Tutsi RPF establishes its own government in Rwanda.
FDLR takes over Zairean refugee camps and keeps raiding Rwanda.

1996-1997: Rwanda sends troops into Eastern DRC to halt Hutu attacks.
Ugandan rebel Lord's Resistance Army takes refuge in Eastern DRC.
Uganda joins Rwanda in supporting Kabila's anti-Mobutu revolt.
This is called the First Congo War.

1997: Kabila's rebel forces drive on Kinshasa and overthrow Mobutu.
Hutus from Laurent Kabila's new DRC keep attacking Rwanda.
What is now DRC accepts military training from DPRK and China.
Rwanda shifts support from Kabila to rebels who oppose his regime.

1998-2002: Several nations send forces to save Kabila's government.
All are Communist proxies: Zimbabwe, Angola, Namibia, Chad, Sudan.
Joseph Kabila takes over after his father Laurent is assassinated.
Rwanda and Uganda agree to pull troops from DRC if FDLR disarmed.
This is called Second Congo War.

2009: Tutsi CNDP rebels sign another peace accord with DRC regime.
Many CNDP fighters are absorbed into DRC army and then abused.

2012: DRC army Tutsis mutiny to form M23.
M23 takes Goma in Eastern DRC to protect its mostly Tutsi population.

2013 (late): M23 pushed into Uganda by DRC, U.N., and FDLR forces.
All U.N. troops are from Chinese allies: South Africa, Tanzania, Malawi.
Since 1998, some 5.4 million DRC residents have died.
That total likely includes another Tutsi genocide in the Eastern DRC.
All nations aiding Kabila's DRC (both times) are now Chinese proxies.

Table 23.1: More Revealing Rwanda/DRC Timeline

(Sources: "Cry Zimbabwe," by Stiff, BBC Country Profile Timelines; Wikipedia Encyclopedia, s.v. "Rwanda," "DRC," "FDLR," "CNCP," "M23," and "Lord's Resistance Army.")

PARTICIPANTS IN SECOND CONGO WAR

Pro-Communist Side	Pro-Western Side
Kabila regime	Anti-Kabila rebels
Zimbabwe	Rwanda
Angola	Uganda
Namibia	Angolan UNITA (U.S. among backers)
Chad	RCD (DRC Banyamulenge Tutsis)
Sudan	
Congo (Brazzaville)	
Tanzania (instructors only)	
China (instructors only)	
North Korea (instructors only)	
Libya (logistical support only)	
FDLR (Hutu Interahamwe)	

Table 23.2: Last Vestige of U.S. Involvement
(Sources: "Cry Zimbabwe," by Stiff, pp.253-254; "Obituary: Jonas Savimbi, UNITA's Local Boy," BBC News, 25 February 2002)

training. Upon his return, he became head of the country's armed forces, with the rank of major general.[8]
— *Encyclopedia Britannica*

In effect, Laurent and his son Joseph—along with all those who support them—have simply been exploiting the Hutu-Tutsi rivalry to more easily achieve their political and economic goals. So far, the U.S. has been unable to do much about it. (See Table 23.2.)

The Problem with Letting Mugabe Lead Coalitions

Chapter 4 makes reference to a 20,000-person massacre in Zimbabwe shortly after its birth in 1980. Yet, there was no mention of who actually committed that massacre. Soviet-backed ZIPRA and Chinese-backed ZANLA had both been trying to defeat the Rhodesian regime. As such, the remnants of either could have been responsible for the mass killing as Zimbabwe's newly elected government. Now, further research has definitively revealed the culprit.

In *Cry Zimbabwe,* well-respected South African researcher Peter Stiff tells the full story of Zimbabwe's first few years as a nation. As might be expected, remnants of ZIPRA and ZANLA had eventually come to blows—most obviously in the town of Bulawayo. Then, the defeated ZIPRA troops had dispersed northward into Matabeleland (the area between Bulawayo and Victoria Falls) to carry on a more guerrilla-like existence. At least that's how it looked after ZIPRA weapons caches were discovered in Bulawayo.[9]

When ZANU's Mugabe became Zimbabwe's prime minister following the 1980 U.N.-sponsored elections, his main political opposition was from ZAPU led by Joshua Nkomo, with its power base in Matabeleland.[10] Because ZIPRA had been the military wing of pre-election ZAPU, Mugabe was thus faced with a dual threat from the same region. He then formed 5th Brigade to deal with the combined problem.

Initially trained by the North Koreans, 5th Brigade had been specifically prepared to eliminate guerrillas by drying up their popular support. Deployed to Matabeleland in 1983, this poorly disciplined brigade ended up fighting civilians.[11]

> Evidence points to the conclusion that 5-Brigade was trained to deliberately target civilians. Wherever they went in the first few months of 1983 they carried out a "grotesquely violent campaign against civilians, civil servants, [ZAPU] party chairmen, and only occasionally armed insurgents *(Breaking the Silence,* Catholic Commission for Justice and Peace, Harare, 1997)." . . .
>
> . . . 5-Brigade was going around villages with lists of ZAPU supporters and the names of those who had fought with ZIPRA during the Bush War. They ask where they are and if they are there they shoot them. If they are not there, they shoot other villagers at random (firsthand account confirmed by Worrall of *The Guardian* [U.K.]).[12]
>
> — *Cry Zimbabwe,* by Peter Stiff

In other words, 5th Brigade went after local political processes from the bottom up by terrorizing all villagers in the region. Stiff refers to what subsequently occurred as a "genocide" in at least three separate places within his book.[13] Any policemen or soldiers from other units who questioned those excesses were told that 5th Brigade answered only to Mugabe.[14] Officially designated as the *Gukurahundi* ("the early rain which washes away the chaff before the spring rains" in the Shona language), 5th Brigade members had no difficulty seeing what Mugabe had in mind during his welcoming address.[15]

> "The knowledge you have acquired will make you work with the people, plough and reconstruct [their society]."[16]
> — Mugabe during his first speech to 5th Brigade

With 5th Brigade clearly in charge, representatives of Mugabe's ZANU-PF then entered Matabeleland to hold compulsory political rallies that would often conclude with Red-Guard like examples of what happens to people who don't want to cooperate. A ZANU-PF membership card became every Matabeleland resident's best chance at survival. The number of civilians who subsequently "disappeared" through 5th Brigade activity began to soar.[17]

While it is extremely doubtful that 5th Brigade ever dumped 20,000 corpses into the same mass grave, its combined killings within Matabeleland could have easily exceeded that number. The similarity between the Shona meaning of *Gukurahundi* and the 1994 Rwandan radio message to "cut the tall trees" is more than chilling.[18]

More about Genocide in the DRC

Since 2009, an estimated 45,000 human beings have expired every month in the DRC's eastern part from unnatural causes. "The presence of ex-Rwandan genocidists, local militias, and mineral warlords have led to the massacres of thousands of people."[19] While most of that region's mining activity occurs in Katanga Province down near the Zambian border, there are also large deposits of gold, coltan (for tantalum), tin, and diamonds up near Goma and Bukavu in the more northerly Kivu Provinces. Most of the DRC's ongoing loss of life has occurred in this Kivu region. (See Maps 23.2 and 23.3.)

The word "genocide" may have first been attached to events in the Kivus by General Laurent Nkunda, eventual leader of the CNDP. He was the DRC army officer of Tutsi extraction who had led dissident troops in June 2003 to capture Bukavu, the capital of South Kivu. Following the 13 August killing of 160 Congolese Tutsi refugees at a Burundian camp, Nkunda had threatened to recapture Bukavu to prevent the "completion" of a genocide of the Congolese Tutsi, known as the Banyamulenge.[20] Of course, Nkunda was quickly accused of war crimes by the Kinshasa government. With this much military activity in any given locale, there are bound to be some atrocities. However, what the world has apparently failed to remember is that the DRC army has had its own rather spotty record in this regard.

> Numerous armed groups remain active and their fighters continue to carry out brutal attacks on civilians, while few efforts have been made to bring commanders of the M23 and other armed groups implicated in abuses to justice. State [DRC] security forces have also been responsible for serious abuses, including extrajudicial killings, rapes, and enforced disappearances. While a growing number of [DRC army] soldiers have been arrested and tried for sexual violence and other serious abuses in recent years, impunity remains widespread, especially for senior level officers.[21]
>
> — *Human Rights Watch,* May 2015

Much of the death in this region has reportedly happened to women and children. One therefore wonders if the use of rape as a weapon has in any way affected the fatality statistics. According to *BBC News,* DRC soldiers have been "ordered to rape" women in any way associated with the opposition.[22]

China's Ongoing Need for Natural Resources

According to *Genocide Watch,* the mineral wealth of the DRC's eastern provinces is the principal cause of the ongoing conflict. "Numerous militias controlled by rapacious warlords, as well as Congolese government troops, exploit these minerals, while engaging in human rights violations on a large scale, including forcing civilians to work in the mines."[23]

Thus, mineral "fever" rather than tribal tension is ultimately to blame for this region's ongoing bloodshed. While Rwanda and Uganda have tailored their regional foreign policy around human rights issues, the DRC and its various allies have based theirs more on natural-resource protection. This became clearly evident as Laurent Kabila assumed leadership of the new nation. As early as 1998, he accused Rwanda of exploiting DRC minerals, and then was assisted by the SADC countries of Angola, Namibia, and Zimbabwe in pushing Rwandan and Ugandan forces out of his country.[24] *Genocide Watch* only vaguely alludes to the difference in motivation between the two sides. It does specify, however, which side has committed the most excesses.

> "Rwandan and Ugandan troops stayed in the DRC and many other African countries sent armies to exploit the vast mineral resources of DRC, driving civilians into the jungle, resulting in over four million civilian deaths and rapes of 200,000 women."[25]
>
> — *Genocide Watch,* 3 October 2012

How the U.N. Sees Things

The U.N. has been focusing so heavily on the M23 rebels that it has apparently forgotten about the human rights abuses of the *FLDR* and DRC army. While the DRC government has often promised to disarm the *FLDR,* it never actually accomplished this. The *FDLR* is now, and always has been, a Hutu militia proxy of Kinshasa. Bringing peace to a region is one thing, but actively supporting a repressive regime is something else. That the U.N. has become more and more attentive to Chinese interests over the years doesn't help.

General Nkunda, now in Rwandan protective custody, has no trouble seeing the PRC waiting in the wings to profit from all that eastern DRC bloodshed. He further states that the Joseph Kabila regime fared poorly in its "roadway for copper" deal with Beijing.[26]

How the Minerals Are Currently Exiting the DRC

Bloomberg News claims that all copper currently departing

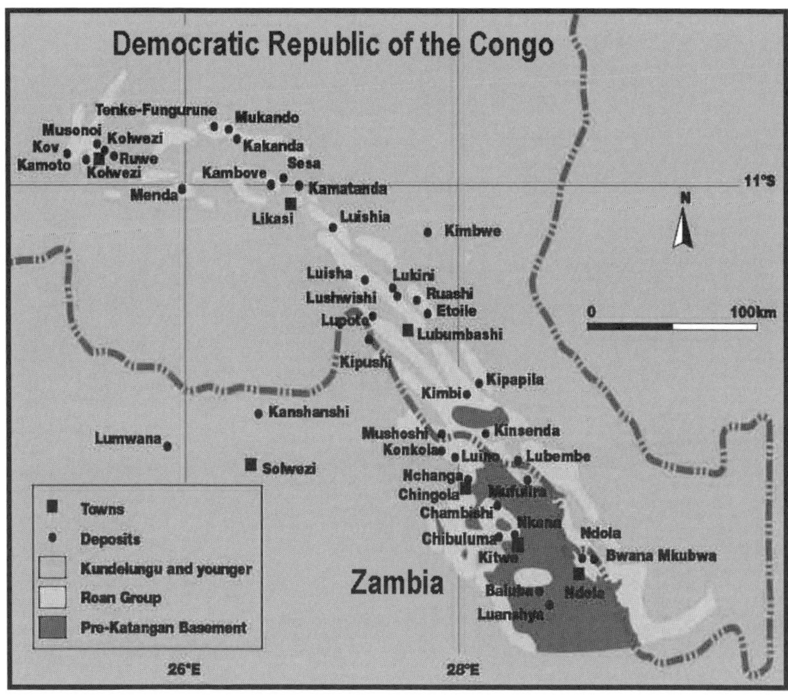

Map 23.2: Exact Location of Strategically Vital Copper Belt
(Source: Map from the website of "Transcontinent Exploration & Mining Company Ltd," copyright ©2006-2013)

Zambia does so by truck. Some goes east along the road paralleling the TANZAM railway to Dar es Salaam, but most goes south on the main highway through Lusaka, then Zimbabwe, and then on to Durban in South Africa.[27] This main north-south thoroughfare stretches up into the DRC Copper Belt and supposedly has a parallel rail line throughout much of its length.[28] (Look again at Map 23.2.)

China's $9 billion trade deal with the DRC (to which General Nkunda was referring) will provide vast supplies of copper and cobalt to the PRC in return for a 1,000 mile road stretching from the DRC-Zambia border to the northeastern Congo. (Refer again

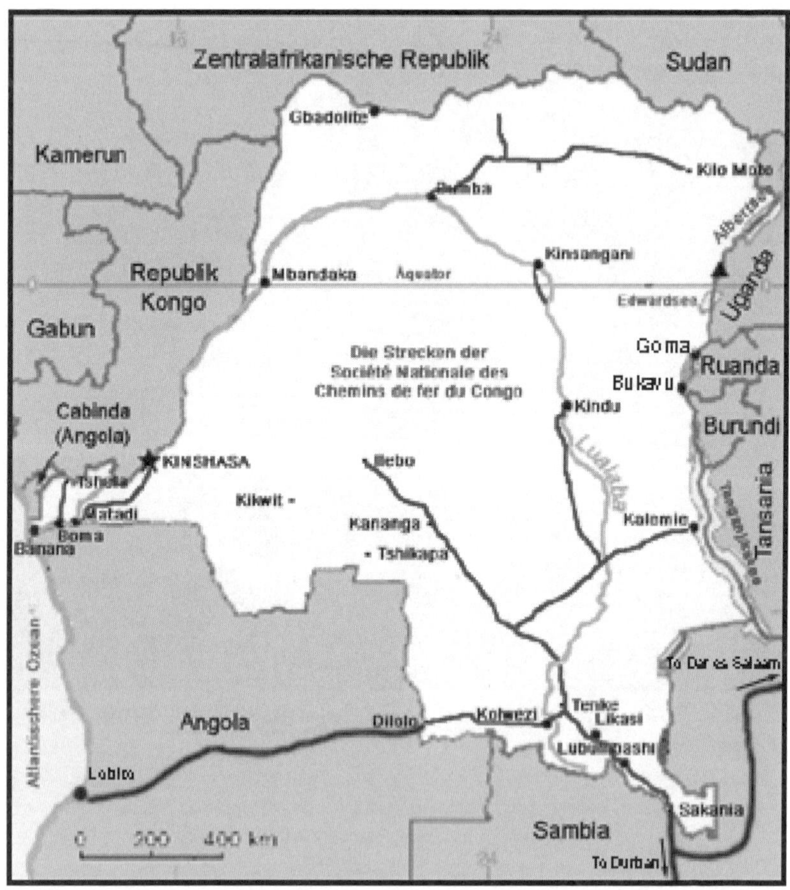

Map 23.3: Existing Rail Lines to the Sea from Copper Belt
(Source: Map based on Wikipedia Encyclopedia image designators "SNNC.png," "600px-Railways_in_Angola.png," and "500px-Railways_in_Tanzania.svg.png.")

to Map 23.3.) Kabila's first hint as to the inadvisability of such a deal should have been the relative scarcity of copper and cobalt in that part of the Congo. China must have had some other strategic reason for the road. Perhaps, it was just to help local proxies maintain control over the region.

Transporting ore (or ingots) by rail would be normally cheaper than doing so by truck. However, the heavy seasonal rains in this part of Africa make railroad maintenance a continuous struggle, as with the TANZAM mud slides. Map 23.3 shows the DRC's existing rail network. Yet, like the Tanzanian portion of the TANZAM, the train tracks leading out of the Copper Belt may not be in very good condition. That's why most ore or partially smelted metal is still leaving by truck. China may have never intended to use the Benguela or TANZAM railroads for DRC mineral removal. Highways are more obscure and resistant to blockage. In other parts of the world, the PRC regularly establishes alternative resource conduits in case its continual 4GW incursions provoke a shooting war.

24 COUNTERING CHINA'S INFLUENCE

- Could U.S. troops help to stem the Communist tide?
- What new mission might they perform?

Grandson of GI who helped village militiamen in Vietnam.

(Source: "Soldier Crouched,"by MSG.W.Vance,F.E.Warren Air Force Base Media Gallery ©,at url: http://www.warren.af.mil/shared/media/ggallery/hires/AFG-100830-003.jpg)

The Dark Continent Situation As a Whole

Africa has natural resources that are absolutely vital to U.S. security. For this reason alone, it cannot be forfeited to the Chinese. While the Islamist threat has also come to parts of the continent, that from the new Communist superpower is far more pervasive and dangerous. Almost all of southern Africa is now under heavy PRC influence. Pro-Chinese dictators currently run Angola and Zimbabwe, and formerly Marxist parties are still in control of South Africa, Namibia, Congo Republic, Tanzania, and Mozambique. Unless the West does something to reverse this trend, almost every nation in Africa will eventually fall under the economic and then political domination of the PRC. Along with self-determination at the polling place and market, its various populations will sacrifice other human rights. At least, that's what *Freedom House* has been implicitly indicating through its yearly ratings.

Just because the Allies' battlefield attempt to save southern Africa from Communism was sidelined by U.N.-monitored elections doesn't mean the struggle is over. 4GW is like that. Temporary setbacks are to be expected in every arena. Only necessary now is a different—and this time more nonmartial—strategy. With Apartheid no longer an issue, the next attempt to save Africa may enjoy more success.

The Most Logical Approach

If the PRC has been destabilizing the Dark Continent (whether or not by design), then America must stabilize it. If much of that destabilization has come through internal strife, then the U.S. must do something to promote law and order in the affected regions. If a flood of Chinese small arms has been contributing to the violence, then America must limit their spread. If Chinese-sponsored drug smuggling has been corrupting local officials, then the U.S. must do more to interdict its principal conduits. Clearly, the Departments of State, Justice, and Defense must now arrive at a joint strategy, in which the Pentagon is no longer limited to strictly warfighting operations.

In essence, local security is the key to combatting the Chinese takeover of the Dark Continent. With more local security, there would be fewer voting irregularities, less of a PLA peacekeeper presence, and not as much dependency on PRC funding. A few defunct African industries might even recover enough to undersell the same Chinese imports that initially ruined them. That would, in turn, create a number of local jobs. As each citizen's economic prospects improved, he or she would be less likely to contribute to the chronic unrest.

Then, with more contented residents in the petroleum- and mineral-producing regions of Africa, Western corporations might return to compete with the Chinese Dragon. As soon as the economic playing field was again level in most nations, so would be their political future. The two are so closely related as to be almost symbiotic. Not to heal the former means automatically to sacrifice the latter.

How More Local Security Might Be Achieved

Local security is normally acquired through the parent nation's criminal-justice system. If the police and courts can't provide it, then troops are sent in. But, there doesn't have to be active warfare. As long as each terrorist act is separately investigated, the overall populace won't be bothered by that troop presence. That's largely how the British were able to win their 1950's guerrilla war in Malaya—by quickly dispatching a tiny paramilitary team to track down the perpetrators of each terrorist crime.

On the Dark Continent (as in other places), the police forces within underpopulated or volatile areas often lack enough military skill to protect themselves, much less go after heavily armed smugglers. This is how the U.S. could help—by sending a squad-sized military contingent to live and work with each police outpost. Something like this has already been successful during the Vietnam War, when scores of lone U.S. infantry squads were stationed with village militias to help train and advise them.[1] By 1970, III Marine Amphibious Force was calling these small enlisted detachments an "aid to local law enforcement."[2]

The young Marines at these villages simply reported any unseemly behavior by their indigenous counterparts up their own chain of command. Superiors then took each issue up with South Vietnamese authorities. Left unopposed within the highest levels of U.S. government, these brilliantly inspired Combined Action Platoons (CAPs) would have interrupted Mao's "bottom-up" takeover methodology enough to win the war. But Gen. Westmoreland's traditional "search and destroy" sweeps sadly gained more favor with President Johnson, and the CAP Program was never fully expanded. The rest is history. Out of over 100 CAP units, one or two had their compounds temporarily overrun and another had its squad leader assassinated. That's not bad for low-ranking Marines with no formal training in Unconventional Warfare (UW). Think how well they might have done with advanced instruction on how initially to surprise attackers, breakout of an encirclement, and then escape and evade (E&E) any pursuers.[3]

To reverse the Chinese takeover of Africa, the Pentagon must forget about its firepower edge and revisit this less destructive way of countering an enemy incursion. With enough Marine squads augmenting indigenous police outposts in the same general area, most drug or arms smuggling across that area would cease. The squads' relative proximity to one another would provide enough mutual protection to forego a supporting-arms umbrella. If one unit got into trouble, it could just E&E over to the next. All would live off the local economy without any regular replenishment. Thus, there would be no need for logistics bases, supply networks, air bases, or artillery parks—no U.S. military footprint of any kind within the host country. The Marines would be little more than "foreign-aid" workers in the law enforcement sector.

Though Gen. Westmoreland would later admit in his memoirs that the CAP Program had been one of the more "ingenious innovations developed in South Vietnam,"[4] *Publishers Weekly* more clearly assesses its wasted potential.

> Between 1965 and 1971, the [U.S.] Marines in Vietnam allocated 4% of their resources to an experimental effort that turned into one of the rare American successes of the war. The . . . (CAP) program was based on the belief that winning the support of the Vietnamese people was of primary importance. The CAP concept . . . was a simple one: a squad of Marines . . . joined forces with the local militia to protect villagers from the Viet Cong—denying the latter recruits, food, and intelligence.[5]
>
> — *Publishers Weekly Review*

Lower-intensity modern wars are more successfully prosecuted by treating every insurgent like a criminal suspect. Just as American policemen are not allowed to inflict much collateral damage, neither should deployed U.S. troops. In the proposed case, the lone Leatherneck squads would have ways other than bombardment to save themselves from capture or annihilation.

U.S. Efforts So Far in Africa

After Washington's ill-fated deployment to Somalia (under U.N. auspices) in the early 1990's, it has mostly depended on the AU to contest *al-Qaeda's* presence in that country. As evidenced by Maps 1.5 and 13.6, much more of Somalia is now supposedly under government control. Still, large swaths of coastline aren't—to include an area just north of Mareeg that used to be connected to Ethiopia's lawless Ogaden region through an "unaligned" corridor. One wonders how much of this likely portal to a transcontinental drug conduit is actually occupied by either the Somali government or AU. Official payoffs are commonplace in Africa, and drug running produces big money. To be absolutely sure that large quantities of Afghan opiates are not flowing through this *al-Shabaab* heartland *en route* to the U.S., DEA personnel would have to be physically stationed inside the Cadaado and Beledweyne corridors (look again at Map 1.5). Such an assignment would be far too risky without American troops nearby. More interdiction at the conduit's relatively narrow East African portal would permit less monitoring of its more widespread West African network. Its ultimate prize would be fewer Afghan opiates reaching the U.S. homeland.

If allowed some counter-narcotics involvement, the Pentagon could also monitor—with drones—the heavily drug-traveled areas between U.S. squads. This is wide-open country, and drones could be of more use destroying narcotics shipments than the leaders of "bottom-up" *jihadist* organizations that don't really need leaders. Drug runners are no harder to identify from 30,000 feet than militant factions. Both would be heavily armed. With very little military footprint, drones would also provide some way of covering a severely endangered squad until its relief force could arrive by long-range helicopter. Without some semblance of a conventional retrieval plan, it's unlikely that America's military leaders will risk the political baggage of so novel an approach to outposting a foreign nation.

As for Africa's Other Unstable Areas

Within most parts of Africa, drones would not be welcome nor very productive. There, additional violence is not considered the best path toward peace. That's been the Chinese approach, albeit through more ordnance to opposing forces. America's contribution must be less combative in nature.

There are those in Washington who now think drones have changed warfare forever. Unmanned aircraft can closely watch individual perpetrators in open terrain, but they are of limited use in all-out conventional or unconventional warfare. How much help would they have been at Iwo Jima, where the average U.S. grunt never saw who he was fighting? [6] Would drones have changed the outcome in Vietnam, where at any given moment there were hundreds of separate firefights in progress? Even when they become capable of watching several separate events in the same general vicinity, there won't be enough of them to make any real difference in a widespread conflict. There was many a time on Vietnam's coast plain where American company commanders were refused aerial support of any kind after a previously planned assault became severely contested.[7] The problem was simple. All the hundreds, if not thousands, of Allied gunships in country at the time were otherwise occupied.

Though aerial drones can decisively eliminate a fair number of individual enemy personnel, his comrades will still control the ground and thus end up winning the war. That's why most African nations would never permit U.S. drones over their territory. It is not because of possible collateral damage from the drones, but rather their minimal effect over any chronic problem. How have most *al-Qaeda* affiliates fared over the years, after having their leaders repeatedly targeted by American drones?

For most of the Dark Continent, a more host-country-friendly approach will be needed. Standoff surveillance and bombardment have far too many limitations. Below is an example of why tiny groups of GIs must be allowed to get much closer to the action.

Joseph Kony Progress

At the end of 2014, the Pentagon was no closer to apprehending (or killing) Joseph Kony, leader of the Lord's Resistance Army (LRA), than it was in November of 2011.[8] There are two reasons for this lack of success. First was its almost total reliance on electronic (instead of human) intelligence to locate him. Then, it made the mistake of outsourcing the job of following up along the ground on any promising leads.

> U.S. military commanders said Sunday that they have been unable to pick up his [J. Kony's] trail but believe he is

Figure 24.1: It Must Be U.S. Mantrackers Chasing Key Offenders
(Source: FM 90-5 [1982], p. 5-4)

> . . . hiding in . . . dense jungle, relying on Stone Age tactics to dodge his pursuers' high-tech surveillance tools.[9]
> — *Washington Post,* 29 April 2012

Kony is far too crafty to leave an electronic signature. Even to find him, an old fashioned police manhunt would be necessary. It must start with a widespread network of "paid snitches." Then, local authorities can never maintain enough operational secrecy to bring him to justice. U.S. forces must conduct the human intelligence gathering, mantracking, and eventual assault themselves. (See Figure 24.1.) That's the lesson of Tora Bora.

> LRA fighters have slipped deeper into the bush, splintering into smaller bands to avoid detection and literally covering their tracks. . . .
> . . . [H]is 200 or so fighters rely on foot messengers and preordained rendezvous points to communicate.

> Kony's methods have proven effective against the U.S. military's satellites . . . and other forms of [electronic] surveillance. Commanders warn that it could take years to find him.[10]
>
> — *Washington Post,* 29 April 2012

The Difference with This New Program

America will not be able save the Dark Continent from the Chinese and Islamists without widely dispersing some of its own armed forces along the ground. If separate elements cannot be entrusted to the U.N., then they must be brought to bear some other way. Police outposts often require paramilitary capabilities just to survive. Why couldn't one specially prepared U.S. infantry squad be assigned to augment, advise, and train the members of each indigenous police detachment in certain regions. That would put them squarely in the path of any drugs or arms being smuggled through the area. Without drug revenues and arms resupply, most Africa rebellions would simply dry up. U.S. businesses would return to the area. And, the precipitous slide into Islamism or Communism would be abated.

Simply training Dark Continent security forces at rear-area base camps will not get the job done. Americans will have to be physically present in the midst of the heaviest action to make any real difference. In Kony's case, they never even left their compounds.

> Since October, U.S. troops have fanned out to five outposts in four countries, advising thousands of troops from Uganda, the Central African Republic, South Sudan, and Congo. . . .
>
> The Americans said they rarely leave the vicinity of their camp. . . .
>
> The U.S. forces carry arms but are not permitted to engage in combat, except in self-defense.[11]
>
> — *Washington Post,* 29 April 2012

Young Americans can do almost anything they are permitted to do. With limited additional training, not many would be lost from such a mission to Africa. The political backlash from losing a few troops now will be nothing like that from not having enough strategic metals to win WWIII.

Where Should the Marine Squads Be Stationed?

Many U.N. commands within Africa have come under the increasing influence of their Chinese components. The PRC has so far contributed only support personnel to any U.N. contingent in the DRC. But, that contingent's mission has already changed from one of warring-faction separation to offensive operations. It has recently been fighting alongside the North-Korean-trained DRC army,[12] and against M23. Initially to preserve the DRC regime, Zimbabwe, Angola, Namibia, Chad, and Sudan deployed military units to the DRC from 1998 to 2002.[13] Now, three other Chinese allies—South Africa, Tanzania, and Malawi—are providing all the combat troops for the new U.N. Intervention Force in the war-torn eastern part of that nation.[14] And, in South Sudan, the PRC just added its own infantry battalion to the U.N. force.[15] Thus, one can say that the PRC has started to take a more direct approach to military intervention in the region. There are other U.N. missions with Chinese components at the Western Sahara, Côte d'Ivoire, Liberia, Sudan, Mali, and now possibly the CAR.[16] U.S. military teams should not try to work in the same areas.

In fact, any country with close PRC ties would not be initially suitable for this new U.S. "Local Security Program." Most of southern Africa would be excluded, as would Guinea-Bissau, Tanzania, both Sudans, and Chad. Tanzania and South Africa now provide large numbers of troops to U.N. peacekeeping efforts,[17] and Chad has joined Sudan as a veritable Chinese proxy.[18] Though Nigeria has in the past accepted military advisers and ordnance from the PRC, it might still be interested in a little U.S. help against *Boko Haram*.[19]

That leaves interdiction of arms and drugs smuggling through the Sahel region as the most likely mission for these specially prepared Leatherneck squads. At the west end of the conduit, appropriate places for their initial deployment might be at police outposts along Trans-African Highway 5 in Niger, Nigeria, and Cameroon. On the eastern end, they could be placed along the main roads to the Indian Ocean through Ethiopia's Ogaden region and Somalia's government or AU-controlled areas. Later detachments could be sent to Guinea and Senegal, plus the northern extremities of Ghana, Togo, and Benin. Places where French forces already have such a mission could be avoided—Mali, Chad, Burkina Faso, Mauritania, and all countries north of Senegal.[20]

The AU has been of more overall help to America on the Dark Continent than the U.N. Thus, wherever AU troops are currently from or deployed (without any U.N. partners) might make a suitable location for the tiny U.S. contingents. Within Somalia, the bulk of AU troops come from Uganda, Burundi, Djibouti, Kenya, Ethiopia, and Sierra Leone.[21] At the top of the list for the new U.S. program would therefore be Somalia, Ethiopia, and Kenya. All three lie along the initial stages of the Afghan opiate conduit.

It's Time for America to Save the World

By limiting the arms and drug smuggling across Africa's Sahel region, U.S. troops would be concurrently countering both Communist and Islamist expansion—while only visibly confronting the latter. China has been profiting from the destabilization these narcotics shipments have brought to *en route* petroleum nations and final drug market, whereas the *jihadist* transporters have mostly made money.

More than just Africa stands to be rescued by such an initiative. Unless the current flood of Afghan heroin into the U.S. is somehow slowed, the next Chinese target to be fully subverted may be America herself.

> Pope Benedict was Pope during . . . the six apparitions of Our Lady [at Fatima] in 1917. He tried earnestly to negotiate a peace to end WWI. . . . As a final attempt to win peace, he asked that a novena to the Blessed Mother be offered in May 1917 to ask her intercession [with Jesus] for the peace of the world. On the eighth day of the novena, which was May 13, 1917, Our Lady made her first appearance to the three shepherd children [at Fatima]. . . .
>
> . . . Our Blessed Lady spoke to the children about another possible world war and the rising and spread of Communism throughout the world, causing great evil.[22]
>
> — World Apostolate of Fatima

Afterword: Wake-Up Call for Americans

Too Many Similarities for Comfort

This book provides evidence of many of the same kinds of "non-martial" intrusions to the Dark Continent that America has been experiencing over the last few years. While Washington's attention has been riveted on *al-Shabaab, Boko Haram,* and other Islamist factions at the north end of Africa, the still-Communistic Chinese have been consolidating their death grip over its southern two-thirds. To do so, they have applied distorted versions of democracy and capitalism, fomented war while seeming to pursue peace, and gained economic (and ultimately political) sway through massive immigration.

While the U.S. news media has largely failed to mention "Communism" for almost 25 years, this atheistic antithesis to free elections and free enterprise remains as unconcerned with human rights as it was in 1950. Communism did not go away with the Soviet Union as many young Americans have now come to believe. It is still alive and well in East Asia, just less blatantly aggressive. Despite repeated evidence of the PRC's sinister intentions against America (everything from ransoming a captured spy plane to continuous cyber attacks against its agencies and businesses),[1] Washington's leaders have remained fully conciliatory. By accepting large amounts of fiscal assistance from China, they have further invited political blackmail.

The PRC has been no more of the friend to its own citizens than those of the foreign nations it has pretended to help. China's inhabitants have suffered terribly under the ruling hand of the CPC (up to 75 million dead overall [2]). So too have the residents of the PRC's first African satellite—Zimbabwe. Now the populations of Angola, Tanzania, Zambia, Mozambique, and even South Africa are coming under similar duress. The underlying reasons should have all Americans worried. For it is through a mixture of overt and covert activities that the PRC has also been striving to gain strategic political influence within the "Yankee" homeland. It does so not only to alter America's foreign policy, but also its worldwide defense posture. In effect, only America now stands in the way of China's global "hegemony."

Washington's Most Glaring Example of Former Manipulation

The Asian gentleman who had coffee with the Clintons in the White House in 1996 was none other than the head of the PRC's largest state-owned investment group. According to the *New York Times,* he was also the chairman of Poly Technologies—a company well known to U.S. intelligence officials as being owned and run by the PLA.[3] What would shortly occur after this "innocent" meeting has placed its details under increasing scrutiny.

> Hutchison [another Chinese firm] has worked closely with . . . (COSCO) . . . the PLA-controlled [shipping] company that almost succeeded in gaining control of the . . . naval station at Long Beach [in California]. . . .
>
> Li Kashing [head of Hutchison] has served on the board of directors of China International Trust and Investment Corp., a PLA-affiliated giant run by Wang Jun. . . . [In February 1996] Wang Jun enjoyed coffee at the White House in exchange for a modest donation to the Clinton-Gore 1996 slush fund.[4]
>
> — *Washington Times,* 1 March 1999

Within 13 months of this "chance" White House encounter, Hutchison Whampoa (by then widely recognized as a "Chinese military company"[5]) had purchased the right to take over all of U.S. Naval Station Rodman alongside the Panama Canal. Before that same deal was complete in 1999, Hutchison would also own part of nearby U.S. Air Station Albrook and the U.S.-built port facilities at both ends of that strategically vital waterway.[6]

Other Evidence of Chinese Tampering with U.S. Security

America doesn't have to be formally invaded by a Communist

army to be taken over by its parent nation. In 2008, the National Intelligence Estimate—a collective opinion of all 16 U.S. spy agencies—forecast that by 2025 " 'state capitalism' such as that practiced in . . . China could be ascendant [in America]."[7] Yet, the rest of the U.S. government seems unperturbed by the prospect. It should be, for whichever way America's economy goes, so will go its politics.

Besides having a loan from the PRC so large as to openly invite political coercion, Washington continues to allow campaign contributions from undisclosed sources. Many of the enormous department store chains that have mostly replaced America's local commercial enterprises now carry mostly Chinese goods. Even America's internal security apparatus has been repeatedly compromised. This unwanted intrusion goes far beyond "hacking" into their electronic databases. Haven't four chapters of this book just demonstrated PRC collusion in America's ongoing drug deluge? Too many drugs on U.S. streets equate to less personal safety on the way to the grocery store and school.

Sadly, the evidence of America being intentionally destabilized by its biggest foreign competitor doesn't stop there. Almost every "dual-faced" Chinese endeavor in Africa is now evident in U.S. neighborhoods. Many help to explain the differences of opinion between various societal factions. According to the prestigious Council on Foreign Relations, "the proliferation of light weapons is a destabilizing force throughout the world."[8] That is precisely what the PRC has done to the U.S.

> The enormous Poly Group [a PLA company later taken over by China's State Council] . . . was involved in a deal that put thousands of commercial assault rifles into circulation in the United States a few years ago.[9]
>
> — *Los Angeles Times,* August 1998

Yes, this is the same Poly Technologies that would visit the White House in the Spring of 1999. State-owned companies tend to work on State-dictated projects.

The Real Smoking Gun

Herein has been detailed a Hong Kong triad's oversight of a

smuggling conduit that has been secretly carrying Afghan opiates across the Dark Continent and then on—via Venezuela—to its biggest market in the U.S. Nothing in Hong Kong happens without the CPC's knowledge and permission. Beijing already has more cash than it knows what to do with. Thus, one can logically conclude that Mainland China has been intentionally facilitating this flow of narcotics to undermine its only remaining opposition to global domination. That various Islamist factions have been actually transporting/protecting those drug loads does nothing to alter this conclusion.

Afrique has also shown at least three of the formerly Marxist regimes within southern Africa to now be veritable Socialist dictatorships—Angola, Congo Republic (Brazzaville), and Zimbabwe. Of the two Copper Belt nations, only Zambia is "partially free" with a downward *Freedom House* trend due to its ruling party's ongoing suppression of the Chinese-backed political opposition. The DRC (with most of those Copper Belt minerals) is "not free," nor is the country just to the east of it—Rwanda. Only partially free are other nations through which the natural resources of Central Africa must pass on their way to market—Tanzania, Mozambique, Burundi, and Uganda. Thus, there seems to be a definite correlation between the PRC's commodity extraction plan and the humanitarian progress of local governments along the way.

Much of China's oil comes from the Republic of the Congo, both Sudans, and Chad. Thus, one can also assert that almost all oil-source and transit-route countries have also remained unstable (by either coincidence or design).

Deeply involved with any such "international intrigue" within Africa is undoubtedly the PLA. Its main mission after the Korean War was to rebuild the physical infrastructure of its own homeland. Then, it was allowed to amass as many as 20,000-30,000 civilian enterprises to help fund its many programs. While its smuggling record would eventually lead to several half-hearted attempts by Beijing to break this corporate connection, the PLA probably still dabbles in overseas construction, natural-resource extraction, and the trading of other highly lucrative commodities. Nor is most other PRC business activity true capitalism. The vast majority of large Chinese companies are state-owned. All others have CPC members within their top management staffs. Any state-owned or otherwise CPC-influenced company would gladly assist its armed forces with their global defense responsibilities.

Any U.S. leader who is still unable to see the parallels between Africa's gradual subjugation and America's worsening internal "quagmire" may know too little about world history to be holding a national-security position.

The PLA's Recent Change in Strategy

By attempting to fight in the "allegedly modern" Western style, the PLA got badly embarrassed during its fully supported punitive strike against North Vietnam in 1979. However, it more easily learns from its mistakes than the Pentagon does. Thus, the PLA's current worldwide strategy may be more about construction and immigration than armed revolt, with the final objective remaining the same—political domination. For any Western administration that still considers bombing and sabotage the only acts of war, such a PLA scheme might pose considerable problems.

When the Oriental tactic of "death by a thousand razor cuts" is applied through non-martial means, its separate blows and their collective impact can be almost imperceptible to the inhabitant of a targeted-nation. This holds particularly true where the attacker is not interested in physically occupying that nation, just controlling its politics.

Why Washington Can't See How Much Trouble Africa Is Really In

4GW has been defined as a conflict waged within martial, economic, political, and religious/spiritual arenas simultaneously. The Pentagon has never been very good at 4GW because of the strict separation of responsibilities between Washington's various agencies. Meanwhile, the Asian Communists—with their Sun-Tzu-like heritage of "winning battles without actually fighting"—have become very good at 4GW. Thus, though somewhat counter-intuitive to most Western observers, future cooperation between the civilian corporations and armed forces of the PRC on the Dark Continent should be expected. And the number of Chinese immigrants *en route* to that strategically vital location is nothing short of shocking.

> The [PLA] navy . . . [remains the] guardian of China's ever-expanding economic interests. These range from . . . (seeing

> most of the South China Sea as an exclusive economic zone) to protecting . . . Chinese shipping, preserving the country's access to . . . raw materials supplies, and safeguarding the soaring numbers of Chinese citizens who work abroad ([only] about 5m today, but expected to rise to 100m by 2020).[10]
>
> — *The Economist,* 7 April 2012

Those same Western observers have taken solace in the fact that China spent only a bit over 2% of its Gross Domestic Product (GDP) on national defence in 2012, whereas America dedicated a full 4.7% of its GDP.[11] However, there's a good chance that the PLA has retained a few covert business extensions to help make up the difference. That would make perfect sense if those same extensions were now the leading edge of its worldwide (mostly economic but eventually political) active-defense plan. It has often been said that the best defense is an offense. Thus, the term "active defense" implies some sort of offense. By appearing to match the Pentagon technologically without any real need to ever use such fancy gear in an all-out war, the PLA would have the perfect diversion for a non-martial attack on the world (to include the U.S. mainland).

America's Achilles Heel

On 24 November 2014, CBS's prestigious "60 Minutes" disclosed that America's road and rail network was old and falling apart, particularly its bridges.[12] The PRC's growing capabilities and lower prices on such construction may soon add to America's woes. Already, the CRBC has helped to repair the Oakland Bay Bridge (probably with its metal surface matting).[13] After many of Africa's most astute leaders, like Sata of Zambia, were led to believe that a Chinese built transportation network was to their advantage, no Chinese company should ever be allowed to bid on a U.S. road or bridge project.

In fact, the Dark Continent's desperate struggle for fiscal independence provides several examples of what should not be happening in America. After many of Africa's local manufacturers have been driven out of business by cheap Chinese goods, no large U.S. department store chain should be carrying more than 20% of its overall sales inventory in products from the PRC. Nor should a Chinese company have been allowed to purchase America's biggest pork producer, after unhealthy growth hormones were obviously present in the Chinese-produced chickens of Zambia. The PRC firm that bought the U.S. company has a poor food safety record.[14] With America's cancer rate on the rise, the last thing U.S. citizens need is too many growth hormones in a primary source of protein.

The PRC Intrusion with Potentially Immediate Consequences

Almost unbelievably, there has been a CEIEC office allowed in Pomona, California.[15] Well known for advanced electronics of a military nature, CEIEC has shown up in more than one contested region over the years. Besides Taliban-controlled Afghanistan and Sadam Hussein's Iraq, it has been in at least four African nations.[16] (Look back at Table 21.1.) That means it might, at some point, be in a position to influence some fairly significant strategic matters in America. The string of suspicious electrical blackouts that plagued the Eastern U.S. around 2003 has been traced back to the CEIEC's suspected mentor—the PLA.

> One prominent expert told National Journal he believes that China's People's Liberation Army played a role in the power outages. Tim Bennett, the former president of the Cyber Security Industry Alliance, a leading trade group, said that U.S. intelligence officials have told him that the PLA in 2003 gained access to a network that controlled electric power systems serving the northeastern United States. The intelligence officials said that forensic analysis had confirmed the source, Bennett said. "They said that, with confidence, it had been traced back to the PLA." These officials believe that the intrusion may have precipitated the largest blackout in North American history, which occurred in August of that year. A 9,300-square-mile area, touching Michigan, Ohio, New York, and parts of Canada, lost power; an estimated 50 million people were affected.[17]
>
> — *National Journal Magazine,* 31 May 2008

Dealing with PRC Subterfuge in America

No internal problem should be solved by Washington, without

Figure A.1: Tiny Law Enforcement Augment
(Source: "On the Town," by SGT.[Ret.] J.T.Manuszak ©, U.S. Army Ctr. of Mil. Hist., from url: http://www.history.army.mil/art/Somalia/Manuszak_Somalia_files/image003jpg)

it first considering the extent to which that same difficulty has affected other nations. If the Communist expansionists' ultimate objective is political subversion, then why must all participants in their "immigrant invasion" be of Chinese origin. Wouldn't arrivals of any nationality be just as likely to back the political party promising expedited citizenship?

Despite these and other challenges, preserving what Pope John Paul II once called the "world's best hope" must ultimately be left up to the U.S. government. But that government does not operate in some impenetrable vacuum. Its policies must always be shaped by a well-informed constituency. Should that constituency ever forget to provide enough governmental guidance, it may wake up some morning to all the personal rights of a citizen of Zimbabwe or the PRC. This research can only offer a solution for what ails Africa. While many of America's symptoms are similar, their appropriate treatments may be quite different (and well beyond the scope of this book).

The Answer for the Most Severe of the African Incursions

American corporations will not go where there is too much danger, even to save a friendly country from "non-martial" takeover. The Pentagon must find some way to create a token U.S. military presence in such places. Further to counter the full array of "instability-fomenting" PRC elements throughout a place as big as Africa, it will never have enough commandos. It must instead rely on its infantry establishment. Both segments of U.S. military society will need more advanced tactical training to permit safely operating beyond any firepower umbrella.

Besides more proficient "boots" to safely put "on the ground" in squad size to help block the drug conduits, the Pentagon will need others in the highly contested mineral- and petroleum-producing areas. In both locales, the squads could act as law-enforcement assistance teams (police outpost reinforcements). That, in turn, would ensure enough local security to lower the amount of street crime and election tampering. (See Figure A.1.) The Communists and Islamists have both been attempting to "sway" local politics through tiny resident cadres. Why shouldn't the West have a few of its own?

This is the easiest way to counter Communist and Islamist expansion, because both opponents prefer to work from the bottom up. That means most of their subversion will first occur at the local level. Doesn't the IRGC have its own business extensions and one squad per neighborhood in its new deployment around Bagdad? That's how it is able to achieve maximum penetration of a large population.[18]

As for All the Other Places on the Dark Continent

No U.S. military involvement should even be contemplated for the other countries of Africa. There, the most productive type of assistance lies in alerting their respective governments to the latest nuances in the Communists' and Islamists' *modus operandi* with regard to foreign expansion. Such a source of good advice will not probably be possible until all U.S. intelligence agencies and the U.S. State Department become more familiar with the Eastern way of war.

Figure A.2: Africans Must Learn to Fight without High-Tech Gear
(Source: "On Watch," by SGT. [Ret.] J.T.Manuszak ©, U.S. Army Ctr. of Mil. Hist., from url: http://www.history.army.mil/art/Somalia/Manuszak_Somalia_files/image001.jpg)

Why America's Current Plan for Africa Will Be Insufficient

For the U.S. military just to train and advise indigenous forces on a grander scale cannot possibly get the job done for two reasons: (1) those forces lack their own supporting arms; and (2) the Pentagon has too few (if any) light-infantry experts to show them how to fight any other way. (See Figure A.2.)

Afrique has only detailed the ongoing situation on the Dark Continent. It is within Posterity Press' other 14 titles that one can most easily find enough light-infantry methodology to correct that teaching (and modern-warfighting) shortfall. For the average American unit, this vital transformation can be accomplished at no additional cost in dollars or leader man-hours, but not by civilian contractors. Such contractors are usually expensive and know too little about small-unit maneuvers. All U.S. infantry and special-operations units must be allowed to conduct their own training—through a pre-tested model for ongoing "tactical experimentation." Only then will they continually acquire enough small-unit expertise and initiative to save the rest of the world. See the Appendix for the full description of such a model.

Appendix: The Military Interface

Situational Awareness Only Part of the Light-Infantry Solution

Within U.S. military reading circles of late, there has been great interest in the preempting of enemy attacks through a little man-tracking, face-reading, and hostile-pattern interpreting. Those things are certainly important to the individual fighter, as well as his small unit. But, for their practitioner to achieve a state of advanced warfighting skill, they cannot be combined with maneuvers that are still "pre-machinegun" in format. No amount of situational awareness will allow the average battlefield quarry to "brainstorm on the spot" the foolproof response to an impending attack. A seemingly logical procedure may still not work without tactical-evolution modifications during its design, and rehearsal prior to its use.

The Pentagon's Part in the Proposed Mission for Africa

To stop the Communists and Islamists from taking over the Dark Continent, America will have to augment hundreds of indigenous police outposts with lone U.S. infantry squads. To remain safe, those squads must know how to do two things without any help from U.S. firepower: (1) break out of an encirclement; and (2) E&E away. (See Figure AA.1.) For such capabilities, they will need nontraditional "bottom-up" (as opposed to regular "top-down") training. This training must be based on a couple of things that only Asians and Germans have so far come to respect: (1) the collective wisdom of infantry noncommissioned officers (NCOs) or riflemen; and (2) field experimentation with tactical technique through casualty and surprise assessment. That's because true "light-infantry" expertise cannot be achieved through standardized procedure. Lowest-echelon initiative and tactical-decision making are among its prerequisites. (See Figure AA.2.) Such things can only derive from more open-ended entry-level preparation.

No More Boards, Think-Tanks, or Warfighting Labs Really Necessary

By following a copyright-free method already "Fleet" tested and fully

Figure AA.1: Semi-Autonomous Squads

(Source: "Road March," by SGT. J.T.Manuszak ©, U.S.Army Ctr.of Mil.Hist., from this url: http://www.history.army.mil/art/Somalia/Manuszak_Somalia_files/image009.jpg)

refined by Posterity Enterprises, each U.S. rifle company could develop its own portfolio of squad, fire team, buddy team, and individual "combat plays." With three of each (that in the manuals, *Last Hundred Yards,* and just developed) for the most likely scenarios, tiny elements could more closely obey their circumstances and become hard to predict in their actions. As in football, each composite element would not need to exactly follow the group maneuver, just use it as a guideline. Then, their parent platoon, company, or battalion would have a much better chance at momentum. The latest version of this new training regimen has been published as an appendix to *Global Warrior*.

The resulting competition between units would create a learning dynamic that standardized training has never produced. In modern war, large formations are seldom attempted in difficult terrain. They are too slow, and vulnerable to mass casualties from precision enemy weaponry. That means each American rifle company needs no longer to be the mirror image of all the others.

With such a training regimen, U.S. troops would have fared far better in Vietnam, Iraq, and Afghanistan. The famous Raiders of WWII were trained in much the same spirit by Lt.Col. Carlson. In effect, Mao's "bottom-up" way of fighting is the most logical means of contending with Asian armies and militias. After being institutionalized by the PLA in 1947, this substitute style of warfare has been adopted by almost every underfunded rebel faction worldwide. (See Figure AA.3.) That's because it requires so little firepower. Thus, for every U.S. squad that learns to operate through this alternative combat mode, "fratricide-risking" supporting arms will seldom become necessary.

Figure AA.2: Every Trooper Must Have "Beat-Cop" Initiative
(Source: "American Soldier...,"by MSGT[Ret] P.G.Varisano ©,U.S.Army Ctr.of Mil.Hist.,from url: http://www.history.army.mil/art/Somalia/Varisano_Somalia_files/image013.jpg)

Poorly Advised Censorship

While the Iraqi and Afghan Wars were still going strong, American enlisted personnel purchased over 160,000 copies of the first 12 Posterity Press titles from their Stateside and overseas exchanges. They did so, not because they liked to read, but because those tactics/intelligence manual supplements were helping them not only to win, but also survive. Until the Pentagon once again allows these books (and their successors) to be sold at its exchanges, the U.S. public should not expect any reduction to the Communist and Islamist takeover of Africa. Totally precluding all U.S. "boots on the ground" is not the answer. As at Tora Bora, indigenous forces frequently suffer too many "leaks" to achieve any decisive victory on their own. Weren't American special operators finally needed to take down Osama bin Laden? There aren't enough U. S. commandos in existence to conduct the proposed strategy for the Dark Continent alone, much less anywhere else on the planet. That is more logically the job of units that regularly establish combat outposts—the American infantry. To accomplish such a mission, U.S. infantry squads would need only more instruction on law enforcement, breakout tactics, and E&E.

The Traditionalists Have Not Been Wrong, Just Non-Comprehensive

Why nonrate expertise is so vital to MW and 4GW has been hard for high-level U.S. leaders to see. America's traditional way of war need not be replaced, just supplemented a little. Here's how the top PLA leaders deal with the same potential inertia. For all units of every size, they require a capability of quickly alternating between Maneuver, Attrition, and Guerrilla Warfare. In this way, they continually validate all three, while still discouraging opposition to the one that just happens to be situationally appropriate. Without learning to fight like a guerrilla, young GIs may never acquire as much assault technique, individual initiative, and decision-making experience as these Eastern counterparts. Nor will their unit commanders ever fully practice MW or 4GW. That's what Lt.Col. Carlson discovered at the start of WWII with his Mao-oriented Marine Raider initiative. The specifics of how he better prepared them to fight the Japanese is in *Gung Ho!*

Just as MW and 4GW have been based upon common sense, so too must be learning how fully to practice them. Firepower and surprise are interchangeable on the field of honor. With more surprise-oriented squads, American unit commanders would enjoy more tactical options on both offense and defense. Esoteric mental gymnastics would no longer permeate Quantico and the Army's Training and Doctrine Command (TRADOC).

They have taken their inspiration from three fallacious assumptions: (1) that enough firepower can accomplish anything in war; (2) that the U.S. military bureaucracy has been continuously streamlining itself; and (3) that America's small-unit maneuvers have kept pace with those in Asia.

The Change Is Manageable

To handle the ongoing Communist and Islamist threat to the Dark Continent (and other parts of the world), the thought processes of all U.S. military leaders must only shift to the counter-intuitive "little-picture." There's a reason all who now emulate Asian Communists have become so proficient at MW and 4GW. They simply acknowledge the potential contribution of a more self-sufficient rifleman. He is their "secret weapon," while the Pentagon continues to focus on technology. Besides constant

Figure AA.3: Nontraditional Training Worked for Marine Raiders
(Source: Courtesy of Edward Molina © 2012)

practice at initiative and tactical-decision-making, that Oriental rifleman gets instruction on a wide variety of "sub-basics"—like, how to move quietly through dry leaves or soggy ground. Against someone who has mostly learned how to operate his weapon and follow orders, he will have the decided edge in any "one-on-one" encounter. As soon as every entry-level U.S. infantryman or commando is prepared to the same extent, all that Asian "battlefield edge" will go away. (See Figure AA.4.)

Such discussions are not meant to insult anyone, only keep America's top leaders adequately informed. Because of the way U.S. governmental agencies operate, many of their upper-echelon personnel are never fully

Figure AA.4: There Is Nothing a Young GI Can't Learn to Do!
(Source: "Special Ops," by Ken Chandler, F.E.Warren Air Force Base Media Gallery ©, from url: http://www.warren.af.mil/shared/media/ggallery/hires/AFG-110411-007.jpg)

apprised of shortfalls at the bottom. Add to this the aversion Western bureaucracies have with airing their own dirty laundry, and one should expect a few unresolved deficiencies. That doesn't mean their leaders are content with them. For any chronic need, history provides the best solution. Does the side that occupies the ground win most wars, or is it the one that tries to control what happens on the ground from the air? The short war with Serbia was a rare exception. That with Libya didn't turn out as well. All other foreign involvements have involved U.S. ground troops. Why they ran into more resistance than expected is simple. Their underfunded foes had come to rely on more "light-infantry" expertise.

This is one U.S. shortfall that can not be rectified with money. Once the Pentagon has acknowledged that "light-infantry" expertise is the key to winning any modern war, then all American units must be allowed to identify and correct their own deficiencies through "on-the-job training." Only general guidance on how that might be accomplished will be of help. Any attempt to standardize the result will be self-defeating. This is the lesson that America's "military-industrial complex" has had so much difficulty accepting. Until it does so, Americans should not plan to win any more wars—big or small.

NOTES

SOURCE NOTES:

Pictures on pages xxiv, 73, 291, 336, 338, 340, and 341 are from U.S. ARMY CENTER OF MILITARY HISTORY ARTWORK (http://www.history.army.mil/html/artphoto/artwork.html). They are part of the Somalia Artwork Gallery with the following image designators: "image015.jpg," "image007.jpg," "Mogadishu.jpg," "image003.jpg," "image001.jpg," "image009.jpg," and "image013.jpg," respectively. See each caption for title, artist, and exact url. Only for an educational nonprofit is reprinting of these pictures fair usage. Others must be more mindful of possible copyright.

Picture on page 5 reproduced after written assurance from Cassell PLC, London, that the copyright holder for *UNIFORMS OF THE INDO-CHINA AND VIETNAM WARS,* text by Leroy Thompson, color plates by Malcolm McGregor and Michael Chappell, could no longer be contacted. The illustrations are from pages 147 of the Cassell publication.

Maps on pages 10, 18, 21, 23, 29, 37, 38, 39, 40, 41, 44, 61, 67, 70, 72, 74, 102, 118, 129, 130, 134, 138, 142, 143, 144, 145, 149, 151, 162, 171, 178, 180, 182, 184, 186, 189, 190, 195, 208, 233, 235, 239, 240, 250, 252, 257, 258, 262, 285, 304, and 307 reprinted after written assurance from GENERAL LIBRARIES OF THE UNIVERSITY OF TEXAS AT AUSTIN that they are all in the public domain.

Picture on page 12 reprinted from WARBOATS.COM, as shown in figure 190. Probably of Soviet military-manual origin, this technical image is from the following url: http://www.warboats.org/soviet.htm. There was no copyright notice posted at the website.

Pictures on pages 24, 77, 132, 176, 183, 187, and 316 reprinted under provisions of GNU Free Documentation License, from *WIKIPEDIA ENCYCLOPEDIA,* s.v. "Somalia," "Zhou Enlai," "Sahel," "Trans-African Highway Network," "Ndjamena-Djibouti Highway," and "Rail Transport in the DRC." As an educational nonprofit, Posterity Press considers reproduction of these images fair usage, but others must be more mindful of possible copyrights. Copyright © n.d. All rights reserved.

Images on pages 30, 95, 105, 120, 147, and 187 reprinted from WIKIMEDIA.ORG. All are in the public domain. They come from these urls: (1) http://upload.wikimedia.org/wikipedia/commons/a/ad/Sudan_Map_Oelgas.png; (2) http://commons.wikimedia.org/wiki/File:Flag_of_the_United_Nations.svg; (3) http://commons.wikimedia.org/wiki/File:Flag_of_the_People%27s_Republic_of_China.svg; (4) http://upload.wikimedia.org/wikipedia/commons/4/44/Ali-Baba.jpg; (5) http://commons.wikimedia.org/wiki/File:AQMI_Flag.svg; and (6) http://upload.wikimedia.org/wikipedia/commons/archive/9/9f/20110324011204!Somalia_map_states_regions_districts.png.

Picture on pages 35, 126, 215, and 238 reproduced after written assurance from Cassell PLC (London, U.K.), that copyright holders for *WORLD ARMY UNIFORMS SINCE 1939,* text by Andrew Mollo and Digby Smith, color plates by Malcolm McGregor and Michael Chappell, can no longer be contacted. The illustrations are from Part II, Plates 63, 110, 81, 124, and 90, respectively, of an Orion Books reprint. Copyrights © 1975, 1980, 1981, 1983 by Blandford Books Ltd. All rights reserved.

Pictures on pages 39, 43, 68, and 255 reproduced after written assurance from Cassell PLC (London, U.K.), that the copyright holders for *UNIFORMS OF THE ELITE FORCES,* text by Leroy Thompson, color plates by Michael Chappell, can no longer be contacted. The illustrations are from Plate 23 (Number 69), Plate 23 (Number 68), Plate 32 (Number 94), Plate 32 (Number 95), and Plate 31 (Number 93) respectively, of an Orion Books reprint. Copyright © 1982 by Blandford Press Ltd. All rights reserved.

Images on pages 50, 57, 58, 59, 89, 105, 121, 209, 243, 299, 305 reprinted from *WIKIPEDIA ENCYCLOPEDIA,* s.v. "Mozambique," "Red Guards," "Mining," "China," "Saladin," "West Africa Coast Initiative," "Bornu Empire," "Zambia," "DRC." All are in public domain with these image designators: "640px-Emblem_of_Mozambique.png," "Red_Guards.jpg," "Struggle_session_poster_1.jpg," "Lead_mining_Barber1865p321cropped.jpg," "Isle of Graia3.jpg," "800px-Flag_of_the_Peoples_Republic_of_China.png," "Drugtrade.png," "Group_of_Kanem-Bu_warriors.jpg," "Flag_of_the_Democratic_Republic_of_the_Congo.svg.png.

Map on page 131 reprinted with permission of FORDHAM UNIVERSITY (fordam.edu/halsall). Entitled "The Muslim Empire: 750 CE," it comes from *Medieval Sourcebook* at the following url: http://www.fordham.edu/halsall/sbookmap.html, and originally from H.G. Wells, *A Short History of the World* (London: 1922). Copyright © indeterminate. All rights reserved.

Picture on page 193 reproduced with permission of the SWEDISH ARMED FORCES and written assurance from Sorman Information/Media (Vaxjo, Sweden) that the illustrator can no longer be contacted. Image is from *Soldf: Soldaten I Falt,* by Forsvarsmakten, with illustrations by Wolfgang Bartsch. It appears on page 31 of the Swedish publication. Copyright © 2001 by Wolfgang Bartsch. All rights reserved.

Image on page 209 is U.S. GOVERNMENT drawn from http://search.usa.gov. As such, it is in the public domain. See each caption for exact url.

Pictures on pages 231 and 280 reprinted with permission of MICHAEL LEAHY. They're from covers of *Terrorist Trail* and *Homeland Siege* from Posterity Press. Copyright © by Michael Leahy. All rights reserved.

Map on page 242 reprinted under provisions of Creative Commons Attribution 3.0 Unported License, from *WIKIPEDIA ENCYCLOPEDIA,* s.v. "Bornu Empire." It is from Gabagool in April 2009. As an educational nonprofit, Posterity Press considers reproduction of this images to be fair usage, but others must be more mindful of a possible copyright. Copyright © n.d. All rights reserved.

Map on page 253 reprinted after being unable to contact LAMU HOLIDAY HOMES (Kenya) for the nonprofit fair usage of image designator "lamu-archipelago-bild1.jpg." There was no copyright notice at the website.

Map on page 254 reprinted after asking permission of LAMU PORT PROPERTIES (Kenya) for the nonprofit fair usage of the map "Lamu Port Urban Area Vision 2030" with image designator "visibility.jpg." Copyright © 2012. All rights reserved.

Map on page 259 reprinted after being unable to contact KENYA MINISTRY OF TRANSPORT for nonprofit use of the image designator "_58831456_kenya_infrastructure_464.gif." Though retrieved from a BBC news story, this government-produced map is likely in the public domain.

Picture on page 283 reprinted after being originally retrieved in 2009 as a public-domain image with designator “1950-sl_ec06.jpg” from this url: http://timpanogos.wordpress.com/2007/09/13. Repro@iisgl.nl writes that THE PEOPLE'S REPUBLIC OF CHINA may have trouble claiming copyrights retroactively to any image created prior to the mid-1980's. As an educational nonprofit, Posterity Press considers its reproduction to be fair usage, but others must more mindful of a possible copyright. Copyright © n.d. All rights reserved.

Picture on page 286 reprinted after written assurance from GLOBAL SECURITY that it does not own or know of a copyright. This image appears at globalsecurity.org under “PLA History,” and has file designator “C14053PictPowPpleArmy53.jpg.” The same picture appears at Wikipedia.org, s.v. “People's Liberation Army,” with file designator “peoples_army.jpg” and would be covered by provisions of GNU Free Documentation License. It's not for sale as part of the 1ISH Collection at ChinesePosters.net. Repro@iisgl.nl writes that China may have trouble claiming copyrights retroactively to any image created prior to the mid-1980's. As an educational nonprofit, Posterity Press considers its reproduction to be fair usage, but others must more mindful of a possible copyright. Copyright © n.d. All rights reserved.

Pictures on page 297, 319, and 344 are from F.E. WARREN AIR FORCE BASE MEDIA GALLERY (http://www.warren.af.mil/art). They have image designators “AFG-060725-004.jpg ,” “AFG-100830-003.jpg” and “AFG-110411-007.jpg.” See caption for title, artist, and exact url. For only the first and second pictures can reprinting be considered fair usage by an educational nonprofit. The third picture is more closely protected. As such, its use required personal permission from the artist, Kenneth Chandler. Copyright © by Kenneth Chandler, n.d. All rights reserved.

Map on page 315 reproduced after being unable to reach TRANSCONTINENT EXPLORATION & MINING COMPANY LTD. As an educational nonprofit, Posterity Press considers its undersized reproduction to be fair usage, but others must more mindful of its prominently displayed copyright. Copyright © 2006 -2013. All rights reserved.

Pictures on pages 343 reprinted with permission of EDWARD MOLINA. They're from the initial draft of various cover images for *Gung Ho* from Posterity Press. Copyright © by Edward Molina, n.d. All rights reserved.

ENDNOTES

Preface:

1. Memorandum for the record from H.J. Poole.
2. Ibid.
3. *Intelligence, MCDP 2* (Washington, D.C.: U.S. Marine Corps, 1997).
4. "Pakistan Is Handing Over De-Facto Control of the Strategic Gilgit-Baltistan Region," *Rediff News* (India), 28 August 2010.

Acknowledgments:

1. *The Latin Mass,* vol. 23, no. 3., Fall 2014, p. 2.

Chapter 1: *Most African Turmoil Still over Commerce*

1. *Tequila Junction: 4th Generation Counterinsurgency,* by H. John Poole (Emerald Isle, NC: Posterity Press, 2007), chapt. 2; *Tactics of the Crescent Moon: Militant Muslim Combat Methods* by H. John Poole (Posterity Press, 2004), chapt. 2; *Terrorist Trail: Backtracking the Foreign Fighter,* by H. John Poole (Posterity Press, 2006), chapt. 2.
2. George Robert Elford, *Devil's Guard* (New York: Dell, 1985), pp. 312-329.
3. Ibid., p. 313.
4. *The Battle of Dien Bien Phu,* Visions of War Series, vol. 10, Videocassette #4010, 50 minutes (New Star Video, 1988).
5. Ibid.
6. Ibid.
7. "China-Africa Relations in the 21st Century," by Jennifer Parneti, *Joint Forces Quarterly,* March 2009.
8. "Tribal Militants Claimed Responsibility for Another Attack on an Energy Installation," *Christian Science Monitor,* World News in Brief, 8 June 2006, p. 7; *ABC's Nightly News,* 18 April 2006; MEND photograph, in "Curse of the Black Gold: Hope and Betrayal in the Niger Delta," *National Geographic,* February 2007, pp. 88-117.
9. "Islam in Africa Newsletter (vol. 1, no. 1)," by Moshe Terdman and Reuven Paz, *Israeli Project for the Research of Islamist Movements* (www.e-prism.org), May 2006.
10. *ABC's Nightly News,* 7 January 2007.
11. *CIA World Factbook,* s.v. "Angola," "Republic of Congo," "Chad," "Algeria," "Nigeria," "Sudan."

12. Peter Stiff, *The Silent War* (Alberton, South Africa: Galago Publishing, 1999), p. 151; Ian Greig, *The Communist Challenge to Africa* (Johannesburg: SA Freedom Foundation, 1977), p. 103, in *The Silent War,* by Stiff, p. 47.

13. Tanzania-Zambia Railway Authority's website, http://www.tazarasite.com; *Wikipedia Encyclopedia,* s.v. "Tanzam Railway," "TAZARA Railway," and "Uhuru or 'Freedom' Railway."

14. "P-6 Class Boat," *Command: Modern Air/Naval Operations* website (http://www.harpoondatabases.com); "PT Project 183 Bolshevik ('P-6') Class," *Command: Modern Air/Naval Operations* website (http://www.harpoondatabases.com), wargame.

15. Stiff, *The Silent War*, p. 144; Greig, *The Communist Challenge to Africa*, p. 36, in *The Silent War,* by Stiff, p. 149.

16. *CIA World Factbook,* s.v. "Mozambique."

17. *BBC Country Profiles,* s.v. "Angola."

18. Ibid., s.v. "Tanzania."

19. Ibid., s.v. "Zambia."

20. "Soviet Policies South and East of Suez," by T.B. Miller, Council on Foreign Relations, *Foreign Affairs* on line, October 1970.

21. Jamie Monson, *Africa's Freedom Railway: How a Chinese Development Project Changed Lives and Livelihoods in Tanzania* (Bloomington: Indiana Univ. Press, 2009), p. 58.

22. Ibid., p. 22.

23. Deborah Brautigam, *The Dragon's Gift: The Real Story of China in Africa* (London: Oxford Univ. Press, 2010), p. 163; *Wikipedia Encyclopedia,* s.v. "China Civil Engineering Construction Corporation."

24. "Angola Restore Copper Rail Line After Four Decade Halt," by Colin McClelland, *Bloomberg News* on line, 25 March 2013; *Wikipedia Encyclopedia,* s.v. "TAZARA Railway" and "Benguela Railway."

25. Richard Miniter (contributor), "The King and O: Al-Qaeda Shifts to Africa, But Is Obama Listening," Opinion Editorial, *Forbes Magazine* on line, 19 November 2013.

26. Ibid.

27. "Osama bin Laden Timeline," *CNN's News* on line, n.d.

28. Aaron Mannes, *Profiles in Terror: Guide to Middle East Terror Organizations* (Lanham, MD: Rowman & Littlefield, 2004), p. 21.

29. Rohan Gunaratna, *Inside al-Qaeda: Global Network of Terror* (Lahore: Vanguard, 2002), pp. 154-156.

30. Ibid., p. 159.

31. Ibid., p. 158; Interview, U.S. intelligence community, February 2000, in *Inside al-Qaeda,* by Gunaratna, p. 158.

32. Watts Roba Gibia Nyirigwa, "Why 2011 Referendum Is the Only Hope for South Sudanese: Part One," *Khartoum Monitor*, 31 May 2006, p. 5; *Wikipedia Encyclopedia,* s.v. "National Congress (Sudan)"; "Sudan Unity Requires Secular State," *Khartoum Monitor,* 1 June 2006, p. 4.

33. Stephen E. Hughes, *Warring on Terrorism: A Comprehensive Dispatch Briefing,* part I, internet piece (Soda Springs, ID, 2005), p. 6.

34. Ibid.

35. Ibid.

36. Gunaratna, *Inside al-Qaeda,* p. 153.

37. Ibid., p. 153.

38. Ibid., p. 151.

39. John Hunwick, "Africa and Islamic Revival: Historical and Contemporary Perspectives," *MSA News* on line, n.d., p. 1.

40. Gunaratna, *Inside al-Qaeda*, p. 158.

41. "Eliminating Terrorist Sanctuaries," *Project of Government Oversight* (http://pogo.org), Ctr. for Defense Info., 10 December 2001.

42. Gunaratna, *Inside al-Qaeda*, pp. 152, 153; Paul Clammer, *Sudan (*Bucks, U.K.: Bradt Travel Guides Ltd., 2005), p. 37.

43. Samuel P. Huntington, *The Clash of Civilizations and the Remaking of World Order* (London: Simon & Schuster, 1997), p. 177; Mannes, *Profiles in Terror,* p. 22; Hughes, *Warring on Terrorism,* pp. 10, 36; Gunaratna, *Inside al-Qaeda*, p. 139.

44. Ibid.

45. Yossef Bodansky (Director of Research of the Internat. Strategic Studies Assn. and Congressional Task Force on Terrorism and Unconventional Warfare), *Offensive in the Balkans,* chapt. 8 (Alexandria, VA: Internat. Media Corp., 1995), pp. 71-78, from "In Bosnia the West . . . Took the Side of . . . Fundamentalist Islam," *Serbian News Network* on line, n.d.; *Israeli Project for the Research of Islamist Movements* (www.e-prism.org), in "The State Sponsorship of the Islamic Terrorist Network," by Stephen E. Hughes, unpublished study (Salt Lake City, 2003).

46. Ibid.

47. Hughes, *Warring on Terrorism,* p. 36.

48. Mannes, *Profiles in Terror,* p. 22.

49. "Al-Qaeda's New Front," *PBS's Frontline,* NC Public TV, 25 January 2005.

50. *Tactics of the Crescent Moon: Militant Muslim Combat Methods,* by H. John Poole (Emerald Isle, NC: Posterity Press, 2004), p. 187.

51. Gunaratna, *Inside al-Qaeda*, pp. 158, 159.

52. Mannes, *Profiles in Terror,* p. 22; Huntington, *The Clash of Civilizations and the Remaking of World Order,* p. 176.

53. Gunaratna, *Inside al-Qaeda*, p. 31.

54. "Iran Shifting Its Attention . . . ," *New York Times,* 13 December 1991, p. A7.

55. *World Almanac of Islamism,* s.v. "Sudan"; *Wikipedia Encyclopedia,* s.v. "Foreign Relations of Sudan (as viewed in 2006)."

56. Kenneth Katzman, *Warriors of Islam: Iran's Revolutionary Guard* (Boulder, CO: Westview Press, 1993), p. 177; Huntington, *The Clash of Civilizations and the Remaking of World Order,* p. 177.

57. Ibid.; John L. Esposito, *Unholy War: Terror in the Name of Islam* (London: Oxford Univ. Press, 2002), p. 10.

58. Ibid., p. 7.

59. Azzam, as quoted in *Unholy War: Terror in the Name of Islam,* by John L. Esposito (London: Oxford Univ. Press, 2002), p. 7.

60. Mannes, *Profiles in Terror,* p. 21.

61. Interview, U.S. intelligence community, February 2000, in *Inside al-Qaeda,* by Gunaratna, p. 158.

62. Gunaratna, *Inside al-Qaeda,* p. 158.

63. Ibid., pp. 154, 158.

64. *World Almanac of Islamism,* s.v. "Sudan"; *Wikipedia Encyclopedia,* s.v. "Foreign Relations of Sudan (2006)."

65. Gunaratna, *Inside al-Qaeda,* p. 159.

66. "Islamists Training in Somalia," by Bill Gertz, Emergency Net News, *ERRI Daily Intelligence Report,* vol. 11, no. 363, 31 December 2005, through *Geostrategy-Direct.*

67. "Pakistani Islamists Sign Deal With China," by Farhan Bokhari, *CBS's News* on line, World Watch, 18 February 2009.

68. "Al-Qaeda on Pakistan: Dr. Ayman al-Zawahiri's Morning and the Lamp," Jamestown Foundation, *Terrorism Monitor,* vol. 8, issue 11, 19 March 2010.

69. "Fighting in Somalia's Puntland Kills at Least 27," *Reuters News* on line, 3 September 2011.

70. Gunaratna, *Inside al-Qaeda,* pp. 154-156.

71. Scott Baldauf and Ali Mohamed, "Cash Lures Somali 'Holy' Warriors," *Christian Science Monitor,* 19 April 2010, p. 19.

72. Jamal Osman, "Exclusive: Inside an al-Shabaab Training Camp," *Channel 4 News* on line (U.K.), 16 December 2013.

73. Ibid.

74. "Somalia: Al-Shabab Loses Their Strongest Military Base in the Central of Somalia to SNA and AU Troops," *Somali News* on line, 13 March 2014.

75. *CIA World Factbook,* s.v. "Chad."

76. "Law and Order in Chad," as retrieved in April 2015 from url: http://www.mapsofworld.com/chad/government-and-politics/law.html.

Chapter 2: *Religious Beliefs Only Partially at Issue*

1. *Encyclopedia Britannica (*2003), p. 306, as quoted in *Wikipedia Encyclopedia*, s.v. "Religion in Africa."
2. *Federation of American Scientists,* s.v. "Sudan People's Liberation Army (SPLA)."
3. "S. Sudan's Machar Unable to Control Rebels," from AFP, as reprinted by *Al Jazeera,* 1 June 2014.
4. "Sudan, Oil, and Human Rights," *Human Rights Watch,* 2003.
5. *BBC Country Profiles,* s.v. "South Sudan."

Chapter 3: *The Formerly Socialist Bloc of Nations*

1. "Dar-es-Salaam Once a Home for Revolutionaries," Times Media Group, *Sunday World* (Zambia), 29 April 2014.
2. Ibid.; Stiff, *The Silent War,* pp. 18, 244.
3. Stiff, *The Silent War,* pp. 46, 281.
4. Ibid., p. 243.
5. Ibid., p. 281.
6. Ibid., p. 30.
7. Bikash Sangraula, "Nepal Grapples with Next Steps," *Christian Science Monitor,* 2 May 2006, p. 6; Stiff, *The Silent War,* p. 315.
8. Stiff, *The Silent War,* pp. 97, 125, 457; *Wikipedia Encyclopedia,* s.v. "Angolan Civil War."
9. Stiff, *The Silent War,* pp. 17, 315.
10. Ibid., p. 314; "China's Military Presence in Africa," by Chuka Enuka, *Journal of Political Studies* (Univ. of Punjab), vol. 18, issue 1, p. 17.
11. "A Controversial Legacy," by T.P., *The Economist,* 11 December 2013.
12. Ibid., p. 18.
13. Ibid., p. 120.
14. Ibid., p. 125.
15. Ibid., pp. 124-129, 135.
16. Ibid., p. 137.
17. Ibid., pp. 144, 145.
18. Ibid., p. 149.
19. Ian Greig, *The Communist Challenge to Africa* (Johannesburg: South African Freedom Foundation, 1977), p. 36, in *The Silent War,* by Stiff, p. 149.
20. Stiff, *The Silent War,* p. 530.
21. Ibid.
22. Ibid., p. 532.

23. Fred Bridgland, *War for Africa* (Gibraltar: Ashanti, 1991), p. 17, and Helmoed-Romer Heitman, *War in Angola – The Final South African Phase* (Ashanti, 1990), pp. 15-16, in *The Silent War,* by Stiff, p. 533.

24. Stiff, *The Silent War,* p. 548.

25. *BBC Country Profiles,* s.v. "Angola (December 2005)."

26. Greig, *The Communist Challenge to Africa,* p. 103, in *The Silent War,* by Stiff, p. 47.

27. Stiff, *The Silent War,* p. 46.

28. Lt.Col. R.F. Reid-Daly, *Pamwe Chete: The Legend of the Selous Scouts* (Weltevreden Park, South Africa: Covos-Day, 1999), pp. 436-445.

29. Stiff, *The Silent War,* p. 268.

30. Ibid., p. 289; Reid-Daly, *Pamwe Chete,* pp. 67, 436-445.

31. Stiff, *The Silent War,* pp. 101, 126.

32. *CIA World Factbook,* s.v. "Democratic Republic of the Congo."

33. Ibid., s.v. "Zimbabwe."

34. Ibid., s.v. "Angola"; Bill Gertz, "Notes from the Pentagon," *Washington Times,* 5 March 2004.

35. Stiff, *The Silent War,* p. 289.

36. *CIA World Factbook,* s.v. "Mozambique," "Namibia," and "Republic of the Congo."

37. *BBC Country Profiles,* s.v. "Angola."

38. Stiff, *The Silent War,* p. 136.

39. *CIA World Factbook,* s.v. "Angola."

40. Stiff, *The Silent War,* p. 46.

41. *BBC Country Profiles,* s.v. "Tanzania."

42. M.Gen.Loots interview of 1987, in *The Silent War,* by Stiff, p. 47.

43. *BBC Country Profiles,* s.v. "Zambia."

44. Ian Greig, *The Communist Challenge to Africa* (Johannesburg: SA Freedom Foundation, 1977), p. 103, in *The Silent War,* by Stiff, p. 47.

45. *CIA World Factbook,* s.v. "Mozambique."

46. *BBC Country Profiles,* s.v. "Angola."

47. Ibid., s.v. "Tanzania."

48. Ibid., s.v. "Zambia."

49. *CIA World Factbook,* s.v. "Angola" and "Zimbabwe."

50. Ibid., s.v. "Botswana," "Tanzania," "Zambia," "South Africa," "Mozambique," and "Namibia."

51. *Freedom House*, s.v. "Freedom in the World 2014—Africa."

52. *CIA World Factbook,* s.v. "Tanzania."

53. *Freedom House*, s.v. "Freedom in the World 2014—Tanzania."

54. "Tanzania," Chinese Foreign Ministry (China.org.cn), 10 October 2006.

55. Stiff, *The Silent War,* pp. 155, 156.

56. David Hoile, *Mozambique – A Nation in Crisis* (London: Claridge Press, 1989), p. 36, in *The Silent War,* by Stiff, p. 156.

57. *CIA World Factbook,* s.v. "Mozambique."

58. "Mozambique," Chinese Foreign Ministry (China.org.cn), 10 October 2006.

59. Ibid., s.v. "Angola."

60. Ibid.

61. *Freedom House,* s.v. "Freedom in the World 2013—Angola"

62. "Zimbabwe: No Money to Print Currency," from *IRIN News* (U.N.), as reprinted in *Khartoum Monitor,* 31 May 2006, p. 10.

63. Daniel Pepper, "Zimbabwe's Army Takes over Black Farms," *Christian Science Monitor,* 5 June 2006, pp. 1, 10.

64. "China Winning Resources and Loyalties of Africa," *The Financial Times* (U.K.), 28 February 2006.

65. "Zimbabwe: Shadows and Lies," *PBS's Frontline / World,* NC Public TV, 27 June 2006.

66. Ryan Truscott, "Short Lives Lead to Short-Term Goals in Zimbabwe," *Christian Science Monitor,* 9 June 2006, p. 4.

67. *Library of Congress Country Studies,* s.v. "South Africa: Human Rights and National Reconciliation."

68. Ibid.

69. "51st National Congress: Declaration," ANC's website (www.anc.org.za/), 20 December 2002.

70. "Left Seizes Control of South Africa's ANC," *The Sunday Times* (U.K.), 25 January 2009; *CIA World Factbook,* s.v. "South Africa."

71. "Zimbabweans Denied Refugee Status in SA amid Fears of Policy Change," by Alex Bell, *SW Africa Radio* (Zimbabwe), 6 September 2013.

72. "Relations with South Africa," Chinese Foreign Ministry (China.org.cn), 14 June 2006.

73. *Freedom House,* s.v. "Freedom in the World 2014—China."

74. "The Tripartite Alliance Has Sold Its Soul," *Mail & Guardian* (South Africa), 27 September 2013.

75. *BBC Country Profiles,* s.v. "Zambia."

76. *Encyclopedia Britannica,* s.v. "Movement for Multiparty Democracy."

77. "China's Stake in Zambia's Election," by Louise Redvers, *BBC News* on *NPR,* Public Radio East (New Bern, NC), 18 September 2011.

78. Ibid.

79. *BBC Country Profiles,* s.v. "Zambia."

Chapter 4: *China's "Cultural Revolution" in Africa*

1. *Merriam Webster Dictionary* (http://www.merriam-webster.com/dictionary), s.v. "Maoism."

2. Constantine Menges, *China: The Gathering Threat* (Nashville, TN: Nelson Current, 2005), p. 55; R.J. Rummel, *Death by Government* (N.p., n.d.), pp. 100-101, op. cit., p. 54; Seventy-year-old Chinese man (in Shanghai airport), in conversation with author in June 2000.

3. Ibid.

4. Roderick MacFarquhar and Michael Schoenhals, *Mao's Last Revolution* (Cambridge, MA: Harvard Univ. Press, 2006), p. 124.

5. Ibid., p. 515.

6. Ibid., pp. 125, 126.

7. Ibid.

8. Ibid.

9. Ibid.

10. "What Was the Cultural Revolution," by Kallie Szczepanski, *About.com,* n.d.

11. *BBC Country Profiles,* s.v. "Tibet."

12. "A Chronology of Tibet's History," *PBS's Frontline,* NC Public TV, n.d.

13. "The Killing Fields," videocassette, 142 minutes. Warner Brothers, 1984.

14. "From the Killing Fields to Compassion," by David R. Aquije, *Maryknoll Magazine,* January/February 2014, pp. 14-17.

15. Stiff, *The Silent War,* p. 268; Hoile, *Mozambique—A Nation in Crisis*, p. 36, in *The Silent War,* by Stiff, p. 156.

16. "Report on the Massacre at Nyadzonya by the Rhodesian Forces on 9 August 1976," ZANU HQ (Chimoio), 19 August 1976 (as captured by the SAS during Chimoio Raid on 23 November 1977), in *Pamwe Chete,* by Reid-Daly, pp. 241-247.

17. Truscott, "Short Lives Lead to Short-Term Goals in Zimbabwe," p. 4.

18. "Zimbabwe Vets Copying Chinese Red Guards," by Jeromy Lovell, *IOL News* (South Africa), 25 April 2000.

19. *Dark Star Safari: Overland from Cairo to Capetown,* by Paul Theroux (N.p.: Mariner Books, 5 April 2004), pp. 261, 262.

20. "Land Tenure and Mining in Tanzania," by Siri Lange, Christian Mechelsen Inst. (Norway), n.d.

21. Stiff, *The Silent War,* p. 136.

22. "(Angola) Summary," *Human Rights Watch,* n.d.

23. *BBC Country Profiles,* s.v. "Zambia."

24. Ibid., "Zambia Timeline."

25. "Zambia," *Country Reports on Human Rights Practices for 2013,* Undersecretary for Civilian Security and Democracy, Bureau of Democracy, Human Rights, and Labor, U.S. Dept. of State, n.d.

26. Ibid.

27. "Zambia: PF Cadres Were Armed with Guns and Machetes—HH," *Lusaka Times* (Zambia), 13 April 2014.

28. Patriotic Front's website, http://pf.org.zm/.

29. "Zambia," U.S. Dept. of State, Country Reports on Human Rights Practices for 2013; "PAC Attends a Patriotic Front Conference," *South African History* on line, 26 October 1991.

30. "Zambia Election: Michael Sata Takes Presidential Oath," *BBC News* on line, 23 September 2011.

31. "China Praises Achievements of Sudan's National Congress Party," from Xinhua, *Peoples Daily* on line, 24 November 2005.

32. "China's Foreign Aids and Human Rights Concerns—Thoughts Provoked by Darfur Humanitarian Crisis," Chinese Foreign Ministry (China.org.cn), 29 October 2009.

33. *Global Security* (globalsecurity.org), s.v. "Sudan - Popular Defense Forces (PDF)."

34. Nyirigwa, "Why 2011 Referendum Is the Only Hope for South Sudanese: Part Two," p. 5.

35. "Sudan: The Forgotten War," by Elizabeth Diaz, *Time,* 23 February - 2 March, 2015, p. 40.

36. *CIA World Factbook,* s.v. "Congo Republic."

37. "Relations with the Republic of the Congo," Chinese Foreign Ministry (China.org.cn), 14 June 2006.

38. *BBC Country Profiles,* s.v. "Republic of Congo Timeline."

39. *Freedom House,* s.v. "Freedom in the World 2014—Congo Republic (Brazzaville)."

40. *BBC Country Profiles,* s.v. "Somalia."

41. "Somali," Chinese Foreign Ministry (China.org.cn), 10 October 2006.

42. "Ethiopia, China to Broaden Areas of Cooperation," from Xinhua, *China Daily* on line, 28 February 2008; *Wikipedia Encyclopedia,* s.v. "Ethiopia," "Derg," and "Ethiopia-Chinese Relations."

43. *Foreign Intervention in Africa: From the Cold War to the War on Terror,* by Elizabeth Schmidt (Cambridge, U.K.: Cambridge Univ. Press, 2013), p. 158; *Chinese and African Perspectives on China in Africa,* by editors Axel Harneit-Sievers, Stephen Marks, and Sanusha Naidu (N.p.: Pambazuka Press, 2010), p. 93.

44. *Foreign Intervention in Africa,* by Schmidt, p. 158.

45. "China and African Peacekeeping," by Richard Weitz, *Second Line of Defense* (Arlington, VA), 7 March 2013.

46. "Rwanda: Boom Town - Kigali's Chinese Investment," by Daniel Nzohabonimana, *AllAfrica (Pambazuka) News,* 14 February 2014.

47. Ibid.

48. Ibid.

49. Ibid.

50. "Mining in Africa toward 2020," Global Mining Inst. (kpmgafrica.com), n.d.

51. "2009 Minerals Yearbook, Tungsten Table 15," *U.S. Geological Survey* (http://www.usgs.gov), n.d.; *Wikipedia Encyclopedia,* s.v "Tungsten."

52. *Freedom House,* s.v. "Freedom in the World 2014—Rwanda."

53. "Hotel Rwanda," DVD, 121 minutes, MGM, 2004.

54. "Mining in Africa toward 2020," Global Mining Inst.

55. "China-funded Burundi palace project to begin in 2014," Forum on China-Africa Cooperation, 30 September 2013.

Chapter 5: *The PRC's Building and Immigration Program*

1. "The Congo's Killing Fields," by Kevin Clarke, *U.S. Catholic,* July 2008; "45,000 Die Each Month in Congo," World Briefs Wire Reports (AP), *Jacksonville Daily News* (NC), 23 January 2008, p. 4A.

2. "China in Angola: An Emerging Energy Partnership," by Paul Hare, Jamestown Foundation, *China Brief,* vol. 6, issue 22, 8 November 2006; "China and Angola Strengthen Bilateral Relationship," by Loro Horta, *Power and Interest News Report,* 23 June 2006.

3. *China's Rising Power in Africa,* Part 3, "China, Congo Trade for What the Other Wants," by Gwen Thompkins, *NPR,* 30 July 2008.

4. Ibid.

5. Scott Baldauf, "In Congo, a Doctor Keeps Helping as Victims Keep Coming," *Christian Science Monitor,* 24 October 2008, pp. 1, 11; "Oil for China, Guns for Darfur," by Moira Herbst, *Bloomberg Businessweek,* 14 March 2008.

6. Scott Baldauf, "Congo's Riches Fuel Its War," *Christian Science Monitor,* 4 November 2008, pp. 1, 10.

7. "Two Weeks after Being Asked for Help, Angola's Government Said," World News in Brief, *Christian Science Monitor,* 13 November 2008; "Angolan, Congolese Troops Join Forces," World Briefs Wire Reports (AP), *Jacksonville Daily News* (NC), 7 November 2008.

8. "While Congo's Government Is 'Open for Dialogue' with All," World News in Brief, *Christian Science Monitor,* 5 November 2008, p. 7.

9. "Islam in Africa Newsletter," by Terdman and Paz; "Tribal Militants Claimed Responsibility for Another Attack on an Energy Installation," World News in Brief, *Christian Science Monitor,* 8 June 2006, p. 7.

10. Longtime owner of Khartoum hotel, in conversation with author on 31 May 2006; "China in Angola," by Hare; "China and Angola Strengthen Bilateral Relationship," by Loro Horta, *Power and Interest News Report,* 23 June 2006.

11. *China's Rising Power in Africa,* "Series Overview," by Didrik Schanche, *NPR,* 28 July 2008.

12. Ibid., Part 4, "Chinese-Built Zambian Smelter Stirs Controversy," by Ofeibea Quist-Arcton, *NPR,* 1 August 2008.

13. Ibid., Part 5, "Army of Shopowners Paved China's Way in Africa," by Ofeibea Quist-Arcton, *NPR,* 1 August 2008.

14. "Hostility toward Workers Cools Angola-China Relationship," by Benoit Faucon and Sherry Su, *Wallstreet Journal,* business edition, 10 August 2010; *CIA World Factbook,* s.v. "Angola"; Bill Gertz, "Notes from the Pentagon," *Washington Times,* 5 March 2004.

15. "China Tightens Grip on Africa with $4.4bn Lifeline for Guinea Junta," by Jonathan Clayton, *The Times* on line (U.K.), 13 October 2009.

16. Longtime owner of Khartoum hotel; "Hostility toward Workers Cools Angola-China Relationship," by Faucon and Su.

17. *Terrorist Trail: Backtracking the Foreign Fighter,* by H. John Poole (Emerald Isle, NC: Posterity Press, 2006), pp. 17-38, 197-208, 223-246.

18. "The Chinese Military-Industrial Complex Goes Global," by David Welker, *The Multinational Monitor,* vol. 18, no. 6, June 1997; "Cameroon: China Invades Country with Cheap, Fragile Goods," *AllAfrica News,* 28 August 2008.

19. Bill Gertz, *The China Threat* (Washington, D.C.: Regnery Pub., 2002), pp. 82, 94; "Beijing Orders Army to Give Up Its Businesses," by Henry Chu, *L.A. Times* on line, 23 July 1998; *Trip Atlas* (tripatlas.com), s.v. "Peoples Liberation Army"; Menges, *China: The Gathering Threat,* pp. 395, 398.

20. "China in Africa," IDE-JETRO (Inst. of Developing Economies—Japan External Trade Organ.), n.d., par. 6.

21. "Global Double Crossing," by Charles R. Smith, *Newsmax* (West Palm Beach, FL), 27 February 2003.

22. Charles R. Smith, "U.S. Bombs Chinese Network in Afghanistan, PRC Sold Taliban Advanced Air Defense System," *Newsmax* (West Palm Beach, FL), 20 October 2001; Mohan Malik, *Dragon on Terrorism: Assessing China's Tactical Gains and Strategic Losses Post-September 11* (Carlisle, PA: Strategic Studies Inst., U. S. Army War College, October 2002), p. 12.

23. CEIEC's website (ceiec.com.cn), intro. video (as viewed in 2005).

24. "China Railway Construction Corp. Plans $3.4B IPO," by Vivian Wai-yin Kwok, *Forbes Magazine,* 4 January 2008.

25. "China Corrects Diplomatic Faux Pas, but Maintains Presence in Gilgit-Baltistan," by B. Raman, Chennai Centre for China Studies, C3S Paper No. 586, 5 September 2010.

26. "China Railway Construction Seeks End-Feb HK IPO-Source," *Reuters News* on line, 15 January 2008.

27. CRSSG's website, crssg.com/english.

28. *Global Security* (www.globalsecurity.org), s.v. "PLA Training"; *Wikipedia Encyclopedia,* s.v. "Modernization of the Peoples Liberation Army."

29. Ibid., s.v. "People's Liberation Army."

30. *Global Security* (globalsecurity.org), s.v. "People's Liberation Army."

31. "The Armed Forces: Instrument of Peace, Strength, Development and Prosperity," by Joseph Babatunde Fagoyinbo (N.p.: AuthorHouse, 2014), p. 364, from *Wikipedia Encyclopedia,* s.v. "People's Liberation Army."

32. Chinese Posters (hosted by Internat. Inst. of Social History in Amsterdam), s.v. "Military Industrial Complex" (from the following url: http://chineseposters.net/themes/military-industrial-complex.php).

33. "Do I Look Dangerous to You," Part I, Partners in Crime Series, by Frederic Dannen, *The New Republic,* 14 & 21 July 1997.

34. "Modernizing the People's Liberation Army of China," by Carin Zissis, Council on Foreign Relations, *Backgrounder,* 5 December 2006.

35. *Wikipedia Encyclopedia* s.v. "Category: Central-Owned Enterprise of the People's Republic of China (as viewed in 2005)."

36. CEIEC's website, ceiec.com.cn; CRBC's website, crbc.com/cn; and CSCEC's website, app.cscec.com.cn; "Company Overview of China Road And Bridge Corporation," *Bloomberg Businessweek,* n.d.

37. Hutchison Whampoa's website, hutchison-whampoa.com (as viewed in 2005).

38. Ibid.

39. CCCCLTD's website, ccccltd.com.cn.

40. "State Owned Assets Supervision and Administration Commission of the State Council," by the PRC, n.d.; "China to Seal $9bn DR Congo Deal," by Tim Whewell, *BBC News* on line, 14 April 2008.

41. "End of the Line for 'Lunatic Express?' Kenya Begins Multi-Billion Dollar Railway," by Stephanie Ott, *CNN's News* on line, 6 January 2014.

42. "Pakistan Is Handing Over De-Facto Control of the Strategic Gilgit-Baltistan Region," *Rediff News* (India); "More Than Troops, Chinese Projects in PoK Worry India," by Pranab Dhal Samanta, *Indian Express* (Delhi), 5 September 2010.

43. CRBC's website, http://www.crbc.com.

44. "Hostility toward Workers Cools Angola-China Relationship," by Faucon and Su; "China's Largest Port Builder Delays $3 Billion Shanghai Offering," *Bloomberg Businessweek,* 8 July 2011; "Angola Restore Copper Rail Line after Four Decade Halt," by McClelland; "Beijings Embrace," *Africa Confidential,* vol. 47, issue 14, 7 July 2006.

45. Brautigam, *The Dragon's Gift,* p. 163.

46. "Picking Up Steam: The Expansion of Chinese Railways in Africa," by Yun Sun, Brookings Inst., 26 September 2014; "China in Africa," IDE-JETRO, par. 10; "World Rail Market March 2009," *Railway Gazette,* 8 March 2009.

47. "State Owned Assets Supervision and Administration Commission of the State Council"; CEIEC's website, ceiec.com.cn.

48. "The Chinese Military-Industrial Complex Goes Global, by Welker, *Multinational Monitor,* vol. 8, no. 6, June 1997, as retrieved in July 2015 from the following url: http://www.multinationalmonitor.org/hyper/mm0697.05.html.

49. China Xinxing Import And Export Corporation's website, en.cxxc-china.com; *Wikipedia Encyclopedia,* s.v. "List of State-Owned Enterprises in China."

50. "China in Africa," IDE-JETRO, par. 10.

51. Ibid.

52. Ibid.

53. Ibid.

54. Ibid.

55. CRBC's website, crbc.com/c; "CRBC Cements Sino-Kenya Ties," *ChinaDaily,* 9 May 2014.

56. "China in Africa," IDE-JETRO, par. 10.

57. Ibid.

58. Ibid.

59. "Congo and China," Global Witness (U.K/), n.d.

60. "China in Africa," IDE-JETRO, par. 10.

61. Ibid., IDE-JETRO, pars. 5 and 8.

62. Ibid., par. 10.

63. Ibid.

64. Bill Gertz, "Notes from the Pentagon," *Washington Times,* 5 March 2004; "China Puts 700,000 Troops on Alert in Sudan," *Newsmax* (West Palm Beach, FL), 27 August 2000; "China Winning Resources and Loyalties of Africa."

65. "China-Africa Relations in the 21st Century."

66. "China's Military Rise: The Dragon's New Teeth," *The Economist,* 7 April 2012.

67. *CIA World Factbook; Wikipedia Encyclopedia,* s.v. "List of African Countries by Population."

Chapter 6: *Peacekeepers Wherever There Is Instability*

1. "Should the United Nations Wage War to Keep the Peace," by James Verinia, *National Geographic* on line, 27 March 2014.

2. "China Puts 700,000 Troops on Alert in Sudan," *Newsmax* (West Palm Beach, FL), 27 August 2000.

3. "China's Discreet Hold on Pakistan's Northern Borderlands," by Selig Harrison, *New York Times,* 26 August 2010.

4. "Pakistan Is Handing Over De-Facto Control of the Strategic Gilgit-Baltistan Region."

5. "Profit In Peacekeeping – China's Strategic Gain," by Andrew Ludwig, *The Diplomat* (Tokyo), 27 May 2014.

6. "China-Africa Relations in the 21st Century," by Parneti.

7. "China's Military Rise: The Dragon's New Teeth."

8. Ibid.; "China in Africa," IDE-JETRO, par. 4.

9. "China and African Peacekeeping," by Weitz.

10. "China Offers 'Troops' to U.N. Mali Peacekeeping Mission," *BBC News* on line, 24 May 2013; "Peacekeeping Fact Sheet," U.N.'s website, 30 September 2014.

11. "China Sends Peacekeeping Police Squad for South Sudan," from Xinhua News Agency, *Global Times* (Beijing), 12 November 2011.

12. Ibid.; "Troop and Police Contributors," U.N.'s website, n.d.

13. "China and African Peacekeeping," by Weitz.

14. Ibid.

15. "China-Africa Relations in the 21st Century," by Parneti.

16. Ibid.

17. "The 'Big Six' Arms Exporters," *Amnesty Internat.,* 11 June 2012.

18. "China's Arms Exports Flooding Sub-Saharan Africa," by Colum Lynch, *Washington Post,* 25 August 2012.

19. "China-Africa Relations in the 21st Century," by Parneti.

20. "China and African Peacekeeping," by Weitz.

21. Ibid.; "China's Involvement in African Conflict Zones," by David H. Shinn, Jamestown Foundation, 20 May 2009.

22. *China into Africa: Trade, Aid, and Influence,* ed. Robert I. Rotberg (N.p.: Brookings Inst. Press and World Peace Foundation, 2008), p. 161.

23. "Arming Genocide in Rwanda: The High Cost of Small Arms Transfers," by Stephen D. Goose and Frank Smyth, Council on Foreign Relations, *Foreign Affairs* on line, September/October 1994 issue.

24. *China into Africa,* ed. Rotberg, p. 163.

25. "China's Involvement in African Conflict Zones," by David H. Shinn, Jamestown Foundation, 20 May 2009.

26. "Chad: How China Created an African Power," by Raluca Besliu, *The Globalist* (Washington, D.C.), 26 December 2013.

27. *CIA World Factbook,* s.v. "Democratic Republic of the Congo."

28. Ibid., s.v. "Zimbabwe."

29. "Chad: How China Created an African Power," by Besliu.

30. "Stratfor: China's Weapons Push in Africa," by Jamie Etheridge, *ABC's News* on line, 25 August 2012.

31. "South Africans a Proud Part of U.N. Peacekeeping Operations," by Kim Helfrich, *Defence Web* (South Africa), 3 June 2014.
32. "South Africa's Peacekeeping Role in Burundi," ACCORD (South Africa), *Occasional Papers,* issue 2, 2007.
33. "Troop and Police Contributors," U.N.'s website, n.d.
34. "Fighting an Invisible Enemy in DRC," *IRIN News* (U.N.), 9 April 2014; *Wikipedia Encyclopedia,* s.v. "United Nations Force Intervention Brigade."
35. "South Africa Sends More Troops to Central African Republic," *The Guardian* (U.K.) on line, 27 March 2013.
36. "New Era of China-Namibia Friendship," by Chinese Ambassador to Namibia, Embassy's website, 7 April 2014.

Chapter 7: *China's New Modus Operandi*

1. "Taiwan Confident of Keeping Burkina Faso Ties after Army Takeover," *Reuters News* on line, 3 November 2014.
2. Stiff, *The Silent War,* pp. 289, 290.
3. *NPR's "Morning Edition" News,* 22 April 2009; *Terrorist Trail,* by Poole, pp. 17-38, 197-208, 223-246.
4. "Zuma's Missing Years Come to Light," *The Times* (U.K.), 22 February 2009.
5. Ibid.
6. *Terrorist Trail,* by Poole, p. 205; *Wikipedia Encyclopedia,* s.v. "Second Congo War."
7. "China Winning Resources and Loyalties of Africa."
8. Daniel Pepper, "Congolese Hopeful Ahead of July 30 Vote," *Christian Science Monitor,* 29 June 2006, p. 7;
9. "China's Stake in Zambia's Election," by Redvers.
10. "Beijing's Blue Berets: U.N. Peacekeeping and the Evolution of Chinese Diplomacy," by Anna Richardson, *The Atlantic* on line, 13 May 2013 [for DRC loan]; "China Tightens Grip on Africa with $4.4bn Lifeline for Guinea Junta," Clayton [for Guinea loan]; "Angola" from Chinese Foreign Ministry, *CIA World Factbook* s.v. "Angola," Gertz' "Notes from the Pentagon" [for Angola credit]; "Mozambique" from Chinese Foreign Ministry [for Mozambique debt reduction].
11. "China-Funded Burundi Palace Project to Begin in 2014," Forum on China-Africa Cooperation.
12. "Relations with South Africa," Chinese Foreign Ministry (China.org.cn), 14 June 2006.
13. *Unrestricted Warfare,* by Qiao Liang and Wang Xiangsui (Beijing: PLA Lit. and Arts Pub. House, February 1999), FBIS translation from the internet.

14. "China's Discreet Hold on Pakistan's Northern Borderlands."

15. Ibid.

16. "Asian Juggernaut," by Brahma Chellaney (New York: HarperCollins, 2006), from *Wikipedia Encyclopedia,* s.v. "Trans-Karakoram Tract."

17. "China Puts 700,000 Troops on Alert in Sudan"; Gertz, "Notes from the Pentagon"; "China Winning Resources and Loyalties of Africa."

18. *Tequila Junction,* by Poole, part one.

19. Stiff, *The Silent War,* pp. 289, 290.

20. *NPR's "Morning Edition" News,* 10 March 2015.

21. "Chinese President Arrives in Brazzaville for State Visit," *Xinhua News* on line, 29 March 2013.

Chapter 8: *African Parts of Former Muslim Empire*

1. *Encyclopedia Britannica*, s.v. "Caliphate."

2. *Jewish Virtual Library* (http://www.jewishvirtuallibrary.org), s.v. "Islam: The Muslim Empire."

3. Ibid., s.v. "Islam: The Caliphate."

4. Ibid., s.v. "Tunisia," "Algeria," and "Morocco"; *Wikipedia Encyclopedia,* s.v. "Caliphate."

5. Jewish Virtual Library (http://www.jewishvirtuallibrary.org), s.v. "Egypt."

6. *Encyclopedia Britannica*, s.v. "Caliphate"; *Wikipedia Encyclopedia,* s.v. "Caliphate."

7. Jewish Virtual Library (http://www.jewishvirtuallibrary.org), s.v. "Egypt."

8. *Encyclopedia Britannica*, s.v. "Mamluk."

9. Ibid.

10. *Encyclopedia Britannica*, s.v. "Caliphate"; *Wikipedia Encyclopedia,* s.v. "Caliphate."

11. Ibid.

12. *Encyclopedia Britannica*, s.v. "Aghlabid Dynasty."

13. *Encyclopedia Britannica*, s.v. "Caliphate"; *Wikipedia Encyclopedia,* s.v. "Caliphate."

14. *Encyclopedia Britannica*, s.v. "Idrisid."

15. Mannes, *Profiles in Terror,* p. 21.

Chapter 9: *Salafist Interest in Northeastern Africa*

1. Hunwick, "Africa and Islamic Revival," p. 7; *Encyclopedia Britannica,* s.v. "Muslim Brotherhood."

2. Ibid.

3. Gunaratna, *Inside al-Qaeda*, pp. 152, 153; Paul Clammer, *Sudan (*Bucks, England: Bradt Travel Guides Ltd., 2005), p. 37.

4. Huntington, *The Clash of Civilizations and the Remaking of World Order*, p. 177; Mannes, *Profiles in Terror*, p. 22; Hughes, *Warring on Terrorism,* pp. 10, 36; Gunaratna, *Inside al-Qaeda*, p. 139.

5. Ibid.

6. "Al-Qaeda's New Front," *PBS's Frontline,* NC Public TV, 25 January 2005.

7. Yossef Bodansky (Director of Research of the Internat. Strategic Studies Assn. and Congressional Task Force on Terrorism and Unconventional Warfare), *Offensive in the Balkans* (Alexandria, VA: Internat. Media Corp., 1995), chapt. 8, pp. 71-78.

8. Hunwick, "Africa and Islamic Revival," p. 8; *Sudan Update* (www.sudanupdate.org), s.v. "National Islamic Front" and "Hassan al-Turabi."

9. Gunaratna, *Inside al-Qaeda,* pp. 154-159; "Islamists Training in Somalia," by Gertz.

10. "Sudan Arrested Chadian Rebel to Support of His Rival," *Khartoum Monitor,* 1 June 2006, p. 1.

11. *CIA World Factbook,* s.v. "Democratic Republic of the Congo."

12. Gertz, "Notes from the Pentagon"; "China Puts 700,000 Troops on Alert in Sudan"; "China Winning Resources and Loyalties of Africa."

13. "The 'Big Six' Arms Exporters," *Amnesty Internat.;* "China's Arms Exports Flooding Sub-Saharan Africa," by Lynch; "China-Africa Relations in the 21st Century," by Parneti; "China and African Peacekeeping," by Weitz; "China Winning Resources and Loyalties of Africa"; Longtime owner of Khartoum hotel, in conversation with author on 31 May 2006.

14. "Chad: How China Created an African Power," by Besliu.

15. *CIA World Factbook,* s.v. "Democratic Republic of the Congo."

16. "Stratfor: China's Weapons Push in Africa," by Etheridge.

17. "Al-Qaeda in East Africa and the Horn," by David H. Shinn, *Journal of Conflict Studies,* vol. 27, no, 1, 2007, as republished in *Horn Affairs,* 2013.

18. "Attack's in Egypt's Sinai Kill at Least 25," World Roundup (AP), *Jacksonville Daily News* (NC), 30 January 2015, p. B1.

19. "Al-Qaeda in East Africa and the Horn," by Shinn.

20. "Yemen Clashes with Shiite Rebels," by Ahmed Al-Haj (AP), *Jacksonville Daily News* (NC), 20 January 2015, p. A8; *ABC's Nightly News,* 23 January 2015.

21. "Rogues' Gallery," by Bobby Ghosh, *Time,* 2 May 2011.

22. Art Theyson, "New Warfront Opens in Iraq Three Months before Handover," *DEBKAfile* (Israel), 5 April 2004.

23. Ginny Hill, "Cold War Roots of Yemen Conflict," *BBC News* on line, 17 September 2009.

24. Ibid.

25. "Yemen: A Hezbollah Withdrawal," *STRATFOR Weekly,* 10 February 2010.

26. "Iranian Proxies: An Intricate and Active Web," by Scott Stewart, *STRATFOR Weekly,* 3 February 2010.

27. Lebanese *Hezbollah* portion of Islami Davet Islamic Politics and Cultural website (Turkey), as viewed on 26 November 2010.

28. "Yemen's War," *The Economist,* 19 November 2010.

29. Anthony H. Cordesman (Strategy Chair), "Iran's Developing Military Capabilities," working draft (Washington, D.C.: Ctr. for Strategic and Internat. Studies, 14 December 2004), pp. 35-38.

30. *NPR's "Morning Edition" News,* 2 February 2011.

31. "Bahrain Protests Joined by Arab Anger in Libya," News Briefs/Wire Reports (AP), *Jacksonville Daily News* (NC), 17 February 2011.

32. *LookLex Encyclopedia* (http://i-cias.com), s.v. "South Yemen"; *Wikipedia Encyclopedia,* s.v. "South Yemen."

33. "Both Iran and Israel Have Military Bases in Eritrea, Global Intel. Reports," by Anshel Pfeffer, *Haaretz News* on line, 12 December, 2012; "Yemen's War."

34. Gunaratna, *Inside al-Qaeda*, p. 158.

35. John L. Esposito, *Unholy War: Terror in the Name of Islam* (London: Oxford Univ. Press, 2002), p. 10.

36. Interview, U.S. intelligence community, February 2000, in *Inside al-Qaeda,* by Rohan Gunaratna, p. 158.

37. Gunaratna, *Inside al-Qaeda,* p. 158.

38. Dr. Mohammed Mahmoud, Tufts Univ., "Islam and Islamization in Sudan: The Islamic National Front," from *Religion, Nationalism, and Peace in Sudan* (paper presented at U.S. Inst. of Peace Conference, 16-17 September 1997), p. 4.

39. Katzman, *Warriors of Islam,* pp. 82-84.

40. Zeyno Baran, "Muslim Brotherhood Takes Up Arms—in Support of Hizbullah," from access@g2-forward.org, 2 August 2006; Syed Saleem Shahzad, "We are just Hit-and-Run Guerrillas," *Asia Times* on line, 10 August 2006.

41. "Iran: U.S. Concerns and Policy Responses," by Kenneth Katzman, CRS Report for Congress, Order Code RL32048, 26 October 2010, pp. 20, 38, 40, 42, 45.

42. Ibid., p. 35.

43. Anthony H. Cordesman (Strategy Chair), "Iran's Revolutionary Guards, the Al Quds Force, and Other Intelligence and Paramilitary Forces," working draft (Washington, D.C.: Ctr. for Strategic and Internat. Studies, 16 August 2007), p. 9.

44. Jon Swain, David Leppard, and Brian Johnson-Thomas, "Iran's Plot to Mine Uranium in Africa," *The Sunday Times* (U.K.), 6 August 2006.

Chapter 10: *Islamist Initiatives in Northwest Africa*

1. *ABC's Nightly News,* 20 January 2015.
2. "Libya Hotel Attack: Five foreigners among Nine Killed," *BBC News* on line, 28 January 2015; "Egypt Bombs Islamic State Targets in Libya after 21 Egyptians Beheaded," by Ahmed Tolba and Yara Bayoumy, *Reuters News* on line, 16 February 2015.
3. *CIA World Factbook,* s.v. "Libya."; "Ex-Libyan General Battling Islamist Militias Faces Dwindling Support amid Stalemate," by Erin Cunningham, *Washington Post* on line, 8 July 2014; "Libya Prime Minister Abdullah al-Thinni Resigns," *BBC News* on line, 29 August 2014; "The New Danger in Benghazi," by Ethan Chorin, Opinion Editorial, *New York Times* on line, 27 May 2014.
4. "Struggle over Libya's Oil Risks Breaking Up Country: Rival PM," by Ulf Laessing, *Reuters News* on line, 28 November 2014.
5. "U.S. Shifts Troops in Response to Libya," from McClatchy Tribute, *Jacksonville Daily News* (NC), 17 May 2014; "Libyan Capital under Islamist Control after Tripoli Airport Seized," by Chris Stephen and Anne Penketh, *The Guardian* (U.K.) on line, 24 August 2014.
6. "Will Libya's Militias Defeat Democracy," by Rana Jawad, *BBC News* on line, 22 July 2014; "Profile: Libya's Ansar al-Sharia," by Faisal Irshaid, *BBC News* on line, 13 June 2014; "Libya's Muslim Brotherhood Struggles to Grow," by Mary Fitzgerald, *Foreign Policy,* 1 May 2014.
7. "Gadhafi's Mercenaries Spread Guns and Fighting in Africa," by Bazi Kanani, *ABC's News* on line, 3 April 2012.
8. "Crisis-Hit Mali Swears in Transitional President," by Leela Jacinto, *France24* on line, 12 April 2012.
9. "French Troops Deployed in Last Mali Rebel Strongholds," by Richard Valdmanis and John Irish, *Reuters News* on line, 30 January 2013.
10. *NPR's "Morning Edition" News,* 31 December 2010.
11. "Boko Haram, Dawood Tie Up to Sell Drugs in India," *Rediff News,* 21 July 2014; "U.S. Designates Dawood Ibrahim as Terrorist Supporter," U.S. Treasury Dept. Press Release, 16 October 2003; *NPR's "Morning Edition" News,* 19 July 2014; "U.S., Liberia Join Forces in Operation Relentless," *DEA News Bulletin,* 1 June 2010; *Wikipedia Encyclopedia,* s.v. "List of Active Rebel Groups."

12. "Algeria 2013 Crime and Safety Report," Bureau of Diplomatic Security, U.S. Dept. of State, 18 June 2013; *NPR's "Morning Edition" News,* 19 July 2014; "U.S., Liberia Join Forces in Operation Relentless," *DEA News Bulletin,* 1 June 2010; *Wikipedia Encyclopedia,* s.v. "List of Active Rebel Groups."

13. *CIA World Factbook,* s.v. "Tunisia."

14. *BBC News* on *NPR,* Public Radio East (New Bern, NC), 20 July 2014.

15. "Algerians Vote on Bouteflika's Re-Election Bid," *BBC News* on line, 17 April 2014.

16. *CIA World Factbook,* s.v. "Morocco."

17. *CIA World Factbook,* s.v. "Western Sahara."

18. "LatAm Drug Traffickers Set Up in Guinea-Bissau, Expand in Africa," by Charles Parkinson, *Insightcrime.org,* 29 August 2013.

19. "Guinea Bissau: Hezbollah, al Qaida and the Lebanese Connection," by Marco Venaschi, Pulitzer Ctr., 19 June 2009.

Chapter 11: *Any Changes to the Muslim Method*

1. "3 African Nations Battle Boko Haram," by Haruna Umar and Michelle Faul (AP), *Jacksonville Daily News* (NC), 5 February 2015, p. B1.

2. "Boko Haram: The Other Islamic State," by Jeremy Ashkenas, Derek Watkinis, and Carchie Tse, *New York Times* on line, 15 January 2015.

3. "The Horrific Aftermath of Boko Haram Massacre on Nigerian Villages," by Laurie Hanna, *Daily Mail* (U.K.) on line, 15 January 2015.

4. "Nigerian Forces Repel Extremists' Attack," by Haruna Umar and Michelle Faul (AP), *Jacksonville Daily News* (NC), 2 February 2015.

5. "3 African Nations Battle Boko Haram," by Umar and Faul.

6. *Unrestricted Warfare,* by Qiao Liang and Wang Xiangsui.

7. "The War on ISIS," *Time,* 9 March 2015, p. 26.

8. "Who Are Nigeria's Mend Oil Militants," by Caroline Duffield, *BBC News* on line, 4 October 2010; *ABC's Nightly News,* 7 January 2007; "Nigeria's MEND Rebels Threaten Future Attack on Oil Industry," by Elisha Bala-Gbogbo, *Bloomberg News* on line, 27 January 2014.

9. "The War on ISIS," p. 26; *Wikipedia Encylopedia,* s.v. "Movement for the Emancipation of the Niger Delta."

10. Ibid., p. 29.

11. "How ISIS Is Winning the Propaganda War," Explainer, *Time,* 6/13 July 2015, p. 14.

12. "Assyrian Christians: A Look at the Religious Group Captured by ISIS," by Alexander Mallin and Pat O'Gara, *ABC's News* on line, 1 March 2015; "Egypt Bombs Islamic State Targets in Libya after 21 Egyptians Beheaded," by Tolba and Bayoumy.

13. "The War on ISIS," p. 30.

14. "The Battle for Nigeria," by Aryn Baker, *Time,* 16 February 2015, pp. 36, 37; *Wikipedia Encyclopedia*, s.v. "Al-Qaeda in the Arabian Peninsula," "al-Qaeda in the Islamic Maghreb," *"al-Shabaab* (militant group)," and *"Boko Haram."*

15. "The War on ISIS," pp. 28, 29.

16. Ibid., p. 29.

17. Ibid., pp. 26-31.

18. *NPR's "Morning Edition" News,* 1 July 2015.

Chapter 12: *Afghan Opiate Entrance to Africa*

1. "Production of Opium by Afghans Is Up Again," by Rod Nordland, *New York Times* on line, Asia Pacific ed., 15 April 2013.

2. DEA Chief Jack Dawn in testimony before the Senate Intel. Committee, and CIA assessment in September 1988, as quoted in *Seeds of Terror: How Heroin Is Bankrolling the Taliban and al-Qaeda,* by Gretchen Peters (New York: Thomas Dunne Books, 2009), pp. 28, 51; "The Spoils of War: Afghanistan's Multibillion Dollar Heroin Trade," by Prof. Michel Chossudovsky, *Global Research,* 15 February 2014.

3. "Significant Findings of NDTA 2011," Community Anti-Drug Coalitions of America, n.d.

4. *2013 National Drug Threat Assessment Summary,* U.S. Dept. of Justice, Nat. Drug Intel. Ctr., n.d., pp. 5, 6.

5. *National Drug Threat Assessment (for) 2011,* U.S. Dept. of Justice, Nat. Drug Intel. Ctr., August 2011, p. 10.

6. "Africa a New Conduit for Europe's Drugs," by Rukmini Callimachi (AP), *Washington Post* on line, 29 July 2007.

7. Texas police officer, in telephone conversation with author in May 2011.

8. *Transnational Organized Crime in Eastern Africa: A Threat Assessment,* UNODC, September 2013.

9. Ibid.

10. Ibid.

11. Ibid.

12. Ibid.

13. Ibid.

14. "FBI Informant Says Agents Missed Chance to Stop 9/11 Ringleader Mohammed Atta," by Brian Ross and Vic Walter, *ABC's News* on line, 10 September 2009.

15. "Statement of the Honorable Thomas Harrigan, Deputy Administrator, DEA, before the Senate Caucus on Internat. Narcotics Control Regarding Countering Narcotics Threats in West Africa," 16 May 2012.

16. Ibid.

17. "Chinese Gangs Fuel Meth Scourge in U.S.," by Joshua Philipp, China Society Internat., *Epoch Times*, 12 September 2013.

18. "The International Heroin Market," Office of National Drug Control Policy, The White House, n.d.

19. *Homeland Siege: Tactics for Police and Military,* by H. John Poole (Emerald Isle, NC: Posterity Press, 2009), chapt. 4.

20. "Heroin Makes a Comeback," by Zusha Elinson, *Wall Street Journal,* 8 August 2013.

21. "90%: Afghanistan, the Unholy Trinity, and Critical Thought," by Louis DeAnda, Inst. for Defense and Govt. Advancement, 26 July 2012.

22. "White House Czar Calls for End to 'War on Drugs'," by Gary Fields, *Wall Street Journal* on line, 14 May 2009; "Drug Policy Changes Under New Director," *NPR's News* on line, 3 November 2009; Drug Czar, as quoted on *NPR's "Morning Edition" News*, mid-2010.

23. "Heroin Makes a Comeback," by Elinson.

24. DEA Chief Jack Dawn in testimony before the Senate Intel. Committee, and CIA assessment in September 1988, as quoted in *Seeds of Terror,* by Peters; "The Spoils of War: Afghanistan's Multibillion Dollar Heroin Trade," by Prof. Michel Chossudovsky, *Global Research,* 15 February 2014.

25. *CIA World Factbook,* s.v. "Illicit Drugs—World."

26. "The Opium Kings," *PBS's Frontline*, NC Public TV, n.d.

27. "Terrorism and Transnational Organised Crime Threatens Hard-Won Progress in Africa," by Yousuf Malik, *Defence IQ* (U.K.), 20 October 2014.

28. "Do I Look Dangerous to You," by Dannen.

29. Ibid.

30. "A Means of Maintaining Social Order," Part II, Partners in Crime Series, by Frederic Dannen, *The New Republic,* 14 & 21 July 1997; *Unrestricted Warfare, by* Qiao Liang and Wang Xiangsui.

31. "Do I Look Dangerous to You," by Dannen.

Chapter 13: *Middle of the Smuggling Corridor*

1. "Drug Trafficking Patterns to and from Eastern Africa," UNODC, n.d.

2. Longtime owner of Khartoum hotel.

3. "Drug Trafficking Patterns to and from Eastern Africa," UNODC, n.d.
4. Ibid.
5. *CIA World Factbook,* s.v. "Ethiopia."
6. Ibid., s.v. "Kenya."
7. "Drug Trafficking Patterns to and from Eastern Africa," UNODC, n.d.
8. *CIA World Factbook,* s.v. "Nigeria."
9. Ibid., s.v. "Burkina Faso" and "Mali."
10. Ibid., s.v. "Benin."
11. Ibid., s.v. "Togo."
12. Ibid., s.v. "Ghana."
13. Ibid., s.v. "Cote D'Ivoire."
14. Ibid., s.v. "Liberia."
15. "Guinea-Bissau: How Cocaine Transformed a Tiny Nation," by Jessica Hatcher, *Time,* 15 October 2012.
16. *CIA World Factbook,* s.v. "Guinea-Bissau."
17. *BBC Country Profiles,* s.v. "Guinea-Bissau."
18. *CIA World Factbook,* s.v. "Senegal."
19. *NPR's "Morning Edition" News*, 19 July 2014.
20. "Guinea Bissau: Hezbollah, al Qaida and the Lebanese Connection," by Venaschi.
21. "Antonio Indjai, Chief of the Guinea-Bissau Armed Forces, Charged . . . with . . . Narco-Terrorism Conspiracy," *DEA News Bulletin,* 18 April 2013.
22. "U.S., Liberia Join Forces in Operation Relentless," *DEA News Bulletin,* 1 June 2010.
23. *World Drug Report 2010,* UNODC, 25 June 2010, p. 84.
24. "Benin 2012 OSAC Crime and Safety Report," Bureau of Diplomatic Security, U.S. Dept. of State, 25 February 2012.
25. "Benin 2014 Crime and Safety Report," Bureau of Diplomatic Security, U.S. Dept. of State, 1 July 2014.
26. "Togo 2014 Crime and Safety Report," Bureau of Diplomatic Security, U.S. Dept. of State, 24 July 2014.
27. *World Drug Report 2010,* map 5, UNODC.
28. "Niger 2012 OSAC Crime and Safety Report," Bureau of Diplomatic Security, U.S. Dept. of State, 29 February 2012.
29. "Nigeria Braced for War with Drug Lords," by David Orr, *The Independent* (U.K.), 4 October 1995.
30. "Drug Trafficking Rising in Central Africa, Warns Interpol," by Ntaryike Divine Jr., *Voice of America,* 8 September 2012.
31. "Algeria 2013 Crime and Safety Report," Bureau of Diplomatic Security, U.S. Dept. of State, 2013.
32. "Chad 2013 Crime and Safety Report," Bureau of Diplomatic Security, U.S. Dept, of State, 16 April 2013.

33. "Political Situation in Somalia 15 March 2011," map, from *Wikipedia Encyclopedia*, s.v. "Somalia."

34. "Ogaden National Liberation Front (ONLF)," Council on Foreign Relations, *Backgrounder,* 1 November 2007.

35. "Sudan Rebels Threaten Khartoum Attack," by Ahmed Younis, Asharq al-Awsat (U.K.), 28 May 2014.

36. "Sudan, Chad, and the Central African Republic," Council on Foreign Relations, *Backgrounder*, 2 January 2007.

37. "Niger 2012 OSAC Crime and Safety Report," Bureau of Diplomatic Security, U.S. Dept. of State.

38. *Terrorist Research & Analysis Consortium* (http://www.trackingterrorism.org), s.v. "National Movement for the Liberation of Azawad (MNLA)"; "Can Niger Offer Mali Lessons on the Tuareg," *IRIN News* (U.N.), 11 April 2013.

39. *NPR's "Morning Edition" News*, 19 July 2014; "Tuareg, Tamasheq in Burkina Faso," Joshua Project, n.d.

40. *World Almanac of Islamism,* s.v. "Boko Haram."

41. Ibid.; *Wikipedia Encyclopedia,* s.v. "List of Active Rebel Groups."

42. *Terrorist Research & Analysis Consortium* (http://www.trackingterrorism.org), s.v. "National Movement for the Liberation of Azawad (MNLA)."

43. *NPR's "Morning Edition" News*, 19 July 2014; "U.S., Liberia Join Forces In Operation Relentless"; *Wikipedia Encyclopedia,* s.v. "List of Active Rebel Groups."

44. *NPR's "Morning Edition" News,* 21 May 2015.

45. "Background Note: Panama." U.S. Dept. of State, November 2007.

46. "Mexico's Internal Drug War," by Sam Logan, *Power and Interest News Report (PINR),* 14 August 2006.

47. *CIA World Factbook,* s.v. "Mexico (2008)."

48. *CIA World Factbook,* s.v. "Mexico (2015)."

49. David J. Danelo, *The Border: Exploring the U.S.-Mexican Divide* (Mechanicsburg, PA: Stackpole Books, 2008), pp. 50-55.

Chapter 14: *The West Coast Portal to America*

1. "Africa a New Conduit for Europe's Drugs," by Callimachi; "Drug Trafficking Rising in Central Africa, Warns Interpol," by Divine.

2. *World Drug Report 2010,* UNODC, p. 84.

3. Ibid., p. 242.

4. "Everyone Wants Cut in Afghan Drug Trade," from McClatchy News Service, *Jacksonville Daily News* (NC), 10 May 2009, p. A8.

5. Excerpt from *Funding Evil: How Terrorism Is Financed and How to Stop It, by* Rachel Ehrenfield (Chicago: Bonus Books, 2005), in *Warring on Terrorism,* by Hughes, pp. 24-26.

6. "Guinea Bissau: Hezbollah, al Qaida and the Lebanese Connection," by Venaschi.

7. Ibid.

8. Gunaratna, *Inside al-Qaeda,* pp. 164, 165.

9. "Lebanon: Existence of Organized Crime in Lebanon, Its Involvement in the Production of Narcotics and Drug Trafficking, Government Actions to Combat Organized Crime," Immigration and Refugee Board of Canada, 11 September 2003; "Text of the Hezbollah International Financing Prevention Act of 2014," Congressional Bill, 23 July 2014.

10. "Guinea Bissau: Hezbollah, al Qaida and the Lebanese Connection," by Venaschi.

11. "Drug Seizures in West Africa Prompt Fears of Terrorist Links," by Jamie Doward, *The Guardian Observer* (U.K.), 28 November 2009.

12. "Hamas and Iran Rebuild Ties Three Years after Falling Out over Syria," by Harriet Sherwood, *The Guardian* (U.K.) on line, 9 January 2014; "The Al-Qaeda-Hezbollah Relationship," by Eben Kaplan, Council on Foreign Relations, *Backgrounder,* 14 August 2006; "Top Iranian Defector on Iran's Collaboration with Iraq, North Korea, Al-Qa'ida, and Hizbullah," Middle East Media Research Inst., Special Dispatch No. 473, 21 February 2003; "Terror-Cell Alliance at Work in U.S.," by Faye Bowers, *Christian Science Monitor,* 15 July 2002.

13. *Tequila Junction,* by Poole, pp. 71-73.

14. "Do I Look Dangerous to You," by Dannen.

15. "Colombia's Most Powerful Rebels," *BBC News,* NC Public Radio, 19 September 2003.

16. "Terrorist and Organized Crime Groups in the Tri-Border Area," by Rex Hudson, Fed. Research Div., Library of Congress, July 2003.

17. Gunaratna, *Inside al-Qaeda,* pp. 164, 165.

18. "Guinea Bissau: Hezbollah, al Qaida and the Lebanese Connection," by Venaschi.

19. "Transnational Activities of Chinese Crime Organizations," by Glenn E. Curtis, Seth L. Elan, Rexford A. Hudson, and Nina A. Koll, Fed. Research Div., Library of Congress, April 2003.

20. Gunaratna, *Inside al-Qaeda,* pp. 164, 165.

21. "U.S. Designates Dawood Ibrahim as Terrorist Supporter," U.S. Treasury Dept. Press Release, 16 October 2003.

22. "Boko Haram, Dawood Tie Up to Sell Drugs in India."

23. "Nigeria Braced for War with Drug Lords," by Orr; *World Almanac of Islamism,* s.v. "Boko Haram."

24. *World Drug Report 2010,* UNODC, 25 June 2010, p. 244.

25. "China Tightens Grip on Africa with $4.4bn Lifeline for Guinea Junta," by Clayton.

26. "New Drug Threat to West Africa, Warns President of Guinea," by Colin Freeman, *The Telegraph* (U.K.) on line, 15 June 2013.

27. *World Drug Report 2010,* UNODC, 25 June 2010, p. 244.

28. Ibid., p. 242.

29. Memorandum for the record by H.J. Poole.

30. "Venezuela," *Insightcrime.org,* 18 September 2012.

31. "Mexican Cartels Buying Afghan Heroin," from PVNN, *Banderas News* (Mexico), n.d.

32. Al Santoli, "The Panama Canal in Transition: Threats to U.S. Security and China's Growing Role in Latin America," *American Foreign Policy Council Investigative Report,* 23 June 1999; *National Drug Threat Assessment (for) 2009,* "Drug Trafficking Organizations"; *Attorney General's Report*, "Gang-Drug Trafficking Organization Connections Affecting Suburban Areas"; "Partners in Crime (Series)," by Frederic Dannen, *The New Republic,* 14 & 21 July 1997.

33. "African Criminal Enterprises," FBI, n.d.

34. Ibid.; *Wikipedia Encyclopedia,* s.v. "Nigerian Organized Crime" and "Igbo."

35. *Transnational Organized Crime in Western Africa,* U.N. Office on Drugs and Crime, p. 16.

36. DEA Chief Jack Dawn in testimony before the Senate Intel. Committee, and CIA assessment in September 1988, as quoted in *Seeds of Terror,* by Peters, pp. 28, 51.

37. "West Africa Coast Initiative," U.N. Office on Drugs and Crime, n.d.

38. "Ebola, Anarchy, and Failing States," by Benjamin Syme Van Ameringen, *Geopolitical Monitor,* 24 November 2014.

39. "West Africa Coast Initiative," U.N. Office on Drugs and Crime, n.d.

40. "LatAm Drug Traffickers Set Up in Guinea-Bissau, Expand in Africa," by Parkinson.

41. *NPR's "Morning Edition" News,* 24 June 2015.

42. Danelo, *The Border,* pp. 47, 63; *National Drug Threat Assessment (for) 2008,* "Drug Transportation."

43. *NPR's "Morning Edition" News,* 24 June 2015.

Chapter 15: *Where Both Factions Work Together*

1. BBC *Country Profile,* s.v. "Peru."; *Wikipedia Encyclopedia,* s.v. "Shining Path," "FARC," "Maoism"; "Socio-Economic Structure of the FARC-EP"; "Seventh Guerrilla Conference of the FARC-EP"; and "Jacobo Arenas."

2. *Tequila Junction,* by Poole, pp. 164, 165.

3. *Unrestricted Warfare,* by Qiao Liang and Wang Xiangsui, p. 122.

4. *ABC's Morning News,* 14 December 2005; Lee Keath, AP, "Shiites Nominate New Premier," *Jacksonville Daily News* (NC), 22 April 2006, p. 5A; Robin Wright and Peter Baker, "Iraq, Jordan See Threat to Election from Iran," *Washington Post,* 8 December 2004, p. A01.

5. *Terrorist Trail,* by Poole, pp. 17-38, 197-208, 223-246.

6. U.S. oil company executive who lives with his Venezuelan wife in one of that nation's coastal cities, in talk with author on 19 August 2008.

7. Bill Gertz, "Chinese Military Trains in West," *Washington Times,* 15 March 2006; Gertz, *The China Threat*, p. 97.

8. "Country Profile: Venezuela," Library of Congress, Fed. Research Div., March 2005.

9. *Global Security* (globalsecurity.org), s.v. "Committee for the Defense of the Revolution."

10. Peter Brookes, "Venezuelan Vagaries," *Armed Forces Journal,* July 2007, pp. 12, 13.

11. Caracas art store owner, in conversation with author on 16 August 2008.

12. *Global Security* (globalsecurity.org), s.v. "Reserves / Popular Defense Units (UDP - Unidades de Defensa Popular)."

13. *Global Security* (globalsecurity.org), s.v. "Sudan - Popular Defense Forces (PDF)."

14. Ibid.

15. "Sudan: The Forgotten War," by Diaz, p. 40.

16. Sepehr Zabih, *The Iranian Military in Revolution and War* (London: Routledge, 1988), pp. 210-212.

17. Ibid., p. 14.

18. Ibid., p. 160.

19. Kenneth Katzman, *Warriors of Islam: Iran's Revolutionary Guard* (Boulder, CO: Westview Press, 1993), pp. 82-84.

20. Sudan's al-Bashir Given Red Carpet Treatment by China," by Malcomb Moore, *The Telegraph* (U.K.) on line, 29 June 2011.

21. "Omar al-Bashir Q&A: 'In Any War, Mistakes Happen on the Ground'," by Sam Dealey, *Time* on line, 14 August 2009.

22. "Relations with South Africa," Chinese Foreign Ministry (China.org.cn), 14 June 2006.

23. "China's Diplomatic Victory in Sudan's Darfur," by Jonathan Holslag, *Sudan Tribune* on line, 2 August 2007.

24. "Sudan-China Model Economic Relations Sudan Vision," Embassy of Sudan in Washington, D.C., February 2015.

Chapter 16: *Intentional Instability*

1. "Democratic Republic of Congo: Background and U.S. Policy," by Alexis Arieff, Congressional Research Service, 24 February 2014.
2. "China's Involvement in African Conflict Zones," by Shinn.
3. "Understanding M23 and the Current Conflict in the DR Congo," by Maurice Musoni, *United to End Genocide,* 29 November 2012.
4. "Rwandan Arms, Fighters Still Sustaining M23 Rebel Forces in Congo," *CBC News* (Canada), 23 July 2013.
5. "Report of . . . Experts on the Illegal Exploitation of Natural Resources . . . of the Democratic Republic of the Congo," Letter from the (U.N.) Secretary General to President of the Security Council, 12 April 2001; "Fighting an Invisible Enemy in DRC," *IRIN News* (U.N.), 9 April 2014; "China's FM in First Visit to New Ally Malawi," *The Namibian,* 16 January 2009.
6. "China and African Peacekeeping," by Weitz.
7. "Thousands Flee Renewed Violence in DRC," by Malcomb Webb, *Al Jazeera News* on line, 18 May 2012; "DR Congo Government, CNDP Rebels 'Sign Peace Deal'," *AFP,* 23 March 2009.
8. "Congo Conflict: 'The Terminator' Lives in Luxury While Peacekeepers Look On," by David Smith, *The Guardian* (U.K.) on line, 5 February 2010.
9. "Hotel Rwanda," DVD, 121 minutes, MGM, 2004.
10. "Thousands Flee Renewed Violence in DRC," by Webb; "Congo Conflict," by Smith.
11. "South Sudanese Rebels Slam China's Conflicting Roles," from AllAfrica News, *Sudan Tribune,* 18 July 2014.
12. "S. Sudan Troops Burning Villages," World Roundup (AP), *Jacksonville Daily News* (NC), 22 May 2015., p. B1.
13. "China to Send 700 Combat Troops to South Sudan," by David Smith, *The Guardian* (U.K.), 23 December 2014.

Chapter 17: *The Jihadist Threat as a Diversion*

1. *ABC's Nightly News,* 18-22 March 2015.
2. "Thousands Flee from Tunisia after Fatal Attack," World Roundup (AP), *Jacksonville Daily News* (NC), 28 June 2015, p. B1; "Tunisia Searches for Attack Accomplices," World Roundup (AP), *Jacksonville Daily News* (NC), 29 June 2015, p. A8; "Kuwait Says Saudi Responsible for Mosque Suicide Bombing," Scott Neuman, *NPR's News* on line, 28 June 2015.
3. *ABC's Nightly News,* 16 July 2015.

4. "Rebels Attack in Southern Yemen," World Roundup (AP), *Jacksonville Daily News* (N.C.), 20 March 2015, p. B1; "Yemen Suicide Bombings Leave over 130 Dead after Mosques Targeted," by Ian Black, *The Guardian* (U.K.) on line, 20 March 2015; *NPR's "Morning Edition" News,* 26 March 2015; "Saudi-Led Coalition Airdrops Arms," World Roundup (AP), *Jacksonville Daily News* (NC), 4 April 2015, p. B1.

5. "The Battle for Nigeria," by Baker.

6. Sun Tzu, *The Art of War,* trans. Samuel B. Griffith, foreword by B.H. Liddell Hart (New York: Oxford Univ. Press, 1963).

7. Ibid.

8. *World Almanac of Islamism,* s.v. "Boko Haram."

9. "Cameroon Army Arrests Mayor of Fotokol, 300 Boko Haram Members, Find Huge Stockpile of Ammunitions in His Residence," *Udumakalu Word Press* (Nigeria), 14 October 2014.

10. "Chad Army Says Kills 120 Boko Haram Militants in Cameroon," *Reuters News* on line, 31 January 2015; "3 African Nations Battle Boko Haram," by Haruna Umar and Michelle Faul (AP), *Jacksonville Daily News* (NC), 5 February 2015, p. B1.

11. "Police Arrest 60 for Bombing in Chad Capital," World Roundup (AP), *Jacksonville Daily News* (NC), 29 June 2015, p. A8; "Rebels Gun Down 97 People Praying," News Roundup (AP), *Jacksonville Daily News* (NC), 3 July 2015, p. B1.

12. "Boko Haram: Spotlight on Human Trafficking," *World Policy Journal* (New York), 22 May 2014.

13. "Nigeria's Boko Haram 'Abducts More Women and Girls'," *BBC News* on line, 23 October 2014.

14. "Islam in Africa Newsletter," by Terdman and Paz; "Tribal Militants Claimed Responsibility for Another Attack on an Energy Installation"; *ABC's Nightly News,* 18 April 2006.

15. "Islam in Africa Newsletter," by Terdman and Paz.

16. MEND photograph, in "Curse of the Black Gold: Hope and Betrayal in the Niger Delta," *National Geographic,* February 2007, pp. 88-117.

17. "Islam in Africa Newsletter," by Terdman and Paz.

18. *ABC's Nightly News,* 18 April 2006.

19. "Who Are Nigeria's Mend Oil Militants," by Duffield; *ABC's Nightly News,* 7 January 2007; "Nigeria's MEND Rebels Threaten Future Attack on Oil Industry," by Elisha Bala-Gbogbo, *Bloomberg News* on line, 27 January 2014.

20. "Death Toll Rises from Car Bomb in Nigerian Capital Abuja," from AP, *The Guardian* (U.K.) on line, 1 May 2014; "Islamic Group Says It Was Behind Fatal Nigeria Attack," by Adam Nossiter, *New York Times* on line, 28 August 2011.

21. *World Almanac of Islamism,* s.v. "Boko Haram."

22. "The Battle for Nigeria," by Baker, pp. 36, 37.

23. *Encyclopedia Britannica,* s.v. "Bornu" and "Kanem-Bornu" and "Kukawa."

24. *World Almanac of Islamism,* s.v. "Boko Haram."

25. "The Battle for Nigeria," by Baker, p. 37.

26. "Boko Haram, Dawood Tie Up to Sell Drugs in India"; *NPR's "Morning Edition" News*, 19 July 2014; "U.S., Liberia Join Forces in Operation Relentless"; *Wikipedia Encyclopedia,* s.v. "List of Active Rebel Groups."

27. *World Drug Report 2010,* p. 84.

28. *World Almanac of Islamism,* s.v. "Boko Haram."

29. "Boko Harma Attacks Two Towns in Niger," from AP, *Jacksonville Daily News* (NC), 7 February 2015, p. B-1.

30. "Niger Campaigners Call for More Details on Oil Deal with China," from AFP, *Energy Daily,* 30 July 2008.

Chapter 18: *Oil & Mineral Removal through Aid Projects*

1. "Critical Raw Materials," *British Geological Survey,* n.d.; *CBS's "60 Minutes,"* 22 March 2015.

2. "2009 Minerals Yearbook, Tungsten Table 15," *U.S. Geological Survey,* n.d.; *Wikipedia Encyclopedia,* s.v "Tungsten."

3. "Somika—Cobalt," Societe Miniere du Katanga, n.d.

4. "Cobalt Faces a Looming Supply Disruption Threat," by Phil Burgert, *Futures Magazine* on line, 9 February 2012.

5. "Africa: Developed Countries' Leverage On the Continent," by Ravinder Rena, *AllAfrica News* on line, 7 February 2008; "Africa, China's New Frontier," *The Times* on line (U.K.), 10 February, 2008; "Chromium," SearchMining.net, n.d.

6. "China in Africa," IDE-JETRO, par. 8.

7. "China Tightens Grip on Africa with $4.4bn Lifeline for Guinea Junta," by Clayton.

8. Ibid.

9. Hutchison Whampoa's website, www.hutchison-whampoa.com/en.

10. "China, South Sudan to Further Reciprocal Cooperation," *Xinhua News Service* on line, 1 July 2014.

11. "China, Congo Trade for What the Other Wants," by Gwen Thompkins, *China's Rising Power in Africa,* part 3, *NPR,* 30 July 2008.

12. "The Mega-Port That Threatens to Sink Sudan," by Tom Stevenson, *Al Jazeera News* on line, 13 October 2013.

13. "Future Kenya Port Could Mar Pristine Land," by Jeffrey Gentleman, *New York Times* on line, 11 January 2010.

14. "Construction of Lamu Port Berths Set for June," by Martin Mwita, *The Star* on line (Nairobi), 10 March 2014; "Lamu Port Construction to Commence Soon," by Danson Kagai, *Kenya Construction Business Review* on line, 27 July 2011.

15. CCCC's website, http://en.ccccltd.cn; *Wikipedia Encyclopedia,* s.v. "List of State-Owned Enterprises in China."

16. CRBC's website, http://www.crbc.com.

17. "Pakistan Is Handing Over De-Facto Control of the Strategic Gilgit-Baltistan Region," *Rediff News* (India); "More Than Troops, Chinese Projects in PoK Worry India," by Pranab Dhal Samanta, *Indian Express* (Delhi), 5 September 2010, reprinted by Yahoo News, 5 September 2010.

18. "Kenya Attack: Mpeketoni near Lamu Hit by al-Shabab Raid," *BBC News* on line, 16 June 2014.

19. "Kenyan Coastal Region of Lamu Hit by Deadly Attacks," *BBC News* on line, 6 July 2014.

20. "Construction of Lamu Port Berths Set for June."

21. "Kenyan Coastal Region of Lamu Hit by Deadly Attacks."

22. Lamu Port Agency's website, http://lamuportagency.com.

23. "End of the Line for 'Lunatic Express?' Kenya Begins Multi-Billion Dollar Railway," by Ott.

24. "Mozambique: Government Seeks Funding for Nacala Deep Water Port," *AllAfrica News* on line, 22 June 2012; "Multipurpose Port Terminal in Nacala, Mozambique to be Operational This Year," *Macauhub News* on line, 27 January 2014.

25. "'Into Africa'—How Chinese Funding Helps Fuel an African Rail Boom," *SmartRailWorld* on line, 29 November 2013.

26. Ibid.

27. "Cameroon's $1b China-Funded Port to Boost West African Cargo Flows," by Emmanuel Tuanjong, *Wall Street Journal* on line, 14 May 2014.

28. "LAPSSET: A Peep at the East African Trade Corridor," *Ventures Africa* on line, 10 January 2014.

29. "Angola's Chinese-Built Rail Link and the Scramble to Access the Region's Resources," *China Africa Reporting Project* on line, 26 February 2014.

30. "China, Congo Trade for What the Other Wants."

31. "Report of . . . Experts on the Illegal Exploitation of Natural Resources . . . of the Democratic Republic of the Congo," Letter from the (U.N.) Secretary General to President of the Security Council, 12 April 2001; "Fighting an Invisible Enemy in DRC," *IRIN News* (U.N.), 9 April 2014; "China's FM in First Visit to New Ally Malawi," *The Namibian,* 16 January 2009; "Viewpoint: Why DR Congo's Volcano City of Goma Matters," by Theodore Trefon, *BBC News* on line, 20 November 2012.

32. "China, Congo Trade For What The Other Wants."

33. "Beijing's Blue Berets: U.N. Peacekeeping and the Evolution of Chinese Diplomacy," by Richardson; "Viewpoint: Why DR Congo's Volcano Ci."

34. "Report of . . . Experts on the Illegal Exploitation of Natural Resources . . . of the Democratic Republic of the Congo."

35. Ibid.

Chapter 19: *China's Sun-Tzu-Like Agenda*

1. *Unrestricted Warfare,* by Qiao Liang and Wang Xiangsui, pp. 221, 222.
2. Ibid.
3. "China in Africa," IDE-JETRO, intro.
4. Ibid., par. 2.
5. Ibid., par. 3.
6. "China and African Peacekeeping," by Weitz.
7. Ibid.; "China's Involvement in African Conflict Zones," by Shinn; "South Sudanese Rebels Slam China's Conflicting Roles."
8. "China-Africa Relations in the 21st Century," by Parneti; "Sudan's Use of Chinese Arms Shows Beijing's Balancing Act," by Jared Ferrie, *Bloomberg News* on line, 30 April 2012; *China and Africa: A Century of Engagement,* by David H. Shinn and Joshua Eisenman (Philadelphia: Univ. of Pennsylvania Press, 2012), pp. 174-178.
9. "New Cold War in Africa," by Nick Terse, The Nation Inst. (N.Y.) *The Investigative Fund,* 31 July 2014.
10. "China in Africa," IDE-JETRO, par. 3.
11. Ibid., par. 5.
12. Ibid., par. 7.
13. *Unrestricted Warfare,* by Qiao Liang and Wang Xiangsui, p. 55.

Chapter 20: *Proof of PRC Drug Trade Involvement*

1. "Beijing Orders Army to Give Up Its Businesses," by Henry Chu, *L.A. Times* on line, 23 July 1998.
2. "Peoples Liberation Army Inc.: Big Business, Big Trouble," by Liz Sly, *Chicago Tribune* on line, 16 August 1998.
3. *CIA World Factbook,* s.v. "China."
4. Menges, *China: The Gathering Threat,* pp. 395, 398; Santoli, "The Panama Canal in Transition"; Gertz, *The China Threat,* pp. 82, 94.

5. "Guinea-Bissau: China Sees a Risk Worth Taking," by Loro Horta, Ctr. for Strategic and Internat. Studies (Washington, D.C.), 9 December 2014.

6. *CIA World Factbook,* s.v. "Guinea-Bissau," "Burkina Faso," "Mali," and "Niger."

7. "Guinea-Bissau: China Sees a Risk Worth Taking," by Horta.

8. Ibid.

9. "Africa a New Conduit for Europe's Drugs," by Callimachi (AP).

10. "DEA Charges Four with Trafficking Heroin from Africa," by Jerry Seper, *Washington Times* on line, 5 June 2013.

11. Ibid.

12. "Afghan Opium Production Explodes Despite Billions Spent, Says U.S. Report," by Spencer Ackerman, *The Guardian* (U.K.) on line, 30 April 2014.

13. "DoD Report: Losing War on Afghan Drug Trade," by Richard Sisk, Military.com, 18 November 2013.

14. *NPR's "Morning Edition News,"* 29 June 2015.

15. "Why West Africa Cannot Break Its Drug Habit," by Rose Skelton, *BBC News* on line, 21 June 2010.

16. Ibid.

17. "Africa Reemerging as Heroin Trafficking Hub: U.N.," by Sylvia Westall, *Reuters News* on line, 30 July 2011.

18. *A History of the DEA: 1985-1990,* p. 62.

19. *A History of the DEA: 1990-1994,* p. 80.

20. *A History of the DEA: 1994-1998,* p. 98.

21. *A History of the DEA: 1999-2003*, pp. 117, 133.

22. "The Opium Kings," *PBS's Frontline*, NC Public TV, n.d.

23. *A History of the DEA: 2003-2008,* pp. 172, 173.

24. "Heroin Makes a Comeback," by Elinson; *CIA World Factbook,* s.v. "Illicit Drugs—World."

25. DEA Chief Jack Dawn in testimony before the Senate Intel. Committee, and CIA assessment in September 1988, as quoted in *Seeds of Terror,* by Peters; "The Spoils of War: Afghanistan's Multibillion Dollar Heroin Trade," by Professor Michel Chossudovsky, *Global Research,* 15 February 2014.

26. Santoli, "The Panama Canal in Transition."

27. *CIA World Factbook,* s.v. "China."

28. "Chinese Gangs Fuel Meth Scourge in U.S.," by Philipp; *CIA World Factbook,* s.v. "Mexico."

29. "Do I Look Dangerous to You," by Dannen.

30. "Chinese Gangs Fuel Meth Scourge in U.S.," by Philipp.

31. "Chinese Organised Crime and Africa," by Gary K. Busch, *Gangsters Inc.,* 30 July 2014.

32. "China Uncooperative in Stopping Meth Flow," Joshua Philipp, China Society Internat., *Epoch Times*, 3 March 2014.

33. "Heroin Makes a Comeback," by Elinson.
34. "Unrestricted Warfare and Drug Smuggling," by John Poole, *The Counter Terrorist,* January/February 2014.

Chapter 21: The *PRC's Overall Occupation of Africa*

1. "China in Africa," IDE-JETRO, par. 6.
2. "China 'Offers Troops' to U.N. Mali Peacekeeping Mission"; "China to Send 700 Combat Troops to South Sudan," by Smith.
3. "China Puts 700,000 Troops on Alert in Sudan"; Gertz, "Notes from the Pentagon"; "China Winning Resources and Loyalties of Africa."
4. "China's Expanding Peacekeeping Role," by Bates Gill and Chin-hao Huang, Stockholm Internat. Peace Research Inst., January 2009.
5. "Inside China: Long March to Africa," by Miles Yu, *Washington Times,* 6 March 2014.
6. "China to Open Its First Military Base Abroad in Indian Ocean," *NDTV* (India), 12 December 2011.
7. "China Mulls Building Naval Base in Namibia, Namibian Times Says," by David Tweed, *Bloomberg News* on line, 27 November 2014; "Chinese Paper Advises PLA Navy to Build Overseas Military Bases," *China Defense Mashup* (Beijing), 8 January 2013.
8. *NPR's "Morning Edition" News,* 1 June 2015; "China Defends Land Reclamation in the Spratly Islands," *Military Times* on line, 24 November 2014.
9. "China in Africa," IDE-JETRO, par. 6.
10. *NPR's "Morning Edition" News*, 29 October 2014.
11. "Zambia's President, 'King Cobra' Sata, Dies in London," *Reuters News* on line, 29 October 2014.
12. "Zambian President Michael Sata Dies in London," *BBC News* on *NPR,* Public Radio East (New Bern, NC), 29 October 2014.
13. "Michael Sata Obituary," by Stephen Chan, *The Guardian* (U.K.), 29 October 2014.
14. *China and Africa: Engagement and Compromise,*" by Ian Taylor, (New York: Routledge, 2006), pp. 96-102; Lady formerly married to South African army major, in conversation with author on 12 April 2015; *Wikipedia Encyclopedia,* s.v. "1986 Mozambiquan Tupolev Tu-134 Crash."
15. Memorandum for the record from H.J. Poole.
16. South African business woman of Indian descent, in conversation with author on 6 May 2015.

17. "S. African Police Arrest Thousands," World Roundup (AP), *Jacksonville Daily News* (NC), 22 May 2015, p. B1.

18. "Special Report: Congo," Internat. Rescue Committee, December 2014.

19. Menges, *China: The Gathering Threat,* p. 55; R.J. Rummel, *Death by Government* (N.p., n.d.), pp. 100-101, op. cit., p. 54.

20. *Tracking Chinese Development Finance* (http://china.aiddata.org.), s.v. "DRC," "Angola," "Somalia," and all other countries in their respective categories on Table 21.1.

21. Ibid.

22. Ibid.

23. "Chinese Presence in Tibet: Population Transfer," *Tibet Online,* n.d.; "Uighurs and China's Xinjiang Region," by Preeti Bhattacharji, Council on Foreign Relations, *Backgrounder,* 29 May 2012.

24. "Chinese Presence in Tibet: Population Transfer."

25. Ibid.

26. Menges, *China: The Gathering Threat,* p. 55; R.J. Rummel, *Death by Government* (N.p., n.d.), pp. 100-101, op. cit., p. 54; Seventy-year-old Chinese man (at Shanghai airport), in conversation with author in June 2000.

27. Truscott, "Short Lives Lead to Short-Term Goals in Zimbabwe," p. 4.

28. Hoile, *Mozambique—A Nation in Crisis*, p. 36, in *The Silent War,* by Stiff, p. 156.

29. "Land Tenure and Mining in Tanzania," by Lange.

30. "China's Policy in Africa 1958-71," by Alaba Ogunsanwo (London: Cambridge Univ. Press, n.d.).

31. *Global Policy Forum* (www.globalpolicy.org), s.v. "Sudan/Darfur."

32. "China Ends One Notorious Form of Detention, But Keeps Others," *NPR News* on line, 5 February 2014.

33. Ibid.

34. Ibid.

35. Ibid.

36. "Opening Statement by Dr. Graham T. Allison before the United States Senate Committee on Armed Services at a Hearing Convened to Discuss 'China, the U.S., and the Asia-Pacific'."

Chapter 22: *Research Projection vs. On-Site Reality*

1. *BBC Country Profiles,* s.v. "Zambia."

2. Airport representative for Lusaka's best hotel, in conversation with author on 6 May 2015; Contract driver for Lusaka's best hotel, in conversation with author on 8 May 2015.

3. Anonymous resident #1 of Lusaka, in conversation with author on 8 May 2015.

4. *CIA World Factbook,* s.v. "Zambia."

5. Acting manager of Lusaka's National Museum, in conversation with author on 7 May 2015.

6. Contract driver for Lusaka's best hotel, in conversation with author on 8 May 2015.

7. Anonymous resident #2 of Lusaka, in conversation with author on 7 May 2015.

8. Memorandum for the record from H.J. Poole.

9. "Sata's Legacy Buried at Embassy Park—Mucheleka," *Sunday Post,* 10 May 2015.

10. *CIA World Factbook,* s.v. "Zambia."

11. *Encyclopedia Britannica,* s.v. "Movement for Multiparty Democracy"; "China's Stake in Zambia's Election," by Redvers.

12. "Sata's Legacy Buried at Embassy Park—Mucheleka."

13. "100 Days of President Lungu's Decision Making," *Zambia Daily Mail*, 7 May 2015, p. 4 of four-page insert.

14. "Govt. Hides $192m Loan," *Saturday Post* (Lusaka), 9 May 2015, p. 1.

15. "$192m Loan Expose Angers Govt.," *Sunday Post* (Lusaka), 10 May 2015.

16. Contract driver for Lusaka's best hotel, in conversation with author on 8 May 2015.

17. "Mumena Extols Lungu over Mineral Royalty," by Nkombo Kachemba, *Zambia Daily Mail,* 8 May 2015.

18. "Grand Coalition Abandon UPND," *Sunday Nation* (Lusaka), 10 May 2015, p. 1.

19. "Sata's Legacy Buried at Embassy Park—Mucheleka."

20. "Yan'an Chronicles: Election Campaign Reached Villages," *Along the Frontier Series,* episode #63, documentary from China Central Television, as viewed through Lusaka CCTV9 on 8 May 2015.

21. "Lungu Blasts U.N.," *Sunday Nation,* 10 May 2015.

22. Contract driver for Lusaka's best hotel, in conversation with author on 8 May 2015.

23. Memorandum for the record from H.J. Poole.

24. TANZAM station manager in Kapiri Mposhi, Zambia, in conversation with author on 8 May 2015.

25. Contract driver for Lusaka's best hotel, in conversation with author on 8 May 2015.

26. Ibid.

27. "Zambia: Developing a Railway Strategy," by Glory K. Jonga, CPCS Transcom, 1 April 2011.

28. "New Firm Sub-Contracted to Work on Chingola-Solwezi Road," *Lusaka Times* on line, 30 January 2014.

29. "State Owned Assets Supervision and Administration Commission of the State Council," by the PRC, n.d.

Chapter 23: *The DRC Situation Comes into Focus*

1. South African Development Community (SADC) website (http://www.sadc.int/).
2. Peter Stiff, *Cry Zimbabwe: Independence—20 Years On* (Alberton, South Africa: Galago Publishing 2000), p. 468.
3. South African Development Community (SADC) website, "SADC Institutions—Summit Troika of the Organ."
4. Menges, *China: The Gathering Threat,* p. 428; *Wikipedia Encyclopedia,* s.v. "Non-Aligned Movement"; "U.S. Hopes China Will Help Moderate Havana Meeting," *China Confidential,* 11 September 2006.
5. "Zimbabwean President Robert Mugabe on an Official Visit to China," *Vatican Radio,* 25 Aug. 2014.
6. "100 Days of President Lungu's Decision Making."
7. *Encyclopedia Britannica,* s.v. "Laurent Kabila."
8. Ibid., s.v. "Joseph Kabila."
9. Stiff, Cry Zimbabwe, p. 100.
10. Ibid., p. 208; *Encyclopedia Britannica,* s.v. "Joshua Nkomo."
11. Stiff, *Cry Zimbabwe,* pp. 180-182.
12. Ibid., p. 182.
13. Ibid., pp. 154, 180, and 194.
14. "Breaking the Silence: A Report of the Disturbances in Matabeleland the Midlands, 1980-1988," Catholic Commission for Justice and Peace in Zimbabwe (Harare, 1997), in Stiff, *Cry Zimbabwe,* p. 182.
15. Stiff, *Cry Zimbabwe,* p. 181; *Wikipedia Encyclopedia,* s.v. "Gukurahundi."
16. Mugabe as quoted at "Breaking the Silence," p. 45, in Stiff, *Cry Zimbabwe,* p. 181.
17. Stiff, *Cry Zimbabwe,* p. 193.
18. "Hotel Rwanda," DVD, 121 minutes, MGM, 200417.
19. *Genocide Watch—DRC* (http://www.genocidewatch.org/drofcongo.html), s.v. "DRC Country Profile, 1 Dec. 2012."
20. "DRC: Interview with Rebel General Laurent Nkunda," *IRIN News* (U.N.), 2 September 2004.
21. *Human Rights Watch* (https://www.hrw.org/ and genocidewatch.net), s.v. "DRC."
22. "DRC Soldiers 'Ordered to Rape' Women," *BBC News,* 11 April 2013.

23. *Genocide Watch – DRC* (http://www.genocidewatch.org/drofcongo.html), s.v. "Genocide Emergency: Democratic Republic of the Congo, 7 February 2012, updated 25 April 2012."

24. "Crisis in the Democratic Republic of the Congo," International Coalition for the Responsibility to Protect, n.d.

25. *Genocide Watch – DRC* (http://www.genocidewatch.org/drofcongo.html), s.v. "Genocide and Mass Atrocity Warning: Democratic Republic of the Congo – the Kivus, 3 October 2012."

26. "DRC: Interview with Rebel General Laurent Nkunda."

27. "Grindrod to Build $989 Million Zambia Mine Railway Route," by Matthew Hill, *Bloomberg News* on line, 3 February 2014.

28. Contract driver for Lusaka's best hotel, in conversation with author on 8 May 2015.

Chapter 24: *Countering China's Influence*

1. *Gung Ho: The Corps' Most Progressive Tradition,* by H. John Poole (Emerald Isle, NC: Posterity Press, 2012), chapt. 14.

2. Assn. of the Combined Action Program's website; Jack Shulimson, *U.S. Marines in Vietnam . . . 1966,* HQMC, 1982, p. 239, in *Our War Was Different* by Hemingway, p. 6; "Fact Sheet on the Combined Action Force," III MAF, 31 March 1970.

3. *Gung Ho,* by Poole, chapt. 14.

4. William C. Westmoreland, *A Soldier Reports* (New York: Da Capo Press, 1989), as quoted in *Wikipedia Encyclopedia,* s.v. "Combined Action Platoon."

5. *Publishers Weekly Review* at Amazon.com of *Our War Was Different,* by Hemingway (Annapolis, MD: Naval Inst. Press, 1994).

6. Navaho codetalker, in "Japanese Codetalkers," *In Search of History,* Hist. Channel, 30 March 1999; Marine infantryman, as quoted in *Iwo Jima: Legacy of Valor,* by Bill D. Ross (New York: Vintage, 1986), p. 135.

7. Memorandum for the record from H.J. Poole.

8. "Rare Access to the Hunt for African Warlord Joseph Kony," *BBC News* on line, 24 November 2014.

9. "Joseph Kony Hunt is Proving Difficult for U.S. Troops," *Washington Post,* 29 April 2012.

10. Ibid.

11. Ibid.

12. "Fighting an Invisible Enemy in DRC," *IRIN News* (U.N.), 9 April 2014; "Report of . . . Experts on the Illegal Exploitation of Natural Resources . . . of the Democratic Republic of the Congo"; "Democratic Republic of Cong," by Arieff.

13. *CIA World Factbook,* s.v. "Democratic Republic of the Congo" and "Zimbabwe."

14. "Fighting an Invisible Enemy in DRC"; "China's FM in First Visit to New Ally Malawi," *The Namibian,* 16 January 2009.

15. "China to Send 700 Combat Troops to South Sudan," by Smith.

16. "China and African Peacekeeping," by Weitz; "Peacekeeping Fact Sheet," U.N.'s website, 30 September 2014.

17. "Troop and Police Contributors," U.N.'s website, n.d.

18. *Global Security* (globalsecurity.org), s.v. "People's Liberation Army"; *Wikipedia Encyclopedia,* s.v. "People's Liberation Army."

19. "China and African Peacekeeping," by Weitz; "China's Involvement in African Conflict Zones," by Shinn.

20. *NPR's "Morning Edition" News,* 19 July 2014.

21. African Union Mission in Somalia's (AMISOM's) website (http://amisom-au.org), s.v. "Frequently Asked Questions."

22. "Popes Connected with Fatima," The World Apostolate of Fatima, *Soul,* Fall 2014, pp. 5, 6.

Afterword: *Wake-Up Call for Americans*

1. "U.S. Surveillance Plane Lands in China after Collision with Fighter," *CNN's Headline News,* 1 April 2001; "Spy Plane" article series from *Washington Post*: (1) "China Says It Will Return Disassembled U.S. Plane," 25 May 2001; (2) "Surveillance Plane to Be Returned to U.S. in Pieces," 30 May 2001; (3) "U.S., China Agree on Plan to Return Spy Plane: U.S. Team Arrives in China to Begin Dismantling Jet," 7 June 2001; (4) "Disassembled Navy Plane Scheduled to Leave China Today," 3 July 2001; (5) "China Bills U.S. Over Collision: $1 Million in Surveillance Plane Dispute Termed 'Exaggerated' ," 7 July 2001; and (6) "U.S. to Pay China $34,567 for Costs of Downed Plane," 10 August 2001; *Homeland Siege,* by Poole, pp. 4-7.

2. AFP-published estimate in *Twentieth Century Atlas—Death Tolls;* Jean-Louis Margolin estimate in *The China Threat,* by Gertz, p. xxi; *Wikipedia Encyclopedia,* s.v. "Cultural Revolution."

3. "Businessman at White House Social Has Close Ties to China's Military Power," by David E. Sanger, *New York Times* on line, 21 December 1996.

4. "Who Needs the Panama Canal," by Robert Morton, *Washington Times,* nat. weekly edition, 1-8 March 1999, as reprinted in *World Tribune,* 4 March 1999.

5. China's State Commission of Science, Technology and Industry for National Defense, as quoted in "Chinese Military to Make Billions through Capitalism," *Geostrategy Direct,* 16 January 2008.

6. Gertz, *The China Threat,* pp. 76, 78, 80, 91, 92; "The Panama Canal and United States Interests," ed. Jesse Helms, Congressional Hearing, 16 June 1998, p. 12.

7. "Analysts: By 2025, U.S. Won't Be Top World Power," by Tom Gjelten, *NPR's "Morning Edition" News,* 21 November 2008 (a review of *Global Trends 2025: The National Intelligence Council's 2025 Project).*

8. "Arming Genocide in Rwanda: The High Cost of Small Arms Transfers," by Goose and Smyth.

9. "Beijing Orders Army to Give Up Its Businesses," by Chu.

10. "China's Military Rise: The Dragon's New Teeth."

11. Ibid.

12. *CBS's "60 Minutes,"* 23 November 2014.

13. "China's Largest Port Builder Delays $3 Billion Shanghai Offering," *Bloomberg Businessweek,* 8 July 2011.

14. "Chinese Meat Firm With Terrible Food Safety Record Buys The Largest Pork Producer In The U.S," by Aviva Shen, *Ctr. for American Progress Action Fund,* 31 May 2013.

15. CEIEC website (http://www.ceiec.com), s.v. "Business Network," as retrieved in November 2014 from the following partially encoded url: http://www.ceiec.com/content/%E9%A9%BB%E5%A4%96%E6%9C%BA%E6%9E%84.

16. Ibid.; Smith, "U.S. Bombs Chinese Network in Afghanistan, PRC Sold Taliban Advanced Air Defense System; Mohan Malik, *Dragon on Terrorism: Assessing China's Tactical Gains and Strategic Losses Post-September 11* (Carlisle, PA: Strategic Studies Inst., U. S. Army War College, October 2002), p. 12.

17. Shane Harris, "China's Cyber-Militia," *National Journal Magazine,* 31 May 2008.

18. Katzman, *Warriors of Islam,* pp. 82-84; "Iran's Revolutionary Guards," by Greg Bruno, Jayshree Bajoria, and Jonathan Masters, Council on Foreign Relations, *Backgrounder,* 14 June 2013; 9. "Quds Force Leader, Commanding Iraqi forces against ISIS, Alarms Washington," by James Rosen, *Fox News* on line, 5 March 2015.

Glossary

ABC	American Broadcasting Company	U.S. TV network.
AIAI	*Al-Itihadd al-Islamiya*	Somali chapter of Muslim Brotherhood.
AIM	Armed Islamic Movement	Muslim Brotherhood try within Sudan to organize regional *jihad*. Same as PAIC and INF.
ANC	African National Congress	PRC-backed South African rebels that switched to Soviet. Now part of ruling tri coalition with SACP and COSATU.
AP	Associated Press	U.S. news service
AQAP	*Al-Qaeda* in the Arabian Peninsula	Radical Sunni rebels in Yemen
AQIM	*Al-Qaeda* in the Islamic Maghreb	Radical Sunni rebels in Algeria and areas to immediate south.
AU	African Union	Coalition of nations
BBC	British Broadcasting Corporation	Radio & TV network
CAP	Combined Action Platoon	U.S. squad as part of local militia platoon.
CAR	Central African Republic	African nation.
CBC	Canadian Broadcasting Corporation	Canada's TV network
CBS	Columbia Broadcasting System	U.S. TV network.
CCCCLTD	China Communications Construction Company Limited	State-owned firm of PRC. Parent of CRBC and CHEC.
CCECC	China Civil Engineering Construction Corporation	State-owned firm in PRC. Subsidiary of CRCC.
CDR	Committees for the Defense of the Revolution	Cuban community watch network.

CEIEC	China National Electronics Import and Export Corporation	Telecommunications provider from PRC. May be PLA-owned.
CHEC	China Harbor Engineering Company	State-owned firm of PRC. Subsidiary of CCCCLTD.
CIA	Central Intelligence Agency	U.S. spy agency.
CNDP	National Congress for the Defence of the People	DRC Tutsi rebel forerunner to M23.
CNODC	China National Oil and Gas Development Exploration Corporation	State-owned firm from PRC operating in Niger.
COSATU	Congress of South African Trade Unions	Now part of ruling tri-partite coalition with ANC and SACP.
COSCO	China Ocean Shipping Company	State-owned boat conglomerate of PRC.
CPC	Communist Party of China	PRC's ruling party.
CPPCC	Chinese People's Political Consultative Conference	PRC agency that shows other nations how to run a national assembly (congress)
CRBC	China Road and Bridge Corporation	State-owned firm of PRC. Subsidiary of CCCCLTD.
CRCC	China Railway Construction Corporation	State-owned firm of PRC
CRECG	China Railway Engineering Corporation/China Railway Group	State-owned firm of PRC
CRSSG	China Railway Shisiju Group Corporation	State-owned firm of PRC.
CS	Confidential Source	Anonymous witness.
CSCEC	China State Construction Engineering Corporation	State-owned firm of PRC.
D.C.	District of Columbia	U.S. capitol location
DEA	Drug Enforcement Administration	U.S. narcotics agency
DIA	Defense Intelligence Agency	U.S. military espionage outfit.
DMI	Department of Military Intelligence	PLA spy agency.
DNA	Deoxyribonucleic acid	Molecule encoding genetic instructions.
DPRK	Democratic People's Republic of Korea	North Korea
DRC	Democratic Republic of the Congo	African nation.

DTO	Drug Trafficking Organization	Organized-crime purveyor of narcotics.
E&E	Escape and Evasion	Eluding pursuit.
EIJM	Eritrean Islamic Jihad Movement	Eritrean insurgents.
ELF	Eritrean Liberation Front	First Eritrean rebels. supported by China.
EPLF	Eritrean People's Liberation Front	Offshoot of the ELF supported by Soviets.
EPRDF	Ethiopian People's Revolutionary Democratic Front	Ruling party of Ethiopia.
E.U.	European Union	Coalition of nations
FAPLA	People's Armed Forces for Liberation of Angola	MPLA's military wing.
FARC	*Fuerzas Armadas Revolucionarias de Colombia*	Maoist rebels in Colombia.
FBI	Federal Bureau of Investigation	U.S. law enforcement agency.
FDLR	*Forces Democratiques de Liberation du Rwanda*	DRC Hutus against Tutsi influence in the region. Still contains perpetrators of 1994 Rwandan genocide.
FFM	*Frente Francisco de Miranda*	Venezuelan youth movement.
FMCR	Fleet Marine Forces Reserve	Inactive status for enlisted Marines who leave active duty after 20 years.
FMS	Foreign Military Sales	Arms trade to other countries.
FNLA	National Liberation Front of Angola	PRC-backed rebels in Angola.
4GW	Fourth Generation Warfare	Four-arena conflict: martial, economic, political, religious.
FRELIMO	Mozambique Liberation Front	PRC-backed rebels in Mozambique.
FUDOC	United Front for Democratic Change	Chadian insurgents.
GDP	Gross Domestic Product	Value of providing goods and services as adjusted for price changes.
GI	Government Issue	Colloquial term for U.S. service member.

GNC	General National Congress	First publicly elected congress in Libya.
HIND	Soviet airplane designator	Helicopter gunship.
HRW	Human Rights Watch	Nonprofit monitoring organization.
INF	Islamic National Front	Same as PAIC, AIM.
INTERPOL	International Criminal Police Organization	Transnational law enforcement agency.
IRGC	Iranian Revolutionary Guard Corps	Iranian commandos.
ISIS	Islamic State of Iraq and Syria	Self-proclaimed caliphate to which other radical factions pledge allegiance.
ISL	Islamic State of the Levant	Same as ISIS.
JCP	Justice and Construction Party	Party representing Muslim Brotherhood in modern-day Libya.
JEM	Justice and Equality Movement	Islamist insurgents in northern Sudan. Belongs, with SPLM-N, to Sudan Revolutionary Front.
LAPSSET	Lamu Port and New Transport Corridor Development to Southern Sudan and Ethiopia	Petroleum conduit from Sudan's Abeyei Oil Fields to new Kenyan super-port.
LIFG	Libyan Islamic Fighting Group	Insurgents in Western Libya.
LRA	Lord's Resistance Army	Ugandan rebels who operate regionally with child soldiers.
LROR	Libya Revolutionary Operation's Room	Militia that recently seized Libyan capital
M23	March 23 Movement	Tutsi rebel army in Eastern DRC that is made up of former government soldiers. Opposes Hutu FDLR.
MCC	China Metallurgical Group Corporation	State-owned firm in PRC.
MDC	Movement for Democratic Change	Opposition party in Zimbabwe.
MEND	Movement for the Emancipation of the Niger Delta	Non-Islamic rebels in Nigeria.
MIG-19	Soviet airplane designator	Jet fighter-bomber.

MIG-23	Soviet airplane designator	Jet fighter-bomber.
MK	*Umkhonto we Sizwe*	Armed wing of ANC.
MMD	The Movement for Multiparty Democracy	PRC-backed political party in Zambia.
MNLA	National Movement for the Liberation of Azawad	Rebels in Mali.
MOFCOM	Ministry of Commerce	Defacto head of PRC economic/business intelligence effort.
MOOTW	Military Operations Other Than War	PLA term
MPLA	People's Movement for the Liberation of Angola	Soviet-backed rebels in Angola.
MSS	Ministry of State Security	PRC spy agency.
MUJO	Unity Movement for Jihad in West Africa	Rebels in Mali.
MW	Maneuver Warfare	Way of fighting in which tactical surprise often takes the place of firepower
NAM	Nonaligned Movement	Loose alliance of developing nations
NBC	National Broadcasting Company	U.S. TV network.
NCO	Noncommissioned Officer	Corporal or junior sergeant in military.
NCP	National Congress Party	Sudan's current ruling party.
NDTA	National Drug Threat Assessment	Official prediction as to the danger of illicit narcotics in America.
NIF	National Islamic Front	Former ruling party of Sudan.
9/11	11 September 2001	Day Twin Towers fell in New York City.
NPR	National Public Radio	U.S. radio network.
NSS	National Seizure System	Tabulation of drug seizures by DEA.
OAS	Organization of American States	Western Hemisphere alliance of nations
OIC	Organization of Islamic Conference	Pakistan-inspired and Saudi-dominated political alliance.
ONLF	Ogaden National Liberation Front	Tribes of Somali descent that inhabit Ethiopian desert.

P-6	Soviet ship designator	PT boat.
PAC	Pan Africanist Congress	ANC offshoot in South Africa that kept PRC backing.
PAIC	Popular Arab and Islamic Conference	Same as AIM and INF.
PBS	Public Broadcasting System	U.S. TV network.
PDF	Popular Defense Force	Para-military wing of Sudan's ruling party.
PDRY	People's Democratic Republic of Yemen	What was Marxist South Yemen.
PF	Patriotic Front	Zambia ruling party
PFDJ	People's Front for Democracy and Justice	Eritrea's ruling party
PIJ	*Palestinian Islamic Jihad*	Levant militants.
PLA	People's Liberation Army	Entire PRC military.
PRC	People's Republic of China	Mainland China.
PT	Patrol Torpedo	Small boat carrying torpedoes.
RaFD	Rally of Democratic Forces	Chadian insurgents.
RCD	Rally for Congolese Democracy	Banyamulenge Tutsi DRC rebels.
RENAMO	Mozambique National Resistance	Initially Rhodesian-backed anti-Reds in Mozambique.
RPF	Rwandan Patriotic Front	Rwanda's ruling party
S-2	Headquarters staff designator	Intelligence section.
SA	South African	Anything from South Africa.
SACP	Communist Party of South Africa	Now part of ruling tri-partite coalition with ANC, COSATU.
2GW	Second Generation Warfare	Way of fighting that attempts to win through killing as many foe as possible.
SIPRI	Stockholm International Peace Research Institute	Swedish think-tank.
SPAF	Sudan Police Auxiliary Forces	Paramilitary police of Sudan before the South split off.
SPDF	Sudan People's Democratic Forces	Machar's new army in southern Sudan. Later became part of SPLA.

SPLA	Sudan People's Liberation Army	Rebel army in southern Sudan before its independence.
SPLA-Nasir	Sudan People's Liberation Army (Nasir)	Breakaway faction from SPLA that got Khartoum support. Same a SPLA-United or SSIM/A.
SPLA-United	Sudan People's Liberation Army (United)	Breakaway faction from SPLA that got Khartoum support. Same as SPLA-Nasir or SSIM/A.
SPLM	Sudan People's Liberation Movement	Ruling party of South Sudan.
SPLM-N	Sudan People's Liberation Movement-North	Islamist insurgents in northern Sudan. Belongs—with JEM—to Sudan Revolutionary Front.
SSLA	South Sudan Liberation Army	South Sudane rebels. Same as SSLM/A
SSLM/A	South Sudan Liberation Movement/Army	South Sudan rebels before independence. Same as SSLA, SPLA-United, and SPLA-Nasir.
SWA	Southwest Asian	Anything from there.
SWAPO	Southwest Africa's People's Organization	Soviet-backed rebels in Namibia.
T-62	Soviet armor designator	Tank.
TANZAM	Tanzania-Zambia (Railway)	Rail line between Dar es Salaam and Kapiri Mposhi in Zambia's "Copper Belt." Same as TAZARA.
TAZARA	Tanzania-Zambia Railway Authority	Same as TANZAM.
TV	Television	Visual way of electronically communicating.
UDP	Popular Defense Unit	Venezuelan home guard.

UFDD	Union of Forces for Democracy and Development	Arab-dominated rebels in Chad.
U.K.	United Kingdom	Great Britain
U.N.	United Nations	International body of nations.
UNIP	United National Independence Party	Only political party in Zambia until 1990. That of Kenneth Kaunda.
UNITA	National Union for the Total Independence of Angola	U.S., Zairean, and SA backed rebels in Angola.
UNODC	U.N. Office of Drugs and Crime	U.N. law enforcement department.
UNPKO	U.N. Peacekeeping Operation	U.N. attempt to split up warring parties.
U.S.	United States	America .
USMC	United States Marine Corps	America's amphibious landing force in readiness.
USSR	Union of Soviet Socialist Republics	Former Soviet Union
UW	Unconventional Warfare	Infantry aspects are E&E and how to fight like a guerrilla.
WIFJ	World Islamic Front for the Jihad against Jews and Crusaders	Osama bin Laden's attempt to promote worldwide *jihad.*
WWI	World War I	First global conflict.
WWII	World War II	Second global conflict
WWIII	World War III	Next global conflict.
ZANLA	Zimbabwe African National Liberation Army	Military wing of ZANU.
ZANU	Zimbabwe African National Union	PRC-backed rebels in Rhodesia.
ZANU PF	Zimbabwe African National Union Patriotic Front	Modern-day political party in Zimbabwe.
ZAPU	Zimbabwe African People's Union	Soviet-backed rebels in Rhodesia.
ZIPRA	Zimbabwe People's Revolutionary Army	Military wing of ZAPU.

Bibliography

U.S. Government Publications, Databases, News Releases, Images

"African Criminal Enterprises." Federal Bureau of Investigation, n.d. As retrieved in July 2014 from the following url: http://www.fbi.gov/about-us/investigate/organizedcrime/african.

"Algeria 2013 Crime and Safety Report." Bureau of Diplomatic Security. U.S. Department of State, 2 February 2014. As retrieved in November 2014 from the following url: https://www.osac.gov/Pages/ContentReportDetails.aspx?cid=14130.

"Antonio Indjai, Chief of the Guinea-Bissau Armed Forces, Charged . . . with . . . Narco-Terrorism Conspiracy." Drug Enforcement Administration News Bulletin, 18 April 2013. As retrieved in August 2014 from the following url: http://www.justice.gov/dea/divisions/hq/2013/hq041813.shtml.

Attorney General's Report to Congress on the Growth of Violent Street Gangs in Suburban Areas, April 2008. As retrieved in October 2008 from the National Drug Intelligence Center website, www.usdoj.gov/ndic.

"Background Note: Panama." U.S. Dept. of State, November 2007. From from its website, www.state.gov.

"Benin 2012 OSAC Crime and Safety Report." Bureau of Diplomatic Security. U.S. Department of State, 25 February 2012. As retrieved in November 2014 from the following url: https://www.osac.gov/Pages/ContentReportDetails.aspx?cid=12062.

"Benin 2014 Crime and Safety Report." Bureau of Diplomatic Security. U.S. Department of State, 1 July 2014. As retrieved in November 2014 from the following url: https://www.osac.gov/pages/ContentReportDetails.aspx?cid=15928.

"Chad 2013 Crime and Safety Report." Bureau of Diplomatic Security. U.S. Department of State, 16 April 2013. As retrieved in November 2014 from the following url: https://www.osac.gov/Pages/ContentReportDetails.aspx?cid=13895.

CIA World Factbook. As updated every three months. From its website (www.cia.gov), during the period July 2014—July 2017.

"Country Profile: Venezuela." Library of Congress. Federal Research Division, March 2005.

"Democratic Republic of Congo: Background and U.S. Policy." By Alexis Arieff. Congressional Research Service, 24 February 2014. As retrieved in November 2014 with the following document designator: fas.org/sgp/crs/row/R43166.pdf.

"Fact Sheet on the Combined Action Force." III Marine Amphibious Force (MAF), 31 March 1970. As retrieved from the Association of the Combined Action Program's website (http://www.cap-assoc.org/).

A History of the DEA. As retrieved in August 2014 from the following url: http://www.justice.gov/dea/about/history.shtml.

Intelligence. MCDP 2. Washington, D.C.: U.S. Marine Corps, 1997.

"The International Heroin Market." Office of National Drug Control Policy. The White House, n.d. As retrieved in July 2014 from url: http://www.whitehouse.gov/ondcp/global-heroin-market.

"Iran: U.S. Concerns and Policy Responses." By Kenneth Katzman. Congressional Research Service Report for Congress. Order Code RL32048, 26 October 2010.

Library of Congress Country Studies. Federal Research Division. From this url: http://lcweb2.loc.gov/frd/cs/cshome.html.

Malik, Mohan. *Dragon on Terrorism: Assessing China's Tactical Gains and Strategic Losses Post-September 11.* Carlisle, PA: Strategic Studies Institute, U. S. Army War College, October 2002.

National Drug Threat Assessment (for) 2008. National Drug Intelligence Center, October 2007.

National Drug Threat Assessment (for) 2009. National Drug Intelligence Center, December 2008. As retrieved from the NDIC website (www.usdoj.gov/ndic), in March 2009.

National Drug Threat Assessment (for) 2011. U.S. Department of Justice. National Drug Intelligence Center, August 2011. As retrieved in July 2014 with the following document designator: www.justice.gov/archive/ndic/pubs44/44849/44849p.pdf.

"Niger 2012 OSAC Crime and Safety Report." Bureau of Diplomatic Security. U.S. Department of State, 29 February 2012. As retrieved in November 2014 from the following url: https://www.osac.gov/Pages/ContentReportDetails.aspx?cid=12091.

"The Panama Canal and United States Interests." Edited by Jesse Helms. Congressional Hearing, 16 June 1998. As retrieved in December 2014 from the following url: https://books.google.com/books?id=W4LQOICV3McC&pg=PA12&lpg=PA12&dq=chinese+buy+rodman+naval+airstation&source=bl&ots=qapm4wD7wu&sig=CQAc1yxqu6jOl_Cf3nig5YLloP4&hl=en&sa=X&ei=K96nVOavM8y-ggTW-4JI&ved=0CCsQ6AEwBQ#v=onepage&q=chinese%20buy%20rodman%20naval%20airstation&f=false.

"Statement of the Honorable Thomas Harrigan, Deputy Administrator, Drug Enforcement Administration before the Senate Caucus on International Narcotics Control Regarding Countering Narcotics Threats in West Africa." U.S. Department of Justice, 16 May 2012. As retrieved in August 2014 with this document designator: http://www.justice.gov/dea/pr/speeches-testimony/2012-2009/051612_testimony.pdf.

"Terrorist and Organized Crime Groups in the Tri-Border Area." By Rex Hudson. Federal Research Division. Library of Congress, July 2003.

"Text of the Hezbollah International Financing Prevention Act of 2014." Congressional Bill, 23 July 2014. As retrieved in December 2014 from url: https://www.govtrack.us/congress/bills/113/hr4411/text.

"Togo 2014 Crime and Safety Report." Bureau of Diplomatic Security. U.S. Department of State, 24 July 2014. As retrieved in November 2014 from the following url: https://www.osac.gov/Pages/ContentReportDetails.aspx?cid=15890.

"Transnational Activities of Chinese Crime Organizations." By Glenn E. Curtis, Seth L. Elan, Rexford A. Hudson, and Nina A. Koll. Federal Research Division. Library of Congress, April 2003.

"2009 Minerals Yearbook, Tungsten Table 15." *U.S. Geological Survey* (http://www.usgs.gov), n.d. As retrieved in July 2014 with the following document designator: myb1-2009-tungs.pdf.

2013 National Drug Threat Assessment Summary. U.S. Department of Justice. National Drug Intelligence Center, n.d. As retrieved in July 2014 with document designator: http://www.justice.gov/dea/resource-center/DIR-017-13%20NDTA%20Summary%20final.pdf.

"U.S. Designates Dawood Ibrahim as Terrorist Supporter." U.S. Treasury Department Press Release, 16 October 2003.

"U.S., Liberia Join Forces in Operation Relentless." U.S. Dept. of Justice. Drug Enforcement Administration News Bulletin, 1 June 2010.

"Zambia." *Country Reports on Human Rights Practices for 2013*. Undersecretary for Civilian Security and Democracy. Bureau of Democracy, Human Rights, and Labor. U.S. Department of State, n.d. As retrieved in October 2014 with this document designator: http://www.state.gov/documents/organization/220386.pdf.

Civilian Publications

Analytical Studies, Databases, and Websites

ABC's News on line. From its website (http://www.abcnews.go.com).

African Union Mission in Somalia's website, http://amisom-au.org.
Al Jazeera News. From its website (www.america.aljazeera.com).
Association of the Combined Action Program's website, http://www.cap-assoc.org/.
BBC News and Country Profiles. From website (http://news.bbc.co.uk).
Bodansky, Yossef (Director of Research of the International Strategic Studies Association and Congressional Task Force on Terrorism and Unconventional Warfare). *Offensive in the Balkans*. Alexandria, VA: International Media Corporation, 1995. From "In Bosnia the West . . . Took the Side of . . . Fundamentalist Islam" at the Serbian Network website, www.srpska-mzeza.com.
Brautigam, Deborah. *The Dragon's Gift: The Real Story of China in Africa*. London. Oxford University Press, 2010.
Brookes, Peter. "Venezuelan Vagaries." *Armed Forces Journal*, July 2007.
CBS's News on line. From its website (http://www.cbsnews.com).
CCCCLTD's website, www.cccltd.com.cn.
CEIEC's website, www.ceiec.com.cn.
China and Africa: A Century of Engagement. By David H. Shinn and Joshua Eisenman. Philadelphia: University of Pennsylvania Press, 2012. As retrieved in December 2014 from this url: http://books.google.com/books?id=hu7n1YNNrqcC&pg=PA162&source=gbs_toc_r&cad=3#v=onepage&q&f=false.
China and Africa: Engagement and Compromise." By Ian Taylor. New York: Routledge, 2006. As retrieved in April 2015 from the following url: https://books.google.com/books?id=vWyjYAUW1ekC&pg=PA96&lpg=PA96&dq=did+samora+machel+like+the+chinese&source=bl&ots=k5nyRqD1Mu&sig=2wgkq9Ni5a5P4WhW1xoz2zUvKCU&hl=en&sa=X&ei=YqwrVc3aHMemNvqYgcgJ&ved=0CCkQ6AEwBA#v=onepage&q=did%20samora%20machel%20like%20the%20chinese&f=false.
"China in Africa." IDE-JETRO (Institute of Developing Economies—Japan External Trade Organization), n.d. As retrieved in October 2014 from the following url: http://www.ide.go.jp/English/Data/Africa_file/Manualreport/cia_10.html.
China into Africa: Trade, Aid, and Influence. Edited by Robert I. N.p.: Brookings Institution Press and World Peace Foundation, 2008. As retrieved in November 2014 from the following url: http://books.google.com/books?id=V70fPqj0YO4C&pg=PA161&lpg=PA161&dq=chinese+small+arms+to+rwanda&source=bl&ots=JFyOwpSTWG&sig=IywOrVNxxV1A-bsS_0tKnjwQCDY&hl=en&sa=X&ei=gcZrVJOGItejyATo54L4CQ&ved=0CEQQ6AEwCQ#v=onepage&q=chinese%20small%20arms%20to%20rwanda&f=false.

"China's Policy in Africa 1958-71." By Alaba Ogunsanwo. New York: Cambridge University Press, 2010. As retrieved in March 2015 from this url: https://books.google.com/books?id=3Dn0fbuz4mEC&pg=PA207&lpg=PA207&dq=cultural+revolution+in+zambia&source=bl&ots=wIDe_wva0f&sig=en68ZcBA-ncrKSk9sMFKSm8jRtY&hl=en&sa=X&ei=HBD7VJ6JIcOegwSbqYRY&ved=0CBcQ6AEwATgK#v=onepage&q=cultural%20revolution%20in%20zambia&f=false.

China Xinxing Import And Export Corporation's website, en.cxxc-china.com.

Chinese and African Perspectives on China in Africa. By editors Axel Harneit-Sievers, Stephen Marks, and Sanusha Naidu. N.p.: Pambazuka Press, 2010. As retrieved in April 2015 from this url: https://books.google.com/books?id=qj75bAEcSLYC&pg=PA266&lpg=PA266&dq=Chinese+and+African+Perspectives+on+China+in+Africa+2009&source=bl&ots=0ue049lPGH&sig=YFS1nNWBboqFjBDiHb7FduaOVRc&hl=en&sa=X&ei=eNw7VeDLEoubNq-ugcgH&ved=0CCYQ6AEwAw#v=onepage&q=Chinese%20and%20African%20Perspectives%20on%20China%20in%20Africa%202009&f=false.

Chinese Foreign Ministry's website, www.China.org.cn.

Chinese Posters' website, http://chineseposters.net.

Clammer, Paul. *Sudan.* Bucks, U.K: Bradt Travel Guides Limited, 2005.

CNN's News on line. From its website (http://www.cbsnews.com).

CRBC's website, www.crbc.com/cn.

CRSSG's website, www.crssg.com/english.

CSCEC's website, www.app.cscec.com.cn.

Danelo, David J. *The Border: Exploring the U.S.-Mexican Divide.* Mechanicsburg, PA: Stackpole Books, 2008.

Dark Star Safari: Overland from Cairo to Capetown. By Paul Theroux. N.p.: Mariner Books, 5 April 2004. As retrieved in October 2014 from the following url: http://books.google.com/books?id=096tukdt0dQC&pg=PA261&lpg=PA261&dq=red+guards+in+tanzania&source=bl&ots=NdAlzjw-ix&sig=AOjFreN0dKYBOw9llMCXSRTFpAQ&hl=en&sa=X&ei=FIZGVJCmBPaZsQTX-ILYAQ&ved=0CBYQ6AEwAQ#v=onepage&q=red%20guards%20in%20tanzania&f=false.

Elford, George Robert. *Devil's Guard.* New York: Dell, 1985.

Encyclopedia Britannica. From its website (http://www.britannica.com).

Esposito, John L. *Unholy War: Terror in the Name of Islam.* London: Oxford University Press, 2002.

Federation of American Scientists. From its website (http://fas.org/).

Foreign Intervention in Africa: From the Cold War to the War on Terror. By Elizabeth Schmidt. Cambridge, U.K.: Cambridge University Press, 2013. As retrieved in April 2015 from the following url: http://books.google.com/books/about/Foreign_Intervention_in_Africa.html?id=k2-2w-lVZUYC.

Fox News on line. From its website (http://www.foxnews.com).
Freedom House. From its website (http://freedomhouse.org/).
Genocide Watch (http://www.genocidewatch.org/ and http://www.genocidewatch.net/).
Geostrategy-Direct. From its website (http://geostrategy-direct.com).
Gertz, Bill. *The China Threat*. Washington, D.C.: Regnery Publishing, 2002.
Global Policy Forum (New York). From its website (www.globalpolicy.org).
Global Security's website, www.globalsecurity.org.
Gunaratna, Rohan. *Inside al-Qaeda: Global Network of Terror*. Lahore: Vanguard, 2002.
Gung Ho: The Corps' Most Progressive Tradition. By H. John Poole. Emerald Isle, NC: Posterity Press, 2012.
Hemingway, Al. *Our War Was Different*. Annapolis, MD: Naval Institute Press, 1994.
Homeland Siege: Tactics for Police and Military. By H. John Poole. Emerald Isle, NC: Posterity Press, 2009.
Hughes, Stephen E. "The State Sponsorship of the Islamic Terrorist Network." Unpublished study. Salt Lake City, 2003.
Hughes, Stephen E. *Warring on Terrorism: A Comprehensive Dispatch Briefing, Part I*. Unpublished study. Soda Springs, ID, 2005.
Human Rights Watch's website, www.hrw.org/.
Huntington, Samuel P. *The Clash of Civilizations and the Remaking of World Order*. London: Simon & Schuster, 1997.
Hutchison Whampoa's website, www.hutchison-whampoa.com.
Jewish Virtual Library's website, http://www.jewishvirtuallibrary.org.
Katzman, Kenneth. *Warriors of Islam: Iran's Revolutionary Guard*. Boulder, CO: Westview Press, 1993.
Lebanese *Hezbollah* portion of Islami Davet Islamic Politics and Cultural website (Turkey), www.islamicinvitationturkey.com. As viewed on 26 November 2010.
LookLex Encyclopedia (Norway). From its website (http://i-cias.com).
MacFarquhar, Roderick and Michael Schoenhals. *Mao's Last Revolution*. Cambridge, MA. Harvard University Press, 2006.
Mannes, Aaron. *Profiles in Terror: Guide to Middle East Terror Organizations*. Lanham, MD: Rowman & Littlefield, 2004.
Menges, Constantine. *China: The Gathering Threat*. Nashville, TN: Nelson Current, 2005.
Merriam Webster Dictionary. From its website (http://www.merriam-webster.com/dictionary).
Monson, Jamie. *Africa's Freedom Railway: How a Chinese Development Project Changed Lives and Livelihoods in Tanzania*. Bloomington: Indiana University Press, 2009.
NPR's News on line. From its website (http://www.npr.org/).

"Partners in Crime (Series)." By Frederic Dannen. *The New Republic,* 14 & 21 July 1997. As retrieved in November 2014 from the following url: http://www.newrepublic.com/article/politics/90738/partners-in-crime.

Patriotic Front's website (Zambia), http://pf.org.zm/.

Reid-Daly, Lt.Col. R.F. *Pamwe Chete: The Legend of the Selous Scouts.* Weltevreden Park, South Africa: Covos-Day Books, 1999.

Ross, Bill D. *Iwo Jima: Legacy of Valor.* New York: Vintage, 1986.

Seeds of Terror: How Heroin Is Bankrolling the Taliban and al-Qaeda. By Gretchen Peters. New York: Thomas Dunne Books, 2009.

South African Development Community (SADC). From its website (http://www.sadc.int/).

Stiff, Peter. Cry Zimbabwe: Independence—20 Years On. Alberton, South Africa: Galago Publishing, 2000.

Stiff, Peter. *The Silent War.* Alberton, South Africa: Galago Publishing, 1999.

"Sudan, Oil, and Human Rights." *Human Rights Watch,* 2003. As retrieved from these urls: http://www.hrw.org/reports/2003/sudan1103/6.htm and http://books.google.com/books?id=3WQkACoP3FkC&pg=PA16&lpg=PA16&dq=his+army+in+the+south+in+2000+as+Sudan+Peoples+Democratic+Forces++%282000-02%29&source=bl&ots=iaU9cEy5ju&sig=T9UDA_G1aAbl7g2_Zs1OGSh-Gg4&hl=en&sa=X&ei=YGkPVOuGAtKAygSY0IHYBQ&ved=0CBoQ6AEwAQ#v=onepage&q=his%20arm%20in%20the%20south%20in%202000%20as%20Sudan%20Peoples%20Democratic%20Forces%20%20%282000-02%29&f=false.

Sudan Update. From its website, www.sudanupdate.org.

Sun Tzu. *The Art of War.* Translated by Samuel B. Griffith. Foreword by B.H. Liddell Hart. New York: Oxford University Press, 1963.

Tactics of the Crescent Moon: Militant Muslim Combat Methods. By H. John Poole. Emerald Isle, NC: Posterity Press, 2004.

Tanzania-Zambia Railway Authority. From its website (http://www.tazarasite.com).

Tequila Junction: 4th-Generation Counterinsurgency. By H. John Poole. Emerald Isle, NC: Posterity Press, 2008.

Terrorist Research & Analysis Consortium. From its website (http://www.trackingterrorism.org).

Terrorist Trail: Backtracking the Foreign Fighter. By H. John Poole. Emerald Isle, NC. Posterity Press, 2006.

Tracking Chinese Development Finance. From its website (http://china.aiddata.org).

Transnational Organized Crime in Eastern Africa: A Threat Assessment. United Nations Office on Drugs and Crime, September 2013. As retrieved in July 2014 with the following document designator: TOC_East_Africa_2013.pdf.

Transnational Organized Crime in Western Africa: A Threat Assessment. United Nations Office on Drugs and Crime, February 2013. As retrieved in July 2014 with the following document designator: West_Africa_TOCTA_2013_EN.pdf.

Trip Atlas. From its website (tripatlas.com).

Twentieth Century Atlas—Death Tolls. From its website (users.erols.com/mwhite28/warstat1.html).

United Nations' website, www.un.org/en/.

Unrestricted Warfare. By Qiao Liang and Wang Xiangsui. Beijing: People's Liberation Army Literature and Arts Publishing House, February 1999. Foreign Broadcast Information Service (FBIS) translation. As retrieved in November 2014 with this document designator: www.dtic.mil/dtic/tr/fulltext/u2/a509132.pdf.

West Africa Coast Initiative, United Nations Office on Drugs and Crime, n.d. As retrieved in November 2014 from the following url: https://www.unodc.org/westandcentralafrica/en/west-africa-coast-initiative.html.

Wikipedia Encyclopedia. From its website (www.wikipedia.org).

World Almanac of Islamism. From American Foreign Policy Council's website, almanac.afpc.org.

Zabih, Sepehr. *The Iranian Military in Revolution and War.* London: Routledge, 1988.

Videotapes, Movies, DVDs, TV Programs, Slide Shows, CDs, Illustrations

ABC's Morning and Nightly News. WCTI, Channel 12. New Bern, NC.

"Al-Qaeda's New Front." *PBS's Frontline.* NC Public Television, January 2005.

The Battle of Dien Bien Phu. Visions of War Series, volume 10. Videocassette #4010. 50 minutes. New Star Video, 1988.

CBS's "60 Minutes." WNCT, Channel 9. Greenville, NC.

"Hotel Rwanda." DVD. 121 minutes. MGM, 2004.

"Japanese Codetalkers." *In Search of History.* History Channel, 30 March 1999.

"The Killing Fields." Videocassette. 142 minutes. Warner Brothers, 1984.

"The Opium Kings." *PBS's Frontline.* NC Public Television, n.d. As retrieved in August 2014 from the following url: http://www.pbs.org/wgbh/pages/frontline/shows/heroin/transform/.

"Political Situation in Somalia 15 March 2011." Map. *Wikipedia Encyclopedia.* As retrieved in November 2014 from this url: http://upload.wikimedia.org/wikipedia/commons/archive/9/9f/20110324011204!Somalia_map_states_regions_districts.png.

"P-6 Class Boat." *Command: Modern Air / Naval Operations* website. As retrieved in June 2014 from the following url: http://www.harpoondatabases.com/encyclopedia/Entry2493.aspx.

"PT Project 183 Bolshevik ('P-6') Class." *Command: Modern Air / Naval Operations* website. Wargame. As retrieved in October 2014 from the following url: http://www.harpoondatabases.com/encyclopedia/Entry2493.aspx.

World Drug Report 2010. Map 5. United Nations Office on Drugs and Crime. As retrieved in December 2014 with document designator: https://www.unodc.org/documents/wdr/WDR_2010/World_Drug_Report_2010_lo-res.pdf.

"Yan'an Chronicles: Election Campaign Reached Villages." *Along the Frontier Series.* Episode #63. Documentary from China Central Television. As viewed through Lusaka CCTV9 on 8 May 2015.

"Zimbabwe: Shadows and Lies." *PBS's Frontline / World.* NC Public Television, 27 June 2006.

Letters, E-Mail, and Direct Verbal Conversations

Acting manager of Lusaka's National Museum. In conversation with author on 7 May 2015.

Airport representative for Lusaka's best hotel. In conversation with author on 6 May 2015.

Anonymous resident #1 of Lusaka. In conversation with author on 8 May 2015.

Anonymous resident #2 of Lusaka. In conversation with author on 7 May 2015.

Caracas art store owner. In conversation with author on 16 August 2008.

Contract driver for Lusaka's best hotel. In conversation with author on 8 May 2015.

Lady formerly married to South African army major. In conversation with author on 12 April 2015.

Longtime owner of Khartoum hotel. In conversation with author on 31 May 2006.

Seventy-year-old Chinese man (at Shanghai airport). In conversation with author in June 2000.

South African business woman of Indian descent. In conversation with author on 6 May 2015.

TANZAM station manager in Kapiri Mposhi, Zambia. In conversation with author on 8 May 2015.

Texas police officer. In telephone conversation with author in May 2011.

U.S. oil company executive who lives with his Venezuelan wife in one of that nation's coastal cities. In conversation with author on 19 August 2008.

U.S. special operator. In telephone conversation with author on 2 January 2011.

Newspaper, Magazine, Radio, and Website Articles

"Africa a New Conduit for Europe's Drugs." By Rukmini Callimachi (Associated Press). *Washington Post* on line, 29 July 2007.

"Africa, China's New Frontier." *The Times* on line (U.K.), 10 February 2008.

"Africa: Developed Countries' Leverage On the Continent." By Ravinder Rena. *AllAfrica News* on line, 7 February 2008. As retrieved from the following url: http://allafrica.com/stories/200802070635.html.

"Africa Reemerging as Heroin Trafficking Hub: U.N." By Sylvia Westall. *Reuters News* on line, 30 July 2011.

"The Al-Qaeda-Hezbollah Relationship." By Eben Kaplan. Council on Foreign Relations. *Backgrounder,* 14 August 2006. As retrieved in August 2014 from the following url: http://www.cfr.org/terrorist-organizations-and-networks/al-qaeda-hezbollah-relationship/p11275.

"Al-Qaeda in East Africa and the Horn." By David H. Shinn. *Journal of Conflict Studies.* Volume 27, number 1, 2007. Republished as "Research: Al-Qaeda in East Africa and the Horn." *Horn Affairs English,* 5 August 2013. As retrieved in January 2015 from url: http://hornaffairs.com/en/2013/08/05/alqaeda-east-africa-and-the-horn/.

"Al-Qaeda on Pakistan: Dr. Ayman al-Zawahiri's Morning and the Lamp." Jamestown Foundation. *Terrorism Monitor.* Volume 8, issue 11, 19 March 2010.

"Analysts: By 2025, U.S. Won't Be Top World Power." By Tom Gjelten. *NPR's "Morning Edition" News,* 21 November 2008. A review of *Global Trends 2025: The National Intelligence Council's 2025 Project.* As retrieved in 2011 from the following url: www.dni.gov/nic/NIC_2025_project.html.

"Angola." China.org.cn (Chinese Foreign Ministry), 10 October 2006. As retrieved in October 2014 from the following url: www.china.org.cn/english/features/focac/183584.htm.

"Angola." *Freedom in the World 2013.* From Freedom House (a Washington, D.C. based human-rights organization). As retrieved in October 2014 from the following url: http://www.freedomhouse.org/report/freedom-world/2013/angola.

"Angolan, Congolese Troops Join Forces." World Briefs Wire Reports (Associated Press). *Jacksonville Daily News* (NC), 7 November 2008.

"Angola Restore Copper Rail Line after Four Decade Halt." By Colin McClelland. *Bloomberg News* on line, 25 March 2013.

"Angola's Chinese-Built Rail Link and the Scramble to Access the Region's Resources." *China Africa Reporting Project* on line, 26 February 2014. As retrieved in July 2014 from the following url: http://china-africa-reporting.co.za/2014/02/angolas-chinese-built-rail-link-and-the-scramble-to-access-the-regions-resources/.

"(Angola) Summary." *Human Rights Watch,* n.d. As retrieved in October 2014 from the following url: http://www.hrw.org/reports/2007/angola0507/1.htm.

"Arming Genocide in Rwanda: The High Cost of Small Arms Transfers." By Stephen D. Goose and Frank Smyth. Council on Foreign Relations. *Foreign Affairs* on line, September/October 1994 issue.

"Army of Shopowners Paved China's Way in Africa." By Ofeibea Quist-Arcton. Part 5. *China's Rising Power in Africa. NPR* on line, 1 August 2008.

"Assyrian Christians: A Look at the Religious Group Captured by ISIS." By Alexander Mallin and Pat O'Gara. *ABC's News*, 1 March 2015.

"Attack's in Egypt's Sinai Kill at Least 25." World Roundup (Associated Press). *Jacksonville Daily News* (NC), 30 January 2015.

"Bahrain Protests Joined by Arab Anger in Libya." News Briefs/Wire Reports (Associated Press). *Jacksonville Daily News* (NC), 17 February 2011.

Baldauf, Scott. "Congo's Riches Fuel Its War." *Christian Science Monitor,* 4 November 2008.

Baldauf, Scott. "In Congo, a Doctor Keeps Helping as Victims Keep Coming." *Christian Science Monitor,* 24 October 2008.

Baldauf, Scott and Ali Mohamed. "Cash Lures Somali 'Holy' Warriors." *Christian Science Monitor,* 19 April 2010.

Baran, Zeyno. "Muslim Brotherhood Takes Up Arms—in Support of Hizbullah." From access@g2-forward.org, 2 August 2006.

"The Battle for Nigeria." By Aryn Baker. *Time,* 16 February 2015.

"Beijing Orders Army to Give Up Its Businesses." By Henry Chu. *Los Angels Times* on line, 23 July 1998. As retrieved in November 2014 from the following url: http://articles.latimes.com/1998/jul/23/news/mn-6350.

"Beijing's Blue Berets: U.N. Peacekeeping and the Evolution of Chinese Diplomacy." By Anna Richardson. *Atlantic* on line, 13 May 2013.

"Beijing's Embrace." *Africa Confidential* on line, volume 47, issue 14, 7 July 2006.

"The 'Big Six' Arms Exporters." *Amnesty International,* 11 June 2012. As retrieved in November 2014 from the following url: http://www.amnesty.org/en/news/big-six-arms-exporters-2012-06-11.

"Boko Haram Attacks Two Towns in Niger." From Associated Press. *Jacksonville Daily News* (NC), 7 February 2015.

"Boko Haram, Dawood Tie Up to Sell Drugs in India," *Rediff News,* 21 July 2014. As retrieved in August 2014 from the following url: http://www.rediff.com/news/report/boko-haram-dawood-tie-up-to-sell-drugs-in-india/20140721.htm.

"Boko Haram: Spotlight on Human Trafficking." *World Policy Journal* (New York), 22 May 2014. As retrieved in February 2015 from the following url: http://www.worldpolicy.org/blog/2014/05/22/boko-haram-spotlight-human-trafficking.

"Boko Haram: The Other Islamic State." By Jeremy Ashkenas, Derek Watkinis, and Carchie Tse. *New York Times* on line, 15 January 2015. As retrieved in February 2015 from the following url: http://www.nytimes.com/interactive/2014/12/11/world/africa/boko-haram-nigeria-maps.html?_r=0.

"Both Iran and Israel Have Military Bases in Eritrea, Global Intel. Reports." By Anshel Pfeffer. *Haaretz News* on line, 12 December 2012. As retrieved in January 2015 from url: http://www.haaretz.com/news/diplomacy-defense/both-iran-and-israel-have-military-bases-in-eritrea-global-intel-reports.premium-1.484326#!.

"Businessman at White House Social Has Close Ties to China's Military Power." By David E. Sanger. *New York Times* on line, 21 December 1996. As retrieved in November 2014 from this url: http://www.nytimes.com/1996/12/21/us/businessman-at-white-house-social-has-close-ties-to-china-s-military-power.html.

"Cameroon Army Arrests Mayor of Fotokol, 300 Boko Haram Members, Find Huge Stockpile of Ammunitions in His Residence." *Udumakalu Word Press* (Nigeria), 14 October 2014. As retrieved in February 2014 from this url: https://udumakalu.wordpress.com/2014/10/01/cameroon-army-arrests-mayor-of-fotokol-300-boko-haram-members-find-huge-stockpile-of-ammunitions-in-his-residence/.

"Cameroon: China Invades Country with Cheap, Fragile Goods." *AllAfrica News* on line, 28 August 2008.

"Cameroon's $1b China-Funded Port to Boost West African Cargo Flows." By Emmanuel Tuanjong. *Wall Street Journal* on line, 14 May 2014.

"Can Niger Offer Mali Lessons on the Tuareg?" *IRIN News* (United Nations), 11 April 2013. As retrieved in December 2014 from the following url: http://www.irinnews.org/report/97823/can-niger-offer-mali-lessons-on-the-tuareg.

"Chad Army Says Kills 120 Boko Haram Militants in Cameroon." *Reuters News* on line, 31 January 2015.

"Chad: How China Created an African Power." By Raluca Besliu. *The Globalist* (Washington, D.C.), 26 December 2013. As retrieved in November 2014 from the following url: http://www.theglobalist.com/chad-china-created-african-power/.

"China-Africa Relations in the 21st Century." By Jennifer Parneti. *Joint Forces Quarterly,* March 2009.

"China and African Peacekeeping." By Richard Weitz. *Second Line of Defense* (Arlington, VA), 7 March 2013. As retrieved in November 2014 from the following url: http://www.sldinfo.com/china-and-african-peacekeeping/.

"China and Angola Strengthen Bilateral Relationship." By Loro Horta. *Power and Interest News Report,* 23 June 2006.

"China, Congo Trade for What the Other Wants." By Gwen Thompkins. Part 3. *China's Rising Power in Africa. NPR* on line, 30 July 2008.

"China Corrects Diplomatic Faux Pas, but Maintains Presence in Gilgit-Baltistan." By B. Raman. Chennai Centre for China Studies. C3S Paper Number 586, 5 September 2010.

"China Defends Land Reclamation in the Spratly Islands." *Military Times* on line, 24 November 2014.

"China Ends One Notorious Form of Detention, But Keeps Others." *NPR* on line, 5 February 2014.

"China-Funded Burundi Palace Project to Begin in 2014." Forum on China-Africa Cooperation, 30 September 2013. As retrieved in October 2014 from url: http://www.focac.org/eng/zxxx/t1083398.htm.

"China in Angola: An Emerging Energy Partnership." By Paul Hare. Jamestown Foundation. *China Brief,* volume 6, issue 22, 8 November 2006.

"China Mulls Building Naval Base in Namibia, Namibian Times Says." By David Tweed. *Bloomberg News* on line, 27 November 2014. As retrieved in December 2014 from the following url: http://www.bloomberg.com/news/2014-11-27/china-mulls-building-naval-base-in-namibia-namibian-times-says.html.

"China Offers 'Troops' to UN Mali Peacekeeping Mission." *BBC News* on line, 24 May 2013. As retrieved in November 2014 from the following url: http://www.bbc.com/news/world-asia-china-22650668.

"China Praises Achievements of Sudan's National Congress Party." From Xinhua. *Peoples Daily on Line*, 24 November 2005.

"China Puts 700,000 Troops on Alert in Sudan." *Newsmax* (West Palm Beach, FL), 27 August 2000.

"China Railway Construction Corp. Plans $3.4B IPO." By Vivian Wai-yin Kwok. *Forbes Magazine,* 4 January 2008.

"China Railway Construction Seeks End-Feb HK IPO-Source." *Reuters News* on line, 15 January 2008.

"China Sends Peacekeeping Police Squad for South Sudan." From Xinhua News Agency. *Global Times* (Beijing), 12 November 2011.

"China, South Sudan to Further Reciprocal Cooperation." *Xinhua News Service* on line, 1 July 2014. As retrieved in October 2014 from this url: http://news.xinhuanet.com/english/china/2014-07/01/c_133453008_2.htm.

"China's Arms Exports Flooding Sub-Saharan Africa." By Colum Lynch. *Washington Post,* 25 August 2012.

"China's Diplomatic Victory in Sudan's Darfur." By Jonathan Holslag. *Sudan Tribune* on line, 2 August 2007. As retrieved in February 2015 from url: http://www.sudantribune.com/spip.php?article23090.

"China's Discreet Hold on Pakistan's Northern Borderlands." By Selig Harrison. *New York Times,* 26 August 2010.

"China's Expanding Peacekeeping Role." By Bates Gill and Chin-hao Huang. Stockholm International Peace Research Institute, January 2009. As retrieved in June 2015 from the following url: http://www.sipri.org/media/newsletter/essay/jan09.

"China's FM in First Visit to New Ally Malawi." *The Namibian,* 16 January 2009. As retrieved in November 2014 from this url: http://www.namibian.com.na/indexx.php?archive_id=2193&page_type=archive_story_detail&page=3278.

"China's Foreign Aids and Human Rights Concerns—Thoughts Provoked by Darfur Humanitarian Crisis." Chinese Foreign Ministry (China.org.cn), 29 October 2009. As retrieved in February 2015 from the following url: http://www.china.org.cn/china/human_rights/2009-10/29/content_18792532_2.htm.

"China's Involvement in African Conflict Zones." By David H. Shinn. Jamestown Foundation, 20 May 2009. As retrieved in November 2014 from the following url: https://sites.google.com/site/davidhshinn/china-s-involvement-in-african-conflict-zones.

"China's Largest Port Builder Delays $3 Billion Shanghai Offering." *Bloomberg Businessweek,* 8 July 2011. As retrieved in October 2014 from this url: http://www.businessweek.com/news/2011-07-08/china-s-largest-port-builder-delays-3-billion-shanghai-offering.html.

"China's Military Presence in Africa." By Chuka Enuka. *Journal of Political Studies* (University of Punjab), volume 18, issue 1, n.d. As retrieved in December 2014 with this document designator: http://pu.edu.pk/images/journal/pols/pdf-files/chuka%20-%202.pdf.

"China's Military Rise: The Dragon's New Teeth." *The Economist,* 7 April 2012.

"China's Stake in Zambia's Election." By Louise Redvers. *BBC News* on *NPR*. Public Radio East (New Bern, NC), 18 September 2011.

China's State Commission of Science, Technology and Industry for National Defense. As quoted in "Chinese Military to Make Billions through Capitalism." *Geostrategy Direct,* 16 January 2008.

"China Tightens Grip on Africa with $4.4bn Lifeline for Guinea Junta." By Jonathan Clayton. *The Times* on line (U.K.), 13 October 2009.

"China to Open Its First Military Base Abroad in Indian Ocean." NDTV (India), 12 December 2011. As retrieved in December 2014 from the following url: http://www.ndtv.com/article/india/china-to-open-its-first-military-base-abroad-in-indian-ocean-157282.

"China to Seal $9bn DR Congo Deal." By Tim Whewell. *BBC News* on line, 14 April 2008. As retrieved in November 2014 from this url: http://news.bbc.co.uk/2/hi/programmes/newsnight/7343060.stm.

"China to Send 700 Combat Troops to South Sudan." By David Smith. *The Guardian* (U.K.), 23 December 2014. As retrieved in December 2014 from the following url: http://www.theguardian.com/world/2014/dec/23/china-700-combat-troops-south-sudan-africa-battalion-un-peacekeeping.

"China Uncooperative in Stopping Meth Flow." Joshua Philipp. China Society International. *Epoch Times*, 3 March 2014. As retrieved in December 2014 from the following url: http://www.theepochtimes.com/n3/540878-china-uncooperative-in-stopping-meth-flow/.

"China Winning Resources and Loyalties of Africa." *The Financial Times* (U.K.), 28 February 2006.

"Chinese-Built Zambian Smelter Stirs Controversy." By Ofeibea Quist-Arcton. Part 4. *China's Rising Power in Africa. NPR* on line, 1 August 2008.

"Chinese Gangs Fuel Meth Scourge in U.S." By Joshua Philipp. China Society International. *Epoch Times*, 12 September 2013.

"Chinese Meat Firm With Terrible Food Safety Record Buys The Largest Pork Producer In The U.S." By Aviva Shen. *Center for American Progress Action Fund,* 31 May 2013. As retrieved in July 2015 from the following url: http://thinkprogress.org/health/2013/05/31/2076871/chinese-meat-firm-buys-pork-producer/.

"The Chinese Military-Industrial Complex Goes Global." By David Welker. *The Multinational Monitor* (Washington, D.C.), volume 18, number 6, June 1997. As retrieved in July 2015 from this url: http://www.multinationalmonitor.org/hyper/mm0697.05.html.

"Chinese Organised Crime and Africa." By Gary K. Busch. *Gangsters Inc.,* 30 July 2014. As retrieved in April 2015 from this url: http://gangstersinc.ning.com/profiles/blogs/chinese-organised-crime-and-africa.

"Chinese Paper Advises PLA Navy to Build Overseas Military Bases." *China Defense Mashup* (Beijing), 8 January 2013. As retrieved in December 2014 from the following url: http://www.china-defense-mashup.com/chinese-paper-advises-pla-navy-to-build-overseas-military-bases.html.

"Chinese Presence in Tibet: Population Transfer." *Tibet Online,* n.d. As retrieved in March 2015 from the following website: http://www.tibet.org/Activism/Rights/poptransfer.html.

"Chinese President Arrives in Brazzaville for State Visit." *Xinhua News* on line, 29 March 2013. As retrieved in October 2013 from this url: http://news.xinhuanet.com/english/china/2013-03/29/c_132271968.htm.

"Chromium." SearchMining.net, n.d. As retrieved in July 2014 from this url: http://www.searchmining.net/mininginfo/mining101/metals_and_minerals/ferrous_metals/chromium.asp.

"A Chronology of Tibet's History." *PBS's Frontline.* NC Public Television, n.d. As retrieved in October 2014 from the following url: http://www.pbs.org/wgbh/pages/frontline/shows/tibet/etc/cron.html.

"Cobalt Faces a Looming Supply Disruption Threat." By Phil Burgert. *Futures Magazine* on line, 9 February 2012.

"Colombia's Most Powerful Rebels." *BBC News* on *NPR.* Public Radio East (New Bern, NC), 19 September 2003.

"Company Overview of China Road And Bridge Corporation." *Bloomberg Businessweek,* n.d. As retrieved in November 2014 from this url: http://investing.businessweek.com/research/stocks/private/snapshot.asp?privcapId=26447281.

"Congo and China." Global Witness (U.K/), n.d. As retrieved in November 2014 from url: http://www.globalwitness.org/node/8425.

"Congo Conflict: 'The Terminator' Lives in Luxury While Peacekeepers Look On." By David Smith. *The Guardian* (U.K.) on line, 5 February 2010.

"The Congo's Killing Fields." By Kevin Clarke. *U.S. Catholic,* July 2008.

"Construction of Lamu Port Berths Set for June." By Martin Mwita. *The Star* on line (Nairobi), 10 March 2014. As retrieved in October 2014 from the following url: http://www.the-star.co.ke/news/article-158384/construction-lamu-port-berths-set-june-kpa.

"A Controversial Legacy." By T.P. (Beijing correspondent). *The Economist,* 11 December 2013. As retrieved in September 2014 from this url: http://www.economist.com/blogs/analects/2013/12/nelson-mandela-and-china.

Cordesman, Anthony H. (Strategy Chair). "Iran's Developing Military Capabilities." Working draft. Washington, D.C.: Center for Strategic and International Studies, 14 December 2004.

Cordesman, Anthony H. (Strategy Chair). "Iran's Revolutionary Guards, the Al Quds Force, and Other Intelligence and Paramilitary Forces." Working draft. Washington, D.C.: Ctr. for Strategic and International Studies, 16 August 2007.

"CRBC Cements Sino-Kenya Ties." *ChinaDaily,* 9 May 2014. As retrieved in November 2014 from the following url: http://africa.chinadaily.com.cn/weekly/2014-05/09/content_17495498.htm.

"Crisis-Hit Mali Swears in Transitional President." By Leela Jacinto. *France24* on line, 12 April 2012.

"Crisis in the Democratic Republic of the Congo." International Coalition for the Responsibility to Protect, n.d. As retrieved in May 2014 from the following url: http://www.responsibilityto protect.org/index.php/crises/crisis-in-drc.

"Critical Raw Materials." *British Geological Survey,* n.d. As retrieved in July 2014 from the following url: http://www.bgs.ac.uk/ mineralsuk/statistics/criticalRawMaterials.html.

"Curse of the Black Gold: Hope and Betrayal in the Niger Delta." *National Geographic,* February 2007.

"Dar-es-Salaam Once a Home for Revolutionaries." Times Media Group. *Sunday World* (Zambia), 29 April 2014. As retrieved in September 2014 from this url: http://www.sundayworld.co.za/life style/2014/04/29/dar-es-salaam-once-a-home-for-revolutionaries.

"DEA Charges Four with Trafficking Heroin from Africa." By Jerry Seper. *Washington Times* on line, 5 June 2013. As retrieved in July 2014 from the following url: http://www.washingtontimes.com/ news/2013/jun/5/dea-charges-four-trafficking-heroin-africa/.

"Death Toll Rises from Car Bomb in Nigerian Capital Abuja." From Associated Press. *The Guardian* (U.K.) on line, 1 May 2014.

"DoD Report: Losing War on Afghan Drug Trade." By Richard Sisk. Military.com, 18 November 2013.

"Do I Look Dangerous to You." Part I. Partners in Crime Series. By Frederic Dannen. *The New Republic,* 14 & 21 July 1997. As retrieved in November 2014 from the following url: http://www.newrepublic.com/article/politics/90738/partners-in-crime.

"DRC: Interview with Rebel General Laurent Nkunda." *IRIN News* (United Nations), 2 September 2004.

"DR Congo Government, CNDP Rebels 'Sign Peace Deal'." Agence France Press, 23 March 2009. As retrieved in March 2015 from this url: http://reliefweb.int/report/democratic-republic-congo/dr-congo-government-cndp-rebels-sign-peace-deal.

"DRC Soldiers 'Ordered to Rape' Women." *BBC News* on line, 11 April 2013.

Drug Czar. As quoted on *NPR's "Morning Edition" News,* mid-2010.

"Drug Policy Changes Under New Director." *NPR's News* on line, 3 November 2009.

"Drug Seizures in West Africa Prompt Fears of Terrorist Links." By Jamie Doward. *The Guardian Observer* (U.K.), 28 November 2009.

"Drug Trafficking Patterns to and from Eastern Africa." UNODC, n.d. As retrieved in August 2014 from this url: https://www.unodc.org/ easternafrica/en/illicit-drugs/drug-trafficking-patterns.html.

"Drug Trafficking Rising in Central Africa, Warns Interpol." By Ntaryike Divine Jr. *Voice of America,* 8 September 2012. As retrieved in 2014 from url: http://www.voanews.com/content/drug-trafficking-rising-in-central-africa-warns-interpol/1504026.html.

"Ebola, Anarchy, and Failing States." By Benjamin Syme Van Ameringen. *Geopolitical Monitor,* 24 November 2014.

"Egypt Bombs Islamic State Targets in Libya after 21 Egyptians Beheaded." By Ahmed Tolba and Yara Bayoumy. *Reuters News* on line, 16 February 2015.

"Eliminating Terrorist Sanctuaries." *Project of Government Oversight* (http://pogo.org). Center for Defense Information, 10 December 2001.

"End of the Line for 'Lunatic Express?' Kenya Begins Multi-Billion Dollar Railway." By Stephanie Ott. *CNN's News* on line, 6 January 2014.

"Ethiopia, China to Broaden Areas of Cooperation." From Xinhua. *China Daily* on line, 28 February 2008.

"Everyone Wants Cut in Afghan Drug Trade." From McClatchy News Service. *Jacksonville Daily News* (NC), 10 May 2009.

"Ex-Libyan General Battling Islamist Militias Faces Dwindling Support amid Stalemate." By Erin Cunningham. *Washington Post* on line, 8 July 2014.

"51st National Congress: Declaration." African National Congress' (ANC's) website (www.anc.org.za/), 20 December 2002. As retrieved in September 2014 from this url: http://www.anc.org.za/show.php?id=2498.

"Fighting an Invisible Enemy in DRC." *IRIN News* (United Nations), 9 April 2014. As retrieved in November 2014 from this url: http://www.irinnews.org/report/99905/fighting-an-invisible-enemy-in-drc.

"Fighting in Somalia's Puntland Kills at Least 27." *Reuters News* on line, 3 September 2011.

"45,000 Die Each Month in Congo." World Briefs Wire Reports (Associated Press). *Jacksonville Daily News* (NC), 23 January 2008.

"French Troops Deployed in Last Mali Rebel Strongholds." By Richard Valdmanis and John Irish. *Reuters News* on line, 30 January 2013.

"From the Killing Fields to Compassion." By David R, Aquije. *Maryknoll Magazine,* January/February 2014 issue.

"Future Kenya Port Could Mar Pristine Land." By Jeffrey Gentleman. *New York Times* on line, 11 January 2010.

"Gadhafi's Mercenaries Spread Guns and Fighting in Africa." By Bazi Kanani. *ABC's News on line,* 3 April 2012.

Gertz, Bill. "Chinese Military Trains in West." *Washington Times,* 15 March 2006.

Gertz, Bill. "Notes from the Pentagon." *Washington Times,* 5 March 2004.

"Global Double Crossing." By Charles R. Smith. *Newsmax* (West Palm Beach, FL), 27 February 2003.

"Govt. Hides $192m Loan." *Saturday Post* (Lusaka), 9 May 2015.

"Grindrod to Build $989 Million Zambia Mine Railway Route." By Matthew Hill. *Bloomberg News* on line, 3 February 2014.

"Guinea-Bissau: China Sees a Risk Worth Taking." By Loro Horta. Center for Strategic and International Studies (Washington, D.C.), 9 December 2014. As retrieved in December 2014 from url: http://csis.org/story/guinea-bissau-china-sees-risk-worth-taking.

"Guinea Bissau: Hezbollah, al Qaida and the Lebanese Connection." By Marco Venaschi. *Pulitzer Center,* 19 June 2009. As retrieved in August 2014 from this url: http://pulitzercenter.org/blog/untold-stories/guinea-bissau-hezbollah-al-qaida-and-lebanese-connection.

"Guinea-Bissau: How Cocaine Transformed a Tiny Nation." By Jessica Hatcher. *Time,* 15 October 2012.

"Hamas and Iran Rebuild Ties Three Years after Falling Out over Syria." By Harriet Sherwood. *The Guardian* (U.K.) on line, 9 January 2014.

Harris, Shane. "China's Cyber-Militia. " *National Journal Magazine,* 31 May 2008.

"Heroin Makes a Comeback." By Zusha Elinson. *Wall Street Journal,* 8 August 2013.

Hill, Ginny. "Cold War Roots of Yemen Conflict." *BBC News* on line, 17 September 2009.

"The Horrific Aftermath of Boko Haram Massacre on Nigerian Villages." By Laurie Hanna. *Daily Mail* (U.K.) on line, 15 January 2015.

"Hostility toward Workers Cools Angola-China Relationship." By Benoit Faucon and Sherry Su. *Wallstreet Journal* on line, business edition, 10 August 2010. As retrieved in October 2014 from the following url: http://online.wsj.com/articles/SB10001424052748704388504575418990791137242.

"How ISIS Is Winning the Propaganda War." Explainer. *Time,* 6/13 July 2015.

Hunwick, John. "Africa and Islamic Revival: Historical and Contemporary Perspectives." Possibly unpublished study, n.d. As retrieved verbatim from *MSA News* (no longer on line) by University of Georgia.

"Inside China: Long March to Africa." By Miles Yu. *Washington Times,* 6 March 2014. As retrieved in December 2014 from this url: http://www.washingtontimes.com/news/2014/mar/6/inside-china-long-march-to-africa/#ixzz3Ml8h90S3.

"'Into Africa'—How Chinese Funding Helps Fuel an African Rail Boom." *SmartRailWorld* on line, 29 November 2013. As retrieved in July 2014 from this url: http://www.smartrailworld.com/blog/2013/11/29/chinese-funding-helps-fuel-africa-rail-boom-projects-in-kenya-mozambique-ethiopia-rwanda-and-morrocco-profiled.

"Iran Shifting Its Attention . . . ." *New York Times,* 13 December 1991.

"Iranian Proxies: An Intricate and Active Web." By Scott Stewart. *STRATFOR Weekly* (http://www.stratfor.com/geopolitical-weekly), 3 February 2010.

"Iran's Revolutionary Guards." By Greg Bruno, Jayshree Bajoria, and Jonathan Masters. Council on Foreign Relations. *Backgrounder,* 14 June 2013. As retrieved in November 2014 from this url: http://www.cfr.org/iran/irans-revolutionary-guards/p14324.

"Islamic Group Says It Was Behind Fatal Nigeria Attack." By Adam Nossiter. *New York Times* on line, 28 August 2011.

"Islam in Africa Newsletter." By Moshe Terdman and Reuven Paz. *Israeli Project for the Research of Islamist Movements* (www.e-prism.org), volume 1, number 1, May 2006.

"Islamists Training in Somalia." By Bill Gertz. Emergency Net News. *ERRI Daily Intelligence Report,* volume 11, number 363, 31 December 2005. Through *Geostrategy-Direct.*

"Joseph Kony Hunt is Proving Difficult for U.S. Troops." *Washington Post,* 29 April 2012.

Keath, Lee. Associated Press. "Shiites Nominate New Premier." *Jacksonville Daily News* (NC), 22 April 2006.

"Kenya Attack: Mpeketoni near Lamu Hit by al-Shabab Raid." *BBC News* on line, 16 June 2014. As retrieved in July 2014 from this url: http://www.bbc.com/news/world-africa-27862510.

"Kenyan Coastal Region of Lamu Hit by Deadly Attacks." *BBC News* on line, 6 July 2014.

"Kuwait Says Saudi Responsible for Mosque Suicide Bombing." Scott Neuman. *NPR's News* on line, 28 June 2015.

"Lamu Port Construction to Commence Soon." By Danson Kagai. *Kenya Construction Business Review* on line, 27 July 2011.

"Land Tenure and Mining in Tanzania," by Siri Lange, Christian Mechelsen Institute (Norway), n.d. As retrieved in October 2014 with this document designator: http://www.cmi.no/publications/file/3008-land-tenure-and-mining-in-tanzania.pdf.

"LAPSSET: A Peep at the East African Trade Corridor." *Ventures Africa* on line, 10 January 2014.

"LatAm Drug Traffickers Set Up in Guinea-Bissau, Expand in Africa." By Charles Parkinson. *Insightcrime.org,* 29 August 2013.

The Latin Mass, volume 23, number 3, fall 2014.

"Law and Order in Chad." As retrieved in April 2015 from url: http://www.mapsofworld.com/chad/government-and-politics/law.html.

"Lebanon: Existence of Organized Crime in Lebanon, Its Involvement in the Production of Narcotics and Drug Trafficking, Government Actions to Combat Organized Crime." Immigration and Refugee Board of Canada, 11 September 2003. As retrieved in December 2014 from this url: http://www.refworld.org/docid/403dd1fec.html.

"Left Seizes Control of South Africa's ANC." *The Sunday Times* (U.K.), 25 January 2009. As retrieved in November 2014 from url: http://www.thesundaytimes.co.uk/sto/news/world_news/article145659.ece.

"Libyan Capital under Islamist Control after Tripoli Airport Seized." By Chris Stephen and Anne Penketh. *The Guardian* (U.K.) on line, 24 August 2014.

"Libya Prime Minister Abdullah al-Thinni Resigns," *BBC News* on line, 29 August 2014.

"Libya's Muslim Brotherhood Struggles to Grow." By Mary Fitzgerald Foreign Policy, 1 May 2014. As retrieved in January 2014 from this url: http://foreignpolicy.com/2014/05/01/libyas-muslim-brotherhood-struggles-to-grow/.

"Lungu Blasts U.N." *Sunday Nation,* 10 May 2015.

Mahmoud, Dr. Mohammed. Tufts University. "Islam and Islamization in Sudan: The Islamic National Front." From *Religion, Nationalism, and Peace in Sudan* (paper presented at U.S. Institute of Peace Conference, 16-17 September 1997).

"A Means of Maintaining Social Order." Part II. Partners in Crime Series. By Frederic Dannen, *The New Republic,* 14 & 21 July 1997. As retrieved in November 2014 from the following url: http://www.newrepublic.com/article/politics/90738/partners-in-crime.

"The Mega-Port That Threatens to Sink Sudan." By Tom Stevenson. *Al Jazeera News* on line, 13 October 2013. As retrieved in October 2014 from this url: http://www.aljazeera.com/indepth/features/2013/10/mega-port-threatens-sink-sudan-20131013717364177765.html.

"Mexican Cartels Buying Afghan Heroin." From PVNN. *Banderas News* (Mexico), n.d. As retrieved in August 2014 from the following url: http://www.banderasnews.com/1101/nr-afghanheroin.htm.

"Mexico's Internal Drug War." By Sam Logan. *Power and Interest News Report (PINR),* 14 August 2006.

"Michael Sata Obituary." By Stephen Chan. *The Guardian* (U.K.), 29 October 2014. As retrieved in December 2014 from this url: http://www.theguardian.com/world/2014/oct/29/michael- sata.

"Mining in Africa towards 2020." Global Mining Institute, n.d. As retrieved in September 2014 with document designator: https://www.kpmg.com/Africa/en/IssuesAndInsights/Articles-Publications/Documents/Mining%20in%20Africa%20towards%202020.pdf.

Miniter, Richard (contributor). "The King and O: Al-Qaeda Shifts to Africa, But Is Obama Listening," Opinion Editorial. *Forbes Magazine,* 19 November 2013. As retrieved in July 2014 from url: www.forbes.com/sites/richardminiter/2013/11/19/the-king-and-o-al-qaeda-shifts-to-africa-but-is-obama-listening/.

"Modernizing the People's Liberation Army of China." By Carin Zissis. Council on Foreign Relations. *Backgrounder,* 5 December 2006.

"More Than Troops, Chinese Projects in PoK Worry India." By Pranab Dhal Samanta. *Indian Express* (Delhi), 5 September 2010. Reprinted by *Yahoo News,* 5 September 2010. As retrieved from news.yahoo.com and indianexpress.com on 14 September 2010.

"Mozambique." Chinese Foreign Ministry (China.org.cn), 10 October 2006. As retrieved in October 2014 from the following url: htm http://www.china.org.cn/english/features/focac/183432.htm.

"Mozambique: Government Seeks Funding for Nacala Deep Water Port." *AllAfrica News* on line, 22 June 2012. As retrieved in July 2014 from this url: http://allafrica.com/stories/201206230017.html.

"Multipurpose Port Terminal in Nacala, Mozambique to be Operational This Year." *Macauhub News* on line, 27 January 2014. As retrieved in July 2014 from this url: http://www.macauhub.com.mo/en/2014/01/27/multipurpose-port-terminal-in-nacala-mozambique-to-be-operational-this-year/.

"Mumena Extols Lungu over Mineral Royalty." By Nkombo Kachemba. *Zambia Daily Mail,* 8 May 2015.

"New Cold War in Africa." By Nick Terse. The Nation Institute (N.Y.). *The Investigative Fund,* 31 July 2014. As retrieved in December 2014 from the following url: http://www.theinvestigativefund.org/investigations/international/2017/a_new_cold_war_in_africa/.

"The New Danger in Benghazi." By Ethan Chorin. Opinion Editorial. *New York Times* on line, 27 May 2014.

"New Drug Threat to West Africa, Warns President of Guinea." By Colin Freeman. *The Telegraph* on line, 15 June 2013.

"New Era of China-Namibia Friendship." By the Chinese Ambassador to Namibia. Embassy website, 7 April 2014. As retrieved in November 2014 from this following url: http://www.fmprc.gov.cn/ce/cena/eng/dsxx/hdjh/t1144716.htm.

"New Firm Sub-Contracted to Work on Chingola-Solwezi Road." *Lusaka Times* on line, 30 January 2014. As retrieved in May 2015 from the following url: http://www.lusakatimes.com/2014/01/30/new-firm-sub-contracted-work-chingola-solwezi-road-current-hired-firm-capacity-fix-road/.

"Niger Campaigners Call for More Details on Oil Deal with China." From Agence France Press. *Energy Daily,* 30 July 2008. As retrieved in February 2015 from this url: http://www.energy-daily.com/reports/Niger_campaigners_call_for_more_details_on_oil_deal_with_China_999.html.

"Nigeria Braced for War with Drug Lords." By David Orr. *The Independent* (U.K.), 4 October 1995. As retrieved in November 2014 from the following url: http://www.independent.co.uk/news/world/nigeria-braced-for-war-with-drug-lords-1575898.html.

"Nigerian Forces Repel Extremists' Attack." By Haruna Umar and Michelle Faul (Associated Press). *Jacksonville Daily News* (NC), 2 February 2015.

"Nigeria's Boko Haram 'Abducts More Women and Girls'." *BBC News* on line, 23 October 2014.

"Nigeria's MEND Rebels Threaten Future Attack on Oil Industry." By Elisha Bala-Gbogbo. *Bloomberg News* on line, 27 January 2014.

"90%: Afghanistan, the Unholy Trinity, and Critical Thought." By Louis DeAnda. Institute for Defense and Government Advancement (http://www.idga.org/), 26 July 2012.

NPR's "Morning Edition" News. Public Radio East. New Bern, NC.

Nyirigwa, Watts Roba Gibia. "Why 2011 Referendum Is the Only Hope for South Sudanese: Part One." *Khartoum Monitor,* 31 May 2006.

"Ogaden National Liberation Front (ONLF)." Council on Foreign Relations. *Backgrounder,* 1 November 2007. As retrieved in December 2014 from the following url: http://www.cfr.org/ethiopia/ogaden-national-liberation-front-onlf/p13208.

"Oil for China, Guns for Darfur." By Moira Herbst. *Bloomberg Businessweek,* 14 March 2008. As retrieved in November 2014 from this url: http://www.businessweek.com/stories/2008-03-14/oil-for-china-guns-for-darfurbusinessweek-business-news-stock-market-and-financial-advice.

"Omar al-Bashir Q&A: 'In Any War, Mistakes Happen on the Ground'." By Sam Dealey. *Time* on line, 14 August 2009. As retrieved in February 2015 from the following url: http://content.time.com/time/world/article/0,8599,1916262-5,00.html.

"100 Days of President Lungu's Decision Making." *Zambia Daily Mail,* 7 May 2015. Four-page insert.

"$192m Loan Expose Angers Govt." *Sunday Post* (Lusaka), 10 May 2015.

"Opening Statement by Dr. Graham T. Allison before the United States Senate Committee on Armed Services at a Hearing Convened to Discuss 'China, the U.S., and the Asia-Pacific'." As retrived in April 2015 from the following url: http://www.armed-services.senate.gov/hearings/15-04-14-us-defense-policy-issues-pertaining_to-the-asia-pacific-theater.

"Osama bin Laden Timeline." *CNN's News* on line, n.d.

Osman, Jamal. "Exclusive: Inside an al-Shabaab Training Camp." *Channel 4 News* on line (U.K.), 16 December 2013. As retrieved from url: www.channel4.com/news/al-shabaab-somalia-kenya-westgate-al-qaeda.

"PAC Attends a Patriotic Front Conference." *South African History* on line, 26 October 1991. As retrieved in October 2014, from this url: http://www.sahistory.org.za/dated-event/pac-attends-patriotic-front-conference.

"Pakistan Is Handing Over De-Facto Control of the Strategic Gilgit-Baltistan Region." *Rediff News* (India), 28 August 2010.

"Pakistani Islamists Sign Deal With China." By Farhan Bokhari. *CBS's News* on line. World Watch, 18 February 2009.

"Peacekeeping Fact Sheet." United Nations' website, 30 September 2014. As retrieved in November 2014 from this url: http://www.un.org/en/peacekeeping/resources/statistics/factsheet.shtml.

"Peoples Liberation Army Inc.: Big Business, Big Trouble." By Liz Sly. *Chicago Tribune* on line, 16 August 1998.

Pepper, Daniel. "Congolese Hopeful Ahead of July 30 Vote." *Christian Science Monitor,* 29 June 2006.

"Picking Up Steam: The Expansion of Chinese Railways in Africa." By Yun Sun. Brookings Institute, 26 September 2014. As retrieved in October 2014 from this url: http://www.brookings.edu/blogs/africa-in-focus/posts/2014/09/26-chinese-railways-in-africa-sun.

"Popes Connected with Fatima." The World Apostolate of Fatima. *Soul,* Fall 2014.

"Production of Opium by Afghans Is Up Again." By Rod Nordland. *New York Times* on line, Asia Pacific edition, 15 April 2013. As retrieved in July 2014 at url: http://www.nytimes.com/2013/04/16/world/asia/afghanistan-opium-production-increases-for-3rd-year.html?_r=0.

"Profile: Libya's Ansar al-Sharia." By Faisal Irshaid. *BBC News* on line, 13 June 2014.

"Profit In Peacekeeping–China's Strategic Gain." By Andrew Ludwig. *The Diplomat* (Tokyo), 27 May 2014. As retrieved in October 2014 from the following url: http://thediplomat.com/2014/05/profit-in-peacekeeping-chinas-strategic-gain/.

"Quds Force Leader, Commanding Iraqi forces against ISIS, Alarms Washington." By James Rosen. *Fox News* on line, 5 March 2015.

"Rare Access to the Hunt for African Warlord Joseph Kony." *BBC News* on Line, 24 November 2014.

"Rebels Attack in Southern Yemen." World Roundup (Associated Press). *Jacksonville Daily News* (N.C.), 20 March 2015.

"Rebels Gun Down 97 People Praying." News Roundup (Associated Press). *Jacksonville Daily News* (NC), 3 July 2015.

"Relations with South Africa." Chinese Foreign Ministry (China.org.cn), 14 June 2006. As retrieved in October 2014 from the following url: http://www.china.org.cn/english/features/wenjiabaoafrica/171412.htm.

"Relations with the Republic of the Congo." Chinese Foreign Ministry (China.org.cn), 14 June 2006. As retrieved in October 2014 from this url: http://www.china.org.cn/english/features/wenjiabaoafrica/171414.htm.

"Report of . . . Experts on the Illegal Exploitation of Natural Resources . . . of the Democratic Republic of the Congo." Letter from the (United Nations) Secretary General to President of the Security Council, 12 April 2001. As retrieved in January 2015 from the following url: http://www.un.org/news/dh/latest/drcongo.htm.

"Rogues' Gallery." By Bobby Ghosh. *Time,* 2 May 2011.

"Rwanda: Boom Town - Kigali's Chinese Investment." By Daniel Nzohabonimana. *AllAfrica (Pambazuka) News,* 14 February 2014. As retrieved in September 2014 from the following url: http://allafrica.com/stories/201402190316.html?page=3.

"Rwandan Arms, Fighters Still Sustaining M23 Rebel Forces in Congo." *CBC News* (Canada), 23 July 2013. As retrieved in November 2014 from the following url: http://www.cbc.ca/news/world/rwandan-arms-fighters-still-sustaining-m23-rebel-forces-in-congo-1.1339383.

"S. African Police Arrest Thousands." World Roundup (Associated Press). *Jacksonville Daily News* (NC), 22 May 2015.

Sangraula, Bikash. "Nepal Grapples with Next Steps." *Christian Science Monitor,* 2 May 2006.

Santoli, Al. "The Panama Canal in Transition: Threats to U.S. Security and China's Growing Role in Latin America." *American Foreign Policy Council Investigative Report,* 23 June 1999.

"Sata's Legacy Buried at Embassy Park—Mucheleka." *Sunday Post* (Lusaka), 10 May 2015.

"Saudi-Led Coalition Airdrops Arms." World Roundup (Associated Press). *Jacksonville Daily News* (NC), 4 April 2015.

"Series Overview." By Didrik Schanche. *China's Rising Power in Africa. NPR* on line, 28 July 2008.

Shahzad, Syed Saleem. "We are just Hit-and-Run Guerrillas." *Asia Times* on line, 10 August 2006.

"Should the United Nations Wage War to Keep the Peace." By James Verinia. *National Geographic* on line, 27 March 2014. As retrieved in November 2014 from the following url: http://news.nationalgeographic.com/news/2014/03/140327-congo-genocide-united-nations-peacekeepers-m23-kobler-intervention-brigade/.

"Significant Findings of NDTA 2011." Community Anti-Drug Coalitions of America, n.d. As retrieved in July 2014 from the following url: http://www.cadca.org/resources/detail/national-drug-intelligence-center-releases-national-drug-threat-assessment.

Smith, Charles R. "U.S. Bombs Chinese Network in Afghanistan, PRC Sold Taliban Advanced Air Defense System." *Newsmax* (West Palm Beach, FL), 20 October 2001.

"Somalia: Al-Shabab Loses Their Strongest Military Base in the Central of Somalia to SNA and AU Troops." *Somali News* on line, 13 March 2014. As retrieved in July 2014 from the following url: http/:www.raxanreeb.com/2014/03/somalia-al-shabab-loses-their-strongest-military-base-in-the-central-of-somalia-to-sna-and-au-troops/.

"Somali." China.org.cn (Chinese Foreign Ministry), 10 October 2006. As retrieved in October 2014 from the following url: http://www.china.org.cn/english/features/focac/183424.htm.

"Somika—Cobalt." Somika: Societe Miniere du Katanga, n.d. As retrieved in July 2014 from the following url: http://www.somika.com/cobalt-properties-ores-minerals-lubumbashi.php.

"South Africans a Proud Part of U.N. Peacekeeping Operations." By Kim Helfrich. *Defence Web* (South Africa), 3 June 2014. As retrieved in November 2014 from this url: http://www.defenceweb.co.za/index.php?option=com_content&view=article&id=34958:south-africans-a-proud-part-of-un-peacekeeping-operations&catid=61:editor-column.

"South Africa Sends More Troops to Central African Republic." *The Guardian* (U.K.) on line, 27 March 2013.

"South Africa's Peacekeeping Role in Burundi." The African Centre for the Constructive Resolution of Disputes (South Africa). *Occasional Papers*. Issue 2, 2007. As retrieved in November 2014 from this url: http://www.accord.org.za/publications/occasional-papers/492-south-africas-peacekeeping-role-in-burundi.

"South Sudanese Rebels Slam China's Conflicting Roles." From AllAfrica News. *Sudan Tribune,* 18 July 2014. As retrieved in November 2014 from this url: http://allafrica.com/stories/201407190241.html.

"S. Sudan's Machar Unable to Control Rebels." From Agence France Press. As reprinted by *Al Jazeera*, 1 June 2014.

"S. Sudan Troops Burning Villages." World Roundup (Associated Press). *Jacksonville Daily News* (NC), 22 May 2015.

"Soviet Policies South and East of Suez." By T.B. Miller. *Foreign Affairs* on line, October 1970. As retrieved from this url: http://www.foreignaffairs.com/articles/24203/t-b-millar/soviet-policies-south-and-east-of-suez.

"Special Report: Congo." International Rescue Committee, December 2014. As retrieved in January 2015 from the following url: http://www.rescue.org/special-reports/special-report-congo-y.

"The Spoils of War: Afghanistan's Multibillion Dollar Heroin Trade." By Michel Chossudovsky. *Global Research,* 15 February 2014. As retrieved in July 2014 from this url: http://www.globalresearch.ca/the-spoils-of-war-afghanistan-s-multibillion-dollar-herointrade/91.

"Spy Plane" article series from *Washington Post*: (1) "China Says It Will Return Disassembled U.S. Plane," 25 May 2001; (2) "Surveillance Plane to Be Returned to U.S. in Pieces," 30 May 2001; (3) "U.S., China Agree on Plan to Return Spy Plane: U.S. Team Arrives in China to Begin Dismantling Jet," 7 June 2001; (4) "Disassembled Navy Plane Scheduled to Leave China Today," 3 July 2001; (5) "China Bills U.S. Over Collision: $1 Million in Surveillance Plane Dispute Termed 'Exaggerated' ," 7 July 2001; and (6) "U.S. to Pay China $34,567 for Costs of Downed Plane," 10 August 2001.

"State Owned Assets Supervision and Administration Commission of the State Council (SASAC)." By the People's Republic of China, n.d. As retrieved in November 2014 from the following url: http://www.sasac.gov.cn/n2963340/n2971121/n4956567/.

"Stratfor: China's Weapons Push in Africa." By Jamie Etheridge. *ABC's News* on line, 25 August 2012. As retrieved in November 2014 from this url: http://abcnews.go.com/International/story?id=82683.

"Struggle over Libya's Oil Risks Breaking Up Country: Rival PM." By Ulf Laessing. *Reuters News* on line, 28 November 2014.

"Sudan Arrested Chadian Rebel to Support of His Rival." *Khartoum Monitor,* 1 June 2006.

"Sudan, Chad, and the Central African Republic." Council on Foreign Relations. *Backgrounder,* 2 January 2007. As retrieved in December 2014 from the following url: http://www.cfr.org/sudan/sudan-chad-central-african-republic/p12309.

"Sudan-China Model Economic Relations Sudan Vision." Embassy of Sudan in Washington, D.C. As retreived in February 2015 from this url: http://www.sudanembassy.org/index.php?option=com_content&view=article&id=320:sudan-china-model-economic-relations-sudan-vision&catid=13:news-and-events&Itemid=207.

"Sudan Rebels Threaten Khartoum Attack." By Ahmed Younis. *Asharq al-Awsat* (U.K.), 28 May 2014. As retrieved in December 2014 from the following url: http://www.aawsat.net/2014/05/article55332663.

"Sudan's al-Bashir Given Red Carpet Treatment by China." By Malcomb Moore. *The Telegraph* (U.K.) on line, 29 June 2011.

"Sudan's Use of Chinese Arms Shows Beijing's Balancing Act." By Jared Ferrie. *Bloomberg News* on line, 30 April 2012.

"Sudan: The Forgotten War." By Elizabeth Diaz. *Time,* 23 February - 2 March, 2015.

"Sudan Unity Requires Secular State." *Khartoum Monitor,* 1 June 2006.

Swain, Jon and David Leppard and Brian Johnson-Thomas. "Iran's Plot to Mine Uranium in Africa." *The Sunday Times* (U.K.), 6 August 2006.

"Taiwan Confident of Keeping Burkina Faso Ties after Army Takeover." *Reuters News* on line, 3 November 2014.

"Tanzania." Chinese Foreign Ministry (China.org.cn), 10 October 2006. As retrieved in October 2014 from the following url: http://www.china.org.cn/english/features/focac/183419.htm.

"Tanzania." *Freedom in the World 2014.* Freedom House (a District of Columbia based human rights organization). As retrieved in October 2014 from this url: http://freedomhouse.org/report/freedom-world/2014/tanzania-0.

"Terror-Cell Alliance at Work in U.S." By Faye Bowers. *Christian Science Monitor,* 15 July 2002.

"Terrorism and Transnational Organised Crime Threatens Hard-Won Progress in Africa." By Yousuf Malik. *Defence IQ* (U.K.), 20 October 2014. As retrieved in November 2014 from this url: http://www.defenceiq.com/naval-and-maritime-defence/articles/africa-s-robust-economy-driving-defence-spending/.

"Thousands Flee from Tunisia after Fatal Attack." World Roundup (Associated Press). *Jacksonville Daily News* (NC), 28 June 2015.

"Thousands Flee Renewed Violence in DRC." By Malcomb Webb. *Aljazeera* on line, 18 May 2012. As retrieved in March 2015 from this url: http://www.aljazeera.com/indepth/features/2012/05/2012517105421722232.html.

"3 African Nations Battle Boko Haram." By Haruna Umar and Michelle Faul (Associated Press). *Jacksonville Daily News* (NC), 5 February 2015.

"Top Iranian Defector on Iran's Collaboration with Iraq, North Korea, Al-Qa'ida, and Hizbullah." Middle East Media Research Institute. Special Dispatch Number 473, 21 February 2003.

"Tribal Militants Claimed Responsibility for Another Attack on an Energy Installation." World News in Brief. *Christian Science Monitor,* 8 June 2006.

"The Tripartite Alliance Has Sold Its Soul." *Mail & Guardian* (South Africa), 27 September 2013. As retrieved in October 2014 from this url: http://mg.co.za/article/2013-09-27-00-the-tripartite-alliance-has-sold-its-soul.

"Troop and Police Contributors," United Nations' website, n.d. As retrieved in November 2014 from the following url: http://www.un.org/en/peacekeeping/resources/statistics/contributors.shtml.

Truscott, Bryan. "Short Lives Lead to Short-Term Goals in Zimbabwe." *Christian Science Monitor,* 9 June 2006.

"Tuareg, Tamasheq in Burkina Faso." *Joshua Project,* n.d. As retrieved in December 2014 from the following url: http://joshuaproject.net/people_groups/15607/UV.

"Tunisia Searches for Attack Accomplices." World Roundup (Associated Press). *Jacksonville Daily News* (NC), 29 June 2015.

"2009 Minerals Yearbook, Tungsten Table 15." *U.S. Geological Survey* (http://www.usgs.gov), n.d. As retrieved in July 2014 with this document designator: myb1-2009-tungs.pdf.

"Two Weeks after Being Asked for Help, Angola's Government Said." World News in Brief. *Christian Science Monitor,* 13 November 2008.

"Understanding M23 and the Current Conflict in the DR Congo." By Maurice Musoni. *United to End Genocide,* 29 November 2012. As retrieved in November 2014 from this url: http://endgenocide.org/understanding-m23-and-the-current-conflict-in-the-drc-congo/.

"Unrestricted Warfare and Drug Smuggling." By John Poole. *The Counter Terrorist,* January/February 2014 issue. As retrieved in December 2014 from this url: http://onlinedigitalpublishing.com/article/UNRESTRICTED_WARFARE_AND_DRUG_SMUGGLING/1610244/192125/article.html.

"U.S. Hopes China Will Help Moderate Havana Meeting." *China Confidential,* 11 September 2006.

"U.S. Shifts Troops in Response to Libya." From McClatchy Tribune. *Jacksonville Daily News* (NC), 17 May 2014.

"U.S. Surveillance Plane Lands in China after Collision with Fighter." *CNN's Headline News,* 1 April 2001.

"Venezuela." *Insightcrime.org,* 18 September 2012. As retrieved in August 2014 from the following url: http://www.insightcrime.org/organized-crime-profile/venezuela.

"Viewpoint: Why DR Congo's Volcano City of Goma Matters." By Theodore Trefon. *BBC News* on line, 20 November 2012.

"The War on ISIS." *Time,* 9 March 2015.

Warring on Terrorism. By Stephen E. Hughes. Part I (internet piece), 2005.

"What Was the Cultural Revolution." By Kallie Szczepanski. About.com, n.d. As retrieved in October 2014 from the following url: http://asianhistory.about.com/od/modernchina/f/What-Was-The-Cultural-Revolution.htm.

"While Congo's Government Is 'Open for Dialogue' with All." World News in Brief. *Christian Science Monitor,* 5 November 2008.

"White House Czar Calls for End to 'War on Drugs'." By Gary Fields. *Wall Street Journal* on line, 14 May 2009.

"Who Are Nigeria's Mend Oil Militants?" By Caroline Duffield. *BBC News* on line, 4 October 2010.

"Who Needs the Panama Canal." By Robert Morton. *Washington Times,* national weekly edition, 1 -8 March 1999. As reprinted in *World Tribune,* 4 March 1999. As retrieved in November 2014 from the following url: http://www.worldtribune.com/worldtribune/m-5.html.

"Why West Africa Cannot Break Its Drug Habit." By Rose Skelton. *BBC News* on line, 21 June 2010.

"Will Libya's Militias Defeat Democracy?" By Rana Jawad. *BBC News* on line, 22 July 2014.

World Drug Report 2010. United Nations Office on Drugs and Crime. As retrieved on 25 June 2010 from its website, www.unodc.org.

"World Rail Market March 2009." *Railway Gazette,* 8 March 2009. As retrieved in November 2014 from the following url: http://www.railwaygazette.com/news/single-view/view/world-rail-market-march-2009.html.

Wright, Robin and Peter Baker. "Iraq, Jordan See Threat to Election from Iran." *Washington Post,* 8 December 2004.

"Yemen: A Hezbollah Withdrawal," *STRATFOR Weekly* (http://www.stratfor.com/geopolitical-weekly), 10 February 2010.

"Yemen Clashes with Shiite Rebels." By Ahmed Al-Haj (Associate Press), *Jacksonville Daily News* (NC), 20 January 2015.

Yemen Suicide Bombings Leave over 130 Dead after Mosques Targeted." By Ian Black. *The Guardian* (U.K.) on line, 20 March 2015.

"Yemen's War." *The Economist,* 19 November 2010.

"Zambia: Developing a Railway Strategy." By Glory K. Jonga. CPCS Transcom, 1 April 2011. As retrieved in May 2015 from the following url: http://www.cpcstrans.com/files/8313/9170/2914/Zambia20Railway20Strategy20201120042001.pdf.

"Zambia Election: Michael Sata Takes Presidential Oath." *BBC News* on line, 23 September 2011.

"Zambia: PF Cadres Were Armed with Guns and Machetes—HH." *Lusaka Times* (Zambia), 13 April 2014. As retrieved in October 2014 from this url: http://www.lusakatimes.com/2014/04/13/pf-cadres-armed-guns-machetes-hh/.

"Zambian President Michael Sata Dies in London." *BBC News* on *NPR.* Public Radio East (New Bern, NC), 29 October 2014.

"Zambia's President, 'King Cobra' Sata, Dies in London." *Reuters News* on line, 29 October 2014.

"Zimbabwean President Robert Mugabe on an Official Visit to China." *Vatican Radio,* 25 Aug. 2014. As retrieved in May 2015 from the following url: http://en.radiovaticana.va/news/2014/08/25/zimbabwean_president_robert_mugabe_on_visit_to_china/1105127.

"Zimbabweans Denied Refugee Status in SA amid Fears of Policy Change." By Alex Bell. *SW Africa Radio* (Zimbabwe), 6 September 2013. As retrieved in September 2014 from this url: http://www.swradioafrica.com/2013/09/06/zimbabweans-denied-refugee-status-in-sa-amid-fears-of-policy-change/.

"Zimbabwe Vets Copying Chinese Red Guards." By Jeromy Lovell. *IOL News* (South Africa), 25 April 2000. As retrieved in October 2014 from the following url: http://www.iol.co.za/news/africa/zimbabwe-vets-copying-chinese-red-guards-1.35525.

"Zuma's Missing Years Come to Light." *The Times* (U.K.), 22 February 2009.

About the Author

After 28 years of commissioned and then noncommissioned infantry service, John Poole retired from the United States Marine Corps in April 1993. While on active duty, he studied small-unit tactics for nine years: (1) six months at the Basic School in Quantico (1966); (2) seven months as a rifle platoon commander in Vietnam (1966-67); (3) three months as a rifle company commander at Camp Pendleton (1967); (4) five months as a regimental headquarters company (and camp) commander in Vietnam (1968); (5) eight months as a rifle company commander in Vietnam (1968-69); (6) five and a half years as an instructor with the Advanced Infantry Training Company (AITC) at Camp Lejeune (1986-92); and (7) one year as the Staff Noncommissioned Officer in Charge of the 3rd Marine Division Combat Squad Leaders Course (CSLC) on Okinawa (1992-93).

While at AITC, he developed, taught, and refined courses on maneuver warfare, land navigation, fire support coordination, call for fire, adjust fire, close air support, M203 grenade launcher, movement to contact, daylight attack, night attack, infiltration, defense, offensive Military Operations in Urban Terrain (MOUT), defensive MOUT, Nuclear/Biological/Chemical (NBC) defense, and leadership. While at CSLC, he further refined the same periods of instruction and developed others on patrolling.

He has completed all of the correspondence school requirements for the Marine Corps Command and Staff College, Naval War College (1,000-hour curriculum), and Marine Corps Warfighting Skills Program. He is a graduate of the Camp Lejeune Instructional Management Course, the 2nd Marine Division Skill Leaders in Advanced Marksmanship (SLAM) Course, and the East-Coast School of Infantry Platoon Sergeants' Course.

In the 21 years since retirement, Poole has researched the small-unit tactics of other nations and written 14 other books: (1) *The Last Hundred Yards,* a squad combat study based on the consensus opinions of 1,200 NCOs and casualty statistics of AITC and CSLC field trials; (2) *One More Bridge to Cross*, a treatise on enemy proficiency at short range and how to match it; (3) *Phantom Soldier,* an in-depth look at the highly deceptive Asian style of war; (4) *The Tiger's Way,* the fighting styles of Eastern fire teams and soldiers; (5) *Tactics of the Crescent Moon,* insurgent procedures in Palestine, Chechnya, Afghanistan, and Iraq; (6) *Militant Tricks,* an honest appraisal of the so-far-undefeated *jihadist* method; (7) *Terrorist Trail,* tracing the *jihadists* in Iraq back to their home countries; (8) *Dragon Days,* an unconventional warfare technique manual; (9) *Tequila Junction,* how to fight narco-guerrillas; (10) *Homeland Siege,* confronting the 4GW assault by a foreign power's organized-crime proxies; (11) *Expeditionary Eagles,* how to outmaneuver the Taliban; (12) *Global Warrior,* forestalling WWIII with tiny contingents; (13) *Gung Ho,* how supporting arms are not needed to take strongpoint matrices; and (14) *Strategic Rifleman,* how tiny semi-autonomous elements are created.

Since 2000, Poole has traveled extensively into both Communist and Islamist worlds. Within Africa, he has been to Morocco, Egypt, Sudan, and Tanzania. In May 2015, he additionally visited South Africa and Zambia to do last minute research for *Afrique*.

As of September 2015, he had conducted multiday training sessions (on advanced squad tactics) at 41 (mostly Marine) battalions, nine Marine schools, and seven special-operations units from all four U.S. service branches.

Between early tours in the Marine Corps (from 1969 to 1971), he served as a criminal investigator with the Illinois Bureau of Investigation (IBI). After attending the State Police Academy for several months in Springfield, he was assigned to the IBI's Chicago office. There, he worked mostly on general criminal and drug cases.

Name Index

A

B

C

D

E

F

G

H

I

J

K

L

M

N

O

P

Q

No entries

R

No entries

S

T

U

V

W

X

Y

Z